Seed to Seed

Second Edition

Seed Saving and Growing Techniques
for Vegetable Gardeners

by Suzanne Ashworth

Edited by Kent Whealy
Assisted by Arllys Adelmann
Designed and Typeset by Aaron Whaley
Cover Photograph by Becky Whaley

Regional Advisors
Will Bonsall
Peter Hatch
Barbara Pleasant
Glenn Drowns
Suzanne Nelson
Suzanne Ashworth
John Navazio

Photography by David Cavagnaro
(unless otherwise noted)

ISBN 1-882424-58-1 (Softcover)

Library of Congress Control Number: 2002100948

Printed in the United States of America

Seed Savers Exchange
3076 North Winn Road
Decorah, Iowa 52101

Phone - 563-382-5990
Fax - 563-382-5872
Website - www.seedsavers.org

CONTENTS

SECTION II - MAJOR VEGETABLE FAMILIES

INTRODUCTION

An estimated 60 million Americans grow a portion of their own food in a vegetable garden. Their planting needs are supplied by 255 mail order seed companies, countless local outlets for seeds and plants, and the ever-present grocery store seed racks. Indeed, American vegetable gardens seem to magically appear each spring as if conjured up directly from the glossy color photographs in the seed catalogs. At first glance, seeds appear to be little more than a convenient way of transferring vegetables from corporation to backyard vegetable patch, from image to juicy reality.

There has always been a substantial minority of gardeners, however, who bypass the garden seed industry completely by saving their own seeds from year to year. Some of these seed savers, remnants of a recently-lost peasant agriculture which purchased nothing that could be produced at home, are still planting the same vegetable varieties that their great-grandparents once grew. Other new converts to seed saving may be trying to save something special discovered along the way, or obtain unique plant material not available commercially. Still others have simply been touched by the powerful satisfaction that comes from a garden that is genuinely self-perpetuating.

For some years now, I have been one of these seed saving gardeners. Like many of my fellow seed savers, I have often been frustrated by not having access to detailed information on saving seeds from garden vegetables. Do turnips cross with Chinese cabbage, watercress with garden cress, red Malabar spinach with white? During the spring and summer months, hardly a week went by without a question arising about how to save seed from various vegetables.

As these questions became more numerous, I felt sure that somewhere within the walls of this country's libraries was just the book that gardeners in my situation needed. But, with every new interlibrary search, it became more evident that a comprehensive guide to saving vegetable seeds on a small scale was not to be found. Instead, bits and pieces of relevant information were hidden in obscure publications on such diverse topics as food sources for honeybees, hybridization of vegetable crops, and commercial seed production techniques.

What was needed, I realized, was a book that would pull these various sources together and facilitate small-scale seed saving of all common and obscure vegetables grown in the United States and Canada. Eventually, with encouragement from the

Seed Savers Exchange and others, I decided to write *Seed to Seed.*

In creating this reference book, I have tried to be comprehensive enough to satisfy the needs of most seed savers, both beginners and those with more advanced skills. For example, techniques have been included for every vegetable appearing in the annual Yearbooks of the Seed Savers Exchange to assist members in growing pure, high quality seeds. Most vegetatively propagated herbs and most grain or forage crops have been excluded, but all forms of corn are discussed along with amaranths and sunflowers, which often appear in the vegetable garden.

In order to offer proven techniques for saving seeds, I have grown seed crops in my own garden of every vegetable discussed in this book. There have been some problems, of course. Some subtropicals refused to ripen completely, so seed extracting techniques had to be tested using purchased ripe fruits. Rutabagas, celery and parsnips had a hard time in the 110° F. summer heat, cassabanana fruits grew only three inches before succumbing to frost, and pepino and tamarillo rarely set fruits without encouragement from the plant hormone gibberelic acid. After three years of persistent effort, I have grown seed of every species that could conceivably be coaxed into maturity in central California.

During my research, I found that the literature that does exist on the pollination of vegetable crops is often quite contradictory. This confusion is due mainly to site-specific environmental factors, especially the vast differences in the sizes of crops and insect populations. In all cases, the information on pollination, seed viability and isolation distances in *Seed to Seed* has been based on the most recent research available.

The only isolation distances ever published for some crops are the recommendations made by commercial seed producers. Such publications deal with large acreages that produce massive amounts of pollen which attract huge insect populations. These commercial isolation distances have been used throughout this text without any attempt at modification. While these distances will ensure absolute seed purity, some may argue that such distances are excessive for small plantings in home gardens and for the related insect populations, which can vary widely from location to location, and even with the weather from year to year. Extensive research far beyond the scope of this project would be needed, however, to make recommendations that would ensure seed purity for specific garden sites.

Since the Seed Savers Exchange was founded in 1975, techniques for growing and saving seeds in home gardens have been tried and tested by numerous members. *Seed to Seed* only includes proven seed saving techniques that have been revised and refined over the course of several gardening seasons. For example, Glenn Drowns' techniques for the hand-pollination of cucurbits have proven to be as successful as any methods currently being used in the United States. In general, though, extensive research would also be necessary to prove which home methods are successful across a wide range of locations. Again, such research was beyond the scope and time frame of this project, so most home techniques have not been included in *Seed to Seed* unless confirmed by the published literature.

Information on various techniques for saving vegetable seeds is a dynamic and evolving area on which far too little has been written. Certainly, a project of this magnitude cannot hope to answer every question that may arise concerning home seed saving. Still, I sincerely hope that *Seed to Seed* will be widely useful and provide a foundation upon which future research and publications can be based.

Many growers have indicated that regional information on growing to seed would be a great addition to *Seed to Seed*. It wasn't easy defining major growing regions or selecting the growers to represent those regions. Certainly not all regions and microclimates in the United State could be represented. Kent Whealy and I have identified seven major regions with very experienced growers in each. The information from each of these growers will help provide readers with a better idea of the techniques appropriate to their particular growing situation. Some additional seed statistics have also been included to help growers who are attempting to market their seed crops.

Seed to Seed would not have been possible without the help of several talented and dedicated persons. Kent Whealy, director of the Seed Savers Exchange, has offered frequent encouragement and support in getting both editions of the book into print. Kent's

Suzanne Ashworth (Photo by Darrow M. Watt)

editing skills and some of his previously published material have added greatly to the readability and content of the book. I wish to also thank Arllys Adelmann who typed the extensive revisions to the text, and Aaron Whaley who contributed the design, layout and scanning for this *Second Edition* of *Seed to Seed*.

Finally, it seems most appropriate that the research, text and photographs that comprise *Seed to Seed (Second Edition)* should be donated to help support the work of the Seed Savers Exchange. And it is to the members of the Seed Savers Exchange that this book is dedicated.

Suzanne Ashworth
Sacramento, California
February 2002

SECTION I

SAVING VEGETABLE SEEDS

SAVING VEGETABLE SEEDS

The seeds that gardeners hold in their hands at planting time are living links in an unbroken chain reaching back into antiquity. Today's gardeners cannot possibly comprehend the amount of history contained in their seeds, both what has come before and what may potentially come after their brief involvement. Our Stone Age ancestors began identifying and domesticating food plants thousands of years ago, with the simple act of selecting seeds for replanting. Whenever gardeners begin to save their own seeds, they also become part of this ancient tradition.

SAVING OUR GARDEN HERITAGE

Because the United States is a nation of immigrants, today's gardeners are blessed with access to an immense cornucopia of vegetable varieties. Gardeners from every corner of the world invariably brought along cherished vegetable seeds when their families immigrated. Afraid that their treasures might be confiscated, these seeds were often smuggled into this country hidden in the linings of suitcases, under the bands of hats and sown into the hems of dresses. Seeds provided a living reminder of their past and ensured continued enjoyment of foods from the old country. This unique heritage of seeds, steadily accumulating for nearly four centuries, was first brought over by passengers on the Mayflower and is still arriving today with immigrants from every corner of the globe.

HEIRLOOM VARIETIES:
AN ENDANGERED TRADITION

Our grandparents and their ancestors were seed savers by necessity. Their best plants were carefully selected to produce the next year's seeds, which were traded over the back garden fence with neighbors and faithfully passed down to each new generation of gardeners. Few of these family heirloom varieties have ever been available commercially, until just recently. Many have been grown on the same farm by different generations of a family for 150 years or more. This often resulted in the seeds slowly developing resistances to local diseases and insects, and also gradually becoming well adapted to climates and soil conditions in family gardens throughout the United States.

Countless heirloom varieties are still being maintained by gardeners and farmers in isolated rural areas and ethnic enclaves. But today's society has become extremely mobile with young families moving every few years, often to urban homes where gardening may not be possible. The steady erosion of rural populations has been rapidly accelerated by the ongoing farm crisis, leaving ever fewer farmers and gardeners to save the family history growing in their own backyards.

Untold numbers of old-time varieties are lost each year, because elderly gardeners can no longer find family members willing to grow and maintain these living heirlooms. When elderly seed savers pass away, unless their seeds are replanted by other gardeners, their outstanding strains become extinct. Invaluable genetic characteristics are lost forever to future generations of gardeners and plant breeders.

There are a few bright rays of hope in what is otherwise a bleak situation. During this last decade, several grassroots genetic preservation projects have started to reverse these losses by collecting and distributing heirloom varieties. Several of these groups are described in the section entitled "Seed Saving Organizations" at the end of this book.

RAPID LOSSES AMONG
COMMERCIAL NON-HYBRID VARIETIES

Today's commercial vegetable varieties have also evolved from the same ancient tradition of seed saving as the heirloom varieties, but often were further refined by public breeding programs. Until recently, most of the Agricultural Experiment Stations at land-grant universities had active vegetable breeding programs that developed varieties specifically suited for growers in their state. Such programs have largely been abandoned and those that remain are in rapid decline. Enrollments at agricultural colleges have also been steadily decreasing for several decades, with ever fewer students choosing careers in traditional plant breeding. The dynamic breeding programs that characterized the first half of this century will probably never happen again.

Tremendous consolidation has occured and is continuing today within the garden seed industry. Multinational corporations, including many agrichemical conglomerates, are buying out family-owned seed

---

Facing Page: Preservation gardens at Heritage Farm, headquarters of the Seed Savers Exchange, where 2,000 endangered varieties are multiplied each summer.

companies and replacing their regionally-adapted collections with more profitable hybrids and patented varieties. The new corporate owners usually switch to generalized varieties that will grow reasonably well in areas across the country, thus assuring the greatest sales in the company's new nationwide market.

During the period from 1984-1987, 54 of the 230 mail-order seed companies in the United States and Canada went out of business. The majority were smaller companies that had been rich sources of unique varieties. The loss of those 54 companies resulted in 943 non-hybrid varieties (19%) becoming unavailable. The collections being dropped, which sometimes represent the life's work of several generations of seedsmen, are often well adapted to specific regional climates and resistant to local diseases and pests. Far from being obsolete or inferior, these may well be the best home garden varieties ever developed. It is entirely possible that half of the non-hybrid varieties still available from seed companies could be lost during the next decade.

Gardeners who are interested in helping rescue these endangered commercial varieties should send for the catalog of the Seed Savers Exchange (see "Seed Saving Organizations" at the end of this book). In addition to membership information, the catalog offers a book entitled the *Garden Seed Inventory*, compiled by Seed Savers, that lists all of the non-hybrid vegetable varieties available by mail order in the United States and Canada. Concerned gardeners can use this comprehensive inventory to purchase and permanently maintain varieties that are about to be dropped, and then share those seeds with other gardeners.

HYBRID VARIETIES GAIN DOMINANCE

The one factor most responsible for destroying garden diversity has been the massive shift to hybrid varieties. Seed companies favor these proprietary varieties for several reasons. Hybrid seeds are usually much more expensive to produce, and usually sell for several times more than "open-pollinated" (non-hybrid) seeds. Also, seeds saved from hybrids are worthless for replanting, so farmers and gardeners must return to the companies for new seeds every year. And the parentage of hybrid varieties can be kept secret, so competing companies can never reproduce them.

Open-pollinated varieties will come "true-to-type" (produce plants like their parents) if not allowed to cross with similar varieties growing nearby. In contrast, hybrids are the result of deliberately crossing two different parent varieties, usually inbreds. Hybrids should be avoided for seed saving purposes, because they are incapable of producing plants like the previous generation. Seeds saved from hybrids will either be sterile or will begin reverting to one of the parent varieties during succeeding generations.

Hybrid corns are markedly more vigorous and productive than their open-pollinated counterparts, due to a phenomenon known as "hybrid vigor" (the synergistic effect that results when two extremely diverse varieties are crossed). There is much less difference between hybrid and open pollinated varieties of self-pollinated crops. Plants that self-pollinate are naturally inbred and contain less diversity when compared to cross-pollinated crops, therefore the hybridization of such self-pollinated crops results in less hybrid vigor.

Most of today's breeding programs produce hybrid varieties for commercial growers, often designed to facilitate mechanical harvesting and long distance shipping. Commercial hybrids exhibit highly uniform characteristics, often ripening almost simultaneously. Hybrid uniformity is essential for commercial growers who must mechanically harvest huge fields with a single pass, but is often poorly suited for home gardeners who wish to spread canning chores and fresh produce over the longest possible harvest season. Many commercial varieties rely on tough skins and solid flesh to withstand mechanical picking and cross-country shipping. Gardeners, on the other hand, are primarily concerned with tenderness and outstanding flavor.

The old varieties are threatened today, not because of any deficiencies, but because they are not suitable for factory farmers and the food processing industry. As long as food crops are being bred for machines and large commercial growers, the needs of the home gardener will be of marginal importance. The old varieties will survive and flourish only if they continue to be grown by backyard gardeners and sold by local farmers markets, organic food co-ops and CSAs.

PASSING HEIRLOOMS ON TO OTHERS

Seed savers put a great deal of effort into locating and preserving heirloom varieties. Just learning how to grow various seeds isn't enough, unless ways are also found to pass those seeds on to other interested growers. Most gardeners are deservedly proud of their gardens and produce, which can easily spark interest in others. Entering visually unique heirloom varieties in county and state fairs takes little time and often causes quite a stir. Some vegetables may not fit into the limited categories allowed by most fairs, but can sometimes be entered in miscellaneous categories.

Garden clubs, arboretum societies and environmental groups are always looking for speakers and opportunities for field trips. Most seed savers enjoy giving short guided tours of their gardens, answering questions about special gardening techniques, and talking about heirlooms varieties. Stage fright is never a problem during such garden tours, because the heirloom plants provide plenty of cues for discussion. Giving out small samples of seeds or a taste of an unusual variety will always bring rave reviews. Also, a local newspaper interview with pictures of visually unique heirlooms can often help reach an even larger audience and contact like-minded gardeners.

If an unusual variety produces a bumper crop, try taking a sample to a favorite restaurant. The reputations of chefs, who must continually offer new items on their menus, depend on their ability to concoct unique and unusual dishes. Most chefs are enthusiastic about extraordinary or beautiful produce, often bemoaning the fact that produce suppliers don't offer more unusual vegetables. Produce companies counter that their growers can't risk growing an unusual crop without an established market.

Give an interested chef enough of a particular vegetable to allow for several culinary experiments. If the experiments are successful, try to establish how much produce would be used during a growing season. Then either grow the requested produce yourself, or help locate another gardener or farmer who would be willing to work with the restaurant. Some gardeners exchange produce for dinner at the restaurant, rather than become involved with cash receipts and record keeping. Heirloom varieties that find their way into commercial production, no matter how limited, are much less likely to die out.

Whenever far more seeds are produced than can be used, consider selling the surplus to a regional seed company. Many companies can use relatively small amounts of seeds of unusual varieties. The time and labor required to produce the seeds may only result in a cash reimbursement that is almost negligible. Some companies offer other seeds in trade, however, which may be advantageous. If becoming a grower for a small seed company is appealing, contact several companies and compare their requirements and prices. Always insist on a contract, no matter how small the amount of seeds, or the company will be under no obligation to buy what you have grown.

Finally, and perhaps most important of all, always try to involve children in both gardening and seed saving. Efforts to preserve heirloom vegetable varieties will not be passed on to future generations without the participation of children, grandchildren, scout troops and 4-H Clubs. Share the joy of gardening with a child, along with a gift of seeds, such as huge sunflowers and gourds. That gift could easily last a lifetime, and may create the next link in this unbroken chain of seed savers.

GARDENERS AS STEWARDS

Seed to Seed (Second Edition) is an invaluable handbook for both beginning and experienced seed savers who are interested in maintaining unique varieties and conserving our vegetable heritage. Seed saving offers gardeners the opportunity to grow a bit of history in their own backyard. Be forewarned that seed saving often starts out as a hobby, but can quickly become a passion. Many seed savers become enthralled with heirloom varieties and with the sparks of life that the seeds contain.

It seems ironic that today's gardeners have access to such a vast array of the best home garden varieties ever developed, yet so many are in immediate danger of being lost forever. For thousands of years, seed savers have been the stewards and guardians of this invaluable and irreplaceable genetic heritage. The number and quality of vegetable varieties currently available are unequaled throughout history, the end result of a tradition of selecting and improvement stretching back nearly 12,000 years. Vegetable gardeners must do everything in their power to maintain what remains, because extinction is forever. *Seed to Seed (Second Edition)* will hopefully play a valuable and timely role in helping to conserve our vanishing vegetable heritage.

BOTANICAL CLASSIFICATIONS

Each vegetable discussed in this book is grouped according to its botanical FAMILY, *Genus* and *species*. The common name of each vegetable is also included next to its Latin name. Latin names are often unfamiliar, but without them we are unable to identify plants that are not indigenous to our area, or are new to our culture.

For seed savers, botanical nomenclature and classification are even more important. Different varieties of plants within the same species will cross with one another, but crosses are rare between plants that belong to different species. Therefore, knowing the species names of common vegetables is essential for proper preservation of specific plant varieties.

15

Plant classification was one of the most important scientific endeavors of our forefathers. As information and trade increased between villages, cities and countries, it became essential to know if what two separate groups of people called a lace-flower berry was in fact the same plant. More complicated still was the fact that the lace-flower berry was considered poisonous by one group, while another group ate the berries without ill effects. Scholars, attempting to solve these problems, were unable to communicate with one another without detailed pictures of each plant.

In 1727, Charles Linnaeus began classifying plants using a system of binomial nomenclature, a two-word designation for each plant that belonged to the same family. Plant families are large groups of plants that share similar botanical characteristics. Typically, plant families are based on similarities in flower and fruit structure.

Plant families are divided into natural groupings called genera (the plural of genus). Genera are groups of more closely related plants that share even closer similarities in morphology. Plants within a genus are also divided even further into species. The genus is the first of the two Latin words that make up a plant's botanical designation, and the species is the second word in its Latin name. For example, zucchini squash (*Cucurbita pepo*) is classified as belonging to the genus *Cucurbita* and the species *pepo*.

Within the genus *Cucurbita* there are several distinctive species of squash, each of which has unique leaf, flower and fruit characteristics. The plants within each of those species possess such similar characteristics that, in fact, all of the members of a species can be thought of as the maximum interbreeding unit. Each species of squash, for example, contains a number of "cultivars" (cultivated varieties) that will all cross with one another, but will not cross with any varieties that belong to other species of squash.

This taxonomic progression can be seen more easily in the following illustration.

```
Family - CUCURBITACEAE
   Genus - Cucurbita
      Species - pepo
         Variety - Black Beauty zucchini
         Variety - Yellow Crookneck squash
         Variety - Connecticut Field pumpkin
         Variety - Patty Pan scallop
         Variety - Spaghetti squash
```

All of the taxonomic classifications in this book are based on *Hortus Third* (Macmillan Publishing, New York, 1976). *Hortus Third* includes names for 281 families, 3,301 genera and 20,397 species. Each entry includes detailed plant descriptions as well as the names of the botanists who have previously contributed to the identification of the plant. *Hortus Third* is limited to plants grown in North America, including those from Hawaii and Puerto Rico, and reflects the most current horticultural and taxonomic research.

Because of the rapid evolution of such knowledge, entries in *Hortus Third* often conflict with *Hortus Second* and other books based on the classifications in *Hortus Second*. For example, many readers may possibly possess taxonomic texts or seed catalogs which classify onions as Liliaceae. As a result of recent research, however, onions are now considered to be members of the Amaryllidaceae family. When *Hortus Fourth* is published, it will undoubtedly conflict with some of the classifications of *Hortus Third*. Botanical classification is a dynamic and rapidly evolving field and it is important to keep abreast of changes as the state of our knowledge increases.

POLLINATION AND FLOWER STRUCTURE

Before becoming a seed saver, it is necessary to know a few things about the reproductive abilities of plants. Plants, like all other living organisms, have a sex life. Unlike animals, however, most plants carry both male and female reproductive organs, often within the same flower. The male portion of the flower is called the *stamen* and consists of one or more hair-like *filaments*, each of which has a pollen-producing sac at its tip called an *anther*. The anthers gradually ripen and split open, exposing the pollen grains.

The female portion of the flower is call the *pistil* and consists of a stigma, a style and an ovary that contains one or more ovules (egg cells). The *stigma*, that portion of the pistil which is receptive to pollen, can vary in shape from just the tip of the *style* of a tomato to a single strand of corn silk which is receptive along its entire length. When a fertile grain of pollen touches a receptive *stigma*, the pollen grain begins to form a pollen tube that goes down through the *style* until it reaches and fertilizes the ovules within the *ovary*. The ovary eventually develops into the fruit or seedpod, while the fertilized ovules become the seeds for the next generation.

In order to maintain pure seed of a variety, pollen from that variety must reach the stigma of the plant, while contaminating pollen from all other varieties

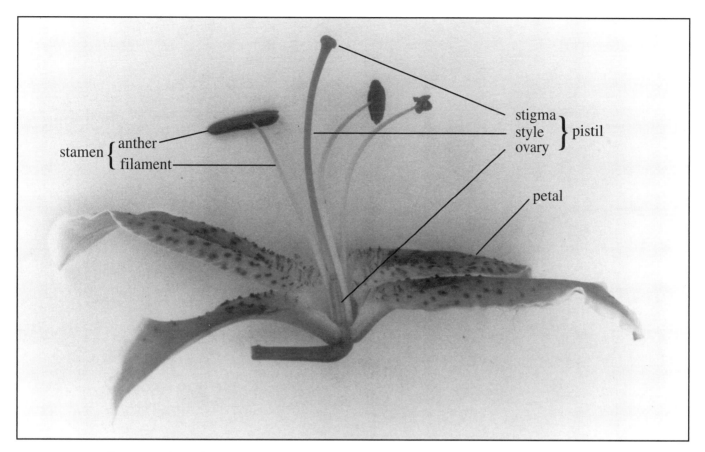

Cross section of a *Lilium rubrum* blossom showing the parts of a perfect flower.

within that species must be excluded. If pollen from a different variety within that species comes in contact with the plant's stigma, resulting in fertilization, the fruit's seeds will be crossed and not true-to-type.

Squash and other "cucurbits" (vine crops) that produce separate male and female flowers on the same plant are referred to as *monoecious* species (which literally means "one house"). Some other species that produce separate male and female plants are *dioecious* ("two houses"). For example, spinach is a dioecious species with male plants that produce only pollen and female plants that produce only seed.

Imagine that a Yellow Crookneck squash and a Dark Green zucchini (which both belong to *Cucurbita pepo*) are growing in the same garden. A honeybee gathering pollen lands on a male flower and collects Dark Green zucchini pollen. Not quite overburdened, the bee then flies to an open female flower on the Yellow Crookneck squash. While the bee is foraging on the flower, some of the Dark Green zucchini pollen is deposited on the stigma of the Yellow Crookneck squash.

The crossed fruit that results will develop and look exactly like all of the other Yellow Crookneck squash on that plant, but any seeds inside that were fertilized by zucchini pollen will carry the genetic code of both parents. If those crossed seeds (known as F1 hybrids or the F1 generation) were saved and replanted, they would produce plants that were uniquely different from the parent plants. A green crookneck zucchini with bumpy skin would be just one possibility. Each plants that was grown from a crossed seed could possibly produce a new and different fruit, but all of the fruits on each individual plant would look exactly alike.

Such crosses can be stabilized after several years (generally 6-12 generations) of continued selection, which is the process used by plant breeders to develop new open pollinated varieties. Such experimentation is beyond the scope of this book and has little to do with preserving the vegetable varieties we already have. In order to preserve our vegetable heritage, cross-pollination must be prevented so that pure varieties can be maintained.

SELF-POLLINATED PLANTS

Self-pollinated plants have functional male and female flower parts within the same flower. Such blossoms are referred to as *perfect flowers* (see the illustration above). Fertilization in perfect flowers usually takes place within each individual flower and usually does not depend on insects or the wind. For

Pollination and Flower Structure

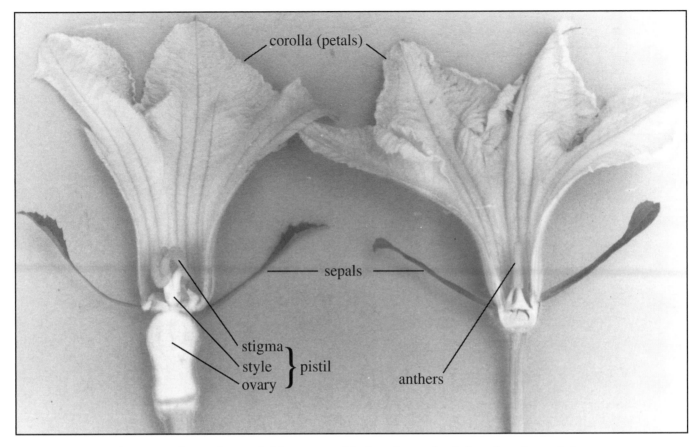

Cross sections of squash blossoms with female on the left and male at right.

example, self-fertilization occurs before the flowers even open. Some self-pollinated plants, such as peppers for example, can also be easily cross-pollinated by insects and must be grown in isolation or in screened cages to prevent such crossing.

There are several genera with perfect flowers that cannot fertilize themselves, and such flowers are said to be *self-incompatible*. The pollen produced by these flowers will not grow in the flower style on the same plant, but it will grow in the style on a different plant. Such plants generally depend on insects to move the pollen from one plant to another.

INSECT-POLLINATED PLANTS

Many vegetables produce separate male and female flowers on the same plant. Such plants are said to have *imperfect flowers*, since each blossom only displays the organs of one sex. A good example is the Cucurbitaceae family, which includes squash, cucumbers, muskmelons and watermelons. Female squash blossoms are easily identified by the ovary located at the flower's base, which is actually the tiny, immature fruit just beginning to form. When the female flower opens (ripens), its multi-segmented stigma is receptive.

Male squash blossoms, also quite easy to recognize, are just a flower at the end of a long, straight stem. The "anthers" (the pollen-producing structures inside the male flower) are also readily apparent and begin shedding pollen when the flower opens. Squash plants rely on insects to move the pollen from the anthers of the male flowers to the stigmas of the female flowers. Insect-pollinated plants must either be grown in isolation away from any other varieties of their species or be hand-pollinated to maintain seed purity.

HONEYBEES are the most efficient pollinators of commercial vegetable crops. Frequently bees are in short supply and must be brought in by the truckload, not only to work the crops but also to produce honey. Without bee pollination, many of our crops would have greatly reduced yields.

Honeybees are covered with dense branched hairs. As the bees brush against the anthers of the flowers while collecting pollen and nectar, grains of pollen become entangled in their hairs. When its body is covered with pollen the bee combs the pollen into pellets that are collected in the pollen baskets on its back legs.

Normally the number of bees foraging for pollen and nectar decreases as the distance from the hive increases. Most foraging is done within one-quarter mile of the hive. If food is scarce, however, bees will travel considerably further. Squash bees, a type of wild bee that has co-evolved with the genus *Cucurbita*, have been known to travel as far as seven miles.

The locations of nearby pollen and nectar sources are made known to the worker bees by a dance-like behavior that conveys direction, distance and other information. Having received these instructions, the worker bees leave the hive and exhibit a behavior called "flower constancy" (the tendency to forage on flowers of the same color and type, instead of foraging on mixed colors and types). For example, a worker bee might be informed of a good source of pollen on bright yellow flowers in a garden just south of the hive. Upon arrival the bee will diligently visit all of the open squash and pumpkin blossoms in the garden, not caring a bit that is has just crossed a Yellow Crookneck squash with a Connecticut Field Pumpkin. Thus, bees are not only beneficial pollinators, but are also extremely efficient cross-pollinators.

BUMBLEBEES, SWEAT BEES AND WILD SOLITARY BEES are also covered with pollen-collecting branched hairs, but are far more random in their search for nectar and pollen than honeybees. (An exception are two species of wild "squash bees" that exhibit a strong preference for cucurbits and forage extensively on squash.) Bumblebees, that are too large to get inside most vegetable flowers, will often hang upside down from the flowers, shaking pollen onto their bodies. Bumblebees, sweat bees and wild solitary bees are minor pollinators on certain crops when compared to honeybees, but are quite capable of causing a significant amount of cross-pollination on the crops that they do frequent.

MOTHS AND BUTTERFLIES are covered with scales rather than hairs, which makes them inefficient pollinators because pollen grains are unable to stick to their scales. Moths and butterflies consume only nectar and do not collect food for nesting or rearing young. Their proboscis, which is usually quite long and delicate, is also unlikely to transfer pollen. The bodies of moths and butterflies seldom come into contact with flower pollen during feeding. Although a few moth species are highly specialized pollinators, moths seldom transfer vegetable pollen.

WASPS are covered with coarse spines that are not adapted to the transfer of pollen. Although wasps feed on the nectar of many flowers, only in a few rare exceptions do they transfer pollen.

FLIES will visit flowers having open, exposed "nectaries" (the part of a flower that secretes nectar), such as various members of the Umbelliferae and the Brassicaceae families. Flies have hairy legs that are capable of transferring pollen and can easily cross-pollinate varieties. The caging and bagging techniques used to exclude bees will also exclude flies.

WIND-POLLINATED PLANTS

Many grains, grasses and trees are dependent upon the wind for pollen dispersal. Although many grasses are self-pollinated, cross-pollination often occurs as a result of the wind. Pollen picked up by the wind can travel for miles on the air currents before coming to rest.

Corn is the most notable plant that relies on the wind for pollination. Corn pollen is produced in the tassel at the top of each stalk, which contains the plant's male flowers. When the wind shakes the plant, pollen falls from the tassels onto the silks that protrude from the ears, which are the plant's female flowers.

Spinach is another example of a plant that is primarily wind-pollinated. Spinach pollen is very fine and can be carried long distances by the wind, easily drifting a mile or more.

——— MAINTAINING VARIETAL PURITY ———

The vegetable varieties gardeners enjoy today are the result of thousands of years of selection and adaptation in diverse worldwide ecological niches. Vegetable seeds have accompanied travelers and immigrants to every corner of the world, being traded from region to region and from continent to continent in order to satisfy mankind's desires for new and different produce. Serious gardeners are never content to grow and eat only one type of pepper or one type of corn. Instead, gardeners are constantly experimenting with different varieties including many that are nearly impossible to grow in their climates. A tremendous heritage is available to today's garden experimenters, but protecting these countless varieties from loss and maintaining their purity is a constant challenge.

ISOLATION DISTANCES

Pure seeds can be saved from cross-pollinated vegetable crops, without resorting to caging or hand-pollination, by isolating a single variety of a species. Such varieties must be isolated by a distance that is large enough to prevent contamination from insect pollination or wind-blown pollen. That distance varies from species to species and is commonly referred to as the plant's "isolation distance."

To produce pure seed, seed savers must properly isolate their own crops and also check the gardens nearby as well. For example, if Nizza zucchini is being grown in isolation and saved for seed while a neighbor a block away is growing Yellow Scallop squash, bees will most likely cross the two varieties. For most gardeners in similar situations, especially those living in communities where vegetable gardens are prevalent, isolation only works for species that are not commonly grown. The more widely grown cross-pollinated vegetable crops usually require hand-pollination, bagging or caging to ensure seed purity.

Isolation distances are given for almost all of the vegetable species in this book. The distances cited are primarily those used by commercial seed producers. For home seed savers these isolation distances will seem excessive. Isolation distances are highly site specific and depend on many factors such as plant population size, pollinator population density, presence of alternate insect forage sources, geographical barriers, vegetation barriers and other habitat-related factors.

These commercial recommendations should be viewed as maximum starting points for individualized experiments to determine isolation distances that would be more appropriate for specific garden sites. Although buildings, trees and tall crops such as sunflowers, amaranth and corn all act as barriers for insects and help decrease the distances required for maintaining purity, this is certainly not to suggest that isolation distances should be ignored. When in doubt, always err on the side of caution. Of course, any experiment should only involve varieties that are widely available.

Pollination experiments are often hard to interpret, because many variables can be involved whose effects on cross-pollination as a function of isolation distance are only partially understood. Some of the variables that would tend to increase the need for isolation include: a greater number of plants, a greater number of varieties, extremely diverse varietal characteristics, and the presence of a large number of highly efficient pollinators. Variables that would tend to decrease isolation distances: the presence of barrier crops, the presence of alternate pollen sources, staggered flowering times (seed collected from first blooms of the first blooming variety), and the collection of seed from the center of block plantings.

TIME ISOLATION

Annual varieties that cannot be isolated by distance can sometimes be isolated by time. To save seeds from more than one variety, plant the first crop as early as possible. When the first crop is beginning to flower, sow the second variety. Time isolation will only succeed if the first crop sets its seeds and stops shedding pollen before the second crop reaches the flowering stage.

Some examples of annual crops that can be easily isolated by time include corn, sunflowers, lettuce and annual Umbelliferae. Corn is a relatively easy crop for time isolation, provided that accurate information on maturity dates is known. For example, an early season Orchard Baby sweet corn could be planted at the beginning of the season. Two weeks later, a late season Country Gentleman sweet corn could be planted. If the weather cooperates and both corn varieties grow normally, the Orchard Baby will have finished tasseling and its silks will have dried up before the Country Gentleman begins to tassel and shed pollen. Both varieties could then be saved for seed even though they were grown in adjacent plots.

Time isolation usually works best using two varieties that have very different maturity dates. Two varieties having equal or similar maturity dates can sometimes still be time isolated, however, when the season is long enough for them to be sown at least four weeks apart. In southern locations, for example, it is possible to sow three varieties of solitary-headed sunflowers, if the plantings are spaced a month apart and the maturity dates are well known. When time isolating three varieties, however, always be careful to allow sufficient time for seeds of the last variety to mature and dry properly.

Weather variability in the spring and fall may cause problems in various time isolation sequences. The earliest variety often does not grow quite as quickly very early in the season because of cooler temperatures, while the second variety may grow more quickly than expected due to warmer weather. That could cause the flowering periods of the two varieties to overlap so that neither variety could be saved for seed. If, due to miscalculation or weather variations, some flowers of both varieties are present simultaneously, the seeds can still be kept from crossing by manually removing the flower buds of the earlier variety from that point on. In some cases, such as okra for example, this might involve simply pruning off the top of the plant.

MECHANICAL ISOLATION

Mechanical isolation involves constructing a physical barrier that prevents unwanted pollination. The mechanical isolation techniques discussed in the following sections are as varied as the plants being

Screen cages prevent insects from crossing various self-pollinated crops.

protected. Sometimes the technique is as simple as tying a cloth bag around a fertile okra blossom until it self-pollinates. Some self-pollinated plants can also be easily cross-pollinated by insects. Populations of peppers, for example, are often grown inside a screened cage to prevent any insect crossing with nearby varieties. Other more elaborate variations, that will be explained shortly, can involve alternate day caging techniques or introducing insects into a cage to pollinate the plants inside.

BAGGING TECHNIQUES

Bagging involves covering the flowering portion of a plant, in order to isolate those flowers from insect pollinators or wind-blown pollen. Except for corn, bagging is usually used to prevent cross-pollination of self-pollinating plants. For example, a cluster of currant tomato blossoms could be bagged with spun polyester cloth to prevent any possible insect crossing. Bagging individual flowers or clusters of blossoms is especially useful in cases where only a small amount of seed is needed and caging methods are not possible.

Spun polyester cloth, often known by the trade name Reemay|, is a popular bagging material as are other lightweight fabrics. Pieces of Reemay| can be tied around individual flower heads or groups of flowers to prevent any insects from entering. Reemay| can also be sewed, heat-sealed or rolled and stapled to make bags for flowers. Always be certain, however, that the base of the bag is tightly secured around the stem. In some cases it may be necessary to wrap a cotton ball or cotton batting tightly around the flower stem before securing the bag with a twist tie, in order to prevent insects from crawling into the bag.

Later when the bag is removed, pods or fruits in-

Maintaining Varietal Purity

side can be marked with pieces of bright yarn so that their seeds will be saved. These bagging techniques do not work for wind-pollinated plants such as spinach whose extremely fine-grained pollen is small enough to pass through Reemay┃ and muslin. Such species are identified throughout the text of this book.

Paper bags are often used, but can become a problem where summer rains are prevalent. Treated paper bags are available from the Lawson Bag Company (see "Supplies for Seed Savers" at the end of this section). Never use clear plastic bags or glassine envelopes, which can cause the flower to cook in the hot sun or become slimy from lack of ventilation. Suitable bagging techniques are discussed for each of the applicable vegetables in Section II and Section III.

CAGING TECHNIQUES

Some crops that are naturally self-pollinating can also be readily contaminated by insect cross-pollination. A good example would be peppers which, given the right conditions, can be crossed by sweat bees at rates exceeding 80%. When a population of peppers is grown under a cage covered with window screen, however, the fruits will all be pure. Because the species is naturally self-pollinating, the fruits will develop normally on pepper plants growing inside of the cage. Eggplants can also be kept pure using exactly the same caging technique.

Pollination cages are usually covered with spun polyester cloth or window screen over a frame made of wood, wire, or lightweight plastic pipe or metal tubing. Both coverings allow air, water and light to pass through to the plants while excluding insects. (Always keep in mind that window screen will block 15-20% of the sunlight, which can be a problem in short season areas.) Larger wood frames covered with nylon mesh or wire window screening can be custom designed to fit eight or more plants into a single cage. A short row of low-growing plants can be caged using half-circles of stiff wire pushed into the ground at intervals and then covered with Reemay┃ whose outer edges are buried in the dirt. Spun polyester cloth can also be wrapped around whole plants and secured with clothespins, or used to cover three-ring tomato cages. Vegetables that respond well to these various caging techniques are identified throughout *Seed to Seed (Second Edition)*.

ALTERNATE DAY CAGING

Alternate day caging is a method of isolating two or more varieties that are flowering simultaneously. This method allows insects to pollinate each variety for one day, then excludes insects during the next day. The trade-off is that seed production is somewhat limited due to the lack of daily pollination. The plants sometimes compensate for this by producing flowers over a longer period of time.

In order to use alternate day caging, a minimum of two cages must be constructed. Every morning one cage is removed and is then replaced that evening; the following day the other cage is removed and replaced. Alternate day caging is ideal if, for example, seeds are being saved from both a cabbage and a kale. Six or more cabbage plants would be covered under one cage, with six or more kale plants under the second cage. These two vegetables both require insects for pollination, but will easily cross with one another. Remember to make absolutely certain that no other varieties of *Brassica oleracea* are flowering in neighboring gardens, or insects could certainly cross the uncovered kale or cabbage.

For maximum seed set, alternate day cage removal and replacement would continue until all of the plants stop flowering. The process can be stopped, however, when a sufficient number of seedpods have formed. Then, to ensure seed purity, leave the cages on both plant groups until all flowering has stopped and the seeds have begun to dry.

Alternate day caging can be expanded to handle up to four varieties. If, for example, four varieties of cabbage are being saved, four cages would be constructed with one cage being removed each day on a four-day rotation. As the number of cages increases, the amount of seed set by each variety will definitely decrease. A two-cage rotation seems to only minimally reduce seed production. A four-cage rotation, however, results in a much greater decrease in the amount of seed that is set.

CAGING WITH INTRODUCED POLLINATORS

Caging with introduced pollinators requires the use of trapped flies or newly emerged bees. The cage needs to be large enough to cover the plants, yet allow the insects some flying space. In commercial applications such cages are often the size of small greenhouses. In a home garden situation this method is rather costly, difficult to put into effect, and is usually outside the means or interests of most gardeners. The technique is certainly an option, however, for advanced seed savers.

Honeybees can be easily trapped by setting out a plate of honey. Typically 20 or more bees can be expected within half an hour. The bees are usually so intent on feeding that the plate can be moved without any covering for a short distance and placed inside the cage. Often the bees will then spend the entire day trying to escape from the cage, doing little or no pollinating. Also, there is always the possibility that trapped bees may be carrying pollen from other crop plants. For these reasons, using trapped bees as introduced pollinators is usually ineffective.

Some government facilities use specially-constructed alternate day hives that are built into one wall of large cages. The bees are allowed to forage outside every second day and are turned into the cage on alternate days. Pollination is often relatively poor because the bees usually spend their day in the cage trying to escape, doing little pollinating. Queenless hives, called nucs, filled with ready-to-hatch bees are sometimes placed inside the cages with greater success. The bees hatch and, having no prior flying experience, are content to fly about as if the cage were their world.

Some plants are naturally pollinated by flies, which can be attracted using rotten meat and trapped. The flies are then introduced into the cage, without the meat of course, but their pollination efficiency is often low and seed set may be only marginally effective. Trapping flies with rotten meat usually ensures that every cat and dog in the neighborhood will also be present. To avoid possible damages to plants or cages by animals, make sure that such trapping occurs well away from the garden.

Although caging with introduced pollinators is not commonly used outside of the Agricultural Experiment Stations, additional information on using such techniques can be obtained from the agricultural or entomology departments of most colleges and universities.

HAND-POLLINATION TECHNIQUES

Next to isolation, either by space or time, hand-pollination is probably the most commonly used method of producing pure seeds in the home garden. Hand-pollination techniques are mainly used for vegetables that require insects for pollination, but are also used for some wind-pollinated crops, especially corn. The various hand-pollination techniques all involve transferring uncontaminated pollen from a male flower onto the receptive stigma of a female flower that has also been protected from contamination. After the pollination has been made by hand, the female blossom must then be protected from any further contamination by foreign pollen. Specific hand-pollination techniques for each of the applicable vegetable species are discussed in Section II and Section III.

SELECTING DESIRABLE CHARACTERISTICS

Vegetable plants and their seeds are in a constantly evolving state of flux, always changing due to either environmental factors (drought, short seasons, disease, pests, etc.) or genetic factors (mutations, genetic shifts, etc.). Seed savers must learn how to select the right plants to save for seed, so that these changes will be for the better.

Seed savers must also learn to closely and attentively observe vegetable plants throughout the entire season, keeping seed selection constantly in mind. Look at the whole plant, not just the fruit. Plant characteristics to consider during selection could include earliness, disease resistance, insect resistance, drought resistance, stockiness, uniformity (or lack of it), and trueness-to-type. Fruit characteristics that can be selected for include color, shape, size, thickness of flesh, productivity, storage ability, flavor and many others.

Vigor is the seed's ability to germinate rapidly with good disease resistance. Only plants that display good vigor should be selected to save for seed. For example, if one plant within a population is always covered with aphids, has smaller leaves and stunted growth, or produced fewer fruits, seed from that plant should definitely not be saved. Also, if all of the best cabbages are harvested for eating each year and only the poorly formed heads are saved for seed production, subsequent crops will eventually include poorly formed heads, more with each generation.

Seed savers can also select for plant characteristics of value in their specific climate, such as bolt resistance in cool season crops. For example, out of a row of 20 lettuce plants, 14 may bolt to seed very early in the season while the remaining six plants bolt two weeks later. Since late bolting is a very desirable characteristic in lettuce, only the six late bolting plants should be allowed to flower. The seed saved from these plants may demonstrate a greater incidence of late bolting than the original crop. If this selection for late bolting continues over a sufficient period of time, a late bolting strain of the original variety will gradually be developed.

POPULATION SIZE

Population size is an extremely important factor to be considered during seed production and should always be kept in mind during selection procedures. Maintaining the genetic diversity within a population is the key to its continued evolution and the ability of the plants to adapt to varying environmental conditions. To avoid detrimentally decreasing the genetic diversity being maintained within a population of plants, seed should be saved from the greatest possible number of plants that meet the selection criteria. For example, never save seed from only the largest or best-looking fruit, which could create a severe and irreversible bottleneck during that generation. Instead, always strive to save equal amounts of seed from as many plants as possible.

The minimum number of plants that need to be grown, in order to maintain a significant representation of the genetic diversity within a given population, varies widely depending on which expert on genetics is being consulted. The miniscule amount of literature that has been published regarding population sizes also varies greatly. The basic general rule is that seed should be saved from 20 inbreeding plants or 100 outbreeding plants. At the same time, however, it has to be noted that many home-scale seed savers must deal with space restrictions, and in some cases severe limitations. Always attempt to grow as many plants as possible in the space available in your garden, and that will usually yield an adequate range of genetic diversity for your particular gardening situation. This technique has worked well for gardeners throughout the last 12,000 years, creating the amazingly diverse richness of the world's food crops.

For the purpose of trying to establish adequate population sizes, each species in this book has been identified as either inbreeding or outbreeding. But the genetic structure of each vegetable species is extremely varied and complex. As a result, most plants are not totally inbreeding or totally outbreeding, but fall somewhere in between depending on an array of complex circumstances. Further discussion of these issues can be found in each applicable vegetable section throughout this book. Also, *Breed Your Own Vegetable Varieties* by Carol Deppe includes additional, valuable information on inbreeding and outbreeding plants.

Deppe's book provides an interesting way of looking at some of the problems involving plant population sizes. She suggests that your reason for saving seeds (and the variability of the variety being saved) can assist in determining the required population size. Also, she feels that saving seed for home use only requires growing as many plants as possible in the available space, since most home seed savers are usually growing seeds in order to produce fresh seed for their own use in their specific climate. Deppe's approach takes into consideration the fact that most seed savers are actually maintaining only a small portion of a much larger seed population for any given variety. At any one time, the entire population of a variety is also being grown by other seed savers, grown and sold by various seed companies, maintained and stored at Seed Savers' Heritage Farm, maintained and stored at one of the USDA's Plant Introduction Stations, and also possibly being maintained by seed banks in other countries.

Larger plant populations are necessary whenever you are a seed source for others. At the very least, suppliers to seed companies and seed repositories will need to follow the basic rule of 100 outbreeding plants and 20 inbreeding plants. In general, naturally diverse populations and truly unique varieties will always require larger growouts than, for example, modern commercial varieties that are usually quite uniform and stable.

Keep in mind that even larger population sizes will be needed if the variety is extremely variable. For example, that would certainly be the case when growing a land race, because those populations contain relatively high degrees of natural variability. Such land race populations are often highly diverse gene pools, allowing native farmers to select from the wide range of genetic combinations within the population, which are needed to respond to that year's particular environmental stresses. Maintaining and preserving these highly variable populations will require growing an even greater number of plants (possibly double or even triple) with some seed being saved from each plant in order to maintain all of the diversity being exhibited.

Other notable exceptions to these general recommendations concerning population sizes involve self-pollinated plants, cucurbits and corns. Self-pollinated crops all have perfect flowers that contain both male and female parts within the same flower. Most self-pollinated plants (except those that are also insect cross-pollinated, such as peppers) are naturally inbred and contain relatively little diversity within any given population. Excellent examples would be any varieties of garden beans, which self-pollinate before their flowers open and have been saved from only a few pods or a few plants for countless generations. Such highly uniform, self-pollinated varieties can often be successfully maintained with populations of very few plants.

Still other exceptions include the "cucurbits" (vine crops such as squash, melons, watermelons, cucumbers and gourds) which are all outbreeding species. Cucurbits display relatively little "inbreeding depression" (the build-up of recessive genes in inadequate populations) even when "selfed" (a plant that is pollinated with its own pollen). A recent USDA report recommended growouts of 24 plants for all types of cucurbits, while other experts suggest minimums that range from 16 down to 8 plants. Imagine the area that the vines of 8 squash plants would cover, and the dilemma for home gardeners with limited space is quite clear. If 8 plants (or less) are grown, be sure to "sib the plants" (spreading pollen between all of the plants during hand-pollinations), and avoid "selfing the plants" which is more genetically limiting in terms of population maintenance.

At the far end of the spectrum from self-pollinated crops (such as beans) are the corns, which are highly sensitive to inadequate population sizes. Significant and irreversible damage can occur in a single generation, if a large enough population is not grown, or if the pollen mixture used during hand-pollinations is not taken from enough plants, or if the seed being saved isn't a good enough mixture from a sufficient number of plants. These problems and other precautions are described in detail when hand-pollination techniques for corns is discussed in Section III.

REACQUIRING GENETIC DIVERSITY

Perhaps you have been growing a small number of plants of a particular variety and saving seed each year for quite some time. Maybe you have noticed that the plants are not as vigorous or are not producing as well as in previous years. This can happen, either gradually or quite quickly, when seed is saved from just a few plants over a number of years. The lack of genetic diversity within a population can also become a problem if you now have (or started with) only a small seed sample or very old seed with low germination. These problems can often be remedied by using some of the following recommendations for reacquiring additional genetic diversity and increasing the size of your seed population.

1. Check the current *Seed Savers Yearbook* to locate other growers maintaining that variety and, if not available, check for similar spellings and contact those seed savers to compare photos and information.

2. Contact the offices of the Seed Savers Exchange to determine if that variety is being permanently maintained in the vast seed collections at Heritage Farm, but has not yet become available through Heritage Farm's listing in *Seed Savers Yearbook*.

3. Check the *Garden Seed Inventory*, because a small seed company may still be offering the variety.

4. Contact the last known seed company that carried the variety. They usually still have some stock of old varieties, even when no longer offered in their catalogs. If the company is out of business, find out who bought the company and contact the new owner.

5. Contact the appropriate USDA Plant Introduction Station to see if seed of the variety is being maintained at any of their repositories, and also check USDA's on-line "GRIN" system (Germplasm Resources Information Network).

ROGUING FOR TRUENESS-TO-TYPE

Commercial seed companies require their contract growers to rogue crops to remove any off-type plants. Onion seed crops, for example, may be rogued four or more times before the plants actually go to seed. During the first season of growth, crews of workers walk through the fields and remove any plants with off-type foliage, bulbs or color. Any plants that bolt to seed during the first year are also removed, because such onions have very poor keeping abilities. During storage, any onions with thick necks, bottle necks, split bulbs, double bulbs or damaged bulbs are removed. Finally, during the second season of growth when bulbs begin to flower, the blossoms are checked for color and shape, and off-types are again removed.

Small-scale seed savers should also rogue their plants, being sure to plant large enough populations so that roguing is meaningful and doesn't lead to inbreeding. Garden plants undergo almost daily inspection during watering, weeding and picking. Off-type plants are easy to spot within a population, and their removal helps eliminate the effects of any slight crossing that may have occurred during a previous generation or any accidental mixing of home-saved seeds.

For many gardeners, who often are concerned with food production and seed saving simultaneously, roguing is a hard thing to do. Letting an off-type plant remain in the garden is fine, if the plant is harvested for food before it flowers. For example, an off-type lettuce is usually just as tasty as its more uniform neighbors. It is a mistake, however, to let any off-type plants stay in the garden long enough to flower and cross-pollinate with neighboring plants being saved for seed. In general, off-type plants can remain in the garden as long as they are in a non-reproductive, vegetative stage, but should be removed before the onset of flowering. Most biennials can therefore be grown for produce during their first season without creating any problems.

With certain vegetables, off-type plants can be extremely difficult to recognize until the fruits form. Imagine, for example, that several plants of Guatemalan Blue Banana squash are being grown for seed.

Maintaining Varietal Purity

Several flowers on each of the plants have been hand-pollinated. The plants initially all look the same, but the banana-shaped fruits on one of the plants are bright pink. To make matters worse, blossoms from the pink-fruited plant were used for the hand-pollinations on some of the blue-fruited plants.

Whether or not this problem can be remedied during the current season depends on the length of the local growing season and if sufficient time remains before frost. First, tear out the pink-fruited plant to avoid any chance of it causing further damage. Then remove all of the small squashes on the blue-fruited plants, including those that were hand-pollinated. The plants will start to flower vigorously shortly thereafter, and the new flowers can again be hand-pollinated.

During this second round of hand-pollinations, only male and female blossoms from the same plant should be used. This technique is called "selfing" (the plant has been pollinated by itself) and should be used whenever seed purity is in question. This situation graphically illustrates the importance of good record keeping, which would have shown whether pollen was taken from the same vine or from a different vine.

Let's follow our imaginary problem through a different set of circumstances. Suppose there wasn't enough time remaining before frost to repollinate, so none of the fruits were removed. Also imagine that the blue-fruited plants represent all of the remaining seed and no more is available. There is still a slight chance of salvaging the variety. First, save the seeds from several hand-pollinated blue-fruited squash that appear to be true-to-type. Select fruits from plants that were farthest away from the uprooted pink-fruited plant and therefore possibly less likely to have received its contaminating pollen. Keep the seed harvested from each fruit separate from the seeds of the other fruits. Next season grow one seed from each of the fruits to check for purity. If a plant produced true-to-type fruits, that probably means other seeds from that fruit are also pure, and could be checked with further growouts. Seeds from fruits that produce off-type plants should be discarded.

SEED CLEANING METHODS

Seed cleaning methods can be divided basically into wet processing or dry processing. The wet processing method is used for any seeds that are embedded in the damp flesh of fruits or berries, such as tomatoes, cucumbers, muskmelons or ground cherries. Seeds that are dry processed include those that are harvested from pods or husks that have usually dried in place on the plant, such as corn, radish, okra, beans or lettuce.

WET PROCESSING,
FERMENTATION AND DRYING

Wet processing is a three-step method that involves *removal* of the seeds from the fruit, *washing* to clean the seeds, and finally *drying*. Large fruits are cut open and the seeds are scraped out. Small fruits are usually crushed or mashed. Depending on the species, the seeds, pulp and juice from the fruits may need to go through a fermentation process. Fermentation occurs in the garden as a natural process to some degree, as unharvested fruits fall to the ground, ferment and rot. During the fermentation process, microorganisms such as bacteria and yeast destroy many of the seed-borne diseases that can affect the next generation of plants. Water should usually not be added to the fermenting mixture, because dilution may slow the fermentation process and can cause premature sprouting of the seeds near the end of the process. (Specific fermentation techniques are described for all applicable species in Section II and Section III.)

The seeds must then be washed to either remove them from surrounding pulp or to separate them from the fermenting mixture. For most fruits this process is basically the same. The seeds and pulp are usually placed in a large bowl or bucket. Add at least twice as much water as the volume of seeds and pulp, and stir the mixture vigorously. Viable seeds tend to be more dense and sink to the bottom, but poor quality seeds tend to float. The debris and hollow seeds can be gently poured off. Add more water and repeat the process until only clean seeds remain. The seeds are then poured into a strainer and washed under running water. Always be sure, however, that small seeds cannot pass through the strainer holes.

The final processing step involves drying the seeds on a non-stick surface. The bottom of the strainer can be wiped on a towel to remove as much moisture as possible. The seeds are then dumped out onto a glass or ceramic dish, cookie sheet, window screen or a piece of plywood. Do not attempt to dry the seeds on paper, cloth or non-rigid plastic, because it can be extremely difficult to later remove the seeds from such surfaces.

It is important to dry the seeds fairly quickly, because warm, wet seeds have a tendency to either germinate or mold. Spread the seeds as thinly as possible on the drying surface and stir the seeds several times during the day. Always remember that damage begins to occur whenever the temperature of the seeds rises above 95° F. For that reason, never dry seeds in an oven. Even at the lowest settings, the temperatures in a stove's oven can vary enough to damage the seeds. It may be possible to place a tray of seeds on the racks inside an oven with just the pilot light on and the door cracked open. Another relatively warm place in most kitchens is on top of the refrigerator.

Never dry seeds in the direct sun if there is any chance that the temperature of the seeds will exceed 95° F. Also, always remember that the air temperature is often not the same as the temperature of the seeds. Even at air temperatures around 85° F., dark colored seeds can sometimes become hot enough to sustain damage. Direct sun can sometimes heat plates and cookie sheets enough to cause seed damage. In humid climates it often helps to place seeds in front of a low-speed fan to hasten the drying process. Ceiling fans are ideal, because the seeds are less likely to blow while drying. Another option is to dry the seeds on window screen that allows for excellent air circulation, stirring as often as once an hour at first.

DRY PROCESSING AND WINNOWING

Plants that produce seeds in pods or husks are usually harvested dry. Bean or pea pods, radish pods and carrot umbels are allowed to dry in the garden whenever possible, depending on the weather. In most cases the dry pods are harvested individually. It is also possible to remove the entire plant, although this makes cleaning much harder. Gardeners in cold climates are sometimes forced to pull entire plants the evening before a hard frost. The plants are then hung for a week or so in a garage or shed that does not freeze. As the plants gradually dry down, the seeds continue to mature and gain some additional strength. The pods can be picked as they dry.

Threshing is the process that breaks the seeds free from their coverings. The dry seed heads or pods are rubbed, beaten or flailed until the seeds fall free. Commercial machines are capable of harvesting, threshing and, to some degree, winnowing the seed crop as it is harvested. For small scale seed saving there are many options. One popular method is to place the dry pods in a feed sack or pillow case, which is then jogged on or flailed. Mashing the pods between two pieces of board works well with smaller seeds. Always be careful, however, because threshing or mashing the seedpods too vigorously can cause split seeds in legumes and can cause hairline cracks in corn. Gradually you will learn to use just the right amount of pressure.

Winnowing is the process used to separate the debris and chaff from the seeds. Most gardeners have seen pictures of Indian women tossing seeds into the air out of baskets, allowing the wind to do the separating. In reality, wind speed is usually quite variable and a considerable amount of seed can be lost easily during a strong gust of wind. Also, when the wind changes direction, it is easy to end up covered with dust and chaff. Good substitutes for the wind include old hair dryers with the heating element removed, the blower from a discarded vacuum cleaner, small high-speed computer fans, household fans, and variable speed squirrel cage blowers.

No matter what winnowing method is used, the area should be covered with a sheet of cloth or plastic. This way seeds that are accidentally blown away with the chaff can be recovered. Always shake out the sheet completely before starting a new variety.

When the seeds and chaff are nearly the same weight, it can be extremely difficult to successfully winnow the seeds. A good example is the feather-like chaff that surrounds lettuce seeds. This can, however, sometimes be separated by repeatedly rubbing the material through a screen of the correct size. In similar cases, another process called reverse screening can also be used. First, a screen is used which is just large enough for the seeds to pass through, but which excludes larger pieces of chaff and plant debris. After this initial screening, all that remains are the seeds and any chaff that was smaller than the seeds. The process is then repeated using a screen that is smaller than the seeds, which removes the remaining chaff.

A method of gravity separation using a bowl can be useful when very small amounts of seeds are being cleaned. The bowl method requires either sturdy lungs or a small fan. Place the seeds and chaff in a bowl and swirl the material around. The chaff and debris will begin to collect on the surface while the seeds remain underneath. Gently tip the bowl and blow the chaff out. This process is repeated until only clean seeds remain.

Another home version of gravity separation works best with rounded seeds and is usually a two-person job. This method requires a smooth board such as a breadboard, a fan of some sort, and either a shallow, flat cake pan or a cookie sheet with low sides. A very light air current is positioned next to the bottom edge of the slightly tilted board. A handful of seeds and chaff is placed near the top of the board. The angle of the board is gradually increased until the round seeds begin to roll down the board and into the cake pan. The chaff does not roll and will be blown up and over the top edge of the board.

Seed Cleaning Methods

HOT WATER TREATMENT

Hot water treatment was commonly used by seed companies to disinfect seeds before chemical seed treatments became popular. This safe and effective technique is seldom used today, but should be quite valuable for seed savers and organic seed producers. Hot water treatment is a method of controlling the seed-borne phase of diseases such as black rot, black leg and black leaf spot in the cabbage family. The treatment can also be used against bacterial canker and target spot in tomato, downy mildew in spinach, black rot and black leg in turnip, and Septoria spot in celery.

The technique requires the use of an accurate thermometer, electric frypan, large saucepan and kitchen sieve. Try a practice run without the seeds. Heat some water in the saucepan to 50° C. (122° F.). Pour a little of this water into the warm electric frypan, leaving the saucepan about 2/3 full, and then set the saucepan into the water in the frypan. Regulate the temperature of the water in the saucepan by either turning up the heat on the frypan or taking the saucepan out of the frypan. When the desired temperature can be steadily maintained, pour in the seeds, stir until all are wetted and not floating, then stir gently throughout the whole process.

Use the following treatment times and temperatures for various crops: treat broccoli, Brussels sprouts, kale and Chinese cabbage seeds for 20 minutes at 50° C. (122° F.); eggplant, spinach and turnip seeds for 25 minutes at 50° C.; celery and pepper seeds for 30 minutes at 50° C.; cauliflower for 25 minutes at 52° C. (126° F.); cabbage seed for 30 minutes at 52° C.; and tomato seed for 25 minutes at 55° C. (131° F.). Then sieve the seeds, spread on a hard surface away from direct sunlight, dry and store.

SEED CLEANING EQUIPMENT

Seed companies and universities often rely on small scale threshing and winnowing equipment to clean small amounts of seeds. Clipper seed cleaners are manufactured in a variety of sizes and have been used on farms and in laboratories for several decades. The Clipper Office Tester and Cleaner, which retails for about $1,500, is a small, compact, desktop machine that is popular with vegetable and flower seed growers and often is used in seed stores for specialized cleaning, grading and sizing. The Clipper is manufactured by the A. T. Ferrell Company, 1440 South Adams Street, Bluffton, IN 46714, phone 260-824-3400.

The I-Tech Seed Winnower, a valuable tool for small-scale seed saving, formerly was manufactured on a limited basis and was available for purchase. This is no longer the case, but detailed plans for making the I-Tech Seed Winnower and a number of other useful small machines for seed savers can be obtained on-line at http://agronomy.ucdavis.edu/LTRAS/itech (Long Term Research on Agricultural Systems unit of U.C. Davis' Agronomy Department). Plans are included for small winnowers (both electric and hand-operated); a grain huller for rice, spelt wheat, quinoa and millet; and also plans for converting a leaf shredder/wood chipper into a grain thresher. These are all public domain designs and are available free of charge.

Many types of seeds can be processed using an assortment of hand-held seed cleaning screens. These screens can be made by assembling frames made of wood lath (1.5" x .25") into 12" squares, and then attaching the screening material to the bottom of each frame. Some hardware stores carry galvanized wire mesh (hardware cloth) in the following sizes: 1/2", 3/8", 1/4", 1/8" and standard window screen. If different-sized meshes are not available locally, Abundant Life Seed Foundation carries six different sizes of seed-cleaning screens from 1/8" down to 1/40". The screens can be purchased either mounted or unmounted (also see "Supplies for Seed Savers" at the end of this section).

━━━━━━━━━ SEED STORAGE TECHNIQUES ━━━━━━━━━

The collection and storage of vegetable seeds necessitates a variety of containers. Seedpods can be easily collected in woven baskets or even bushel baskets, but always make sure that the basket's weave is tight enough to prevent the seeds from falling through. Many traditional Indian baskets are woven with seed collection specifically in mind. Baskets allow the air to circulate around the seeds, which encourages further drying.

Paper bags, feed sacks and cardboard boxes are also commonly used to collect seeds and seedpods. Such containers are especially useful when relatively large portions of the plants are being collected. It is best not to reuse bags or boxes, however, because seeds from the first collection often get stuck in their seams and can become mixed with a second seed harvest.

Fruits, berries and other seeds that are embedded in moist flesh are usually collected in plastic buckets, plastic deli tubs from the grocery store, and various kinds of bowls. One-gallon jugs are also quite useful and can often be obtained from restaurants and bakeries. Five-gallon plastic buckets are available from some fast-food restaurants or drywall contractors. Such containers are especially useful for collection and processing, because the seeds can then be fermented or washed right in the same container. Cooking bowls that are used for fermentation should always be thoroughly cleaned and sterilized with a bleach solution before being used again for food preparation.

AIRTIGHT STORAGE CONTAINERS

Vegetable seeds are at their peak when they reach maximum dry weight on the mother plant. Vigor is the seed's ability to germinate rapidly with good disease resistance. Home-saved seeds will retain maximum vigor when thoroughly dried and stored in a moisture-proof container. The most vigorous seeds at harvest time will keep the longest in storage. The two greatest enemies of stored seeds are high temperature and high moisture. Seeds that are stored at fluctuating temperature and moisture levels will quickly lose their ability to germinate. As a rule of thumb, the sum of the temperature (degrees F.) and relative humidity should not exceed 100. In actuality, humidity is probably more important than temperature, because it allows for the growth of microorganisms that degrade seed quality.

Always realize that seed vigor can be lost during storage well before the seeds die completely. For example, if a seed sample germinates at only 20%, that doesn't mean those seeds which sprouted would have grown normally. That sample's seed vigor has diminished to the point that 80% of the seeds aren't even strong enough to sprout, and the remaining 20% will have so little strength that they probably will grow weakly and may not even reach maturity. Constantly keep in mind that your seeds are living entities and will only grow strongly during subsequent seasons if you do everything possible to see that they are stored in truly excellent conditions. Strong plants in the garden are partially a reflection of good seed storage techniques.

Containers used for seed storage should always be airtight. Glass and metal are the only common materials that are completely moisture-proof. Glass jars with good rubber seals under their lids, such as baby food jars or canning jars with new lids, provide a nearly airtight seal when screwed on really tight. Gallon glass jars that do not have a common-sized canning lid can be modified into excellent storage containers by cutting gaskets for their lids out of used automobile inner tubes.

Lightweight plastic bags are not moisture-proof and make poor storage containers. However, seeds can be put into Self Seal T-Bags|, Seal-A-Meal| bags, Zip Lock bags, small drawstring muslin bags, or paper envelopes, before being stored inside of a large, airtight jar. Each bag of seeds should be securely sealed and carefully labeled. The jar should then be stored in a cool, dry, dark place where the temperature fluctuates as little as possible. Locations at floor level are better than those near the ceiling, which can be significantly warmer. The constant cool temperature of an underground root cellar is excellent, for those lucky enough to have access to such a structure. Finding the right storage location may take a bit of experimentation, but will ensure the long-term vigor and viability of home-saved seeds.

LONG-TERM FROZEN STORAGE

Most seed savers grow out their seeds on a fairly regular basis. Imagine that three varieties of leeks are being maintained, for example, with one variety being grown each year on a rotating basis. Leek seeds will maintain 50% germination for three years, if properly dried and well stored. The proposed three-year rotation would result in each variety reaching 50% germination before being regrown, but 50% is really too low. Seed vigor declines well before germination is actually lost, so always try for at least 70% germination. The three-year rotation cycle and a germination level above 70% can both be attained, if long-term frozen storage techniques are used.

Seeds of all species can be stored for many years with almost no loss of germination and only minimal loss of vigor, when dried to about 8% seed moisture, sealed into an airtight container and frozen. Seeds stored using these techniques will maintain their viability for up to ten times longer than normal germination rates. Freezing does not hurt seeds that have been dried to moisture levels of 8% or less. If the seeds are not thoroughly dry, however, the excess moisture expands when frozen and will rupture the cell walls. A quick and easy test is that seeds will break instead of bending when folded, if their moisture level is 8% or less. Also, hard shelled seeds, such as beans or corn, will shatter instead of mashing when placed on concrete and struck with a hammer.

Color-indicating silica gel is an excellent "desiccant" (moisture absorbing material) for drying seeds. By comparison, powdered milk is less than 10% as

Seed Storage Techniques

effective as a drying agent. Silica gel, which looks like little plastic beads, is often treated with cobalt chloride that indicates how much moisture has been absorbed. The beads are deep blue when completely dry, but gradually change to light pink as moisture is absorbed. Silica gel can be reactivated indefinitely by drying for eight hours in a 200° F. oven. Batches weighing over a pound should be stirred regularly to speed up the drying process. Always dry silica gel slowly, because temperatures that are too high can scorch and ruin it, turning the beads black.

Silica gel can also be easily dried in a microwave, because those ovens work on the moisture in the material. It usually takes only about 25 minutes to dry an 8" x 12" glass dish that is filled with silica gel to a depth of 1.5-2". Progress can be checked by watching through the glass door of the microwave as the silica gel slowly changes from pink to deep blue. Whichever drying method is used, the silica gel is then stored in an airtight container to keep the material dry until it is needed.

The drying process requires a glass jar with an airtight lid, at least half a pound of dry silica gel, and the seeds. Each sample of seeds should be placed in a paper packet and carefully labeled. Determine the total weight of the seeds and packets, and then measure out an equal weight of dark blue silica gel. Place both the seed packets and an equal weight of dry silica gel into the jar and screw the lid on tightly. The silica gel will immediately start absorbing moisture from the seeds.

Both large and small seeds reach optimum moisture levels for storage after seven or eight days in the container. Peas, beans and corns usually contain 6-8% moisture at the end of that period, which is dry enough to greatly increase their storage life while avoiding dormancy problems that can occur when legumes are dried to under 5% moisture. Small, soft seeds such as peppers and tomatoes will reach a lower 4-5% moisture level during that period, because their mass is so small. Small seeds aren't damaged if moisture levels remain above 3%.

After seven days, open the jar and separate the packets of seeds from the silica gel. The seed packets are then stored in another moisture-proof container without any silica gel in order to maintain the low moisture content of the seeds. The second container could be another glass jar or any similar moisture-proof container. Thoroughly dry seeds reabsorb moisture quickly, so always try to minimize the time that the seed packets are exposed to the moisture in the air while being shifted to the second container.

Another type of container that has proven to be really versatile is a flat bag that has laminated walls made from layers of paper, plastic, foil and another layer of plastic. Individual paper packets of dry seeds can be heat-sealed inside of these pouches with a thermo-impulse heat sealer that is available from several of the sources listed in "Supplies for Seed Savers" at the end of this section.

Paper/poly/foil/poly pouches can even be sealed shut with an ordinary clothes iron set on "Wool" and applied to the open end of the bag for three seconds. When the pouches are filled with water and sealed, a person can stand on them without the seals leaking. If that person jumps on them until the pouch breaks, the sealed edges are still perfect. The sealed edge can be cut off with a pair of scissors, seeds can be taken out and the pouch can be resealed. The outside of the pouch can be written on, since that layer is paper, but for safety's sake always put a label inside with the seeds as well. Several small packets can be sealed into each laminated pouch. The pouches can be stored directly in the freezer, take up very little space, and are inexpensive.

The very best place to store an airtight container of thoroughly dried seeds is in a freezer. The next best place is in a refrigerator, followed by any cool area where the temperature fluctuates as little as possible. When retrieving seeds from frozen storage, always allow the sealed jar (or heat-sealed pouch) to reach room temperature before opening. Let the jar set out overnight, whenever there is sufficient time. If the jar is opened before the seeds reach room temperature, moisture will condense on the cold seeds and rehydrate them. When taking seeds from the container, reseal the jar or moisture proof pouch quickly, so that the seeds will regain as little moisture as possible. Also try to limit the number of times seeds are retrieved from the jar, because temperature fluctuations will gradually reduce the viability of the seeds.

When removing seeds from storage that have been dried to low moisture levels, expose the seeds to the air for a few days before planting, if time allows. This will let the seeds slowly pick up some moisture, instead of going immediately from low moisture storage to a very moist planting environment.

Color-indicating silica gel and heat-sealable barrier pouches are available from several of the sources listed in "Supplies for Seed Savers" at the end of this section.

OVERWINTERING BIENNIAL PLANTS

Probably the most difficult task faced by seed savers involves overwintering biennials, especially in northern climates where roots or plants must be dug, stored and then replanted the next spring. In extremely mild climates, overwintering may be as simple as making a fall planting, caring for plants that are left in the soil during the winter, and then harvesting seed during the next summer. In areas where the ground freezes only to a slight extent, special mulching techniques are used to cover plants or roots that are left in the garden over the winter. In northern areas where the ground freezes deeply, gardeners who successfully save vegetables in a root cellar for eating during the winter months will probably also be able to save some of the vegetables a bit longer for use in seed saving. The same techniques are used with only a few minor exceptions.

Saving biennial plants and roots requires some sort of storage area, clean storage containers, clean paper for wrapping and shredding, clean dry leaves (or sphagnum moss, peat moss or sand), water containers for providing moisture and increasing the humidity, a thermometer and humidity gauge. Root cellaring is commonly used to hold vegetables several months after harvest in a cold, moist atmosphere. Care must be taken to prevent the vegetables from either freezing or drying out during storage. Generally root cellaring is most successful when temperatures are held between 32° and 40° F., a temperature range that slows down the microorganisms which cause spoilage and also retards plant growth.

So many variations of root cellaring are used in various climates that whole books have been written on the subject. Specific guidelines for commonly grown biennial vegetables are given in the applicable sections of *Seed to Seed (Second Edition)*. These techniques include preparation for storage, optimum temperature and humidity levels, and expected storage life.

Basement storerooms designed to overwinter vegetables are often no more than a closed-off corner of the basement. Usually the north or east corner is chosen, because temperatures are most likely to be stable in areas least affected by the sun. Storage areas should not contain any heating ducts, oil pipes or water pipes. All of the designs incorporate insulated walls and ceilings, tightly closing doorways, air ducts and passive ventilation systems.

Occasionally garages or sheds are utilized for cold storage. These areas are subject to greater temperature fluctuations, however, and usually are not recommended for winter storage of vegetables. Also, garages used to park cars or other machinery often have emissions that interfere with temperature and air quality. Never use attics for seed storage because such areas are especially prone to temperature fluc-

tuation on sunny winter days.

Many different types of outdoor storage pits are popular in various areas of the country. Cone pits are often constructed by layering straw and vegetables, and then covering the entire mound with a layer of soil 6" or deeper. A special cone is inserted in the top of the mound to allow for ventilation. Often only one type of vegetable is stored in each pit and, once the pit is opened, the entire contents are usually removed. A partially buried barrel laid on an insulating bed of straw and covered with straw and earth is also a popular type of outdoor storage pit. Another variation is the Walter Needham pit that is designed to meet storage needs in extremely cold climates such as Vermont.

Complete descriptions of these special pits and other storage techniques are described in *Putting Food By* by Ruth Hertzberg, *Root Cellaring* by Nancy and Mike Bubel, and USDA Bulletin No. 119: *Storing Vegetables and Fruits in Basements, Cellars, Outbuildings, and Pits.*

GERMINATION TESTING

Usually the time and expense involved with long-term frozen storage are only warranted for seeds that have high germination rates. An exception would be in cases where frozen storage is used to maintain seeds with low germination rates until they can be grown out. In either case, germination testing can be easily done at home and closely mimics commercial testing.

Most vegetable seeds will germinate when exposed to moisture and warmth. Moist conditions are easily provided by using blotter pads or heavy paper towels. Cut the material into 12" x 12" squares and spray with warm water. Lay the moistened squares on a piece of plastic for easy handling and place 10, 25, 50 or 100 seeds, evenly spaced, on the surface. If there is an ample supply, use a minimum of 25 seeds. If an accurate count is needed, use 100 seeds due to sampling error. Cover with another moistened square, roll the layers up and place inside a lightweight plastic bag, such as a bread sack. Always remember that the seeds need air in order to grow. Punch a number of holes in the plastic sack, enough to let in some air without drying out the contents. Don't make the blotters too soggy, especially for melon seeds, which rot easily.

Finding a spot in the home that provides constant warmth at a specific temperature is sometimes difficult. The tops of refrigerators will sometimes suffice, as will areas near appliances with pilot lights. Natural gas inhibits many of the Solanaceae species, however, so do not try to germinate such seeds near gas stoves or water heaters. A 25 or 40 watt light bulb in a

Seed Storage Techniques

plywood box can provide an excellent source of heat at minimal expense, but should be closely checked with a thermometer. The temperature can be regulated by connecting the light bulb to a dimmer switch. The box may also need to be equipped with a heat-activated rheostat in order to maintain a constant temperature.

The importance of proper germination temperatures cannot be overstated. A constant minimum temperature of 75° F. is appropriate for most garden seeds. Some species, however, won't germinate if temperatures are slightly too high or too low. For example, eggplants and peppers germinate best at 80° F., but lettuce won't germinate if temperatures exceed that level. Malabar spinach, on the other hand, requires a constant temperature of at least 85° F.

If the proper level of warmth is constantly provided, most vegetable seeds will start to germinate in about seven days. Check the seeds daily, remoistening with warm water when necessary. After seven days, make the first count of germination and then remove the sprouted seeds. Make a second count a week later and add the first and second counts before figuring the germination percentage. Germination may not be complete for 21-28 days for some vegetables. The germination requirements for each species being tested should be checked before aborting a germination test. The most accessible source for such information is *Knott's Handbook for Vegetable Growers (Third Edition)* by Oscar A. Lorenz and Donald N. Maynard, Wiley and Sons, 1988.

RECORD KEEPING

Gardeners who grow their own vegetable seeds need to keep accurate records of seed sources and plant characteristics. An easy way to keep such records is to develop a card file. Any local office supply store should be able to provide a small metal recipe box, some 3" x 5" cards and dividers. Write all of the different plant types being kept on the dividers, and then fill out a card for each variety of seeds being maintained in your collection.

Each card should include the following information: type of plant, variety name (synonyms if any), name and address of source, date obtained, germination percentage if known, date the seeds were stored, year the seeds were last grown, accession number, and any pertinent history or cultural notes. If more seed needs to be obtained for some unforeseen reason, the source information could be invaluable. For computer storage, the information that is most important for retrieval includes: plant type, variety name, accession number, year last grown and date stored.

Accession numbers are particularly important when different varieties with the same name have been obtained from different sources.

Data taken on the plants throughout the gardening season can also be written onto the cards. Such information might include: days to maturity (number of days from sowing to dry seed, or from transplant to ripe fruit); plant height and habit; fruit size, color and shape; productivity; disease resistances or susceptibilities; flavor; and storage qualities.

Detailed records called descriptor lists often become important as seed savers begin maintaining ever larger collections of rare and heirloom varieties. Descriptors are used by researchers worldwide to give as much data as possible about a plant. With practice it is relatively easy to visualize a plant and its fruit by looking only at the data on a descriptor list.

Descriptor lists are often specially formulated for each vegetable species, however there are usually a number of similarities. Each set of descriptors will show: botanical and common names, accession number or seed source, location where the data was taken, name of the evaluator, number of days to maturity from seeding or transplanting, maturity in relation to the maturity of a standard open pollinated variety, plant characteristics at the time of first flower, description of the flower's color and size and shape, description of the leaf's size and color and shape, dimensions and color of a mature fruit, disease problems, insect problems, and possibly even a taste comparison to a standard variety.

Taking descriptor data requires a substantial investment in time and energy, and therefore such data is usually kept only by serious seed hobbyists on rare and little-known varieties. Descriptor lists are as varied as the individual growers and their data requirements. It would be wonderful if standard descriptors were developed and if all growers maintained complete descriptor lists, however that would require more time than most seed savers can afford.

A photograph taken on a grid of 1" squares showing fruits, flowers and a cluster of leaves can partially replace lengthy descriptor lists. Such photos are usually taken from a tripod with the camera aimed downward and the grid resting on the ground. A fairly inexpensive grid can be made from four photographer's "gray cards" taped together and marked off in 1" squares with a waterproof marker. This middle-gray background gives the perfect meter reading in the light available at the time. The best light for grid photos occurs on bright but overcast days. Never take such photos in full sun, which always results in dark shadows and bright highlights.

SUPPLIES FOR SEED SAVERS

Often it is difficult for seed savers to find the supplies that they need, especially in small quantities and at reasonable prices. The following companies offer various supplies that should be of interest to gardeners who are saving vegetable seeds.

Abundant Life Seed Foundation (PO Box 772, Port Townsend, WA 98368, e-mail abundant@olypen.com, phone 360-385-5660, fax 360-385-7455) is a nonprofit corporation dedicated to acquiring, propagating and preserving plants and seeds of native and naturalized flora of the North Pacific Rim. Their seed catalog offers stainless steel screens for seed cleaning, available in six different meshes (1/8" to 1/40"), either mounted or unmounted. The screens can even be used to wash berry and other fruit seeds from their pulp without rusting. A suggested donation of $30 for membership will bring you their seed catalog (also available separately for a suggested $2 donation), book list, periodic newsletters and a 10% discount on purchases.

Johnny's Selected Seeds (184 Foss Hill Road, Albion, ME 04910-9731, phone 207-437-4301, fax 800-437-4290, www.johnnyseeds.com) carries several varieties of spunbonded polypropylene floating row covers for frost and wind protection and insect control, and also wooden and metal row or plant markers. Their catalog is free.

Lawson Bag Company (PO Box 8577, Northfield, IL 60093, phone 847-446-8812) makes all sizes of pollinating bags for corn, sorghum, wheat, grasses, millet and sunflowers. Their tassel and shoot bags, which are used for the hand-pollination of corns, are made of sturdy paper and tough adhesive, and are designed to withstand the elements. Although Lawson is primarily a supplier to large companies and government programs, the company offers smaller quantities (lots of 1,000) of their #402 tassel bags and #217 shoot bags to amateur growers. These are the sizes of bags that are most commonly used by seed savers. The tassel bag expands to about 5" x 5" x 14.5" and the shoot bag to 2" x 1" x 7". Call or send for their price list.

Packaging Aids Corporation (PO Box 9144, San Rafael, CA 94912, phone 415-454-4868, fax 415-454-6853) sells a wide array of industrial-scale impulse heat sealers, including Audion Pronto ($386) which can be wall-mounted or attached to a table, and Audion Sealboy ($489 with cutter, $409 without), a table model for manual operation.

Peaceful Valley Farm Supply (PO Box 2209, Grass Valley, CA 95945, phone toll-free 888-784-1722, fax 530-272-4794, www.groworganic.com) is a source for Agribon and Tufbell floating row covers of varying sizes and weights, as well as row cover snap clamps and galvanized wire for hoops. Their catalog is free.

Synthetic Industries (Performance Fabrics Division, PO Box 977, Gainesville, GA 30503, phone 770-532-9756) manufactures a caging material that is used extensively by the Plant Introduction Station in Ames, Iowa. This is a woven synthetic screen that will last up to five years. For additional information, e-mail hilda_burke@sind.com.

Seed Savers Exchange (3076 North Winn Road, Decorah, IA 52101, phone 563-382-5990, fax 563-382-5872, www.seedsavers.org) has developed a complete line of supplies for seed saving, processing and storage, which are available on their web site and in upcoming catalogs. Their catalog is free.

Southern Exposure Seed Exchange (PO Box 460, Mineral, VA 23117, phone 540-894-9480) offers the best line of supplies for seed savers in the United States. Their catalog includes heat-sealable barrier pouches in two sizes, an industrial quality thermo-impulse heat sealer for all types of material, and color-indicating silica gel. Other items available include small and large ziplock plastic bags, ear shoot bags, four sizes of airtight Seed Saver Vials™, self-seal seed packets with sift-proof corners, drawstring muslin bags, row marking stakes, hand-held corn and popcorn shellers, and Reemay™ in 67" x 50" rolls. Their catalog is $2 (free to previous customers).

Territorial Seed Company (PO Box 158, Cottage Grove, OR 97424, phone 541-942-9547, fax 888-657-3131, www.territorialseed.com) offers two floating row covers (AG-19 Garden Fabric and Reemay™), a frost blanket to protect young plants, and a summer insect barrier. They also carry desiccant packages, a seed saving kit, and a variety of potting and transplanting supplies. Their catalog is free.

SECTION II

MAJOR VEGETABLE FAMILIES

THE AMARYLLIDACEAE FAMILY

James Beard, premier American chef, once said that without alliums there would be food, but no cuisine. Alliums are such an important crop that many cultures have used allium flowers in deity worship ceremonies. Onions, leeks and garlics have all been grown since prehistoric times and have spread worldwide. There are more than 400 species of alliums. Many species that are grown only as flowers in the United States are eaten in other parts of the world.

FAMILY TAXONOMY

Nearly all gardeners can identify members of the genus *Allium*. A strong onion or garlic odor is their most common characteristic. The odor is caused by sulfur compounds in the leaves and bulbs of the plants. The hollow round leaves that are so characteristic of onions are also found in many other allium species. Flat leaves that bend at a 45Υ angle in the middle are characteristic of leeks and garlics.

Topsetting onions and rocambole produce small bulbs called bulbils at the top of their flower stalk. Most garlics, shallots, multiplier onions and potato onions are "multicentric" (dividing vegetatively under the ground to form many bulbs). It is very unusual for any of these types of onions to produce seed, but some occasionally do when subjected to extreme variations in the weather. Possibly such plants are responding to a little understood survival mechanism.

Common chives grow in low clumps and do not form bulbs. Garlic chives look like miniature clumping leeks and have a garlic-like flavor. Common chives and garlic chives both form seed.

POLLINATION CHARACTERISTICS AND TECHNIQUES

Allium flowers are perfect, but are unable to self-pollinate. The anthers open first and shed pollen before the style and stigma are receptive. The anthers continue to shed pollen for three days, and the style and stigma are receptive for six days. The individual flowers open over a period of 30 days with the largest number open during the second week. Thus, on each seed head, some anthers are shedding pollen and some of the stigmas are receptive at any one time.

Allium flowers are visited by many types of insects. Flies and bees are the primary pollinators; wind is not a pollination vector. Different varieties within the same species are commercially isolated by 1-3 miles depending on the geography.

Most home seed savers isolate varieties rather than deal with caging or daily hand-pollination. Another relatively easy method is alternate day caging, which can be used when working with more than one variety (see "Alternate Day Caging" in Section I).

Amaryllidaceae in the Garden		
Genus	Species	Common Name
Allium	*ampeloprasum*	leek
	cepa	common (seed-producing) onion, shallot, multiplier onion, potato onion, topsetting onion
	fistulosum	Japanese bunching onion
	sativum	garlic, rocambole
	schoenoprasum	common chives
	tuberosum	garlic chives (Chinese chives)

Hand-pollination needs to be done every day for at least two weeks and preferably for 30 days, if good seed is to be produced. The immature flower heads are bagged before any of the individual flowers open. At least 10 flower heads of each variety should be bagged. Reemay bags or weather resistant corn tassel bags may be used. The bags should be secured with removable strings or plastic twist ties.

Each morning between 9:00 a.m. and noon, remove the bags from as many flower heads as can be kept free of insects. Use a camel hair brush to transfer pollen between the open flowers, moving from head to head and back again. Cover each flower head twice in rotation, which will help to ensure that some flowers are pollinated with pollen from another plant. Rebag the flowers and repeat the process daily. The bags can be removed when all of the seeds have set. Be sure to tag the hand-pollinated flower heads for identification during harvest.

Facing Page: Some common members of the Amaryllidaceae Family.

Caging with introduced pollinators, another method of pollination, is also described in Section I.

GENERAL PRODUCTION AND PROCESSING TECHNIQUES

It is very important to examine all alliums that are to be saved and replanted for seed production. Plants with off-type foliage should be removed early in the growing season. Also remove any plants that bolt or start to flower during the first season. Save only the best, most true-to-variety bulbs (or bulbils from the nonseeding alliums).

Garden rotation is very important when growing any nonseeding allium species. Invariably a few bulbils are unknowingly left in the soil after harvest. If a different variety is planted in the same location the following year, differences in the two varieties may not be obvious and the varieties could become mixed.

Two different methods are used for growing biennial alliums. Most common is the seed-to-bulb-to-seed method. Seeds are planted in the spring and mature bulbs are harvested, sorted or rogued in the fall. Only healthy true-to-type bulbs are stored over the winter for replanting the following spring. Shortly after being replanted, each bulb will begin to produce a seed stalk.

In mild winter areas it is also possible to grow alliums using the seed-to-seed method. Seeds are planted in the late summer or early fall, the plants grow throughout the winter, and bolt to seed in the spring. The seed-to-seed method does not allow for the bulbs to be sorted prior to flowering. Off-type bulbs are difficult to see and are usually not removed. It is best to use the seed-to-bulb-to-seed method if there is any question about the purity of seed that is being renewed.

It is easiest to let the seed heads mature on the stalks. In arid climates the stalks and seed heads dry quickly when irrigation is withheld. Harvest should begin as soon as the heads are dry. Many seeds will shatter and be lost if the plants are left in the garden too long. In humid regions of the country, seed heads often are cut off and dried on tarps or pieces of plastic in an area that can be protected from the rains. Seed heads can also be dried in a food dehydrator, but only if the temperature can be accurately controlled. Drying temperatures higher than 95ϒ F. will damage the seeds.

Allium seeds will easily fall out of the seedpods when the heads are dry. The remainder can be removed by jogging on top of the heads or using a small seed thresher. Winnowing is then used to separate any remaining seedpods and other debris.

Allium ampeloprasum - Leek

Leeks are a favorite vegetable in northern European countries. Their soft bulbs and leaves tolerate freezing temperatures and are more resistant to diseases than onions. Wild relatives of leeks can be found as far north as Germany.

Elephant garlic, sometimes known as greathead garlic, is also a true leek. The large bulbs are used like a mild garlic. Most elephant garlics produce a single large bulb, but do not flower. The few that do flower produce several cloves around a large central flower stalk. Flowers of these varieties are usually sterile.

BOTANICAL CLASSIFICATION

Leeks are members of the genus *Allium* and the species *ampeloprasum*. Different varieties of *A. ampeloprasum* have been selected for long white bulbs, resistance to bolting, bluish green leaf color and cold tolerance. Leeks are most commonly grown in France and England where numerous heirlooms are documented.

POLLINATION, CROSSING AND ISOLATION

Leeks are outbreeding plants. Like other seed producing alliums, leeks have perfect flowers. Leeks do not cross with onions or with any other allium species. Leeks will, however, cross with kurrat, a wild leek that grows in Egypt and along the Mediterranean.

SEED PRODUCTION, HARVEST AND PROCESSING

Leeks are true biennials, but will produce flower stalks regardless of the daylength after experiencing cold weather for 4-6 weeks. Some leeks form an onion-like bulb instead of the familiar white leaf base when grown during very long, warm days. Leeks can be overwintered under mulch where winters are not extremely cold. In far northern regions with severe winters, the plants must be dug in the fall, overwintered in a root cellar, and planted the next spring. Leeks will stay in good, plantable condition for many months when stored at 32° F. and 80-90% humidity.

Leek varieties are easily crossed by insects. Isolation of one mile is recommended for seed production. Bagging with hand-pollination, alternate day caging, and caging with introduced pollinators can all be used to ensure pure seed crops. (These pollination techniques are explained in detail in Section I.)

Leeks that are left in the ground during the winter will often produce side shoots known as leek pearls. These pearls can provide an emergency method of preserving a variety that has been damaged or cross-pollinated. Leek pearls are genetically identical to their parent plants, and can be used as leek sets and grown to maturity for seed, if the seed crop from the parent plants has been contaminated.

Leek seeds are more tightly encased in their seedpods than onion seeds. Therefore, leeks do not shatter as readily as onions, so the immediate harvest of the dry seed heads is not as critical. Leek seed may be threshed and winnowed as described in the introductory pages of the Amaryllidaceae family.

SEED STATISTICS

Leek seed will retain 50% germination for three years when stored in cool, dry, dark conditions. Members of the Seed Savers Exchange annually offer about 35 varieties of leeks, and the *Garden Seed Inventory* contains 84 varieties available from commercial seed companies. There are approximately 10,000 seeds per ounce (350 per gram or 160,000 per pound), depending on the variety. Federal Germination Standard for commercially sold leek seed is 60%.

GROWING LEEKS FROM SEED

Leeks are a cool season biennial. They must be grown to maturity during their second season, before a vernalization period, in order to produce quality seed. Plants that produce seed in one growing season should not be used for seed. Seed set is dependent on climate. Either the seed-to-seed method or the seed-to-bulb-to-seed method can be used. Leeks can be direct seeded or greenhouse sown (and kept continually moist) at a depth of .25-.5". The seeds germinate at temperatures from 50-75° F., usually within 8-16 days. Transplant into a 5" trench, 2" inches apart, filling in as the plants grow. This provides some freezing protection in mid-range climates. Plants benefit from cool temperatures and will tolerate some shade.

REGIONAL GROWING RECOMMENDATIONS

Northeast: Leeks can be direct seeded about May

1. The plants like full sun and average water. Dig the plants in late October or early November and store by heeling into dirt (we use buckets) in a cold damp cellar. Replant in early May. During year two the seed heads should be left in the field as long as possible, often until mid-November. Flower stalks are best staked. Pull the whole seed stalks and place upside down in paper bags in a dry place to "after-ripen." Many of the hardier (winter) types may be overwintered in the field with little or no mulch, but results are less consistent than with cellaring. Roots/dirt should be lightly watered in mid to late winter, if appropriate, preferably in such a way as to dampen the soil but not the foliage. Remove the buckets from the cellar a week or two before time for replanting and allow the blanched foliage to "green up" a bit and get tougher.

Mid-Atlantic: Leeks can be direct seeded about March 1, or started in a greenhouse about January 15 and transplanted into the garden about March 1. The plants like full sun and average water, and overwinter with no special care. Thrips are sometimes a pest.

Southeast/Gulf Coast: Start in a greenhouse about September 15 or January 15 and transplant into the garden about November 15 or March 15. We use hoop houses here in Zone 7 for cosmetic reasons rather than enhanced seed production. The plants overwinter in the garden with no special care, but may not flower until the second spring. Plants seeded in the spring will flower the next spring (a year later), but when seeds are started in fall they may not flower until 18 months later.

Upper Midwest: Start in a greenhouse about March 1 and transplant into the garden about April 20. The plants like full sun and average water. Mulch the plants in mid-November with straw and cornstalks; also make use of snow by planting where the snow drifts. At harvest time, watch out for heavy rainfall as the seed is ripening. Winters with minimal snow cover will cause problems, so a portion of the crop should be dug as insurance.

Southwest: Leeks can be direct seeded from January 1 to April 15, or August 15 to October 1. The plants like full sun and average water.

Central West Coast: Leeks can be direct seeded August 15 to September 15. The plants like partial sun and average water, and overwinter in the garden with no special care.

Maritime Northwest: Leeks can be direct seeded from March 20 to April 10, or can be started in a greenhouse about January 20 and transplanted into the garden about March 20. The plants like full sun and average water, and will overwinter in the garden with no special care.

Botanists believe that the onion originated in Iran and Pakistan. Onion carvings and seeds have been found in Egyptian tombs dating back to 3200 B.C. Greeks and Romans wrote about onions as early as 400 B.C. and held festivals during onion harvest. By the Middle Ages, onions had been transported throughout northern Europe and were used as both food and medicine.

Onion bulb formation is dependent on daylength or photoperiod. Onion varieties are classified according to the photoperiod required for bulbing: short day varieties require 12 to 13 hours of daylight; intermediate varieties 13.5 to 14 hours; long day varieties 14.5 to 15 hours; and a few very long day varieties require 16 or more hours of daylight. Onions tend to bulb more quickly during warm days, however temperatures over 104° F. can actually retard bulbing.

Despite these daylength classifications, onion bulbing is really a response to the length of the night, not daylight. Locations closer to the equator have shorter summer days than, for example, some areas of Alaska that have 20 hours of light on some June days. Thus, short day onions grow to full bulb size during the 12 hours of light available in the southern regions of the United States. Intermediate varieties bulb well in the nation's midsection, and long day types grow well in the northern regions. Gardeners in the mild winter regions of the intermediate zones often grow long day onions from spring to summer, and short day varieties from summer to fall.

BOTANICAL CLASSIFICATION

Onions belong to the genus *Allium* and species *cepa*. *A. cepa* includes several groups or subspecies.

The Aggregatum Group includes all of the multicentric onions that divide vegetatively. Shallots, multiplier onions and potato onions are all examples of the Aggregatum Group.

Biennial onions that produce seed comprise the Cepa Group.

The Proliferum Group includes the topsetting onions which are commonly known as Egyptian onions, tree onions or walking onions.

POLLINATION, CROSSING AND ISOLATION

Common onions are inbreeding plants. All varieties of seed-producing onions can be crossed by insects. Some of the top setting onions (*Allium cepa*, Proliferum Group) produce fertile flowers that can contaminate nearby seed-producing onions. There can also occasionally be some crossing between seed-producing onions and some varieties of *A. fistulosum*. Seed-producing onions do not cross with chives or leeks.

Isolation of one mile is adequate for seed purity. Bagging or various caging techniques can be used when more than one variety is grown in the garden. These techniques are described in the introductory pages of the Amaryllidaceae family and also under each applicable species.

SEED PRODUCTION, HARVEST AND PROCESSING

Seed-producing onions are biennial and require two growing seasons to produce seed. Onion bulbs that are going to be replanted for seed production can be harvested after the first season. Only the best bulbs should be stored for replanting in the spring. This is referred to as the seed-to-bulb-to-seed method. In some mild winter climates, onions can be left in the ground to overwinter.

When using the seed-to-bulb-to-seed method, the onions are harvested after the first growing season when the tops begin to dry. The bulbs are then dried or cured for 10-12 days. Avoid drying the bulbs in the sun where temperatures exceed 75° F. or the bulbs will sunburn and spoil in storage. After curing the onions, remove the dry tops or braid into strands. Recent studies suggest that most varieties will keep for 3-6 months at 32° to 45° F. or at 77° to 95°, and at 60-70% humidity. The worst possible storage temperature is 60Υ to 70Υ F., which is about room temperature. At a relative humidity of 40% or lower and a temperature of 37Υ F., some onion varieties can be stored for 10-12 months.

Onions will begin to sprout only after a period of rest, which varies from variety to variety. During this resting period, the bulbs will not sprout even when exposed to optimal growing conditions. Following the resting period, the onions enter a dormant phase. During this period of dormancy, the onions will sprout if the temperature and humidity are both within the proper range.

During the next spring, the best, most true-to-type onions are replanted for seed production. As the days get longer, each onion will form a seed stalk and a flower head that contains hundreds of tiny flowers. As the seeds form, the flower and plant begin to dry. The seeds are encased in tiny pods that shatter easily. Onion seeds should be harvested as soon as the seeds

Egyptian onion (*Allium cepa*, Proliferum Group) with sprouted bulbils.

are mature and the pods start to dry. The seed heads can be bent over into a sack and cut from the stalk to avoid losing any seeds during harvest.

The seed heads should be placed in a protected area, away from direct sunlight, to complete drying. Onion seeds fall free of the seedpods quite easily once the pods are dry. The remaining seeds can be removed with a commercial seed thresher. Other successful seed removal techniques include jogging in place on the seed heads, rubbing them over a wire mesh screen, or rubbing the seed heads together. Winnowing the seeds in a light wind will remove any remaining seedpods and debris.

SEED STATISTICS

Onion seeds will retain 50% germination for two years when stored in cool, dry, dark conditions. Members of the Seed Savers Exchange annually offer about 38 varieties of common onion (and 88 varieties of multiplying onions) and the *Garden Seed Inventory* lists sources for 128 varieties of common onions (and

38 varieties of multiplying onions) that are available from commercial mail-order seed companies. There are approximately 6,500 seeds per ounce (230 per gram or 105,000 seeds per pound), depending on the variety. Federal Germination Standard for commercially sold onion seed is 70%.

GROWING COMMON ONIONS FROM SEED

Seed-producing onions are biennials, requiring two seasons to produce seed. The seed-to-bulb-to-seed method or the seed-to-seed method can be used depending on the climate. Plants producing seed in one season should not be used for seed stock. Onion seed can be either direct seeded or greenhouse started. Lightly cover the seeds in either direct seeding or greenhouse sowing. Optimum germination temperature is 70° F. with germination usually occurring in 10 days. Plant or set out in full sun in northern climates, or afternoon shade in hot climates. The plants should be thinned to 3" (depending on the size of the variety being grown).

Amaryllidaceae

Flower stalks and seed heads of common onions (*Allium cepa*, Cepa Group).

REGIONAL GROWING RECOMMENDATIONS

Northeast: Common onions can be started in a greenhouse in early March and transplant into the garden by mid-May. Likes full sun and average water. Dig the plants in late August when the tops begin to brown, and store as hanging braids or in net bags, in cool drier part of cellar. Replant in early May. In late August of year two, watch carefully to avoid shattering. Flower stalks will often need staking.

Mid-Atlantic: Common onions can be direct seeded about March 1, or started in a greenhouse about January 15 and transplanted into the garden about March 1. The plants like full sun and average water and overwinter in the garden with no special care.

Southeast/Gulf Coast: Start bulb onions in a greenhouse about January 30 and transplant into the garden about March 15. The plants like full sun. Multipliers overwinter in the garden with no special care, and bulblets can be set out in the fall.

Upper Midwest: Common onions can be started in a greenhouse about March 1 and transplanted into the garden about April 20. The plants like full sun and average water, and require mulching (with straw or cornstalks) in mid-November. At harvest time, watch for heavy rainfall as the seed is ripening. Winters with minimal snow cover will cause problems, so a portion of the crop should be dug as insurance.

Southwest: Common onions can be direct seeded September 15 to March 15. The plants like full sun and average water. In low desert, the plants can "oversummer" in the ground, but must be mulched to protect from heat.

Central West Coast: Common onions can be direct seeded March 15 to April 15, or started in a greenhouse about January 15 and transplanted into the garden March 15 to April 15. The plants like full sun and average water, and overwinter in the garden with no special care.

Maritime Northwest: Common onions can be direct seeded March 20 to April 10. The plants like full sun and average water. The plants should be stored in a cool (50-60° F.) location that is dry and dark, and replanted March 20 to April 10 to produce a seed crop.

Allium fistulosum
Japanese Bunching Onion

Japanese bunching onions are inbreeding plants and have been used like green onions for centuries in China and Japan. They do not have a well-developed bulb, but definitely have the hollow, tube-like leaves of an onion. Seed heads are formed after a cold period, although some varieties will form topsets instead. Different varieties of *A. fistulosum* can be insect cross-pollinated, and occasional crossing can also occur between varieties belonging to *A. fistulosum* and *A. cepa.*

SEED STATISTICS

The seeds of Japanese bunching onion seeds will retain 50% germination for two years when stored in cool, dry, dark conditions. Members of the Seed Savers Exchange annually offer about 22 varieties of bunching onions, and the *Garden Seed Inventory* contains 38 varieties of bunching onions available from commercial seed companies. There are 12,500 seeds per ounce (440 per gram or 200,000 per pound), depending on the variety. Federal Germination Standard for commercial seed is 70%.

GROWING JAPANESE BUNCHING ONIONS FROM SEED

Japanese bunching onions are basically biennial, requiring two seasons to produce seed. However, bunching onions will set seed after a short cold period, allowing seed to be set in one year. Bulb formation is not an issue, as with *Allium cepa*, and seed produced in one year may be used as stock seed. Seeds can either be direct seeded or greenhouse started. Lightly cover seeds in either direct seeded or greenhouse sowings. The optimum seed germination temperature is 70Υ F. with germination usually occurring in about 10 days. Plant or set out in full sun in northern climates, or in areas with afternoon shade in hot climates. The plants should be thinned to .5" depending on the variety.

REGIONAL GROWING RECOMMENDATIONS

Northeast: Japanese bunching onions can be direct seeded as early in spring as possible (before May 15) or in late summer (after August 1). The plants like full sun and average water, and overwinter in the garden with no special care.

Mid-Atlantic: Japanese bunching onions can be direct seeded about March 1, or started in a greenhouse about January 15 and transplanted into the garden about March 1. The plants like full sun and average water. Plants overwinter with no special care.

Southeast/Gulf Coast: Start in a greenhouse January 15 and transplant into the garden March 15. Spring-seeded plants benefit from division in the fall, then flower the following spring. However, dividing in the fall and spring is the easiest method of propagation.

Upper Midwest: Japanese bunching onions can be direct seeded in early April. The plants like full sun and average water, and require mulching (with cornstalks or straw) in mid-November. At harvest time, watch for heavy rainfall as the seed is ripening. Winters with minimal snow cover will cause problems, so a portion of the crop should be dug as insurance.

Southwest: Japanese bunching onions can be direct seeded from September 15 to March 15. The plants like partial sun and average water. Plants may die from heat in low desert regions, so mulch to protect from the heat.

Japanese bunching onion (*Allium fistulosum*).

Central West Coast: Japanese bunching onions can be direct seeded about March 15. The plants like full sun (but partial sun is okay) and average water, and overwinter in the garden with no special care.

Maritime Northwest: Japanese bunching onions can be direct seeded March 20 to April 10. The plants like full sun and average water, and overwinter in the garden with no special care.

Allium sativum
Garlic and Rocambole

Garlic is grown vegetatively from the cloves formed in each bulb. Several layers of sheath leaves surround each of the cloves. Each clove contains two mature leaves and a vegetative bud. The outer leaf is a dry sheath with an aborted blade. The second leaf is quite thick and also has an aborted leaf blade. The vegetative bud has a bladeless sprout leaf and one or two foliage leaves that remain at rest after the bulb is mature.

Rocambole, also known as serpent garlic, forms an elongated stalk that twists in a circular loop as it grows. Both the top setting bulbils and the underground cloves can be eaten or replanted. The cloves are usually preferred for replanting, because the top sets may take two seasons to produce full-sized bulbs.

After harvest, garlic bulbs enter a period of rest similar to onions. Following this rest period, garlic cloves begin a period of dormancy. During this dormancy period, sprouting will occur when the temperature and humidity reach the proper range.

In mild climates, garlic is usually planted in the fall and allowed to grow during the cool conditions of winter. This allows the plants to grow to good size before bulbing begins during the lengthening days of spring. In cold climates, fall-planted garlic will remain dormant under mulch until the spring thaw, but still produces bigger bulbs than garlic planted in spring. Garlic harvest begins when the plant's partially dry top bends over. Garlic bulbs are usually dried for one week prior to storage, but never in direct sunlight.

After curing, garlic may be stored in paper bags or hung in braids or in bunches. Bulbs that are to be used for planting stock will keep for 6-8 months when stored in the dark at 35-40° F. and 60% humidity. Higher temperatures can cause rough bulbs and early sprouting. Garlic bulbs are broken apart into individual cloves that are planted.

REGIONAL GROWING RECOMMENDATIONS

Northeast: Garlic cloves can be planted from September 22 to November 1. The plants like full sun and average water, and overwinter in the garden with no special care. Harvest in mid-August, or when the plants are half yellow. Cure in a cool, airy place for about one week. With rocamboles, slightly better yields are attained by breaking off the "scapes" (flower stalks) as soon as they form – unless you wish to use those "bulbils" as propagation material, in which case it requires two full seasons to get large cloves. This is a good way to increase the number of plants quickly.

Mid-Atlantic: Start the bulbs in September for summer harvest (June). The plants like full sun and average water, and overwinter with no special care. Sometimes mites and thrips are pests.

Southeast/Gulf Coast: Set out in late November.

Upper Midwest: Garlic be planted in late August (by cloves). The plants like full sun, are drought tolerant, and overwinter in the garden with no special care.

Southwest: Garlic can be planted September 15 to March 15. The plants like full sun and average water. In low desert, plants can "oversummer" in the ground; mulch with straw to protect from heat.

Central West Coast: Garlic can be planted about September 1. The plants like full sun and average water, and overwinter in the garden with no special care.

Maritime Northwest: Garlic is planted from September 10 to October 1. The plants like full sun and average water, and overwinter with no special care.

Allium schoenoprasum
Common Chives

Common chives look like tiny clumps of onions. The plants are perennial and grow for years. Each year some of the plants will produce purple-flowered seed heads that are insect-pollinated. Several different varieties of chives are stored in USDA collections. These varieties are distinguished from each other mainly by plant height and flower color variations. Seed catalogs in the United States offer generic chives only, with no mention made of any varietal distinctions. Different varieties grown near one another would be insect cross-pollinated. Common chives do not cross with garlic chives or any other allium species.

Allium tuberosum
Garlic Chives (Chinese Chives)

Common chives and garlic chives are both outbreeding plants. Garlic chives look like miniature leeks with flat leaves, and taste like very mild garlic. The plants flower freely in late summer. Their white flowers, often used as a garnish, are insect-pollinated.

Garlic chives are also called Chinese chives and a myriad of names in various Chinese dialects. If different varieties exist and were grown near each other, they would be insect cross-pollinated. Garlic chives do not cross with common chives or any other allium species.

SEED STATISTICS

The seeds of common chives and garlic chives will retain 50% germination for two years when stored in cool, dry, dark conditions. Members of the Seed Savers Exchange annually offer about 2 varieties of chives and 2 varieties of garlic chives, and the *Garden Seed Inventory* lists sources for 11 varieties of chives and 4 varieties of garlic chives available from commercial seed companies. There are 33,000 seeds per ounce (1,155 per gram or 528,000 per pound) depending on the variety. Federal Germination Standard for both types of commercially sold seed is 70%.

GROWING COMMON CHIVES AND GARLIC CHIVES FROM SEED

Common chives and garlic chives are both perennial, tolerating frost but not prolonged freezing temperatures. They are frequently grown as annuals in climates with winter temperatures below 32° F. for extended periods of time. Clumps may be dug, stored over the winter, and set out to flower in the spring. Seed production occurs each spring-summer in perennial plantings. Chive seeds can be direct seeded or greenhouse started. Cover the seeds .25-.5" deep. Seed germinates best at 70° F. with germination usually occurring in 14 days. Plant or set out in full sun or partial shade. Chive plants are usually not thinned, but left to grow in bunches.

REGIONAL GROWING RECOMMENDATIONS

Northeast: Common chives and garlic chives can both be direct seeded anytime, but preferably in early spring. The plants like full sun and average water, and will overwinter in the garden with no special care. Watch the plants of garlic chives carefully near harvesting time, as they are quite shatter-prone.

Mid-Atlantic: Common chives can be started in a greenhouse and transplanted into the garden any time. Garlic chives can be direct seeded about March 1, or started in a greenhouse about January 15 and transplanted into the garden about March 1. The plants like full sun and average water, and will overwinter in the garden with no special care. Aphids are an occasional problem on common chives.

Southeast/Gulf Coast: Common chives and garlic chives can both be started in a greenhouse about January 15-30 and transplanted into the garden about March 15. Both like partial sun, and will overwinter with no special care. Vegetative propagation of common chives by dividing and replanting in the fall (September to October) is easiest. Dividing garlic chives in early spring is the easiest method of propagation.

Garlic chives (*Allium tuberosum*).

Upper Midwest: Start common chives in a greenhouse about March 1 and transplant into the garden about April 15. Common chives and garlic chives both like partial sun, and the plants will overwinter in the garden with no special care. At harvest time, watch for heavy rainfall while the seed of common chives is ripening. Winters with minimal snow cover can also cause problems, so a portion of the crop should be dug as insurance.

Southwest: Common chives and garlic chives can both be direct seeded from September 15 to March 15. The plants like partial sun and average water. Both have difficulty "oversummering" in the ground, so mulch and cover in low desert areas.

Central West Coast: Common chives and garlic chives are direct seeded from March 15 to June 15, or August 30 to October 1. The plants like full sun and average water, and will overwinter in the garden with no special care.

Maritime Northwest: Common chives and garlic chives can both be direct seeded March 20 to April 10, or started in a greenhouse about January 20 and transplanted into the garden about March 20. The plants like full sun and average water, and their seeds are harvested after the flowers dry out.

Amaryllidaceae

The Brassicaceae family (formerly known as the Cruciferae family) is quite large and includes over 350 genera. Cabbage and broccoli usually come to mind when brassica is mentioned, but some very important flowers, condiments and herbs are also members of the family. Garden cress, watercress, radish, horseradish and turnip all share family ties with the more common cole crops.

At times the vernacular associated with Brassicaceae becomes difficult to decipher. Many gardeners refer to broccoli, kale, cabbage and Brussels sprouts as cole crops. Another name, mustards, is sometimes used to refer to the entire family or just to the mustard species. Even the authoritative *Hortus Third* still lists Brassicaceae and Cruciferae as alternate names for one another.

Since recorded time, various forms of Brassicaceae have been savored by mankind. In Rome about 201 B.C., Cato described several different kinds of kales and cabbages. Chinese cabbages and mustards appear in artwork and literature dating many centuries before Christ. Perennial wild cabbage can still be found growing on the coasts of England and France.

Broccoli, a wild cabbage selected specifically for its flower buds, is thought to have been developed in Italy. Continual selection for the best edible shoots and flower buds has resulted in the broccoli varieties grown today. Similar selections have resulted in the development of many of the other cole crops.

FAMILY TAXONOMY

Seedlings of the Brassicaceae family all look very much alike and often are impossible to tell apart. The flowers are also quite similar, each having four petals that form a cross. The outdated, though still commonly encountered family name, Cruciferae, was derived from this cross-like petal formation of flowers.

POLLINATION CHARACTERISTICS AND TECHNIQUES

The Brassicaceae family can be a difficult one for the garden seed saver. All members within each of the species can cross with one another. This means that varieties of broccoli, Brussels sprouts, cabbage, kohlrabi, collards, cauliflower and kale will all cross with each other. The flowers are perfect, but require insects for pollination. Many varieties exhibit self-incompatibility similar to self-sterility in fruit trees, which is nature's way of ensuring diversity. The pollen of self-incompatible varieties cannot grow properly in a flower on the same plant. It will grow normally, however, when moved by an insect to a flower on another plant.

It is never a good idea to save seed from just one plant, but it would be impossible to do so in many of the Brassicaceae genera due to self-incompatibility.

Brassicaceae in the Garden		
Genus	Species	Common Name
Armoracia	*rusticana*	horseradish
Brassica	*hirta*	white flowered mustard
	juncea	Indian mustard, mustard greens
	napus	rutabaga (Swede turnip), Siberian kale, rape
	nigra	black mustard
	oleracea	broccoli, Brussels sprouts, cabbage, cauliflower, collards, kale, kohlrabi
	rapa	turnip, broccoli raab, Chinese cabbage, Chinese mustard
Crambe	*maritima*	sea kale
Eruca	*sativa*	rocket (roquette)
Lepidium	*mayenii*	maca
	sativum	garden cress
Raphanus	*sativus*	radish
Rorippa	*microphylla*	large leaf water cress
	nasturtium	watercress

Facing Page: Checking for ripe pods on seed stalks of cabbage (*Brassica oleracea*).

Insects must carry pollen from one plant's flower to a flower on another plant, not just one flower to another on the same plant. Therefore, the larger the group of plants, the better the pollination and seed production will be. Finally, to confuse matters even further, some summer or East Indian cauliflowers and some Brussels sprouts will self-pollinate.

To ensure seed purity it is necessary to isolate different varieties by 1/2 mile, use caging with introduced pollinators, or use alternate day caging. Spun polyester is an ideal caging material, because it allows air, water and light to pass through to the plants while restricting insect travel.

Alternate day caging requires the construction of a cage for each of the varieties. Each morning an alternate cage is removed, and each evening the cage is replaced. This method allows insects to pollinate each variety for one day and excludes insects the next. Seed production is restricted due to the lack of daily pollination.

Caging with artificial insect introduction requires the use of trapped flies or newly hatched bees. This method sounds far better than it works. Flies trapped with rotten meat can be introduced into the cage, but there is no guarantee that they will visit enough flowers to ensure adequate pollination. (Caging with introduced pollinators is described in detail in Section I.)

GENERAL PRODUCTION AND PROCESSING TECHNIQUES

Always select healthy plants that perform well in your area when saving seed. Plants that have excessive insect damage or are stunted, that show off-color foliage or produce poorly should not be saved for seed production. Weather and insect damage will not affect the genetic makeup of a plant but will affect the quality and quantity of the seeds.

Brassicaceae seedpods must develop fully while still attached to the growing plant. Plants pulled before they are completely mature and stored in hopes of further pod development produce little viable seed. As the seeds approach maturity, the pods begin to dry out and turn light brown. The seedpods of all cole crops have a tendency to shatter. The ripest seedpods will be located at the bottom of each seed stalk and should be hand-harvested as they dry. Progressive collection of the pods can be made over several weeks. If hand harvesting is too time-consuming, cut the entire stalk when the largest number of pods are dry but have not shattered. Maturing seed stalks may need to be netted or bagged to protect the seed crop from birds.

Continue to dry the stalks away from the direct sun. Many of the seedpods will shatter, while others will need to be broken by hand, or by jogging in place on top of a seed bag, or with the use of a seed thresher. The wind, a hair dryer or a fan can be used to winnow the seeds. Be sure to cover the area used for winnowing with a tarp or sheet. If a strong gust of wind accidentally causes seeds as well as chaff to be blown out of the winnowing container, the tarp will recover many of the seeds. Always be careful, however, to completely shake out the tarp when switching from one variety to the next.

Brassicaceae seeds do not normally require any further processing. However, if black rot (*Xanthomonas campestris*) or black leg (*Phoma lingam*) or black leaf spot (*Alternaria brassicae* and *A. brassicola*) is a problem, the seeds can be hot water treated to reduce incidence of the disease. (The technique for hot water treatment of seeds is described in detail in Section I.)

Brassica napus – Rutabaga, Siberian Kale and Rape

Rutabagas (known as Swede turnip in England) appeared in Europe during the Middle Ages. Some gardening books indicate that rutabagas are the result of a cross between a turnip and a cabbage, but this could not be verified in any of the references cited. Rutabagas do not grow well in areas where summer temperatures exceed 75° F. for long periods of time. There are two common forms of rutabagas, one with white flesh and another with yellow flesh.

BOTANICAL CLASSIFICATION

Rutabagas belong to the genus *Brassica* and the species *napus*. Previously Sturtevant incorrectly classified rutabagas as *B. rapa* along with turnips. In more recent taxonomic references (*Hortus*, Yamaguchi, George), rutabagas and turnips have been correctly separated into different species.

Some residual name confusion still exists, however, especially with very old varieties. The names Swede turnip, Finnish turnip or Lapland turnip all refer to vegetables belonging to *B. napus*. Some varieties of agricultural or fodder turnips, however, may be *B. napus* while others are *B. rapa*. Additional research and testing are needed to separate all known varieties of rutabagas and turnips into their correct species.

Brassica napus is commonly divided into three subspecies. Napobrassica Group includes rutabagas which are grown for their roots. Pabularia Group includes rutabagas grown for their foliage, such as Siberian kale and Hanover Salad. The third group includes the rape varieties. Rape is grown as an oil seed, for birdseed and for animal forage.

POLLINATION, CROSSING AND ISOLATION

Rutabagas are inbreeding plants. Rutabaga flowers are self-fertile and are capable of self-pollination. Varieties grown within one mile of each other are easily cross-pollinated by insects. Rutabagas will also cross with some varieties of agricultural turnips or fodder turnips, and with all varieties of winter rape.

To ensure seed purity it is necessary to isolate all varieties belonging to *Brassica napus* by one mile. If two or more varieties are grown within close proximity, caging is necessary. Various caging methods are described in the introductory pages of the Brassicaceae family.

SEED PRODUCTION, HARVEST AND PROCESSING

Rutabagas are biennial, producing seed during their second growing season. The plants are frost tolerant and, if well mulched, can be left in the ground under a snow cover. In areas with extremely cold winters, however, the roots should be dug after the first few frosts. Trim the tops to 2". Rutabagas will keep 2-4 months when stored in sawdust or moss at 32-40° F. and 90-95% humidity.

Rutabagas produce seed stalks 3' tall or more. The plants flower prolifically and are very attractive to bees. The seedpods, which form after the flowers begin to fade, are green initially, but turn tan as the seeds mature and the plant begins to dry. The seedpods shatter beginning with the pods lowest on the stalks. Several hand pickings will result in the greatest seed harvest. If harvesting by hand is too time-consuming, cut the entire stalk when the greatest number of seedpods are dry but have not yet shattered.

Continue to dry the stalks and seedpods away from direct sunlight. Many of the seedpods will shatter. The remaining pods will need to be broken by hand, with a seed thresher, or by jogging in place on a bag of seedpods. Winnowing will remove small pieces of seedpods, leaves and other remaining debris.

Rutabaga seeds do not normally require any further processing. If black rot diseases are a problem, the seeds can be hot water treated to reduce incidence of the disease. (The technique for hot water treatment of seeds is described in Section I.)

SEED STATISTICS

Rutabaga seeds will remain viable for five years when stored under ideal conditions. Members of the Seed Savers Exchange annually offer about 50 varieties of rutabaga, while the *Garden Seed Inventory* lists sources for 26 varieties that are available from commercial seed companies. There are approximately 9,000 rutabaga seeds per ounce (320 per gram or 144,000 per pound), depending on the variety. Federal Germination Standard for commercially sold rutabaga seed is 80%.

GROWING RUTABAGA FROM SEED

Rutabagas are biennial, frost tolerant plants that grow best where summer temperatures are cool. They do not benefit from long, dry, hot summers in mild climates. Rutabaga is usually direct seeded in the late spring in fertile, well dug soil, covering the seeds .5" deep. Plant or set out in full sun in cool climates, or partial shade in hot summer climates. The seed germinates at temperatures ranging from 50-70° F. with germination usually occurring in 5-15 days. The plants should be thinned to 6-8" for food production and for breeding purposes. An early frost will increase the sugar in the roots.

REGIONAL GROWING RECOMMENDATIONS

Northeast: Rutabaga can be direct seeded from June 5-20. The plants like full sun and average water. We use floating row covers to keep flea beetles from decimating young seedlings. Dig the plants in late October and store in a cool damp cellar. Crowns must not wither. Replant in early May. Pods are very shatter-prone at harvest time. In the second year, pits should be at least 2" x 2". The plants are very susceptible to flea beetles (and deer, rabbits, etc.), so row cover is a must, until flowering (June). Flower stalks should be staked.

Mid-Atlantic: Rutabaga can be direct seeded about March 1, or from August 15 to September 15. The plants like full sun and average water, and overwinter in the garden with no special care.

Southeast/Gulf Coast: Rutabaga can be direct seeded from September 1-15. The plants like partial sun, and overwinter in the garden with no special care.

Upper Midwest: Rutabaga can be direct seeded about April 15-20. The plants like full sun and average water. Dig the plants in early March and store in moist sand or peat moss, then replant in early April.

Southwest: Rutabaga is not commonly grown in this region.

Central West Coast: Rutabaga can be direct seeded from August 1 to September 1. The plants like full sun and average water, and overwinter in the garden with no special care.

Maritime Northwest: Rutabaga can be direct seeded about September 5-10. The plants like full sun and average water. We use floating row covers for first 4-6 weeks to protect crop from cabbage root maggot. Plants overwinter in the garden with no special care.

Brassica oleracea - Cabbage

Cabbage is the fourth most produced vegetable in the United States. While we may eat a lot of cabbage, very few of the hundreds of known varieties are still grown. Today's headed cabbage was selected from a wild perennial cabbage that still grows along the coasts of England. Cabbages have evolved into a variety of head shapes and growth habits through centuries of climatic and human selection.

In the 1800s headed cabbages were divided into five categories determined by the shape of the heads: flat, round, egg or sugar loaf, elliptic, and conical. In addition, three colors are mentioned: white, green, and purple. *The Vegetable Garden* by Vilmorin lists 57 varieties available to growers in 1883. Today over 100 varieties are available to the home gardener, but many are just strains that have been "improved" with the wholesale storage market in mind. Many of the varieties listed by Vilmorin are still available in Europe and through seed importers in the United States.

BOTANICAL CLASSIFICATION

Cabbage belongs to the genus *Brassica* and the species *oleracea*. *B. oleracea* includes cabbage, cauliflower, broccoli, Brussels sprouts, kale, collards and kohlrabi. Cabbage belongs to a subspecies of *B. oleracea* known as the Capitata Group.

Cabbage is a biennial and must undergo "vernalization" (a period of cold temperatures) in order to flower. In regions where winter temperatures do not drop below 28° F., it is possible to plant biennial Brassicas in the fall and harvest seed the following summer. In colder areas, cabbage plants must be dug carefully in the fall and stored between 32-45° F. with moderate humidity. The plants are then set out in a prepared garden bed in early spring. The plants can also be dug and transplanted into pots that are kept in a greenhouse, until being planted out in the spring.

POLLINATION, CROSSING AND ISOLATION

Cabbages are outbreeding plants. Cabbage flowers must be insect-pollinated or hand-pollinated to produce viable seed. Most cabbages are self-incompatible. The pollen is viable, but is unable to grow in a flower on the same plant. Pollen carried by insects to a flower on another plant will grow normally. Because the insects must carry pollen from one plant to another, instead of just from one flower to another on the same plant, the larger the group of plants the better the pollination and seed production.

All *B. oleracea* varieties will cross with one another. To save seeds from more than one variety of *B. oleracea*, it is necessary to use caging techniques or isolate plants by a distance of one mile. Alternate day caging or caging with introduced pollinators can also be used. (These techniques are described in detail in Section I.)

SEED PRODUCTION, HARVEST AND PROCESSING

In cold winter areas, late season storage cabbages are best used for winter storage. Choose firm, solid heads and trim off loose outer leaves. Dig the plants very carefully and trim the root system to 12", leaving some lateral roots. The roots can be covered with damp sawdust and the entire head can be wrapped in newspaper. Cabbage will keep for 2-4 months when stored between 32-40° F. and 80-90% humidity.

Cabbage varieties are commonly classified by seasons. Varieties such as Golden Acre and Copenhagen Market are grown as early crops. Midseason varieties include Greenback, King Cole, Roundup, Market Prize and Red Head. Autumn or storing cabbages include such varieties as Danish Ballhead, Rio Verde, Market Prize and Green Winter.

Growing cabbage for seed is one of the most interesting seed saving experiences. In early spring of the second growing season, cut a shallow "X" in the top of the head. This will allow the emerging seed stalk to push up through the cabbage a bit more easily. The seed stalk actually pushes the head open and uncurls itself as it rises out of the head. It is a vegetable birth in the most graphic sense. The stalk will grow 3-4" tall before branching out. For further information on seed production and processing, refer to the information in the introductory pages of the Brassicaceae family.

Cabbage seeds do not normally require any further processing. However, if black rot diseases are a problem, the seeds can be hot water treated to reduce incidence of the disease. (The technique for hot water treatment of seeds is described in Section I.)

SEED STATISTICS

When stored under ideal conditions, cabbage seeds will remain viable for four years. Members of the Seed Savers Exchange annually offer about 29 varieties of cabbage and the *Garden Seed Inventory* lists sources for 108 varieties of cabbage that are available from commercial seed companies. There are approximately 7,000 cabbage seeds per ounce (250 per gram or 112,000 per pound), depending on the variety. Federal Germination Standard for commercially sold cabbage seed is 75%.

GROWING CABBAGE FROM SEED

Cabbages are biennial plants that grow best in mild summer climates. Cabbage may be direct seeded or greenhouse started, covering the seeds .5" deep. The optimum seed germination temperature is 70° F., with germination usually occurring in 5-10 days. Direct seed or set out in full sun where summers are mild, or in afternoon shade in hot, dry climates. Cabbage plants should be thinned to 24-36" for food and seed production purposes. Vernalization is necessary to induce flowering. Seed-to-plant-to-seed methods may be used in climates where winter temperatures do not drop below 28° F. Elsewhere, cabbage plants must be spring sown, stored over the winter and set out to flower the following spring.

REGIONAL GROWING RECOMMENDATIONS

<u>Northeast</u>: Cabbage can be direct seeded in early May. The plants like full sun and average water. We use floating row covers to protect against flea beetles. Dig the plants in early October and store heeled into sand or sawdust in a root cellar. Replant in early May. The seed shatters easily. Overwintering the head is very problematic, however, in this climate it's not absolutely necessary to do so. Sometimes I've had better luck chopping away (and eating) the cabbage but leaving the core and "inner head" as much as possible. Roots should be watered mid to late winter. Second year plants are extremely susceptible to flea beetles and animals, so row cover is used until flowers form.

<u>Mid-Atlantic</u>: Cabbage can be direct seeded about March 1 or from September 1-15, or started in a green-

Dry, completely ripe cabbage seedpods
(*Brassica oleracea*)

house about January 15 or August 1 and transplanted into the garden about March 1 or August 1 to September 15. The plants like full sun and overwinter in the garden with no special care, but cold-season mulch helps cold hardiness.

<u>Southeast/Gulf Coast</u>: Start in a greenhouse about August 1 or January 20, and transplant into the garden about September 10 or February 15 to March 1. Harvesting for food would then be November 10 to December 15 or mid-June.

<u>Upper Midwest</u>: Cabbage can be direct seeded about May 1, or started in a greenhouse about March 1 and transplanted into the garden April 1-15. The plants like full sun and average water. Dig the plants in early November and store in moist sand. Replant in early April. Care must be taken to monitor the weather and not dig the plants too early.

<u>Southwest</u>: Cabbage can be direct seeded from about August 1 to April 15. The plants like full sun

Brassicaceae

and average water.

Central West Coast: Cabbages can be direct seeded from August 15 to September 30. The plants like full sun and average water, and overwinter in the garden with no special care.

Maritime Northwest: Start in a greenhouse about July 15 and transplant into the garden about August 15. Likes full sun and average water. We use float-ing row covers for the first 4-6 weeks to protect the crop from cabbage root maggots. Plants overwinter in the garden with no special care, if the head is not fully formed. By planting cabbage in midsummer so that it goes into winter without a fully formed head (only large wrapper leaves), the plant is able to with-stand the Maritime Northwest winter and will flower by May the following spring.

Brassica oleracea - Broccoli and Cauliflower

Cauliflower and broccoli varieties are available in purple, green, and white. Prior to the turn of the century, purple broccoli was more common than green broccoli. Broccoli was described in garden literature long before cauliflower. In Italy the name broccoli originally referred to the tender shoots produced by various kinds of overwintered cabbages. The shoots were highly regarded and were grown in the royal gardens. Broccoli ceased to be a cabbage as garden-ers selected and cultivated plants that produced the tenderest shoots in the greatest abundance. Centu-ries of selection resulted in varieties similar to the sprouting broccoli of today. As this selection contin-ued, some plants exhibited white curds and were slowly developed into what is now known as cauli-flower.

BOTANICAL CLASSIFICATION

Broccoli and cauliflower belong to the genus *Bras-sica* and the species *oleracea*. *B. oleracea* is a very large species whose different vegetable members can be grouped into eight subspecies according to physi-cal characteristics. Broccoli and cauliflower are mem-bers of the Botrytis Group. Always remember that these groups will cross readily with one another, be-cause they are all *B. oleracea*.

POLLINATION, CROSSING AND ISOLATION

Broccoli and cauliflower are outbreeding plants, and both will cross with all other varieties within the huge *B. oleracea* species, which includes all cabbages (except Chinese cabbage), Brussels sprouts, kale, col-lards and kohlrabi, as well as with each other. Begin-ning seed savers should restrict themselves to one variety of *B. oleracea* per year. That means allowing just one variety of broccoli to flower, for example, and making sure that within a one-mile radius there are no flowering plants of Brussels sprouts, cabbages, cauliflowers, collards, kales or kohlrabies. Advanced seed savers may want to try methods of alternate day caging or caging with introduced pollinators (as described in Section I).

SEED PRODUCTION, HARVEST AND PROCESSING

Broccoli and cauliflower are biennials and both must undergo vernalization in order to flower. In some regions where winter temperatures do not drop be-low 28° F., brassicas can be planted in the fall and seed is harvested the following summer. In addition, some of the shorter season broccolis, when planted in early spring, will flower and produce seed in one sea-son.

In cold winter areas, broccoli and cauliflower plants are carefully dug in the fall and stored between 32-40° F. and 80-90% humidity. Even under the best conditions, however, the plants will quickly succumb to rot, often remaining in good condition for only 4-6 weeks. Broccoli cuttings can sometimes be rooted and grown in a greenhouse until planted out the next spring. Cauliflower seed production is generally lim-ited to mild winter areas.

Seed producers in Japan have developed an inter-esting method for broccoli seed production. The plants are sown in the spring and the central head is harvested at least two months before a killing frost. The central head stump is cut to 4-6" above the ground. The resulting side shoots are cut when 4" tall, treated with a rooting hormone and planted in heated nurs-ery beds. The rooted shoots are planted out the fol-lowing spring. Since these rooted plant cuttings have undergone vernalization, they will bolt in the late spring and produce seed.

When broccoli and cauliflower are grown for seed, the heads should not be harvested for food. Some gardeners cut the central head of broccoli and only let the side shoots go to seed. While this does work, the seed crop is of lesser quality and quantity. The cauliflower head must be intact to produce a good seed crop.

Most broccoli and cauliflower is self-incompatible. To ensure a good seed set and to preserve as much genetic diversity as possible, a minimum of six plants should be used for seed saving. Twenty plants will provide a much greater genetic base.

Broccoli and cauliflower produce seed stalks 4' or taller. The yellow flowers are attractive to bees. For additional information on general production and processing techniques, see the introductory pages of the Brassicaceae family.

SEED STATISTICS

Broccoli and cauliflower seeds will remain viable for five years when stored under ideal conditions. Members of the Seed Savers Exchange annually offer about 13 varieties of broccoli and 4 cauliflowers, while the *Garden Seed Inventory* lists sources for 33 broccolis and 81 cauliflowers that are available from commercial seed companies. There are approximately 6,000-9,000 seeds per ounce (210-320 per gram or 96,000-144,000 per pound), depending on the variety. Federal Germination Standard for commercial broccoli and cauliflower seed is 75%.

GROWING BROCCOLI AND CAULIFLOWER FROM SEED

Broccoli and cauliflower are biennial, frost tolerant plants that are best grown for seed in mild winter climates. Both may be direct seeded or greenhouse started, covering the seeds .5" deep, but it is common for broccoli to be direct seeded while cauliflower is more often transplanted. The optimum seed germination temperature is 70° F. with germination usually occurring in 5-7 days. Plant or set out in full sun. Broccoli should be thinned to 8-12" for food production, or 6-8" for breeding purposes. Cauliflower should be thinned 24-36" for food production, or 18" for breeding purposes.

REGIONAL GROWING RECOMMENDATIONS

Northeast: These instructions are for broccoli, because I have no success with cauliflower. Start broccoli in a greenhouse about April 15 and transplant about May 20. The plants like full sun and average water. We use floating row covers to guard against flea beetles. Plants must be well established early.

Mid-Atlantic: Broccoli and cauliflower can be direct seeded about March 1. The plants like full sun and average water. Spring-mulched plants will endure droughts and heat of summer more effectively. Use compost, rotted leaves or rotted manure. Some

Romanesco, a unique spiral-headed Italian broccoli. (Photo by Kent Whealy)

long-season varieties require growth through the winter months (e.g. Purple Broccoli). Species demands rich fertile soils for best production. Aphids and cabbage loopers are often a problem.

Southeast/Gulf Coast: Start in a greenhouse about August 1 (preferred) or January 30, and transplant into the garden about September 1 or March 10. Spring crops flower in June. Harvest for food October 20 to December 1, or June 1.

Upper Midwest: Cauliflower is not a success here, but broccoli does fine. Start it in a greenhouse about March 1 and transplant into the garden about April 15. The plants like full sun and average water.

Southwest: Broccoli and cauliflower can be direct seeded from August 1 to May 15. The plants like full sun and average water.

Central West Coast: Broccoli and cauliflower are direct seeded March 1 to April 1, or August 15 to September 30. The plants like full sun and average water, and overwinter in the garden with no special care.

Maritime Northwest: Broccoli and cauliflower can be direct seeded from March 20 to April 10. The plants like full sun and average water. We use floating row covers for the first 4-6 weeks to protect the crop from cabbage root maggots. The plants overwinter in the garden with no special care.

Kale and collards may have been the first cultivated brassicas. Early Greek and Roman literature referred to kale-like plants. The first known reference to kale was written by Cato about 201 B.C.

Kale is highly prized in winter gardens and is remarkably hardy in areas with very cold, snowy winters. Ornamental kale, used in flower and vegetable gardens, is edible and used in salads and as a garnish.

Collard greens and kale are opposites in some respects. Kale fades in the summer sun, but collards thrive on heat. A favorite vegetable in the southern United States, collards are tradionally cooked with ham hocks or bacon drippings. Collards are usually grown in mild winter areas and are extremely adaptable, withstanding temperatures as low as 10° F. Can be grown as perennials where weather permits.

BOTANICAL CLASSIFICATION

All collards and most kales belong to the genus *Brassica* and the species *oleracea*. Botanically, kale is a bit confusing. Kales that belong to *B. oleracea* include Common, Scotch, Marrow-Stem, Borecale, Chinese, Tall, Cabbage, Tree, Decorative, Flowering, Kitchen, Ornamental, Cow and Curled. However, Siberian kale, Hanover Salad and Winter Rape kale are *B. napus*, along with rutabagas.

POLLINATION, CROSSING AND ISOLATION

Kale and collards are outbreeding plants. Most kale and all collards will cross with all other members of *B. oleracea*, including cabbage, broccoli, Brussels sprouts, cauliflower, collards and kohlrabi. As just mentioned, the only exceptions are a few kales, including Siberian Kale and Hanover Salad, which are *B. napus* and will cross instead with rutabagas. Variety names have changed over time and are often confused. Several Siberian kales are available from seed companies, but it is not certain yet if these are all *B. napus*. Until those taxonomic questions are answered, do not presume that a kale called Siberian will not cross with other varieties of kale belonging to *B. oleracea* or with other members of the Brassicaceae family.

To ensure seed purity it is necessary to grow only one variety of *B. oleracea*. All varieties and types within the species will cross with one another. To save seeds from more than one variety within any brassica species, it is necessary to use caging techniques or to isolate different varieties by one mile.

SEED PRODUCTION, HARVEST AND PROCESSING

It is possible to eat kale or collards and save seeds from the plants as well. During the first season, small quantities of leaves can be harvested without affecting the seed crop. Kale and collards, which are biennials and produce seed during their second growing season, must undergo vernalization in order to flower. In some mild winter regions it is possible to plant biennial brassicas in the fall and harvest seeds the following summer. Kale is extremely hardy and will overwinter in many areas. In regions with extremely cold winters, the plants can be dug, trimmed and stored in sawdust or sand. Kale plants stored at 32-40° F. and 80-90% humidity will only have a limited life of 1-2 months. Any stored plants that do make it through the winter are set out in a prepared bed in early spring.

Both kale and collards produce seed stalks that are 5' or taller. The plants flower prolifically and are very attractive to bees. Additional information on production and processing techniques is presented in the introductory pages of the Brassicaceae family.

Neither kale nor collard seeds normally require any further processing after harvesting and cleaning. However, if black rot diseases are a problem, the seed can be hot water treated (described in Section I) to reduce incidence of the disease.

SEED STATISTICS

Kale and collard seeds will remain viable for four years when stored in a cool, dry, dark location. Members of the Seed Savers Exchange annually offer about 38 varieties of kale and 11 collards, while the *Garden Seed Inventory* lists sources for 42 kales and 4 collards that are available from commercial seed companies. There are approximately 7,000 seeds per ounce (250 per gram or 112,000 per pound), depending on the variety. Federal Germination Standard for commercially sold kale and collard seed is 75%.

GROWING KALE AND COLLARDS FROM SEED

Kale and collards are biennial plants that will tolerate climates spanning a wide range of conditions. Both may be direct seeded or greenhouse started depending on the climate, covering the seeds .5" deep. The seed germinates at temperatures ranging from 65-85° F. with germination usually occurring in 5-10

Some of the leaf types exhibited by different varieties of kale (*Brassica oleracea*).

days. Plant or set out in full sun in mild summer climates, or afternoon shade in very hot summer climates. Kale and collard plants should be thinned to 12" for food production, or 6-8" for breeding purposes.

REGIONAL GROWING RECOMMENDATIONS

Northeast: Kale and collards can be direct seeded about June 5-30. The plants like full sun and average water. We use floating row covers to protect against flea beetles. Mulch in late October or early November with loose hay or leaves (and cage to prevent blowing and to deter animals). I've had very mixed success with kale. Possibly it would do better heeled into sand or dirt or sawdust (or in buckets) in the cellar.

Mid-Atlantic: Kale and collards can be direct seeded about March 1, or from August 15 to September 15. The plants like full sun and average water, and overwinter in the garden with no special care.

Southeast/Gulf Coast: Kale and collards can be direct seeded about September 1-15. The plants like full sun, and overwinter in the garden with no special care. Collards especially produce plenty of flower buds, and while still green are great to eat. Watch kale closely for cabbage aphids.

Upper Midwest: Kale and collards can be direct seeded from mid-July to early August for seed production. The plants like full sun and average water. Dig the plants in early November and store in moist soil. Replant in early April. Collards don't overwinter as well as kale.

Southwest: Kale and collards can be direct seeded from August 1 to May 15. The plants like full sun and average water.

Central West Coast: Kale and collards can be direct seeded from August 30 to September 30. The plants like full sun and average water, and overwinter in the garden with no special care.

Maritime Northwest: Start in a greenhouse about July 15 and transplant into the garden about August 15. The plants like full sun and average water. We use floating row covers for the first 4-6 weeks to protect the crop from cabbage root maggots. The plants overwinter in the garden with no special care.

Brassicaceae

Brassica rapa - Chinese Cabbage and Chinese Mustard

All types of Chinese cabbage and Chinese mustard are thought to have originated in China and Eastern Asia where they have been cultivated since the fifth century A.D. Chinese cabbage and Chinese mustard readily cross with one another. Selection and crossing, both intentional and accidental, have occurred thousands of times during the last 16 centuries. Distinct types have evolved due to local adaptations as well as traits which were specifically selected. Many of the varieties grown in Asia are not available in the United States. The varieties available here often have different names depending on the country from which they were imported. In addition, attempts to Romanize the Chinese dialect name has resulted in numerous English translations for the same variety.

BOTANICAL CLASSIFICATION

All Chinese cabbages and Chinese mustards belong to the genus *Brassica* and the species *rapa*. Some attempts have been made to change the common name from Chinese cabbage to Asiatic cabbage. The vegetables are found throughout Asia, so Asiatic cabbage actually would be more appropriate.

Many references go into great detail, grouping Chinese cabbages into various subspecies. Lengthy debates over different plant characteristics and growth habits have arisen as various taxonomists have developed different classifications for these proposed subspecies. Herklots, Tsen and Lee, Sun, and Bailey have all done a great deal of work on subspecies classifications.

Most references place Chinese cabbages and Chinese mustards into one of three groups. Chinensis Group includes nonheading varieties of Chinese mustard, celery mustard and pak-choi. Pekinensis Group includes heading Chinese cabbage, celery cabbage and pe-tsai; and the Perviridis Group includes all spinach mustards. It is important to remember that these varieties are all members of the same species, *B. rapa*, and cross readily regardless of subspecies classification.

Confusion surrounding variety names in *B. rapa* is rampant. What one person buys as Chihli cabbage may be what someone else thinks of as Shantung cabbage. A patient, dedicated group with a lot of time is needed to grow, document and compile data on the vast array of *B. rapa* varieties available in this country.

POLLINATION, CROSSING AND ISOLATION

Chinese cabbages and Chinese mustards are outbreeding plants. Both are *Brassica rapa* and will cross with each other as well as with any turnip varieties, which are also *B. rapa*. Remember that this species also includes broccoli raab, a type of turnip grown for its flower stalks. Chinese mustard varieties will not cross with common mustard, which is a weed in many areas of the United States, or with varieties grown for mustard seeds, or with mustard greens.

Most Chinese cabbages are self-incompatible. Insects must move pollen from one plant's flower to a flower on another plant in order to produce viable seed. Thus larger groups of plants improve pollination and seed production. No fewer than six plants should ever be grown for seed production.

To save seed from more than one of any of the brassica species, it is necessary to use caging techniques or to isolate the different varieties by one mile. Reemay™ is an ideal caging material that does not restrict air, water and light to the plants, but does restrict insect travel. Alternate day caging or caging with introduced pollinators (as described in detail in Section I) can also be used.

SEED PRODUCTION, HARVEST AND PROCESSING

When growing Chinese cabbage or Chinese mustard for seed, some of the outer leaves can be harvested without significantly affecting the seed harvest. Always select plants that exhibit the desired characteristics for seed production. Do not use plants for seed production if they bolt prematurely or are of a different color, size or shape from the rest of the population.

Chinese cabbages and mustards are primarily biennial and normally require two growing seasons to produce seed. However, they may go to seed in a single season, if planted in early spring. Such plants have already experienced short days and cool spring temperatures and may bolt when the long, hot days of summer arrive. There is a danger, however, that this shortened method may actually amount to selecting for premature bolting.

In areas with extremely cold winters, Chinese cabbage will need to be overwintered in a root cellar and then replanted the next spring. Before the first killing frost, choose mature, solid plants and carefully dig the roots with some soil attached. Carefully pack the roots and the attached soil in damp sand, while leaving the head exposed. Chinese cabbage will store for 2-4 months at 32-40° F. and 90-95% humidity.

Chinese cabbages and Chinese mustards will produce seed stalks 3' or taller. The plants prolifically produce yellow flowers that are very attractive to bees. After the flowers fade, seedpods form that are initially green but turn tan as the seeds mature. As the plants begin to dry, the pods begin to shatter, starting with ones that are lowest on the stalks. Several hand pickings will result in the greatest seed harvest. If harvesting by hand is too time-consuming, cut the entire stalk when the greatest number of seedpods are dry but have not yet shattered.

Techniques for drying, cleaning and winnowing Chinese cabbage and Chinese mustard seeds are described in detail in the introductory pages of the Brassicaceae family.

SEED STATISTICS

The seeds of Chinese cabbage and Chinese mustard will remain viable for five years under ideal conditions. Members of the Seed Savers Exchange annually offer about 57 varieties of Chinese cabbages (and Chinese mustards), and the *Garden Seed Inventory* lists sources for 90 varieties that are available from commercial seed companies. There are approximately 8,500 seeds per ounce (300 per gram or 136,000 per pound), depending on the variety. Federal Germination Standard for commercially sold Chinese cabbage and Chinese mustard seed is 75%.

GROWING CHINESE CABBAGE
AND CHINESE MUSTARD FROM SEED

Chinese cabbage and Chinese mustard are biennials, but sometimes produce seed in one season (see the caution in the previous text). Both are usually direct seeded, covering .25-.5" deep. The seeds germinate at temperatures ranging from 75-85° F. with germination usually occurring in 5 days. Chinese cabbage and Chinese mustard can be planted year-round in mild climates, either in full sun or partial shade. The plants should be thinned to 8-12" for food production, or 6-8" for breeding purposes.

REGIONAL GROWING RECOMMENDATIONS

Northeast: Chinese cabbage and Chinese mustard can be direct seeded before May 10 or, better yet, started in a greenhouse about April 20-30 and transplanted into the garden about May 15. The plants like full sun and average water. We use floating row covers to guard against flea beetles. Seed heads are shatter-prone. I've had inconsistent success with these crops here.

Mid-Atlantic: Chinese cabbage and Chinese mustard can be direct seeded about March 1, or from September 15 to November 15. The plants like full sun and average water, and overwinter in the garden with no special care.

Southeast/Gulf Coast: Chinese cabbage and Chinese mustard can be direct seeded about March 1. The plants like full sun. Spring sowings will flower without heading first; fall crops head up great but are usually winter-killed. When grown as a food crop, start in a greenhouse about August 15, transplant into the garden about September 15, and harvest from November 1-30.

Upper Midwest: Chinese cabbage and Chinese mustard can be direct seeded about mid-April. The plants like full sun and average water.

Southwest: Chinese cabbage and Chinese mustard can be direct seeded from about September 15 to February 15. The plants like full sun and average water.

Central West Coast: Chinese cabbage and Chinese mustard can be direct seeded throughout the year. The plants like full sun (but partial sun is okay) and average water, and overwinter in the garden with no special care.

Maritime Northwest: Chinese cabbage and Chinese mustard can be direct seeded from about March 20 to April 10. The plants like full sun and average water. We use floating row covers for the first 4-6 weeks of the growing season to protect the crop from cabbage root maggot.

Brassica rapa - Turnip and Broccoli Raab

Grown since prehistoric times, turnips have been savored in every European and Asian culture. Tiny white turnips shaped like eggs are currently popular. In times past, the varieties of choice were the types with larger roots, which were noted for their storage capabilities. These larger types account for much of the name confusion between rutabagas and turnips. Rutabagas, sometimes called Swede turnips or Finnish turnips, belong to a different species, *Brassica*

napus, than the common garden turnips of today.

BOTANICAL CLASSIFICATION

Turnips belong to the genus *Brassica* and the species *rapa*. Sometimes *B. rapa* was referred to as *B. campestris* in some early taxonomic texts. Some varieties of agricultural or fodder turnips may actually be rutabagas, *B. napus*, and would therefore cross with rutabagas but not with turnips. It is unlikely that such varieties would be available to most seed savers.

Turnips are grouped into two subspecies. Varieties grown for their roots are members of the Rapifera Group. Broccoli raab, rapa, Italian turnips and other varieties grown for their flower stalks are members of the Ruvo Group.

Turnips are grown as annuals for their fleshy roots and leafy greens. The root shapes vary greatly and include flat, long, and globe shapes. The flesh color of the roots is usually white or yellow. Skin colors range from white, cream, yellow, red, and purple to black. Flower color usually correlates with the flesh color of the roots. Plants with white-fleshed roots usually produce bright yellow flowers. Yellow-fleshed varieties have flowers with pale orangish yellow petals.

POLLINATION, CROSSING AND ISOLATION

Turnips and broccoli raab are outbreeding plants. Different varieties of turnips will cross with each other as well as with all other members of *B. rapa*. This includes all Chinese cabbages, Chinese mustards and any turnips that are grown for their flower stalks such as broccoli raab. Turnips will not cross with any other brassica species. Most turnips are self-incompatible. Insects must carry pollen from a flower on one plant to a flower on another plant for pollination.

To ensure seed purity, isolate different varieties of *B. rapa* by one mile. Alternate day caging or caging with insect introduction can be used when two or more varieties are grown near one another. (These caging techniques are described in Section I.)

SEED PRODUCTION, HARVEST AND PROCESSING

Most turnips produce seed biennially and must undergo vernalization in order to flower. In some mild winter regions it is possible to plant turnips in the fall and harvest seed the following summer. In colder areas of the country, the crops must be overwintered in a root cellar. Carefully dig the turnip plants before a heavy freeze, trim the tops to 2" and store in cartons of sawdust, sand or leaves. Turnips will keep 2-4 months when stored at 32-40° F. and 90-95% humidity. The stored roots are set out in a prepared garden bed in early spring. The plants can also be transplanted into pots and kept in a greenhouse until spring. Some earlier maturing varieties of turnips have annual seeding characteristics and may be grown to seed in one season.

Turnips produce seed stalks 3' or taller. Flowers appear prolifically and are very attractive to bees.

After the flowers fade, seedpods form that are initially green but turn tan as the seeds mature and the plant begins to dry. The seedpods shatter beginning with the pods lowest on the stalks. Several hand pickings will result in the greatest seed harvest. If harvest by hand is too time-consuming, then cut the entire stalk when the greatest number of seedpods are dry but have not yet shattered.

Additional drying of the stalks can be continued in a protected location away from direct sun. Many of the seedpods will shatter. Others will need to be broken by hand, with a seed thresher, or by jogging in place on top of a seed bag. The seeds can then be winnowed in the wind or with a hair dryer or fan.

Turnip seeds normally do not require any further processing. However, if black rot diseases are a problem, the seeds can be hot water treated to reduce incidence of the disease. (The technique for hot water treatment of seeds is described in detail in Section I.)

SEED STATISTICS

Turnip and broccoli raab seeds remain viable for five years when stored under ideal conditions. Members of the Seed Savers Exchange annually offer about 42 varieties of turnips and 5 broccoli raabs, while the *Garden Seed Inventory* lists sources for 39 turnips and 11 broccoli raabs. There are approximately 8,500 seeds per ounce (300 per gram or 136,000 per pound), depending on the variety. Federal Germination Standard for commercially sold seed is 75%.

GROWING TURNIPS AND BROCCOLI RAAB FROM SEED

Turnips and broccoli raab are biennial, but may produce seed in one season (again, see cautions in preceding text). Both are usually direct seeded, covering the seeds .25-5" deep, and can be planted year-round in mild climates, either in full sun or partial shade. The seed germinates at temperatures ranging from 70-85° F. with germination usually occuring in 5 days. Turnips and broccoli raab should both be thinned to 4-8" for either food and breeding purposes.

REGIONAL GROWING RECOMMENDATIONS

Northeast: Turnips and broccoli raab can be direct seeded about June 10-30. The plants like full sun and average water. We use floating row covers to guard against flea beetles. Dig the plants in late October and store in barrels in a cool damp cellar. Turnips are fussier than rutabagas to overwinter. Too much dampness causes them to rot more easily than rutabaga, yet they are also more vulnerable to drying out and withering at the crown.

Mid-Atlantic: Turnips and broccoli raab can be direct seeded about March 1, or from September 15 to November 15. The plants likes full sun and average water, and overwinter with no special care.

Southeast/Gulf Coast: Turnips and broccoli raab can be direct seeded September 1-15. The plants overwinter in the garden with no special care. Fall-sown crops flower in early spring.

Upper Midwest: Turnips and broccoli raab can be direct seeded about July 25 for seed production. Dig the plants in early November and store in moist sand. Replant in early April.

Southwest: Turnips and broccoli raab can be direct seeded from September 15 to February 15. The plants like full sun and average water.

Central West Coast: Turnips and broccoli raab can be direct seeded from August to November, or February to April. The plants like full sun and average water, and overwinter with no special care.

Maritime Northwest: Turnips and broccoli raab can be direct seeded about September 5. The plants like full sun and average water, and overwinter in the garden with no special care. We use floating row covers for the first 4-6 weeks to protect against cabbage root maggot. The plants overwinter with no special care.

Raphanus sativus - Radish

The little red morsels that today's gardeners call radishes have an impressive history. Radishes were considered so important in ancient Egypt that their pictures were inscribed on many pyramid walls. Greeks presented offerings to Apollo which included turnips made of lead, beets of silver and radishes of gold. Often thought to be native to Asia, radishes appear in artwork and legends in the eastern Mediterranean that date back to 2000 B.C.

Radishes are available in nearly every size, shape and color. Oriental or daikon radishes stay tender and crisp even when grown to more than 20" long. French gardeners favor small red, white or pink radishes which are eaten with butter and French bread. In India radishes have been developed that are grown for their large seedpods. Rat Tail radish has seedpods that can grow up to 12" long. The immature, green seedpods are used as a green vegetable, in curries or made into pickles.

BOTANICAL CLASSIFICATION

Radishes belong to the genus *Raphanus* and the species *sativus*. *R. sativus* is commonly grouped by growing season. Radiculata Group includes the annual small red and white varieties. Longipinnatus Group contains the long white daikon types common in Asia. Rat Tail radishes belong to the Caudatus Group.

POLLINATION, CROSSING AND ISOLATION

Radishes are outbreeding plants that are insect-pollinated and will cross with all varieties of wild and domesticated radishes. They will not cross with any other members of the Brassicaceae family.

Most radishes are self-incompatible. The pollen is viable, but cannot grow in a flower on the same plant. Pollen carried by insects to a flower on another plant will grow normally. Because the insects must carry pollen from one plant to another and not just from one flower to the other, the larger the group of plants the better the pollination and seed production will be.

Any two radish varieties must be separated by 1/2 mile or grown using the caging techniques described in Section I. Wild radishes are common in some rural regions. Care must be taken to remove all wild plants or to isolate seed crops from the wild types.

SEED PRODUCTION, HARVEST AND PROCESSING

It perhaps goes without saying that radishes can't be eaten and saved for seed too. However, the green, immature seedpods can be eaten in small quantities with only a minimal effect on the seed harvest, since radishes are prolific seed producers.

Radish seed stalks grow 3' or taller. White or purple and white flowers appear prolifically and are very attractive to bees. After the flowers fade, the seedpods form. The pods are green at first, but turn tan as the seeds mature and the plant begins to dry. The seed stalks are harvested when the stalk and pods are dry.

Radish seeds are dried and cleaned using techniques similar to other members of the Brassicaceae family. It is a bit harder to remove their seeds from the seedpods, however, so plan on spending more time and getting fewer seeds than from other family members. Gently pounding the pods with a large hammer or a wooden maul will help break open pods that do not yield when rubbed by hand. Radish seeds require no further processing.

Daikon radishes
(*Raphanus sativus*, Longipinnatus Group).

SEED STATISTICS

Radish seeds will remain viable for five years when stored in a cool, dry, dark location. Members of the Seed Savers Exchange offer about 121 different radish varieties, while the *Garden Seed Inventory* lists sources for 155 radish varieties that are being offered by by mail-order from commercial seed companies in the United States and Canada. There are approximately 2,240 radish seeds per ounce (80 seeds per gram or 35,840 per pound), depending on the variety. Federal Germination Standard for commercially sold radish seed is 75%.

GROWING RADISHES FROM SEED

Almost all commonly available radish varieties are annuals, but some varieties that belong to the Longipinnatus Group are biennial. All are easily grown throughout the growing season in nearly every climate, although winter storage types will need time to mature. Radishes are direct seeded in either full sun or partial shade, depending on the season, with seeds covered .5" deep. Seeds will germinate within a wide range of temperatures (45-85° F.) with germination usually occurring in 4-10 days. Radish plants should be thinned to 1-2" for food production and for breeding purposes.

REGIONAL GROWING RECOMMENDATIONS

Northeast: Radishes can be direct seeded early to mid-May or, for daikons, best started indoors in peat pots after April 15 and transplanted into the garden about mid-May. The plants like full sun and average water. We use floating row covers to guard against flea beetles.

Mid-Atlantic: Radishes can be direct seeded about March 1 or September 1. The plants like full sun and average water, and overwinter in the garden with no special care.

Southeast/Gulf Coast: Radishes can be direct seeded from March 1 to April 10 (all types) or September 10-30 (best for daikons). Fall sowings may be winter-killed, except for daikons. Spring sowings are best for seed production.

Upper Midwest: Radishes can be direct seeded anytime after the ground opens until June. Winter radishes should be sown about August 1, dug in early November and stored in moist sand, and then replanted in early April. The plants like full sun and average water.

Southwest: Radishes can be direct seeded from September 1 to May 15. The plants like full sun and average water.

Central West Coast: Radishes can be direct seeded from February 1 to April 30, or from September 1 to November 1. The plants like full sun and average water, and overwinter in the garden with no special care.

Maritime Northwest: Radishes can be direct seeded March 20 to April 10. The plants like full sun and average water. We use floating row covers for the first 4-6 weeks to protect this crop from cabbage root maggot.

Armoracia rusticana
Horseradish

Horseradish is grown from root cuttings and does not produce seeds in most regions of the United States. When harvested, the large roots are dug for market and the small side roots and crowns are saved for replanting. The pungent flavor found in horseradish is caused by allyl isothiocyanate, a sulfur compound.

Horseradish is extremely hardy and will overwinter in the ground in most regions. The roots may also be dug before the ground freezes. The roots should be trimmed and the tops cut to 3" above the crown before storing in damp sand, sawdust or leaves. Horseradish roots will keep 4-6 months when stored at 32-40° F. and 90-95% humidity.

REGIONAL GROWING RECOMMENDATIONS

Northeast: Horseradish can be sown anytime, but best in early spring or late fall. The plants like full sun and average water, and overwinter in the garden with no special care. Propagated by root division.

Mid-Atlantic: Horseradish is grown as a food crop in this region. Can be planted anytime when dormant (November to March). The plants like full sun and are drought tolerant, and overwinter with no special care.

Southeast/Gulf Coast: Horseradish does not flower in this region, but roots can be planted in spring or fall. The plants like partial sun, and overwinter in the garden with no special care. Although the plant never flowers, otherwise it is indestructible, and can be dug and divided anytime.

Upper Midwest: Plant horseradish roots in the spring. The plants like full sun and average water, and overwinter in the garden with no special care.

Southwest: Not commonly grown in this region.

Central West Coast: Plant horseradish from February 1 to June 1 using root pieces, or start in a greenhouse anytime. The plants like partial sun, are drought tolerant, and overwinter with no special care.

Maritime Northwest: Horseradish usually reproduces asexually. Plant roots from March 20 to April 10. The plants like full sun and average water, and overwinter in the garden with no special care.

Brassica hirta
White Flowered Mustard

Brassica hirta varieties have white flowers and are used as spicy salad or cooked greens. The seed-pods are small and contain three or four seeds. White-flowered mustards are cultivated in the Mediterranean as an oil seed crop. They have been naturalized in North America and may be found growing as common weeds. *B. hirta* is not the seed from which the commercial condiment "mustard" is made. White-flowered mustards are self-incompatible and require insects for successful pollination. *B. hirta* varieties do not cross with any other Brassica species.

GROWING WHITE FLOWERED
MUSTARD FROM SEED

White flowered mustard is an annual, inbreeding plant that grows easily from seed wherever its wild relatives are successful. Mustards are direct seeded, either in full sun or partial shade, covering the seeds .25-.5" deep. The seed germinates at temperatures ranging from 75-85° F. with germination usually occurring in about 5 days. The plants should be thinned to 8-12" for food production, or 6-8" for breeding purposes. There are approximately 12,600 seeds per ounce (445 per gram or 202,000 per pound), depending on the variety. Federal Germination Standard for commercial seed is 75%.

REGIONAL GROWING RECOMMENDATIONS

Northeast: White flowered mustard can be direct seeded in mid-May, preferably. The plants like full sun and average water. We use floating row covers to keep flea beetles from decimating the young seedlings. Harvest seed in late August; somewhat prone to shatter.

Mid-Atlantic: White flowered mustard can be direct seeded about March 1, or from August 15 to September 15. The plants like full sun and average water, and overwinter in the garden with no special care.

Southeast/Gulf Coast: White flowered mustard can be direct seeded about September 15 for greens, or planted March 1 for seed. Spring-sown mustards flower early and well. Fall-sown plants make great greens but are usually winter-killed.

Upper Midwest: White flowered mustard can be direct seeded about April 15. The plants like full sun and average water.

Southwest: White flowered mustard can be direct seeded from September 15 to February 15. The plants like full sun and average water.

Central West Coast: White flowered mustard can be direct seeded from March 1 to May 1. The plants like full sun and average water.

Maritime Northwest: White flowered mustard can be direct seeded from March 20 to April 10. The plants like full sun and average water. We use floating row covers for the first 4-6 weeks to protect the crop from cabbage root maggots. Harvest when the pods are dry.

--- *Brassica juncea* ---
Indian Mustard and Mustard Greens

Brassica juncea includes brown mustard, Indian mustard, leaf mustard and mustard greens. The flowers are bright yellow. Some varieties have become common weeds in North America. Southern mustard or curled mustard is a member of the Crispifolia Group; varieties within this subspecies are commonly grown for mustard greens. Varieties in the Foliosa Group have very large, flat leaves and are often used as greens. Longidens Group, often found growing as weeds, has long, narrow leaves with prong-like teeth. Multisecta Group varieties have finely divided leaves and also occur as weeds.

Regardless of these groups or subspecies, all varieties of *B. juncea* will cross with one another. Varieties grown for seed must be isolated from other cultivated and weedy types by 1/2 mile. Varieties grown in close proximity can be caged. *B. juncea* varieties are self-compatible and self-pollinating. Seed is saved using techniques similar to rutabagas.

GROWING INDIAN MUSTARD AND MUSTARD GREENS FROM SEED

Brassica juncea, an inbreeding species, includes varieties that are perennial, annual and biennial. Indian mustard and mustard greens can be direct seeded in either full sun or partial shade, and are easily grown for seed wherever their wild relatives are successful. The seeds are covered .25-5" deep, and germinate at temperatures from 75-85° F., usually within 5 days. The plants are thinned to 8-12" for food production, or 6-8" for breeding purposes. There are approximately 12,600 seeds per ounce (445 per gram or 202,000 per pound), depending on the variety. Federal Germination Standard for commercial seed is 75%.

REGIONAL PLANTING RECOMMENDATIONS

Northeast: *Brassica juncea* can be direct seeded before May 10. The plants like full sun and average water. We use floating row covers to keep flea beetles from decimating young seedlings. Seed pods are very prone to shatter.

Mid-Atlantic: *B. juncea* can be direct seeded about March 1, or from August 15 to September 15. The plants like full sun, are drought tolerant (but like average water), and overwinter in the garden with no special care.

Southeast/Gulf Coast: *B. juncea* can be direct seeded from September 1-15 to produce greens, or March 1-15 for seed. The plants like partial sun. Spring-sown mustards flower promptly and well. Fall-sown make great greens and are often winter-killed.

Upper Midwest: *B. juncea* can be direct seeded April 15. The plants like full sun and average water.

Southwest: *B. juncea* can be direct seeded from September 15 to February 15. The plants like full sun and average water.

Central West Coast: *B. juncea* can be direct seeded from March 1 to May 1. The plants like full sun and average water.

Maritime Northwest: *B. juncea* can be direct seeded from March 20 to April 10. The plants like full sun and average water. We use floating row covers for the first 4-6 weeks to protect the crop from cabbage root maggot. Harvest when the pods are dry.

--- *Brassica nigra* ---
Black Mustard

Brassica nigra varieties produce the millions of seeds required to make the condiment mustard. Although recipes vary, all mustards begin with *B. nigra* seeds in whole, split or ground form. Growing *B. nigra* for the making of mustard is no more difficult than saving the seeds of any other brassica species.

B. nigra varieties have bright yellow flowers and often grow 6' tall. The flowers are insect-pollinated and do not cross with any other brassica species. The plants may be found growing as weeds, so care must be taken to isolate seed crops from weedy types. Isolation of 1/2 mile will ensure seed purity. Seed saving techniques are the same as those used for turnips.

GROWING BLACK MUSTARD FROM SEED

Brassica nigra is an outbreeding annual, and can be easily grown for seed wherever its wild relatives are successful. Direct seed in either full sun or partial shade, and cover .25-5" deep. The seeds germinate best between 75-85° F., usually within about 5 days. The plants should be thinned to 8-12" for food production, or 6-8" for breeding purposes. There are approximately 12,600 seeds per ounce (445 per gram or 202,000 per pound), depending on the variety. Federal Germination Standard for commercial seed is 75%.

REGIONAL GROWING RECOMMENDATIONS

Northeast: *Brassica nigra* can be direct seeded before May 10. The plants like full sun and average water. We use floating row covers to protect against flea beetles.

Mid-Atlantic: *B. nigra* can be direct seeded about March 1, or from September 15 to October 15. The plants like full sun and average water, and overwinter in the garden with no special care.

Southeast/Gulf Coast: *B. nigra* can be direct seeded from February 15 to March 15. The plants like full sun.

Upper Midwest: *B. nigra* plants like full sun and average water.

Southwest: *B. nigra* can be direct seeded from September 15 to February 15. The plants like full sun and average water.

Central West Coast: *B. nigra* can be direct seeded from February 15 to April 15, or September 1 to October 15. The plants like full sun and average water, and overwinter in the garden with no special care.

Maritime Northwest: *B. nigra* can be direct seeded from March 20 to April 10. The plants like full sun and average water. We use floating row covers for the first 4-6 weeks of the growing season to protect against cabbage root maggot.

Brassica oleracea
Brussels Sprouts

Botanically, Brussels sprouts are not really baby cabbages, but for culinary purposes the analogy is perfect. Brussels sprouts grow slowly over a long season and require nearly six months to develop the 3' plants commonly seen in garden magazines and seed catalogs. Despite frost and snow, their fresh garden flavor is maintained well into the winter months. The edible heads or sprouts appear during the first growing season and the seed forms during the second season.

Brussels sprouts are biennial and belong to the genus *Brassica* and the species *oleracea*, and also to the Gemmifera Group. They are self-incompatible and require insects for pollination. Brussels sprouts will cross with any of the groups that make up *B. oleracea*, which include all varieties of cabbage, cauliflower, broccoli, kale, collards and kohlrabi. They will not cross with any other brassica species. Plants grown for seed must be isolated from other *B. oleracea* varieties by one mile. When grown in closer proximity, caging techniques used for other *B. oleracea* varieties can be used.

Brussels sprouts will only keep in storage for a very limited time. The plants succumb to rot quickly and only last 4-6 weeks when stored between 32-40° F. at 80-90% humidity. Harvest and seed cleaning techniques are similar to those used for cabbage.

GROWING BRUSSELS SPROUTS FROM SEED

Brussels sprouts are an outbreeding, frost and snow tolerant biennial, that can be grown for seed wherever the plants are successfully overwintered in the ground. The plants require a very long growing season and are difficult to grow in hot summer climates. Brussel sprouts are usually grown in greenhouses for transplants, but may be direct seeded where transplants would succumb in hot, dry climates. Either plant or set out in full sun in mild climates, or in partial shade in hot summer climates. Seeds are covered .25-5" deep and germinate best at about 70° F., usually within 5-10 days. Plants should be thinned to 24-36" for food production, 12-24" for breeding purposes. There are approximately 7,000 seeds per ounce (250 per gram or 112,000 per pound). Federal Germination Standard for commercially sold seed is 75%.

REGIONAL GROWING RECOMMENDATIONS

Northeast: Brussels sprouts can be direct seeded in early May, or started in a greenhouse in early April and transplanted into the garden in mid-May. The plants like full sun and average water. We use floating row covers to guard against flea beetles. Dig the plants in late October and store in buckets with dirt over the roots. Replant in early May. Seed heads are shatter-prone. It is critical for overwintering to get a heavy woody stock. I have harvested most of the "sprouts" for food with little harm to the seed crop, provided removal does not tear the bud areas too badly. Second year plants are best "hilled up." I've not been consistently successful with this seed crop here.

Mid-Atlantic: Brussels sprouts can be direct seeded from about March 1. The plants like full sun and average water. Aphids are often a problem. Brussels sprouts are very difficult to get to seed maturity here.

Southeast/Gulf Coast: This crop can be grown for seed in this region, but I've never done it. For food, start in a greenhouse about August 1 and transplant into the garden about September 10. Harvest from November 30 to March 1.

Upper Midwest: Start in a greenhouse about March 1 and transplant into the garden about April 1-15. The plants like full sun and average water. Dig the plants in early November and store in moist sand.

Replant in early April.

Southwest: With little or no frost, Brussels sprouts just aren't grown in the Southwest.

Central West Coast: Brussels sprouts can be direct seeded about July 1. The plants like full sun and average water, and overwinter in the garden with no special care. Often it is very difficult to get plants started during dry summer months, so use shade cloth over the seedlings.

Maritime Northwest: Start in a greenhouse about July 15 and transplant into the garden about August 15. The plants like full sun and average water. We use floating row covers for the first 4-6 weeks to protect the crop from cabbage root maggot. Plants overwinter in the garden with no special care.

———————— *Brassica oleracea* ————————
Kohlrabi

Kohlrabi is the common name for *B. oleracea* varieties that belong to the Gongylodes Group. Kohlrabi is sometimes referred to as stem turnip because of the turnip-like enlargement of the stem. The swollen stem resembles a cabbage heart in flavor. Although not widely grown, kohlrabi is versatile and a quick grower. Both white and purple varieties are ready for harvest in seven to eight weeks.

Kohlrabi is a biennial and will cross with all varieties of *B. oleracea*. Kohlrabi plants are dug after frost and the leaves are removed. The roots are clipped to 4-6" and then stored in damp sand or sawdust. The best roots are planted out the next spring for seed production. Seed saving techniques are the same as those used for cabbage.

GROWING KOHLRABI FROM SEED

Kohlrabi is an outbeeding biennial that is difficult to grow for both culinary use and seed production. The plants do not tolerate hot weather, but are frost hardy to about 20° F. A variety of planting times and winter storage techniques must be used in order to meet the plant's biennial seed production requirements. Kohlrabi is usually direct seeded as soon as the ground can be worked in the spring, or in the fall. Plant in full sun or partial shade, depending on the climate. Seeds are covered .25" deep and germinate best between 70-85° F., usually in 5-10 days. Plants should be thinned to 3" for food production, or 4-5" for breeding purposes. There are approximately 8,400 seeds per ounce (300 per gram or 134,000 per pound), depending on the variety. Federal Germination Standard for commercially sold kohlrabi seed is 75%.

REGIONAL GROWING RECOMMENDATIONS

Northeast: Kohlrabi can be direct seeded from late June to early July for small summer types, or early May for giant storage types. The plants like full sun and average water. We use floating row covers to guard against flee beetles. Dig plants mid to late October and store heeled into sand, soil or sawdust in cellar. Replant in early May. Seed heads are shatter-prone. Second year plants should either be set deeper than they originally grew, or else hilled up. The big trick, as with other *B. oleracea*, is to overwinter in good condition. Remove leaves but try not to tear the skin. Water roots in the cellar in mid to late winter, if they seem too dry.

Mid-Atlantic: Kohlrabi can be direct seeded about March 1, or started in a greenhouse about January 15. Plants might require protection in harsh winters. Mulch with compost, leaf litter or straw for winter protection.

Southeast/Gulf Coast: Start in a greenhouse about February 10 or August 15 and transplant into the garden about March 10 or September 10. The plants overwinter in the garden with no special care. Fall crops do not flower until spring.

Upper Midwest: Kohlrabi can be direct seeded in late July for seed production. The plants like full sun and average water. Dig the plants in early November and store the roots in moist sand. Replant in early April.

Southwest: Kohlrabi is not commonly grown in this region.

Central West Coast: Kohlrabi can be direct seeded about February 1 or August 1. Partial sun is okay; likes average water. The plants overwinter in the garden with no special care. It is very very difficult to produce seed for kohlrabi here, because the plants usually burn up in the heat of summer.

Maritime Northwest: Kohlrabi can be direct seeded about September 1. The plants like full sun and average water. We use floating row covers for the first 4-6 weeks to protect the crop from cabbage root maggot. The plants overwinter in the garden with no special care.

———————— *Crambe maritima* ————————
Sea Kale

Sea kale is a perennial and requires care similar to rhubarb or asparagus. Plants grown from cuttings are ready for harvest one or two years sooner than those started from seeds. Sea kale seeds are not difficult to start and may be the only way to secure the plants.

Sea kale is native to the coasts of western Europe. In early spring the plants are covered with an inverted bucket or pot to completely exclude all light. The young stalks become blanched and tender, are cut like asparagus, cooked until tender in salted water, and served with butter or hollandaise. Sea kale is an especially attractive plant and is a nice addition to any edible landscape or flower garden.

Sea kale flowers have a distinctively pleasant odor and are very attractive to insects. Different varieties can be cross-pollinated by insects. Isolation distances are not available but, judging by the types of insects that visit the flowers, the 1/2 mile distance used for other species of Brassicaceae should be sufficient for seed purity. The seed stalks grow about 2' above the plant. Sea kale continues to produce leaves and remains green as the seed stalks dry. Each seed is enclosed in a round seedpod. Care must be taken to avoid smashing the seeds when the seedpods are removed. For home storage and seed trading, it is easiest to store the seeds in the seedpods.

GROWING SEA KALE FROM SEED

Sea kale is an outbreeding perennial that flowers each spring, starting two or three years after planting. The plants will tolerate light frost, but no prolonged temperatures below 32° F. Sea kale may be direct seeded, greenhouse started, or propagated from divisions. Plant or set out in partial shade. Seeds should be covered .5" deep and germinate best at 75° F., usually in about 15 days. Plants should be thinned to 18" for food production and for breeding purposes. There is no Federal Germination Standard for sea kale.

REGIONAL GROWING RECOMMENDATIONS

Northeast: Sea kale cannot be grown in this region.

Mid-Atlantic: Sea kale can be direct seeded about March 15, or started in a greenhouse January 15 or later, and transplanted into the garden March 1 or later. The plants like full sun and average water, and overwinter in the garden with no special care. Mulch (composted rotted manure) helps the plants endure hot, dry summers. The seeds sometimes are difficult to germinate.

Southeast/Gulf Coast: Sea kale is not commonly grown in this region.

Upper Midwest: Sea kale plants like full sun and average water. Dig the plants in November and store in moist soil in basement. Replant about April 15.

Southwest: Sea kale cannot be grown in this region.

Central West Coast: Sea kale can be direct seeded February 1 to March 30. Some shade is necessary. The plants like average water and overwinter in the garden with no special care. This is a perennial plant that flowers every spring here.

Maritime Northwest: Sea kale plants like full sun and average water, and overwinter with no special care. Harvest each fall after the seed forms.

Eruca sativa
Rocket (Roquette)

Rocket (also known as rocket salad or roquette or roka or gargeer) has been grown throughout history. The ancient Romans are known to have used its leaves. In India the pungent seeds add spice to many native dishes. Rocket is currently enjoying a resurgence of popularity as a salad green. In most parts of the United States, rocket is grown in the early spring or in the late fall and winter. Hot temperatures and long days cause the leaves to become extremely hot with a hint of bitterness. For most gardeners, rocket is an acquired taste at best.

Rocket is usually planted by broadcasting the

Rocket (*Eruca sativa*).

seeds. The plants are pulled or snipped beginning when they have six true leaves. The flowers are self-sterile and require insects for cross-pollination. Rocket does not cross with any other genus or species within the Brassicaceae family. Different varieties of rocket will cross with one another and must be isolated by 1/2 mile for seed purity. Seed pollination, harvest and storage techniques are similar to those used for Chinese cabbage.

Turkish rocket, *Bunias orientalis*, is a perennial that is indigenous to Central Europe and Siberia. Further information or seed sources for Turkish rocket are unavailable.

GROWING ROCKET FROM SEED

Rocket is an outbreeding annual that bolts to seed quickly during warm days. Although somewhat frost hardy, rocket does not survive hard freezes. Rocket is direct seeded, either covering very lightly or letting water settle the seeds. Plant or set out in full sun or partial shade, early in the spring or late in the fall for the best culinary quality and seed producing plants. The seeds germinate at a wide range of temperatures (55-80° F.), usually in 5-7 days. There are approximately 15,400 seeds per ounce (545 per gram or 246,000 per pound), depending on the variety. There is no Federal Germination Standard for rocket.

REGIONAL GROWING RECOMMENDATIONS

Northeast: Rocket can be direct seeded about May 1-15. The plants like full sun and average water.

Mid-Atlantic: Rocket can be direct seeded about March 1 or August 15. The plants like full sun and average water, and overwinter with no special care.

Southeast/Gulf Coast: Rocket can be direct seeded about September 1-30, or from February 15 to March 15. The plants overwinter in the garden with no special care. Spring sowings flower very quickly.

Upper Midwest: Rocket can be direct seeded from early April to early June. The plants like partial sun and average water.

Southwest: Rocket can be direct seeded from September 15 to February 15. It is not very tasty in low to no frost areas.

Central West Coast: Rocket can be direct seeded from September 15 to November 1, or February 1 to March 30. The plants like full sun and average water, and overwinter in the garden with no special care.

Maritime Northwest: Rocket can be direct seeded from March 20 to April 1. The plants like full sun and average water.

─────── *Lepidium meyenii* ───────
Maca

Maca grows wild at high elevations in the Peruvian Andes where it is used for both food and medicine. The frost-resistant plants are widely cultivated throughout the central highlands of Peru. Maca forms a rosette of 12-20 leaves. As the outer leaves die, new ones form in the center of the plant. The roots resemble turnips and range in color from cream, yellow, and purple to black. They are traditionally cooked in Peru by roasting in hot ashes. Peruvian Indians believe that frequent consumption of the roots will increase fertility in human beings and animals. The roots have a tangy taste with a slight butterscotch aroma. There is no known source for maca seed in the United States.

Although maca is very rarely grown in the United States, gardeners who like to experiment might possibly be successful using the following growing suggestions. In areas of the Central West Coast, maca tubers should be started in a greenhouse from February 15 to March 15 and transplant into the garden about April 30. The plants like ample water, and some shade is necessary. Dig the plants before frost. store in rice hulls at cool temperatures, and then replant about February 15. This crop is not well adapted in most areas of the United States, but it can be done.

─────── *Lepidium sativum* ───────
Garden Cress

Garden cress resembles its namesake, watercress, in flavor but not habitat. Garden cress does nicely in the home garden and requires care similar to other salad greens. The seed is broadcast thickly where the plants are to grow. Harvest begins at the six-leaf stage by snipping the tops or thinning the plants. Long days and hot weather cause the flavor to decline.

The flowers are very small and rarely visited by honeybees, but crossing between varieties is possible. Isolation distances for garden cress are not available.

The seeds can be harvested like turnips. Those seedpods left to shatter on their own will result in renewable, self-sown beds.

Other garden cress varieties that are available in many seed catalogs include common cress, broad leaf cress, French cress, curled cress, curly moss cress, land cress, mustard cress, upland cress and peppergrass.

GROWING GARDEN CRESS FROM SEED

Garden cress is an outbreeding annual that grows

best in cool, moderate climates with daytime temperatures between 60-70° F. Neither hot nor cold temperatures are well tolerated. Garden cress is direct seeded, covering the seeds very lightly and keeping very moist. The seeds germinate at 50-60° F., usually within 7 days. Plant or set out in full sun or partial shade in cool, wet soil. The plants should be thinned to 4-6" for food production, or 2-3" for breeding purposes. There are approximately 11,200 seeds per ounce (400 per gram or 180,000 per pound), depending on the variety. There is no Federal Germination Standard for garden cress.

REGIONAL GROWING RECOMMENDATIONS

Northeast: Garden cress is not commonly grown in this region.

Mid-Atlantic: Garden cress can be direct seeded March 1. The plants like full sun and average water.

Southeast/Gulf Coast: Garden cress can be direct seeded March 1-30 or September 15-30. I don't know about winter hardiness.

Upper Midwest: Garden cress is direct seeded in early April. Plants like partial sun and average water.

Southwest: Garden cress can be direct seeded from September 15 to February 15. The plants like full sun and average water.

Central West Coast: Garden cress can be direct seeded from February 1 to March 30, or November 1 to December 1. Some shade is necessary; the plants like average water.

Maritime Northwest: Garden cress can be direct seeded about September 1. The plants like full sun and average water, and overwinter with no special care.

—————— *Rorippa microphylla* ——————
Large Leaf Watercress

—————— *Rorippa nasturtium var. aquaticum* ——————
Common Watercress

Many garden books still indicate that watercress must be grown in running water. Numerous time-consuming methods have been devised so that home gardeners can provide running water in streamless gardens. Watercress is found naturally in streams, but only needs to be rooted in mud. Running or still water has nothing to do with the plant's ability to grow.

Common watercress is *Rorippa nasturtium var. aquaticum*. Large leaf watercress is *R. microphylla*. The two species do not cross with one another. Watercress is usually propagated by divisions or cuttings. Watercress from the grocery store will root and may

be used as a source for plants. Seeds are produced in very small, curved seedpods that develop from tiny white flowers. The seedpods shatter easily and are difficult to find and harvest. The tiny dry pods can be rubbed between the hands or rolled lightly with a rolling pin to extract the seeds.

European growers name cress after the areas where it historically has been grown. English connoisseurs may prefer cress from Springhead or Waltham. It is not clear if such designations refer to distinct varieties.

GROWING WATERCRESS FROM SEED

Large leaf watercress and common watercress are both perennials that grows best in cool, moderate climates with daytime temperatures between 60-70° F. Neither hot nor cold temperatures are well tolerated. Watercress is usually started from cuttings, but can also be direct seeded. Cover seeds very lightly and keep very moist. Seeds germinate at 50-60° F., usually in about 7 days. Plant or set out in full sun or part shade in cool, wet soil. Plants should be thinned to 4-6" for food production, 2-3" for breeding purposes. There are approximately 11,200 seeds per ounce (400 per gram or 180,000 per pound), depending on the variety. There is no Federal Germination Standard for watercress.

REGIONAL GROWING RECOMMENDATIONS

Northeast: Large leaf watercress and common watercress are not commonly grown in this region.

Mid-Atlantic: Large leaf watercress and common watercress are not commonly grown in this region.

Southeast/Gulf Coast: No experience growing large leaf watercress. Common watercress grows wild in coldwater streams in the Upper South and is propagated vegetatively.

Upper Midwest: Large leaf watercress and common watercress can be started in a greenhouse about March 1 and transplant into the garden about April 15. Some shade is necessary; needs very wet conditions.

Southwest: Large leaf watercress and common watercress are not commonly grown in this region.

Central West Coast: Large leaf watercress and common watercress can be direct seeded about March 15. Some shade is necessary; needs very wet conditions. Cuttings may be taken before frost, rooted in water and replanted after the threat of frost has passed.

Maritime Northwest: Large leaf watercress and common watercress are not commonly grown in this region.

THE CHENOPODIACEAE FAMILY

The Chenopodiaceae family includes several very widely grown vegetables. Beets, chard and spinach were noted in Aristotle's writings as early as the fourth century B.C. Orach is recorded in ancient Indian history. Although not well known in the United States, quinoa is an important grain crop in the Andes Mountains of South America. Lamb's-quarters and Good King Henry are common in English gardens and are gathered wild throughout Europe and America.

FAMILY TAXONOMY

Members of the Chenopodiaceae family are very diverse in growth habit and even in seed formation. Beet or chard seed is an aggregate containing several seeds formed in an irregular, dry, hardened, woody calyx. Other family members have "panicles" (flower clusters) of single seeds.

POLLINATION CHARACTERISTICS AND TECHNIQUES

Members of the Chenopodiaceae family are wind-pollinated. The pollen is light and can travel up to five miles depending on the variety, air temperature and wind speed. Commercial seed production relies entirely on isolation to keep the seed crop pure.

In the home garden it is possible to bag beets, orach and spinach, if varieties are grown very close together. As the seed stalks form, a wooden or metal support stake is placed in the center of the plants. The seed stalks are all bent in slightly to the stake and covered with a large, water-resistant paper bag. The seed stalks are then wrapped with cotton batting to cushion and seal the bottom of the bag. The batting prevents stray pollen and insects from entering the bag from the bottom. The bag is stapled shut and then tied or taped around the batting to form a secure seal. In most areas the daily winds will be sufficient to mix the pollen inside the bag. Shaking the bags on windless days will help to ensure good pollination and seed set.

GENERAL PRODUCTION AND PROCESSING TECHNIQUES

Except for beetberry, Chenopodiaceae seeds are harvested dry and are usually stripped from the plants by hand while still in the garden. Some beet and prickly-seeded spinaches can be hard on the hands, making gloves a necessity. The plants and their fully mature seeds can be pulled to finish drying under cover in areas where summer rains occur.

——— Chenopodiaceae in the Garden ———		
Genus	Species	Common Name
Atriplex	*hortensis*	orach (mountain spinach)
Beta	*vulgaris*	garden beet, sugar beet, mangel, Swiss chard
Chenopodium	*album*	lamb's-quarters
	bonus-henricus	Good King Henry
	capitatum	beetberry
	quinoa	quinoa
Spinacia	*oleracea*	spinach

Beta vulgaris - Garden Beet, Sugar Beet, Mangel and Swiss Chard

Beets have been providing food for humans and animals since ancient Grecian times. Invading Roman armies took beet roots into northern Europe to provide feed for their horses. The tender green leaves and long-keeping roots made beets an excellent crop for northern European climates. Centuries of selection resulted in varieties that produced tender, abundant greens, which have become the chards of today. Other selections produced tiny red table beets, and huge varieties used for stock feed and sugar production.

In 1700 the Prussians began searching for a way to produce sugar in their short, cold climate. Their attention centered on beets, and by 1775 a forage beet with 6% sugar content had been developed. Today's sugar beets often yield a sugar content of 20% and provide nearly half of the world's sugar.

Facing Page: A single giant leaf of Swiss chard (*Beta vulgaris*), a red-stemmed variety known as rhubarb chard, becomes a child's toy.

69

BOTANICAL CLASSIFICATION

Beta vulgaris includes all forage, sugar and garden beets as well as the chards. Chard varieties are beets that are grown for their greens rather than for root production. *B. vulgaris* is biennial, requiring two seasons to produce seed. Beets will not flower until their roots are mature and have been subjected to at least a month of cold temperatures. In mild winter climates, beets planted in the late summer will "bolt" (produce a seed stalk) during the following spring.

Sugar beets are usually white or cream colored and weigh from 8-15 pounds. Forage or mangel beets can grow much larger and are available in white, yellow, red, and red with white stripes. Table beets have been selected for their small size, sweet flavor, and for a variety of root shapes. Globe and round shapes are by far the most common. Cylindrical varieties are often preferred for canning and pickling because all of the slices are nearly the same diameter. Table beets are available in yellow, gold, pink, red, and red with white stripes.

The larger forage or mangel beets are rapidly vanishing from commercial catalogs and need immediate attention in order to be preserved. Rabbit breeders should be especially interested in growing mangel beets as a feed supplement and might provide a unique maintenance network.

POLLINATION, CROSSING AND ISOLATION

All beets and chards are outbreeding plants that will cross with each other, no matter what their size or use. To make seed saving even more difficult, beets are wind-pollinated. Beet pollen is light and can travel up to five miles depending on the temperature and climate. Crop isolation or seed stalk bagging can be used to ensure seed purity. Isolation of two to five miles is required for absolute purity. In home gardens the bagging technique described on the Chenopodiaceae family pages can be used. A minimum of six beets should be included in each bag or cage.

SEED PRODUCTION, HARVEST AND PROCESSING

As with other biennial root crops, two methods of seed production are commonly used with beets. The

Garden beet (*Beta vulgaris*) flowers, left, and mature seeds, right.

seed-to-seed method is the easiest, especially in mild winter areas. The beet seed is planted and the roots that are left in the ground over the winter produce seed the following year.

When using the seed-to-root-to-seed method, beet seeds are planted in the spring. The roots grow to maturity, are dug before the first killing frost, and are sorted for uniform color, size and shape. Be very careful not to nick or bruise the roots. The tops are cut leaving 2" of greens, and the root tips are trimmed to about 6". The roots are then packed into a layer of damp sand or sawdust, and the green tops are covered with sawdust, shredded newspaper or leaves. Beets will store for 4-6 months between 32-40° F. at 90-95% humidity. The best roots are replanted the following spring for seed production. Some gardeners cut the tops back to within 1" of the roots, while others believe that leaving the tops on provides an added source of nourishment for the roots.

Seed savers in mild winter climates usually use the seed-to-seed method. However, if there is any doubt about seed purity, use the seed-to-root-to-seed method so that the roots can be examined and any off-types can be rogued out.

Beet seed stalks can grow 4' tall and are usually harvested when the majority of the seed clusters have turned light brown. The fully mature seeds can be progressively stripped from the plant as they mature, or the entire seed stalk can be cut when the majority of the seeds are mature, and then dried further. The dried seed stalks can be threshed with a flail, but jogging in place on a bag of dried stalks is faster for large quantities. The seeds are then winnowed to remove any remaining pieces of stems and leaves.

Beet seeds have a different structure from other garden seeds. Each seed is actually a group of flowers that is fused together by the flower petals. This forms a multigerm cluster which usually contains two to five seeds. Plant breeders have recently developed single seeded clusters for some sugar beets, which eliminates the need for thinning.

Some seed companies break apart the seed clusters of garden beets for the same reason. Research suggests that this increases seed injury and reduces germination. Seed clusters can also be broken apart at home. Place the seeds in a bag and gently roll it with a rolling pin. Adjust the pressure until the clusters are broken apart but not crushed.

SEED STATISTICS

Beet seeds will retain 50% germination for six years when stored in a cool, dry, dark location. Members of the Seed Savers Exchange annually offer about 41 varieties of beets, and the *Garden Seed Inventory* lists sources for 78 beets that are available from mail-order seed companies. There are approximately 2,800 seeds per ounce (100 per gram or 45,000 per pound), depending on the variety. Federal Germination Standard for commercially sold beet seed is 75%.

GROWING BEETS FROM SEED

Beets and chards are biennials that must be dug, stored, and replanted in order to produce seed crops in climates with freezing winter temperatures. Beets are usually direct seeded. Swiss chard can either be direct seeded or transplanted from greenhouse starts. The seeds should be covered .5" deep and will germinate at temperatures ranging from 55-80° F., usually in 5-10 days. Plant or set out in full sun. Garden beets should be thinned to 4", sugar beets and mangels to 10", and Swiss chard to 12" spacings.

REGIONAL GROWING RECOMMENDATIONS

Northeast: Sugar beet and Swiss chard can be direct seeded about May 20, garden beet as late as July 10. The plants like full sun and average water. Dig the plants in early October. Store Swiss chard heeled in dirt, sand or sawdust in buckets, others in tight barrels. We have occasionally field-wintered chard with mulch, but it's unreliable. Storage of all types must be very cool and very damp. Warmth and drying cause the spreen (crown) to wither and fail.

Mid-Atlantic: Beets can be direct seeded about March 1 or August 15. Plants prefer full sun and average water, and overwinter in the garden with no special care when mulched.

Southeast/Gulf Coast: Beets can be direct seeded about March 1 or September 1. The plants like partial sun, and overwinter in the garden with no special care. Overwintered plants look rough and are no longer edible, but flowering is excellent. The plants flower in spring after overwintering.

Upper Midwest: Beets can be direct seeded anytime up to late July. The plants like partial sun and average water. Dig the plants in early November and store in moist sand. Replant in early April to produce a seed crop. Stake to prevent the plant from toppling over.

Southwest: Beets can be direct seeded about August 1. The plants like full sun and average water.

Central West Coast: Beets can be direct seeded from September 1 to October 1 for seed, anytime for eating. The plants like full sun and average water, and overwinter in the garden with no special care.

Chenopodiaceae

Maritime Northwest: Beets can be direct seeded about July 15. Likes full sun and average water. We use floating row covers for overwintering chard, which overwinters in the garden with no special care. Reemay™ can help for the coldest period of winter. Beets must be dug about October 1 and stored in a root cellar or in punctured plastic bags with wood shavings in a cooler. Replant about March 15. Beet, sugar beet and mangel don't usually make it through the winter outdoors in the Pacific Northwest due to repeated freeze-thaw cycles and disease. Therefore it is best to dig them in the fall and store them in a cooler or root cellar between 32-40° F. in punctured plastic bags containing several handfuls of wood shavings.

Spinacia oleracea - Spinach

Spinach is known to have been cultivated in Europe since 1351. The species probably originated in central Asia and was mentioned in Chinese agricultural literature in the seventh century.

Spinach is a unique annual vegetable, because its plants produce either all male flowers or all female flowers. Spinach seed is either prickly or smooth, which corresponds to the plant's leaf shape. Prickly-seeded varieties produce flatter leaves, while smooth-seeded varieties generally are more wrinkled.

Seed-set in spinach is daylength sensitive, and long days will cause the plants to bolt to seed. Depending on the variety, plants will begin to bolt when daylight reaches 12.5-15 hours. In addition, plants exposed to alternating cold and hot temperatures will often bolt at even less than 12.5 hours of daylight. Crowded plants will bolt more quickly than those given ample space.

BOTANICAL CLASSIFICATION

Spinach belongs to the genus *Spinacia* and the species *oleracea*. Different varieties of *S. oleracea* have been selected for their resistance to bolting and for dark leaves that are rich in vitamins. Depending on climate and season, either cold tolerant or long day tolerant varieties can be grown.

The concentration of nitrate in spinach leaves can occasionally reach toxic levels. Such high nitrate levels usually occur when large amounts of ammonia fertilizers are used to produce the crop. Spinach also may contain high levels of oxalates that sometimes interfere with calcium intake in humans.

POLLINATION, CROSSING AND ISOLATION

Spinach is an outbreeding plant that is mainly wind-pollinated, which makes it difficult for home seed savers to grow more than one variety to save for seed without the use of bagging. Spinach pollen is very light and can be carried for great distances by the wind.

Commercial spinach seed crops are separated by

Female spinach plant (*Spinacia oleracea*) with seeds, left, and flowering male plant, right.

5-10 miles. Spinach pollen is so fine that it easily penetrates mesh screen, but is severely restricted by spun polyester fabric. The bagging technique described on the Chenopodiaceae family pages can be used with some success.

As was stated earlier, spinach plants are either male or female. Always maintain a ratio of one male to two female plants, and also an absolute minimum of two male and four female plants per cage, which will result in good pollination and will retain a fair amount of genetic diversity within the population. The sex of spinach plants is hard to determine until the seed stalks have formed, which often results in less than an ideal situation when attempting to determine the plants that are to be caged. Close plantings in wide beds will provide the greatest chance that the necessary ratio of male to female plants will be growing in relatively close proximity.

SEED PRODUCTION, HARVEST AND PROCESSING

In home gardens the outer leaves of the spinach rosette are often harvested as a cut-and-come-again vegetable. Commercially, the entire rosette is harvested. When spinach is being grown for a seed crop, a few of the outer leaves can be eaten without decreasing the quality or quantity of the seed.

Commercial spinach seed is usually dried in the field. In areas with prolonged summer rains, the plants can be pulled when the seed is fully formed but not yet dry. When possible, however, spinach seed is much easier to harvest directly from the plants in the garden. Prickly-seeded varieties can be very abrasive to the hands, so heavy gloves are a necessity. Starting at the bottom of the plant, strip off the seeds and leaves in an upward motion and let them fall into a basket or sack.

Seeds and leaves that are completely dry can be winnowed immediately after harvest. If still damp, let them dry for several additional days away from direct sunlight. Winnowing will then remove the remaining leaves and other debris.

Commercially produced prickly-seeded varieties are put through an abrasion process to smooth the seeds. This technique is not necessary and does not aid in germination.

SEED STATISTICS

Spinach seeds will retain 50% germination for five years when stored under ideal conditions. Members of the Seed Savers Exchange annually offer about 20 varieties of spinach, and the *Garden Seed Inventory* lists sources for 46 varieties of spinach that are available from mail-order seed companies in the United States and Canada. There are approximately 2,240 spinach seeds per ounce (80 per gram or 36,000 per pound), depending on the variety. Federal Germination Standard for commercially sold spinach seed is 65%.

GROWING SPINACH FROM SEED

Spinach is a daylength sensitive annual that grows best in cool, mild climates. Spinach is usually direct seeded in the very early spring or late fall. The seeds should be covered .5" deep and will germinate at temperatures between 55-70° F., usually in 6-15 days. Either plant or set out in full sun or partial shade. Plants should be thinned to 3" for both food and breeding purposes.

REGIONAL GROWING RECOMMENDATIONS

Northeast: Spinach can be direct seeded from late April to early May. The plants like average water and full sun, but some shade is necessary if you <u>do not</u> want crop to run to seed (for eating purposes). The seed ripens unevenly and some may shatter, so I sometimes put paper on the ground under the sprawling plants.

Mid-Atlantic: Spinach can be direct seeded from February 1 to April 1, or August 15 to October 1. The plants like full sun and average water, and overwinter in the garden with no special care.

Southeast/Gulf Coast: Spinach can be direct seeded about March 1, or from September 1 to October 10. The plants overwinter in the garden with no special care. The plants flower in spring, with or without overwintering.

Upper Midwest: Spinach can be direct seeded as early as ground can be worked. The plants like partial sun and average water. Many beetles and other insects attack the ripening seeds, so row cover is recommended after pollination.

Southwest: Spinach can be direct seeded from September 15 to February 15. The plants like full or filtered sun and average water.

Central West Coast: Spinach can be direct seeded about March 1-15 or October 1-15. The plants like partial sun and average water, and overwinter in the garden with no special care. This is a difficult crop here due to heat.

Maritime Northwest: Spinach can be direct seeded about April 1 or, if grown as an overwintered crop (which can be done most years), plant between September 15 and October 1 for a mid-summer seed harvest the following year. Do not mulch in this wet winter climate, as many of your plants will rot. The plants like full sun and average water.

Chenopodiaceae

Atriplex hortensis
Orach (Mountain Spinach)

Orach is also known as mountain spinach, French spinach, sea purslane and salt bush. The last two names refer to the plant's ability to withstand saline soils. The Greeks used orach as a medicine and later as a vegetable. Although not commonly cultivated in the United States, orach is widely grown in many parts of the world.

Orach can be used in place of spinach or chard in any recipe. The red variety is quite attractive and is sometimes planted in flower gardens. The three varieties available from seed companies include: red, green, and a light green sometimes called yellow.

Orach has tiny wind-pollinated flowers. Isolation or bagging will prevent cross-pollination between varieties. Orach plants bolt in response to lengthening days and are not truly biennial.

The seeds are enclosed in leafy membranes known as bracts that are easily stripped from the plants as they mature. The plants also produce some tiny black seeds without bracts, that are usually not fertile. After harvest the seeds are dried and stored.

Orach seeds will maintain 50% germination for six years when stored in cool, dry, dark conditions.

GROWING ORACH FROM SEED

Orach is an outbreeding, annual plant that is day-length sensitive and adapted to many climatic conditions. Usually orach is direct seeded. Either cover the seeds very lightly or water in without covering. The seeds germinate at temperature ranging from 50-75° F., usually within about 14 days. Plant in full sun in the spring or late fall. The plants are thinned to 6" for food production, or 12" for breeding purposes.

REGIONAL GROWING RECOMMENDATIONS

Northeast: Orach can be direct seeded before May 15. The plants like full sun and average water. This seems to be an "iffy" seed crop here and is probably more dependable if started indoors.

Mid-Atlantic: Orach can be direct seeded from February 15 to March 15, or started in a greenhouse about January 15 and transplanted into the garden about March 1. The plants like full sun and average water. Plants are never grown in fall for overwintering.

Southeast/Gulf Coast: Orach can be direct seeded March 1 to May. Likes full sun and average water.

Upper Midwest: Orach can be direct seeded as early as ground can be worked. The seed shatters easily in heavy rains and wind.

Southwest: Orach can be direct seeded March 15 to May 15. The plants like full sun and average water.

Central West Coast: Orach can be direct seeded February 1 to April 1. Likes full sun and average water.

Maritime Northwest: Orach can be direct seeded March 20 to April 10. The plants like full sun and average water.

Orach (*Atriplex hortensis*) seed stalk, with leaves of red orach, top, and green orach, bottom.

Chenopodium album
Lamb's-Quarters

Lamb's-quarters is a weed in most temperate and tropical regions of the world. The leaves can be cooked like spinach or eaten raw. Southwest Indian tribes gathered the seeds and ground them into a flour for bread.

C. album is also sometimes called pigweed or

white goosefoot weed. Male and female flowers are produced on the same plant and can be either insect-pollinated or wind-pollinated. Different varieties, if available, would cross with one another.

GROWING LAMB'S-QUARTERS FROM SEED

Lamb's-quarters is an outbreeding annual that grows as a weed in many climates. Usually it is direct seeded. Cover the seeds very lightly or just water in. Germination is erratic. Plant in full sun or partial shade in early spring. The plants should be thinned to 6" for food production, or 4" for breeding purposes.

REGIONAL GROWING RECOMMENDATIONS

Northeast: Lamb's-quarters can be direct seeded about mid-May. Plants like full sun and average water.

Mid-Atlantic: Lamb's-quarters can be direct seeded about March 1, or from September 15 to November 15. The plants like full sun and average water, and overwinter in the garden with no special care.

Southeast/Gulf Coast: This crop grows wild. Seeds sprout in May and mature July to September.

Upper Midwest: Lamb's-quarters can be direct seeded anytime the ground can be worked. The plants like full to partial sun.

Southwest: Lamb's-quarters can be direct seeded March 15 to May 30. The plants like full sun and are drought tolerant.

Central West Coast: Lamb's-quarters can be direct seeded March 15 to April 30. The plants like full sun and average water.

Maritime Northwest: Lamb's-quarters can be direct seeded March 20 to April 10. The plants like full sun and average water.

———— *Chenopodium bonus-henricus* ————
Good King Henry

Until the beginning of the 1900s, Good King Henry was commonly grown in English kitchen gardens. Also known as fat hen plant, *C. bonus-henricus* is perennial and very hardy. Each spring its arrow-head-shaped leaves are used like spinach. The plants can be covered with an inverted flower pot in the early spring in order to blanch the stems which are then harvested and eaten like asparagus.

It is not known if different varieties of Good King Henry exist. If varieties do exist and were grown near one another, they would probably be crossed by either insects or the wind. Tiny black seeds are harvested when the plant begins to die back in the fall.

GROWING GOOD KING HENRY FROM SEED

Good King Henry is an outbreeding perennial that grows as a weed in many climates. Usually it is direct seeded. Cover seeds very lightly or just water in. Germination is erratic. Plant in full sun or partial shade in the early spring. The plants should be thinned to 6" for food production, or 4" for breeding purposes.

REGIONAL GROWING RECOMMENDATIONS

Northeast: Good King Henry is not commonly grown in this region.

Mid-Atlantic: Good King Henry is direct seeded March 1, or September 15 to November 15. Partial sun is okay; some shade is necessary. The plants like average water, and overwinter with no special care.

Southeast/Gulf Coast: Good King Henry is not commonly grown in this region.

Upper Midwest: Good King Henry can be direct seeded as early as possible. The plants like full sun and average water.

Southwest: Good King Henry is not commonly grown in this region.

Central West Coast: Good King Henry can be direct seeded about March 15. Some shade is necessary; likes average water. The plants overwinter in the garden with no special care.

Maritime Northwest: Good King Henry is not commonly grown in this region.

———— *Chenopodium capitatum* ————
Beetberry

Beetberry is native to southern Europe where it is often considered a weed. The small plants produce numerous flower clusters on a short stem. Orangish red fruits develop around tiny, black seeds. The fruits are sweet, but lack any real flavor. In some regions the fruits are called strawberry blite, although any resemblance to strawberries seems limited to color.

Beetberry is primarily wind-pollinated. Different varieties, if grown in close proximity, would likely cross-pollinate. Isolation distances are unavailable.

Mature seeds can be saved from fruits which are bright red or orange in color. The tiny, soft fruits are easy to crush with either fingers or the back of a spoon. The addition of a small amount of water will cause the pieces of the fruit to float and the seeds to sink. Pour off the water and pulp, drain the seeds and set out to dry. Care must be taken to ensure that the extremely small seeds do not pass through kitchen strainers. Information on seed viability is unavailable.

Chenopodiaceae

GROWING BEETBERRY FROM SEED

Beetberry is an outbreeding annual that grows as a weed in many climates. Usually it is direct seeded. Cover the seeds very lightly or just water in. Germination is erratic. Plant in full sun or partial shade in the early spring. The plants should be thinned to 6" for food production, or 4" for breeding purposes.

REGIONAL GROWING RECOMMENDATIONS

Northeast: Beetberry is not commonly grown in this region.

Mid-Atlantic: Beetberry can be direct seeded about March 1 or August 1. The plants like filtered sun and average water.

Southeast/Gulf Coast: Beetberry can be direct seeded from March 1 to May 1. The plants like partial sun and average water.

Upper Midwest: Beetberry can be direct seeded as early as the ground can be worked. The plants like partial sun and average water. Harvest the seed when the berries have dried on the plant, which is easier to do than picking the ripe fruits. Seed is viable for at least five years under normal conditions.

Southwest: Beetberry is not commonly grown in this region.

Central West Coast: Beetberry can be direct seeded from March 15 to September 15. Plants like full sun and average water.

Maritime Northwest: Beetberry is not commonly grown in this region.

———— *Chenopodium quinoa* ————
Quinoa

Quinoa is a native of the Andes Mountains of South American and has been the subject of much recent attention. Grown like orach, quinoa is well adapted to climates above 8,000' in the Andes. Most varieties are short day sensitive and do not produce seed until very late in the season when grown in the United States, although selections from the southern Andes are adapting well to comparable North American latitudes.

Quinoa's green or slightly greenish purple leaves are eaten like spinach. Many different varieties have developed in a vast range of altitudes throughout the Andes. Seed colors include white, ivory, pink, red, and purple. Quinoa seed is very bitter and must be soaked, washed and rubbed in several changes of water before being boiled for cereal or added to stews.

Quinoa's flowers are perfect. Different varieties grown near one another would probably be crossed by insects or the wind. Quinoa is not related to nor does it cross with amaranth.

GROWING QUINOA FROM SEED

Quinoa is an annual, but there is conflicting information on its inbreeding or outbreeding tendencies. Many varieties are short daylength sensitive and must have an adequate frost free period in order to mature in the late fall. Quinoa is usually direct seeded. Cover the seeds very lightly or just water in. The seeds germinate best at 70-80° F. Plant in full sun or partial shade in early spring. The plants should be thinned to 8-12" for seed production.

REGIONAL PLANTING RECOMMENDATIONS

Northeast: Quinoa can be direct seeded about mid-May, or (better) started in a greenhouse late April to early May in individual peat pots and transplanted into the garden after May 20. Plants like full sun and average water. The seedheads often require after-ripening (curing). Cut and hang in a dry, airy place with a tarp underneath, or surround the seedhead with a paper bag.

Mid-Atlantic: Quinoa is not commonly grown in this region.

Southeast/Gulf Coast: Quinoa is not commonly grown in this region.

Upper Midwest: Quinoa can be direct seeded as early as the ground can be worked. Plants like full sun and average water.

Southwest: Quinoa can be direct seeded March 15 to June 15. The plants like full sun and are drought tolerant.

Central West Coast: Quinoa can be direct seeded anytime, but spring is preferred. The plants like full sun and are drought tolerant, and overwinter in the garden with no special care.

Maritime Northwest: Quinoa can be direct seeded March 20 to April 10. The plants like full sun and average water.

Facing page: A village of screen houses at Gatersleben, the world famous seed bank in the former East Germany. Introduced pollinators (orchard mason bees and flies) pollinate up to 19 species in each cage. (Photo courtesy of the Institut für Pflanzengenetik und Kulturpflanzenforschung)

Compositae is sometimes referred to as the salad family. Indeed, the family's claim to fame is lettuce. Millions of tons of lettuce are produced and consumed worldwide each year. Other salad vegetables include the chicories, endives and some of the daisies.

A flower garden would never be the same without daisies, but neither would the vegetable garden. Sunflowers, Jerusalem artichokes and shungiku are delicious and add color to any garden. For most gardeners, a big yellow sunflower represents happiness. Perhaps sunflowers take us back to our childhood when all flowers were drawn with rays and big happy faces.

FAMILY TAXONOMY

The Compositae family is immense and has been divided into groups on the basis of such characteristics as the presence or absence of milky or colored sap, corolla type, morphology of anthers and styles, etc. Compositae members that are used as vegetables make up a very small portion of this family's more than 20,000 species. Only 11 of those species are commonly used as vegetables worldwide.

POLLINATION CHARACTERISTICS AND TECHNIQUES

Compositae flowers are perfect and most are self-compatible. However, many species require insect or mechanical agitation for the pollen to reach the stigma. Studies indicate that plants that are freely visited by insects have a greater number of viable seeds.

Compositae flowers are produced on a seed stalk that grows upward from the center of the plant. Although the flowers are perfect, they are also designed to attract insects. A few varieties are self-incompatible and do require insects for pollination.

Most home seed savers either isolate or hand-pollinate different varieties within each species. It is also possible to control pollination in the Compositae family with caging, alternate day caging, and caging with introduced pollinators. (Those techniques are explained in detail in Section I.)

PLANT SELECTION

At every stage of development, seed savers should check to make sure that each plant is true-to-type. Remove any plants that differ in color, shape or size. If any of the biennial Compositae bolt during the first season, remove the plants and do not save their seeds. Biennial plants that bolt prematurely usually do not produce full-sized, properly formed plants. Including bolters in a population of plants used for seed production increases the chances of many more poorly formed plants in future crops.

Compositae in the Garden

Genus	Species	Common Name
Arctium	lappa	gobo (Japanese burdock)
Chrysanthemum		
	coronarium	shungiku
Cichorium	endivia	endive, escarole
	intybus	chicory (witloof chicory)
Cynara	cardunculus	cardoon
	scolymus	artichoke (globe artichoke)
Helianthus	annuus	sunflower
	maximiliani	edible rooted sunflower
	tuberosus	Jerusalem artichoke (sunroot)
Lactuca	sativa	lettuce, celtuce
Polymnia	sonchifolia	yacon
Scorzonera	hispanica	black salsify (scorzonera)
Tragopogon	porrifolius	salsify
	pratensis	wild salsify

GENERAL PRODUCTION AND PROCESSING TECHNIQUES

All seeds in the Compositae family are harvested dry. Birds are readily attracted to Compositae seeds

Facing Page: Comparative growout of lettuce (*Lactuca sativa*) at Heritage Farm where 850 varieties are being permanently maintained.

and can ruin a seed crop before harvest. Some of the bagging and caging techniques described in each of the following vegetable sections will keep that damage to a minimum. The seeds can be harvested directly from plants that are left standing in the garden. It is usually more convenient, however, to cut the entire seed stalks and store them in feed sacks for threshing.

When the stalks are dry, many of the seeds will fall off. The remainder can be removed by jogging on top of the seed heads, or by using a flail or small seed thresher. Winnowing is usually necessary to remove any remaining leaves and debris.

Cichorium endivia - Endive and Escarole

Endive has been used by the Egyptians for many centuries and is thought to have spread to northern Europe by 1200 A.D. The use of endive plants was described in English cookbooks in the 16th century and in an American recipe book in 1806. Historically, endive has been used as a cooked vegetable, but today the leaves are most often used in salads.

Endive grows as a loose head of leaves with ruffled or serrated edges. The outside leaves are green and slightly bitter. The inner leaves, partially protected from light, are somewhat milder. Escarole, a smooth-leaved form of endive, has more of a heading tendency and is usually less bitter. Both types can survive light frost and extended periods of temperatures in the low 30s. The sugar stored in the plant gradually increases during cool weather, which results in improved quality and reduced bitterness.

BOTANICAL CLASSIFICATION

Endive and escarole belong to the genus *Cichorium* and species *endivia*. *C. endivia* does not include the Belgian endives or witloof chicory, which are both *C. intybus*. Endive is closely related to the chicories and probably developed from a chance cross of two wild chicory species. Endive differs distinctively from chicory, however, being fully self-compatible and self-pollinating.

The standard commercial endive variety is Green Curled Ruffec, that has curled, deeply-cut leaves. Salad King is larger and more tolerant to both heat and cold. Pink Star and Red Endive have anthocyanin in the midribs which causes the leaves to appear pink.

Full Heart Batavia is the most common variety of escarole, but Florida Deep Heart matures slightly earlier. A large number of imported varieties are available in the United States. Most bear the name of the region where they originated. Studies indicate that there are few, if any, differences in leaf color and shape between most varieties.

POLLINATION, CROSSING AND ISOLATION

Endive and escarole are inbreeding plants. En-dive flowers, which are perfect and self-pollinating, open at first light and close by noon. Endive varieties cannot be crossed by chicory, but chicory can be crossed by endive. In 1953, studies with chicory and endive determined that two separate species classifications were appropriate. One endive and one chicory were planted next to one another. Insects freely visited both plants. The seeds produced by each plant were grown the following season. All of the seeds from the endive plant produced endive plants, proving that self-pollination had occurred and that crossing with chicory had not.

Endive, left, and escarole, right,
both *Cichorium endivia*.

Different varieties of endive can be crossed by insects and should be either separated by 1/2 mile or caged to ensure seed purity. Endive flowers bloom over a long period, so the cage must be left in place from the first bloom until the last.

SEED PRODUCTION, HARVEST AND PROCESSING

Endives are biennial, but will bolt to seed during the first season if exposed to cool temperatures and short days. Such bolting often occurs when seeds are sown very early in the season. The plants begin to produce seed stalks as the days lengthen and the temperatures increase.

In mild winter climates, endives are usually planted in the fall. Light leaf harvest during the first growing season will not significantly harm flower or seed production. Endive may be overwintered in the ground under a mulch in many regions of the United States. In climates where the ground freezes solid, the roots are dug before a hard frost. The tops are trimmed to 2" above the crown, and any small or secondary roots are clipped off. The endive roots are then stored in soil or sand and will keep for three months or more at 32-40° F. and 80-90% humidity. Replant the best roots in spring for seed production.

Once the majority of the flowers have set seedpods, withhold water and let the seed stalks dry. Crush the base of a dry flower to check on the seed development. The individual seeds are tightly enclosed and require a good bit of prying to remove. The seeds are ready to harvest when they appear to be dry and are firm.

Two methods of small scale seed cleaning can be used. It is easiest to break the completely dry seedpods off of the stalks one at a time, and then store them in small glass containers without further cleaning. Entire pods can be planted, but thinning will be necessary when the plants appear. The pods can also be broken open to free the individual seeds.

To obtain cleaner seeds, place the seed stalks in a feed sack on a concrete floor and pound the pods with a large hammer or wooden maul. For larger quantities, an I-Tech Seed Winnower crushes the pods quite efficiently (see "Seed Cleaning Equipment" in Section I). The seeds will then need to be winnowed or screened to remove any remaining dust or debris.

SEED STATISTICS

Endive seeds will remain viable for eight years when stored in a cool, dry, dark location. Members of the Seed Savers Exchange annually offer about 12 varieties of endive (and escarole), and the *Garden Seed Inventory* lists sources for 47 varieties that are available from seed companies. There are approximately 14,430 seeds per ounce (510 per gram or 230,000 per pound), depending on the variety. Federal Germination Standard for commercially sold seed is 70%.

GROWING ENDIVE AND ESCAROLE FROM SEED

Endive is a biennial, tolerating temperatures down into the low 30s. The plants do not tolerate heat well. Endive may be direct seeded or greenhouse started to produce transplants, covering the seeds .25" deep. The seeds germinate at temperatures ranging from 60-70° F., usually within 10-14 days. Plant or set out in full sun, or afternoon shade in hot summer climates. The plants should be thinned to 8-12" for both food and seed production.

REGIONAL GROWING RECOMMENDATIONS

Northeast: Endive (and escarole) can be direct seeded in early May or (preferably) started in a greenhouse about mid-April and transplanted into the garden mid to late May. The plants like full sun and average water. We often put hex-wire over plants to foil the deer. Goldfinches are sometimes a problem as the seed matures, and row cover helps after most of flowering is over (but is best omitted if possible).

Mid-Atlantic: Endive can be direct seeded about March 1, or from September 15 to October 15, or started in a greenhouse about January 15 and transplanted into the garden about March 1. The plants like full sun and average water, and overwinter in the garden with no special care.

Southeast/Gulf Coast: Endive can be direct seeded about September 1-20, or from February 20 to March 15. We use hoop houses for cosmetic reasons. The plants overwinter in the garden with no special care, but look pretty bad unless grown under tunnels.

Upper Midwest: Endive should be direct seeded as early as possible to get mature seed the first year, or sow midsummer and overwinter. The plants, which like full sun and average water, should be dug in early November and stored in moist sand, and replanted in early April.

Southwest: Endive is not commonly grown in this region.

Central West Coast: Endive is direct seeded from September 1 to October 15. The plants like full sun and average water, and overwinter with no special care.

Maritime Northwest: Endive can be direct seeded

about April 1, or can be planted from September 15 to October 1 for a midsummer seed harvest the following year. The plants like full sun and average water, and will survive through most Pacific Northwest winters very nicely. Do not mulch in wet winter weather as you may lose the plants to rot.

Cichorium intybus - Chicory (Witloof Chicory)

Chicory is an important salad vegetable throughout Europe. Over half of the chicory grown is in the form of witloof chicory or Belgian endive. The roots are dug, trimmed, and forced to sprout in underground pits or in dark, air-conditioned rooms. The "chicons" (blanched chicory sprouts) are harvested and used alone as a salad ingredient or as a lightly cooked vegetable.

Chicory production is concentrated in France, Holland and Belgium. Red chicory, favored in Italy and commonly referred to as radicchio, has found a place in the American gourmet market. Most chicories are quite bitter and are used in small quantities in salads or as garnishes.

Chicory root is well known as an addition to or substitute for coffee. After a full season of growth, the roots are dug, cleaned, cut into chunks, roasted until nearly black and then ground into a powder. Chicory roots become crisp and very light in weight when thoroughly roasted. Roots that are not roasted completely will gum up the blades of a blender or food processor.

Asparagus chicory, a type that is little known in the United States, sends up new shoots in the spring from roots that have wintered over. The shoots can be blanched by wrapping with paper or covering with an overturned flower pot. The shoots are cut when 46" long and are prepared like asparagus.

BOTANICAL CLASSIFICATION

All chicories belong to the genus *Cichorium* and the species *intybus*. Some varieties of *C. intybus* have escaped from cultivation and have become weeds in many temperate climates. Their light blue flowers open at first light, close by noon, and are easy to spot in any landscape.

POLLINATION, CROSSING AND ISOLATION

Chicory is an outbreeding plant. Chicory flowers are perfect, but are also self-incompatible and require insect cross-pollination. Pollen from one flower will not successfully grow in another flower on the same plant. Insects must move pollen from one plant to the flowers on a different plant. Chicory plants will accept pollen from endive plants, which, of course, will ruin the chicory seeds. All chicory varieties will cross with one another. Cultivated varieties will also cross with any of the wild chicories growing nearby. An isolation distance of 1/2 mile will ensure seed purity.

One chicory variety and one endive variety can be grown for seed if the endive is caged. Alternate day caging can be used when two or more chicory varieties are grown in close proximity. Chicory plants produce abundant flowers over a long period of time, so alternate day caging can be used for up to five varieties. The seed yields will be reduced, but will still be sufficient for most home seed savers. (Alternate day caging is discussed in detail in Section I.)

Hand-pollination of chicory is also possible. The evening before the flowers are to open, bag or tape the flowers on as many different plants as possible. Early in the morning, remove the bags or tapes and gently rub the flowers from two different plants together. If the plants are near one another, this can be done without picking the flowers. Just bend the stalks until the flowers touch. If that is impossible, pick several flowers to use during the hand-pollination process. Rebag or retape the flowers, and also mark each of the hand-pollinated flowers, possibly with a brightly colored piece of yarn.

Bags can be removed after the flowers fall off. If tape was used, it will fall off with the petals. If additional seeds are desired, hand-pollination can be repeated over several days. During harvest, exercise great care to pick only those blossoms that were hand-pollinated.

SEED PRODUCTION, HARVEST AND PROCESSING

Chicory varieties are biennial, producing seed during their second growing season. In mild winter climates, the plants can be left in the ground. A light harvest of leaves during the first growing season will not harm either flower or seed production.

In climates where the ground freezes solid during the winter, the roots should be dug before a hard frost. The tops are trimmed to 2" and any small or secondary roots are removed. Endive roots will keep for three months or more when stored in sand or soil at 32-40° F. and 80-90% humidity.

The best roots are replanted in the spring for seed

production. Once the majority of the flowers have set seedpods, withhold water and let the seed stalks dry. Crush the base of a dry flower to check on the seed development. The individual seeds are tightly enclosed and require a good bit of prying to remove. The seeds are ready to harvest when they appear dry and are firm.

Two methods of seed cleaning are used for small scale seed production. Break the completely dry flowers off of the stalks one at a time, and store them dry in a small glass container without any further cleaning. Entire pods can be planted, but thinning is necessary. The pods can also be broken open to free individual seeds.

To obtain cleaner seeds, place the seed stalks in a feed sack on a concrete floor and pound the pods with a large hammer or wooden maul. When cleaning larger quantities, the I-Tech Seed Winnower is quite efficient (see Section I). After crushing the pods, the seeds will need to be winnowed or screened to remove dust and debris.

SEED STATISTICS

Chicory seeds will remain viable for eight years when stored in a cool, dry, dark location. Members of the Seed Savers Exchange annually offer about 44 varieties of chicory, and the *Garden Seed Inventory* lists sources for 78 varieties that are available from commercial seed companies. There are approximately 14,430 seeds per ounce (510 per gram or 230,000 per pound), depending on the variety. Federal Germination Standard for commercially sold chicory seed is 70%.

GROWING CHICORY FROM SEED

Chicory is a biennial, tolerating temperatures down into the low 30s. The plants do not tolerate heat well. Chicory may be direct seeded or greenhouse started to produce transplants, covering the seeds .25" deep. The seed germinates best at 60-70° F., usually within 10-14 days. Plant or set out in full sun, or afternoon shade in hot summer climates. The plants should be thinned to 8-12" for both food and seed production.

REGIONAL GROWING RECOMMENDATIONS

Northeast: Chicory can be direct seeded before June 15. The plants like full sun and average water. Witloof and coffee types overwinter in the garden with no special care; radicchio and cataloqua types often do best if mulched with leaves or straw in late October. The safest method is to dig the plants in late October, cut off the foliage (at least the big outer leaves), store in soil or sand or sawdust in buckets, then replant in early May. Sometimes gauze covering is needed to foil goldfinches, and we use hex-wire to deter deer. Even when plants are overwintered in the soil (e.g. witloofs), they should be dug and replanted (in the spring) to properly space (about 2' x 2') and to cull/select roots.

Mid-Atlantic: Chicory can be direct seeded about March 1, or September 15 to October 15, or started in a greenhouse about January 15 and transplanted into the garden about March 1. The plants like full sun and average water, and overwinter in the garden with no special care.

Southeast/Gulf Coast: Chicory can be direct seeded September 1-20, or from February 20 to March 15. The plants overwinter with no special care.

Upper Midwest: Chicory should be direct seeded as early as ground can be worked. The plants like full sun and average water. Sometimes the plants can overwinter with mulch, but it is best to dig them in early November, store in moist sand, and replant in early April.

Southwest: Chicory is not commonly grown in this region.

Central West Coast: Chicory can be direct seeded from September 1 to October 15. The plants like full sun and average water, and overwinter in the garden with no special care.

Maritime Northwest: Chicory can be direct seeded about August 1. The plants like full sun and average water, and overwinter with no special care.

Cynara cardunculus - Cardoon

Cardoon is a 4' grayish green perennial thistle with soft-lobed leaves and beautiful bluish purple flowers. Unlike globe artichoke, cardoon's blossoms are not eaten, but the midribs of the plant's leaves are an Italian delicacy. Cardoon is native to southern Europe and is widely grown in France and Spain. Though not common in America, cardoon is easily grown and should be included in vegetable gardens and edible landscapes.

Cardoon requires some special garden preparation. In mild winter climates, cardoon is savored from November through February when there are few other garden chores and the preparation seems worth the time. Six weeks prior to harvest, tie the 4' stalks together about 6" from the top with a heavy twine. Pile leaves or hay against the stalks or wrap the plant with heavy paper to exclude all light. After this blanching period, the entire plant can be cut. Good results are also obtained by cutting only the leaf stalks near the center.

BOTANICAL CLASSIFICATION

Cardoon belongs to the genus *Cynara* and the species *cardunculus*. Sources of *C. cardunculus* are limited in the United States, where little choice of varieties is available. In contrast, Vilmorin described five varieties of cardoon that were commonly available in the Paris markets in 1885. Prickly Tours was described as the most spiny but also the most sought after in Paris. Smooth Solid was free of spines and produced a large plant with broad ribs and green leaves. Long Spanish was very large with broad leaves whose ribs were not as solid as other varieties. Artichoke Leaf was free from spines, had large, dark green leaves and ribs that were not very solid. Red Stemmed had red-tinged ribs that were also not very solid.

POLLINATION, CROSSING AND ISOLATION

Cardoon is an inbreeding plant that is easily grown from seeds. Individual cardoon flowers are self-sterile, having anthers that release pollen five days before the stigmas are receptive. At any given time, however, some of the anthers on the flower head will be releasing pollen and some of the stigmas will be receptive. Bees are readily attracted to cardoon's purple flower heads and quickly become covered with heavy pollen. Cardoon varieties will cross with artichokes.

If two or more varieties are grown for seed, bag the blossoms on as many different plants as possible just before they open. Homemade bags of spun polyester or heavy paper bags work well to protect the blossoms from contamination. A soft brush is used to agitate the blossoms once a day, which ensures that pollen will travel down the style and pollinate the ovule.

SEED PRODUCTION, HARVEST AND PROCESSING

The flower heads are cut from the stalks when the flowers are completely open and begin to show white, downy seed plumes. The flower heads should be stored in a large bag in a dry location away from direct sunlight. When the ends of the stalks are dry and the flower heads are brittle, place one flower head at a time into a feed sack or canvas bag. Lay the sack on a rigid surface, preferably concrete. Pound the base of the blossom with a hammer, allowing the down to float out of the bag. The seeds are heavy and will remain in the bag. The seeds should be removed from the bag after each flower is cleaned to avoid crushing them.

SEED STATISTICS

Cardoon seeds will remain viable for seven years when stored under ideal conditions. Members of the Seed Savers Exchange annually offer about 8 varieties of cardoon, and the *Garden Seed Inventory* lists sources for 7 varieties that are available from commercial seed companies. There are approximately 540 seeds per ounce (20 per gram or 8,640 per pound), depending on the variety. Federal Germination Standard for commercially sold seed is 70%.

GROWING CARDOON FROM SEED

Cardoon is a perennial, tolerating winter temperatures down into the low 20s. Flowering occurs each spring after the plants are well established. Cardoon is usually greenhouse started and then transplanted, covering the seeds .5" deep. The optimum seed germination temperature is 75° F., with germination usually occurring in 10-14 days. Set out in either full sun or partial shade. The plants should be thinned to 60-72" for both food and seed production.

REGIONAL GROWING RECOMMENDATIONS

Northeast: Cardoon cannot be grown in this region.
Mid-Atlantic: Cardoon can be direct seeded about March 1, or started in a greenhouse about January 15 and transplanted into the garden March 1 to April 1. The plants like full sun and average water. Although the plants overwinter with no special care, winter mulch (loose straw, leaf litter) helps hardiness.
Southeast/Gulf Coast: Cardoon can be started in a greenhouse about March 1 and transplanted into the garden about April 1. We use hoop houses, as winter hardiness is unpredictable. Luck is required, as plants resent humid heat in summer and sometimes fail to survive the winter. But when they make it, two-year-old plants are phenomenally productive.
Upper Midwest: Cardoon should be direct seeded as early as ground can be worked, or started in a greenhouse in early January and set out in early April to produce seed the first season. The plants like partial sun and average water, and rarely overwinter.
Southwest: Cardoon cannot be grown in this region.
Central West Coast: Cardoon can be direct seeded about March 15, or roots can be planted anytime (the

plants are perennial). The plants like partial sun and average water, and overwinter in the garden with no special care. They die back after blooming in summer and regrow in the fall.

Maritime Northwest: Cardoon is not commonly grown in this region.

Cynara scolymus - Artichoke (Globe Artichoke)

Artichokes are a delicacy worldwide and an important agricultural crop along the coasts of southern Europe and the western United States. The grayish green thistle-like plants produce flowers whose immature buds are eaten. Artichoke plants thrive in cool, sunny coastal climates and can tolerate temperatures into the low 30s. When produced under less than perfect weather conditions, however, the buds will be much smaller than those seen in grocery stores. In areas where freezing temperatures occur, the plants are trimmed back and the roots are dug for winter storage.

BOTANICAL CLASSIFICATION

Artichokes are a member of the genus *Cynara* and the species *scolymus*. Individual plants of *C. scolymus* will grow 5' tall and 3-5' in diameter. Artichoke leaves are usually spineless.

POLLINATION, CROSSING AND ISOLATION

Artichoke is an inbreeding plant that does not usually come true from seed and is generally not propagated in that manner. Instead, plants that produce the greatest number of tight, tender flower buds are divided after flowering. Seeds are sometimes used to produce a wide variety of new plants, and the best of these are saved and divided.

Individual artichoke flowers are self-sterile, because their anthers release pollen five days before the stigmas are receptive. At any given time, some of the stigmas on the flower head will be receptive to the pollen that is being released. The large purple flower heads are quite attractive to bees. Artichokes will cross with cardoon varieties.

For selective breeding purposes, the individual flowers can be bagged to prevent crossing. It is nec-

The large, thistle-like purple flowers of globe artichoke (*Cynara scolymus*).

Compositae

essary to agitate or brush the tops of the blossoms once a day to ensure that the pollen travels down the style and pollinates the ovule. In mild winter climates, artichoke plants that have gone to seed have propagated huge populations of pernicious weeds. If seeds are not going to be harvested, the artichoke flowers should be destroyed. Preventing the plant from producing seeds also channels more energy into the next crop of flower buds.

SEED PRODUCTION, HARVEST AND PROCESSING

Artichoke flower heads are cut when completely open and beginning to show their white seed plumes. Store the flower heads in a dry location away from direct sunlight until dry and brittle. Place one of the dry flower heads in a feed sack or canvas bag on a concrete surface. Pound the base of the blossom with a hammer and allow the down to float out of the bag. The seed is heavy and will remain behind, but should be removed from the bag after each flower is processed to avoid crushing.

SEED STATISTICS

Artichoke seeds will remain viable for seven years when stored under optimum conditions. Members of the Seed Savers Exchange annually offer about 2 varieties of artichoke, and the *Garden Seed Inventory* lists sources for 12 varieties that are available from commercial seed companies. There are approximately 540 seeds per ounce (20 per gram or 8,640 per pound), depending on the variety. Federal Germination Standard for commercially sold seed is 70%.

GROWING ARTICHOKES FROM SEED

Artichoke is a perennial, tolerating winter temperatures down into the low 30s. The plants are usually produced from division, because plants produced from seeds are variable. Flowering occurs each spring after the plants are well established. Artichokes are usually greenhouse started and transplanted, covering the seeds .5" deep. The optimum seed germination temperature is 75° F., with germination usually occurring in 10-14 days. Set out in full sun or partial shade. The plants should be thinned to 60-72" for both food and seed production.

REGIONAL GROWING RECOMMENDATIONS

Northeast: Artichoke cannot be grown in this region.

Mid-Atlantic: Artichoke can be direct seeded about March 1, or started in a greenhouse about January 15 and transplanted into the garden about March 1. The plants like full sun and average water, and sometimes overwinter in the garden with no special care; loose hay helps. The plants require rich fertile soil, and need to be cut back when hot humid weather arrives in the summer. Overwintering is hit and miss, but can be grown as an annual with some success.

Southeast/Gulf Coast: Artichoke should be started in a greenhouse about March 1 and transplanted into the garden about April 1. We use hoop houses, as winter hardiness is unpredictable. Luck is required, as the plants resent humid heat in summer and sometimes fail to survive the winter. But when they make it, two-year-old plants are phenomenally productive.

Upper Midwest: Artichoke can be direct seeded as early as the ground can be worked, or started in a greenhouse in early January and set out in early April to get seed the first season. The plants like partial sun and average water, and rarely overwinter here.

Southwest: Artichoke cannot be grown in this region.

Central West Coast: Artichoke can be direct seeded about March 15, or roots can be planted anytime (plants are perennial). Some shade is necessary; likes average water. The plants overwinter in the garden with no special care.

Maritime Northwest: Artichoke cannot be grown in this region.

Helianthus annuus - Sunflower

North and South American Indians used sunflower plants in their entirety. The stalks were used for bean poles and animal fodder, and were peeled into thin sheets for use like paper. Immature leaves, flower petals and roots were all cooked as vegetables. Mature leaves were used as a tobacco substitute and for animal feed. Some tribes even used the empty seed compartments in the flower head as containers for dye and paint. Many Indian varieties have retained tribal references in their names, such as Apache Brown Stripe, Hopi Black Dye and Tarahumara White.

Sunflowers are grown commercially for oil and for seed. Oil seed sunflowers have been specifically selected for high oil content. The large seeded varieties are preferred for snacks. In home gardens, sunflowers are often grown as flowers and for bird seed.

BOTANICAL CLASSIFICATION

Cultivated annual sunflowers are members of the genus *Helianthus* and the species *annuus*. Wild populations of *H. annuus*, which are native or introduced throughout much of North America, will cross with any other *H. annuus* cultivar. In addition, cultivated sunflower varieties are often found growing wild, usually spread by birds and animals that have visited commercial fields. These cultivated escapees will also cross with cultivated varieties.

A whole host of other annual and perennial species of *Helianthus* are native to North America, including wild Jerusalem artichokes. None of these, however, will cross with *H. annuus*.

One of the perennial sunflowers, *H. maximiliani*, is sometimes cultivated for its very thin but tasty roots. Maximilian sunflower is being evaluated at The Land Institute in Salina, Kansas for its seed-bearing potential in perennial polycultures, and has also been used recently in various permaculture applications.

POLLINATION, CROSSING AND ISOLATION

Sunflowers are outbreeding plants. Each sunflower head can have from 1,000 to 4,000 individual florets that are perfect and usually open for two days. On the first day the anthers release pollen into the anther tube. On the second day the stigma pushes up, and its two lobes open and are receptive to, but out of reach of, its own pollen. Insects, mainly bees, move the pollen around, causing fertilization.

It takes five to ten days for all of the florets on a single flower head to open. A typical flower head could have dried florets around its outside edge, followed by a ring of receptive stigmas, then another ring of pollen shedding florets, and unopened florets in its center. Some varieties are self-incompatible, requiring the transfer of pollen from one plant to another. Other varieties are self-compatible, so insects must only move the pollen from floret to floret on the same flower head.

To maintain seed purity, different varieties must be isolated by 1/2 to three miles depending on the size of the populations of sunflowers being grown in the area.

Hand-pollination, which is time-consuming but not difficult, requires that the flower heads be bagged before the first florets open. Each day for ten days, remove the bags from two adjacent plants and gently rub the surfaces of the flower heads together. Continue down the row, unbagging and rebagging the flowers as you proceed. This method will effectively pollinate both self-incompatible and self-compatible varieties.

SEED PRODUCTION, HARVEST AND PROCESSING

When the sunflower head is completely filled out and the flower petals have fallen off, the head can be cut and dried in a protected area. Protection from birds is crucial. Blue jays will actually fly into rooms through open doors to steal sunflower seeds.

The seeds can be removed from the flower heads when no longer soft or damp. To clean large numbers of flowers, rub sunflower heads across a 1" x 1" welded wire screen placed over a five-gallon pail. Cut the wire 12" larger than the diameter of the pail and mold the wire down over its sides. Place the container between your knees, which will hold its wire top in place. Rub the sunflower head roughly against the wire, and the seeds will fall into the container below.

Using your thumbs and index fingers, grasp each end of a shelled sunflower seed and try to bend it. Seeds which snap in two instead of bending are sufficiently dry for storage. Most seeds will need some additional drying. Place a 1" layer of seeds in baskets or containers and finish drying in a warm area away from direct sunlight.

SEED STATISTICS

Sunflower seeds will remain viable for seven years when stored in a cool, dry, dark location. Members of the Seed Savers Exchange annually offer about 32 varieties of sunflowers, and the *Garden Seed Inventory* lists sources for 35 varieties that are available from commercial seed companies. There are between 560 and 1,120 sunflower seeds per ounce (20-40 per gram or 8,960-17,920 per pound), depending on the variety. Federal Germination Standard for commercially sold sunflower seed is 75%.

GROWING SUNFLOWERS FROM SEED

Sunflowers are annuals, adapted to a wide range of climates, and are usually direct seeded. Seeds should be covered .5-1" deep. The optimum seed germination temperature is 75° F., with germination usually occuring in 5-10 days. Plant or set out in full sun, thinning to 12-18" for both food and seed production.

REGIONAL GROWING RECOMMENDATIONS

Northeast: Sunflowers can be direct seeded about May 10-20. The plants like full sun and average water. Birds can get there first, so before seed coats turn dark, tie scraps of Reemay™ over individual heads, or just monitor closely and harvest promptly. Cut heads must be cured a week or so in a dry airy bird/rodent-free area, until seeds drop off easily. Sunflower moth larvae often are a serious problem; I have no remedy yet. In late August into September, rainy winds can cause lodging, so I plant in hills (three plants each) and tie tops loosely together. Also, some ripe heads form a basin when they "nod," holding water and rotting. The only remedy is to monitor after rain.

Mid-Atlantic: Sunflowers can be direct seeded from April 15 to June 15. The plants are heavy feeders that require rich fertile soil.

Southeast/Gulf Coast: Sunflowers can be direct seeded from April 1 to May 1.

Upper Midwest: Sunflowers can be direct seeded early, and up until mid-July. The plants like full sun and are generally drought tolerant. Early plantings will be frequently lost to borers; best success is achieved from late June plantings.

Southwest: Sunflowers can be direct seeded from March 15 to June 1. The plants like full sun and average water. Lodging may occur during violent monsoon thunderstorms, so the plants should be staked.

Central West Coast: Sunflowers can be direct seeded April 15 to July 15. The plants like full sun and are drought tolerant.

Maritime Northwest: Sunflowers can be direct seeded April 20. Likes full sun and average water.

——————— *Helianthus tuberosus* - Jerusalem Artichoke (Sunroot) ———————

Jerusalem artichoke is native to America and was taken to Italy by Champlain. How the English managed to corrupt "girasole articocco," its Italian name, into Jerusalem artichoke is an etymological mystery. The plant has nothing to do with Jerusalem or artichokes. In the diaries of their travels, early explorers noted various Indian tribes using Jerusalem artichoke as a vegetable.

Jerusalem artichoke, sometimes known as sunroot, has not been the most popular garden vegetable. The knobby protuberances make the roots difficult to clean. Jerusalem artichoke roots are extremely hardy. Pieces of unharvested tubers resprout in the spring and are almost impossible to eradicate. Many gardeners have tried Jerusalem artichokes with enthusiasm, only to spend the next several years wishing they hadn't.

BOTANICAL CLASSIFICATION

Jerusalem artichoke belongs to the genus *Helianthus* and the species *tuberosus*. *H. tuberosus* should not be confused with white Jerusalem artichoke, *Bomarea edulis*, which is a member of the Amaryllidaceae family.

Jerusalem artichoke varieties include a wide range of shapes and colors. Golden Nugget is shaped like a carrot and has yellow flesh. Smooth Garnet has red skin and white flesh. Fuseau and Long Red are shaped like sweet potatoes. The knobby tubers of French Mammoth White are commonly available in grocery stores.

SEED PRODUCTION, HARVEST AND STORAGE

Although some varieties of Jerusalem artichoke will flower, any seed produced is usually sterile. The plants are traditionally grown from tuber pieces. The roots will overwinter in the ground in most regions, or can be dug, the soil brushed off, and stored in plastic bags or damp sand.

SEED STATISTICS

Jerusalem artichoke roots will keep for two months or more at 32-40° F. and 90% humidity. Members of the Seed Savers Exchange annually offer about 101 varieties of Jerusalem artichokes, and the *Garden Seed Inventory* lists sources for 12 varieties available from commercial seed companies.

GROWING JERUSALEM ARTICHOKES

Jerusalem artichokes are propagated from tubers, and are planted 3-4" deep. Soil is mounded around the plants as the tubers are being produced. Plant in full sun, and then thin to 12-18" for food production.

REGIONAL GROWING RECOMMENDATIONS

Northeast: Jerusalem artichoke can be direct seeded anytime before July 1, but preferably in early May. The plants like average water and full sun, but partial sun is okay. Plants overwinter in the garden with no special care. Some varieties are not full-size until early November. If fall-dug and stored (for food or replanting), tubers must be kept very cool and damp. Tubers are very prone to wither when dry; I use tight barrels. If one wishes to save "true" seed (for breeding new varieties), plants must have been established the previous fall. Even then, many varieties rarely mature seed (or even flower) in this climate.

Mid-Atlantic: Jerusalem artichoke can be direct

seeded from March 1 to April 15, or started in a greenhouse about March 1 and transplanted into the garden about April 15. The plants like full sun and average water, and overwinter in the garden with no special care.

Southeast/Gulf Coast: Set out new roots from March 15 to May 1; propagation is by digging and dividing roots. The plants overwinter with no special care.

Upper Midwest: Jerusalem artichoke is vegetatively propagated. The plants like full sun, are drought tolerant, and overwinter in the garden with no special care.

Southwest: Jerusalem artichoke is not commonly grown in this region.

Central West Coast: The roots of Jerusalem artichoke can be planted from March 15 to April 15. The plants like full sun, are drought tolerant and overwinter in the garden with no special care. Some varieties will produce viable seed here.

Maritime Northwest: Jerusalem artichoke can be direct seeded from March 20 to April 10, but usually is asexually propagated. The plants like full sun and average water, and overwinter in the garden with no special care.

Lactuca sativa - Lettuce and Celtuce

Today's cultivated lettuces probably originated from wild lettuce, *Lactuca serriola*, which was used as a medicinal herb. Lettuce was grown in Egypt about 4500 B.C. and its likeness is carved into the walls of many tombs. The Greeks and Romans also made frequent culinary use of lettuce.

Lettuce is used primarily as a fresh vegetable in salads and on sandwiches. Occasionally lettuce is used as a cooked vegetable and, in some areas of the world, is even used as a tobacco substitute.

BOTANICAL CLASSIFICATION

All varieties of garden lettuce belong to the genus *Lactuca* and the species *sativa*. Some insect crossing does occur between *L. sativa* and *L. serriola*, a wild species, but the extent of such crossing continues to be debated. Some growers think that any crossing between the two species is minimal, while others claim to have seen such crosses at distances that exceed 150'. When crosses do occur, their offspring have intermediate characteristics and are often bitter.

L. sativa and *L. serriola* are thought to have evolved from chance hybrid populations. Crossing between *L. sativa* and an unknown third species may have produced *L. serriola*, or *L. sativa* may have evolved from a cross between *L. serriola* and an unknown third species. Differences between the two species have been further enhanced by the constant cultivation and selection of *L. sativa* varieties.

There are six types of lettuce: crisphead, butterhead, cos, leaf, stem and Latin. Crisphead types (more commonly known as head lettuce) are the ones usually available in grocery stores. The heads are tightly folded with crisp, greenish white leaves.

Butterhead varieties have small, loose, green heads and soft-textured leaves. Butterheads are the most popular lettuces grown in northern Europe. One group of butterhead varieties produces firm heads during lengthening days of summer, while another kind was developed for winter greenhouse production.

Cos or romaine lettuce has elongated leaves that form an upright loaf-shaped head. The outer leaves are dark green with heavy ribs. Cos varieties are very popular in the United States, southern Europe and Mediterranean countries.

Leaf lettuce varieties lack heading tendencies and produce a rosette of leaves. Leaf lettuces are often grouped by leaf shape and color. Numerous green and red varieties, including many beautiful heirlooms, are available to the home gardener.

Asparagus lettuce, also known as celtuce or stem lettuce, is grown for its succulent, thick stem and tender leaves. The plant is thought to have originated in China, where it is used both raw and cooked.

Latin lettuce, grown mainly in the Mediterranean and South America, has elongated leaves that form a loose head. Common varieties of Latin lettuce include Gallega, Criolla Verde, Criolla Blance and Madrilene. Gallega was the first identified source of resistance to lettuce mosaic virus.

POLLINATION, CROSSING AND ISOLATION

Lettuce is an inbreeding plant. Lettuce flowers form in heads of 10-25 individual florets. Each floret is one celled and produces one seed. All of the florets in a head open on the same day, usually in the morning. The style emerges through the anther tube and is pollinated by pollen grains along the sides of the style. Shortly after opening, the florets close and never reopen.

Bees and other hairy insects visit lettuce flowers and cause some crossing between different varieties. Many growers claim that lettuce varieties do not cross at all, while others report up to 5% crossing in varieties grown side by side. Lettuce varieties exhibit many different flower characteristics that greatly affect the

Wild lettuce (*Lactuca serriola*) before flowering.

chances of crossing. Some flowers are open for as little as 30 minutes, others for several hours. Most commercial seed companies require that different varieties be separated by 25', while USDA publications suggest at least 12' of separation between varieties.

Caging will ensure absolute seed purity when two or more varieties are flowering. Just before the flowers open, wrap the seed heads with spun polyester or put a wire cage in place. The fabric or cage can be removed when the plants stop flowering and begin to dry.

SEED PRODUCTION, HARVEST AND PROCESSING

A few outer leaves of each lettuce plant can be picked without affecting the quality or quantity of the seed produced. Lettuce will bolt to seed in response to lengthening days.

The seed stalks of head lettuce varieties often have difficulty pushing up through the heads. Slitting the top of the head or twisting the head may promote the emergence of the seed stalk. If no effort is made to assist the plant, head rot brought on by heat and humidity often proves fatal. Some gardeners strike the top of the head sharply with their open palm, which supposedly fractures each leaf base where it attaches to the stem without damaging the seed stalk. After the head is struck, the leaves are removed. In commercial fields the heads are often slit halfway open with a knife. Probably the most reliable method is to simply peel the leaves away to expose the emerging stalk.

Lettuce seeds ripen irregularly and are ready for harvest from 12-24 days after flowering. To obtain the maximum amount of seed, the plants should be harvested daily during that period by shaking the seed heads into a large grocery sack that is then stored each night in a dry area. Label the sacks clearly to avoid any mixups when working with more than one variety. If maximum yield is not essential, the entire plant can be cut when the greatest percentage of seeds is ripe and placed head first into a bag. When the lettuce seed heads are totally dry, grasp the cut ends of the stalks and shake the heads vigorously within the sack. Rubbing the seed head between your palms will result in additional seed falling into the sack.

More than half of the seed volume will be white lettuce feathers and chaff. The seeds and chaff are about the same size and weight, so attempts at winnowing often result in lots of seed being lost. Use a fine mesh screen that will allow the seeds to pass through but will restrict the feathers. Shake the screen gently while lightly blowing the feathers to the far edge of the screen. The seeds collected below the screen will be clean enough for most home seed savers.

Further cleaning can be accomplished by a reverse screening. Select a screen that is slightly too small for the seeds to pass through. Pour the seeds and remaining chaff on the top of the screen and gently rub the mixture with the palm of your hand. The clean seeds will remain on top of the screen, while the small chaff and the remaining feathers will pass through.

SEED STATISTICS

Lettuce seeds will remain viable for three years when stored in a cool, dry, dark location. Members of the Seed Savers Exchange annually offer about 309 varieties of lettuce, and the *Garden Seed Inventory* lists sources for 457 varieties that are available from commercial seed companies. There are approximately 22,400 lettuce seeds per ounce (790 per gram or 358,000 per pound), depending on the variety. Federal Germination Standard for commercially sold lettuce seed is 80%.

GROWING LETTUCE FROM SEED

Lettuce is an annual, bolting to seed with lengthening days. Lettuce may be direct seeded or greenhouse started. Cover seeds very lightly and water in. Lettuce seed germinates at 60-70° F., usually in 2-10 days. Plant or set out in full sun, or afternoon shade in hot summer climates. The plants should be thinned to 4-8" for both food and seed production.

REGIONAL PLANTING RECOMMENDATIONS

Northeast: Lettuce can be direct seeded in early May, or started in a greenhouse about April 15 and transplanted into the garden about May 15. The plants like full sun and average water. Late heading types usually must be started indoors; loose-leaf types often do fine when direct-sown.

Mid-Atlantic: Lettuce can be direct seeded about March 1 or August 15, or started in a greenhouse about January 15 and transplanted into the garden about March 1. The plants like full sun and average water. Sometimes the plants overwinter in the garden with no special care; winter mulch helps. Leaf hoppers are sometimes a problem.

Southeast/Gulf Coast: Lettuce can be direct seeded from September 1 to October 1, or from February 15 to March 20. We use hoop houses to prevent winter killing. Butterheads and romaines overwinter in the garden with no special care. Spring sowings may bolt without heading.

Upper Midwest: Lettuce should be direct seeded as early as possible (no later than June 10) to produce seed. Partial sun is okay. The plants are drought tolerant at seed stage and like average water otherwise. Staking of flowering plants helps. Heavy rains can occur at seed harvest and cause high seed loss.

Southwest: Lettuce can be direct seeded from August 15 to January 15. The plants like full sun and average water.

Mature seed stalks of lettuce (*Lactuca sativa*), left, and wild lettuce (*L. serriola*), right.

Central West Coast: Lettuce can be direct seeded from February 15 to April 15, or September 15 to October 15. The plants like average water and full sun (partial sun is okay), and overwinter in the garden with no special care.

Maritime Northwest: Lettuce can be direct seeded from March 20 to April 10. The plants like full sun and average water.

──────── *Scorzonera hispanica* - Black Salsify (Scorzonera) ────────

Scorzonera has all but disappeared from American gardens, but is still quite common in Europe. A full season is required to produce large carrot-sized roots with smooth, oyster-flavored white flesh and contrasting black skin. Scorzonera's foliage is quite attractive and very much at home in the flower garden. Plants that are not dug for fall and winter use will send up a bouquet of yellow daisy-like flowers the following spring.

Scorzonera roots remain tasty and tender even when the flower stalks appear, and can be grown for a second year before harvest. The distinctive oyster-like flavor is contained in the skin of the roots. If the skin is peeled while being prepared for cooking, much

of the flavor will be lost. New spring shoots produced by unharvested roots can be cut and used like asparagus. Young leaves can also be used like lettuce in salads.

BOTANICAL CLASSIFICATION

Scorzonera belongs to the genus *Scorzonera* and the species *hispanica*, and is also known as black salsify, Spanish salsify, viper's grass and black oyster plant.

POLLINATION, CROSSING AND ISOLATION

Scorzonera is an inbreeding plant that does not cross with any other vegetable. Few, if any, varieties are available in the United States. Most seed companies just sell scorzonera, with no variety name specified. Scorzonera flowers are perfect, but different varieties could be crossed by insects. Isolation of 1/2 mile will ensure seed purity. When two or more varieties are grown in close proximity, caging can be used. Scorzonera can also be found growing wild in some parts of the United States. Always check the area for wild varieties before relying on isolation.

SEED PRODUCTION, HARVEST AND PROCESSING

Scorzonera is biennial, requiring two seasons to produce seeds. The roots can be mulched and left in the ground in most areas of the country. In climates where the ground freezes solid in the winter, plants are carefully dug, tops clipped to 3" and roots stored in damp sawdust. The roots will keep 2-4 months when stored at 32-40° F. and 90% humidity. For maximum seed production, the early spring shoots should not be eaten.

Scorzonera plants send up a seed stalk of beautiful yellow daisy-like flowers during their second season. As these flowers fade, seeds form inside each flower base. When fully mature, the base of the flower will begin to flatten and the seed will float away in the wind. Seeds must be collected daily for maximum harvest. Once each day, remove the seeds from the freshly opened seed capsules. Break the fluff away from the seeds, and then set the seeds aside for further drying.

Scorzonera seeds should be dried away from direct sunlight for two or three days. Seeds that break in half are ready for storage. If the seeds bend instead of breaking, further drying in a warm location is needed.

SEED STATISTICS

Scorzonera seeds will remain viable for two years when stored under optimum conditions. Members of the Seed Savers Exchange annually offer about 5 varieties of scorzonera, and the *Garden Seed Inventory* lists sources for 5 varieties that are available from commercial seed companies. There are approximately 1,875 seeds per ounce (65 per gram or 30,000 per pound), depending on the variety. Federal Germination Standard for commercial seed is 75%.

GROWING SCORZONERA FROM SEED

Scorzonera is a biennial, but may be grown as a perennial in mild winter climates. Flowers are produced each spring from fully formed roots. The plants are adapted to a wide range of growing and climatic conditions. Scorzonera is direct seeded, with seeds covered .25" deep. The seed germinates at temperatures ranging from 65-75° F. with germination usually occurring in 10-14 days. Plant in full sun. Scorzonera plants look like spurge and other grasses. The plants should be thinned to 2" for root production, but to 12" for perennial plants used for greens and seed production. Take care when thinning.

REGIONAL GROWING RECOMMENDATIONS

Northeast: Scorzonera can be direct seeded before June 10. The plants like full sun and average water. The plants overwinter in the garden with no special care. Once the plants have set enough seed, they must be covered with some kind of row cover to foil goldfinches, which will strip them just before completely ripe. Because the plants flower and mature unevenly, that's difficult, so we often cover or bag individual heads after they've "burst out."

Mid-Atlantic: Scorzonera can be direct seeded about March 1, or started in a greenhouse about January 15 and transplanted into the garden about March 1. The plants like full sun and average water, and overwinter in the garden with no special care.

Southeast/Gulf Coast: Scorzonera can be direct seeded from February 10 to March 10. The plants overwinter with no special care. Overwintered plants bloom in the spring. Edible crops are dug in early winter.

Upper Midwest: Sow as early as possible. The plants overwinter in the garden with no special care.

Southwest: Scorzonera is not comonly grown in this region.

Central West Coast: Scorzonera can be direct seeded from March 15 to May 15 (perennial). The plants like full sun and average water, and overwinter in the garden with no special care.

Maritime Northwest: Scorzonera can be direct seeded about July 15. The plants like full sun and average water, and overwinter with no special care.

——— *Tragopogon porrifolius* - Salsify (and *T. pratensis* - Wild Salsify) ———

Salsify is a European native, where it is commonly referred to as havrerod or haverwortel. A few named varieties do exist. The roots and flower buds have been savored since at least the 13th century. The plant sends up a seed stalk of beautiful bluish purple flowers during its second season of growth. The flowers remain open until noon and have earned a place in the English flower garden as John Go To Bed At Noon flowers.

Salsify, sometimes called vegetable oyster, is easy to grow and is eaten in three different forms. When grown from a spring sowing, the roots are mild and taste slightly of oysters. Roots left to overwinter produce tasty asparagus-like shoots in the spring. Also the unopened flower buds can be used as a green vegetable in the early spring. They are traditionally served lightly sauteed in butter. Salsify is a very versatile vegetable and has been unjustifiably ignored by most gardeners.

BOTANICAL CLASSIFICATION

Salsify belongs to the genus *Tragopogon* and the species *porrifolius*. Another species, *T. pratensis*, is a common weed that is sometimes referred to as wild or yellow-flowered salsify.

POLLINATION, CROSSING AND ISOLATION

Salsify is an inbreeding plant that has escaped from the garden and become a weed in many areas. These garden escapees should not be confused with *T. pratensis*, known as yellow-flowered salsify, which is also a weed. Bluish-purple flowered salsify, *T. porrifolius*, does not cross with the yellow-flowered species.

Most seed companies sell only Mammoth Salsify, or just salsify with no variety name specified. The flowers are perfect, but different varieties of the same species can be crossed by insects. Isolation of 1/2 mile will ensure seed purity. When two or more varieties of the same species are grown in close proximity, caging must be used. Always check for any blue-flowered escapees growing in the wild before relying on isolation.

SEED PRODUCTION, HARVEST AND PROCESSING

T. porrifolius and *T. pratensis* are both biennials and require two growing seasons for seed production. In most regions of the country, salsify roots can be mulched and left in the ground over winter. In areas where the ground freezes and the roots would be damaged, the plants are dug, tops are trimmed to 3", and roots are stored in damp sawdust. Salsify roots will keep 2-4 months at 32-40° F. and 90% humidity. The best roots are then replanted in the spring. Two or three flower buds on each plant can be harvested for eating without significantly reducing the seed production.

Salsify seeds are very easy to save, and germinate readily. As the flowers fade, the seeds form inside their bases. When fully mature, the seed capsules will begin to flatten and the salsify seeds will float away in the wind. Once a day, remove seeds from the newly opened seed capsules.

Break the fluff away from the seeds, and set the seeds aside for further drying. Salsify seeds should be dried for two or three days away from direct sunlight. When the seeds break in half, they are ready for storage. If the seeds bend instead of breaking, further drying is needed

SEED STATISTICS

Salsify seeds will remain viable for four years when properly stored. Members of the Seed Savers Exchange annually offer about 12 varieties of salsify, and the *Garden Seed Inventory* lists sources for 47 varieties that are available from commercial seed companies. There are approximately 2,800 seeds per ounce (100 per gram or 45,000 per pound), depending on the variety. Federal Germination Standard for commercially sold seed is 75%.

GROWING SALSIFY FROM SEED

Salsify is a biennial that produces flowers each spring. The plants are adapted to a wide range of growing and climate conditions. Salsify is direct seeded, covering the seeds .25" deep. The seed germinates at temperatures ranging from 65-75° F. with germination usually occurring in 10-14 days. Plant in full sun. Salsify plants look like spurge and other grasses. The plants should be thinned to 2" for root production, and to 4" for seed production. Take care when thinning.

REGIONAL GROWING RECOMMENDATIONS

Northeast: Salsify can be direct seeded by June 10. The plants like full sun and average water, and overwinter with no special care. Goldfinches usually race us to the harvest, so we often protect individual seedheads with Reemay™ or small paper bags and clips.

Mid-Atlantic: Salsify can be direct seeded about March 1. The plants like full sun, are drought tolerant, and overwinter in the garden with no special care.

Southeast/Gulf Coast: Salsify can be direct seeded from February 10 to March 10. The plants overwinter in the garden with no special care.

Upper Midwest: Salsify can be direct seeded anytime up to August. The plants like full sun, are drought tolerant, and overwinter with no special care.

Southwest: Salsify is not commonly grown in this region.

Central West Coast: Salsify can be direct seeded

Compositae

from March 15 to May 15, or September 1 to October 1. The plants like full sun and average water, and overwinter in the garden with no special care.

Lesser Grown Compositae

Arctium lappa
Gobo (Japanese Burdock)

Gobo is a native of Siberia and is grown extensively in Japan. The tender root can grow to 36" in length and is widely used as an ingredient in many Japanese dishes. The leaves also can be eaten like spinach.

Gobo is an inbreeding biennial and can tolerate both extremely high and low temperatures. After a period of vernalization, gobo produces a flower stalk. The flowers are self-pollinating, but different varieties of gobo could be cross-pollinated by insects. Caging can be used when two or more varieties are being grown for seed. Isolation of at least 1/2 mile will also ensure seed purity.

In some areas of Japan and in the western United States, gobo has escaped from the garden and become a weed. Gobo will not cross with *Arctium minus*, another weed found throughout the United States that is also called burdock or dock.

SEED STATISTICS

Gobo seeds will remain viable for five years when stored in a cool, dry, dark location. Members of the Seed Savers Exchange annually offer about 3 varieties of Japanese burdock (gobo), and the *Garden Seed Inventory* lists sources for 3 varieties that are available from commercial mail-order seed companies. There are approximately 1,750 gobo seeds per ounce (60 per gram or 28,000 per pound), depending on the variety. There is no Federal Germination Standard for gobo.

GROWING GOBO FROM SEED

Gobo is biennial, producing flowers from fully formed roots after a period of vernalization. The well formed, long roots require deeply prepared soil. Gobo is direct seeded, covering the seeds with .25" of soil. Gobo seed germinates at temperatures ranging from 65-75° F. with germination usually occurring in about 10-14 days. The seeds should be planted in a location that gets full sun. The plants can be thinned to 6-8" for food production, and 2-4" when being used for breeding purposes.

Maritime Northwest: Salsify can be direct seeded about July 15. The plants like full sun and average water, and overwinter with no special care.

REGIONAL PLANTING RECOMMENDATIONS

Northeast: Gobo can be direct seeded anytime before June 10, but preferably in early May. The plants like full sun and average water, and overwinter in the garden with no special care.

Mid-Atlantic: Gobo is not commonly grown in this region.

Southeast/Gulf Coast: Gobo is not commonly grown in this region.

Upper Midwest: Gobo can be direct seeded as early as possible. The plants like full sun and average water, and require mulching in mid-November with leaves, straw, etc.

Southwest: Gobo is not commonly grown in this region.

Central West Coast: Gobo can be direct seeded from March 30 to June 30. The plants like full sun, are drought tolerant, and overwinter with no special care.

Maritime Northwest: Gobo can be direct seeded about July 15. The plants like full sun and average water, and will overwinter in the garden with no special care.

Chrysanthemum coronarium
Shungiku

Shungiku, sometimes called garland chrysanthemum, is a very common vegetable in Japan. There are three distinct types based on their leaf structure: narrow, finely parted and dark; medium sized; broad and pale green. The narrow leaf varieties do well in cold climates, while those with broad leaves are better adapted to warm climates. Their tender shoots and new leaves are harvested continually for use in salads and stir-fry dishes.

Shungiku is an inbreeding plant that produces beautiful yellow chrysanthemum-like flowers following vernalization. The flowers are self-pollinating. Insects freely visit the flowers and will cross different varieties of shungiku that are growing within 1/2 mile of each other, but bagging or caging are effective preventions. Shungiku does not cross with annual garden chrysanthemums, *C. carinatum*, or with perennial chrysanthemums. The method used to save shungiku seed is similar to the techniques used for lettuce.

SEED STATISTICS

Members of the Seed Savers Exchange annually offer about 2 varieties of shungiku, and the *Garden Seed Inventory* lists sources for 4 varieties that are available by mail-order from commercial seed companies in the United States and Canada. There are approximately 14,560 shungiku seeds per ounce (515 seeds per gram or 233,000 per pound), depending on the variety.

GROWING SHUNGIKU FROM SEED

Shungiku is an annual, producing seed after a period of vernalization. Shungiku may be either direct seeded or or started in a greenhouse. The seeds should be covered very lightly. Shungiku seed germinates at temperatures ranging from 70-75° F. with germination usually occurring in 7-10 days. Shungiku should be direct seeded or set out in full sun, or in partial shade in hot summer climates. The plants should be thinned to 6" for food production, and 10" for breeding purposes.

REGIONAL PLANTING RECOMMENDATIONS

Northeast: Shungiku is not commonlhy grown in this region.

Mid-Atlantic: Shungiku can either be direct seeded in the spring about March 1 or in the fall from about September 15 to October 15, or started in a greenhouse about January 15 and transplanted into the garden about March 15. The plants like full sun and average water, and will overwinter in the garden with no special care.

Southeast/Gulf Coast: Shungiku can be direct seeded from about September 1-20. The plants will overwinter in the garden with no special care in some areas.

Upper Midwest: Shungiku can be direct seeded as early as possible to get mature seed. The plants like full sun and average water.

Southwest: Shungiku can be direct seeded about September 15.

Central West Coast: Shungiku can be direct seeded September 1 to October 15. The plants like full sun and average water, and overwinter in the garden with no special care.

Maritime Northwest: Shungiku can be direct seeded from about March 20 to April 10. The plants may freeze out in some areas during the winter, but usually will overwinter many years in areas that have mild winters.

——— *Polymnia sonchifolia* ———
Yacon

Yacon plants are grown in the Andes Mountains of South America for their crunchy, sweet tubers. The plants are not daylength sensitive and will grow in the mild climate areas of the United States. Unfortunately, the small daisy-like yellow flowers rarely set seeds. Yacon is propagated from small offshoots and also from tuber cuttings. Yacon cuttings and plants are available from some botanical gardens and tropical nurseries in the United States. Also, yacon is offered annually by some of the members of Seed Savers Exchange, but it is not listed in the current edition of the *Garden Seed Inventory*.

GROWING YACON

Yacon is a perennial grown from tubers, and requires a long growing season with warm temperatures. The plants do not tolerate any frost. Tubers may be dug and stored in climates that experience frost. Short seasons areas with freezing temperatures are not conducive to yacon production. The tubers should be set out in full sun, or in a location with afternoon shade in hot summer climates. Cover tubers with 3-4" of soil. The plants should be thinned to 12-18" for food production.

REGIONAL GROWING RECOMMENDATIONS

Northeast: Yacon cannot be grown in this region.

Mid-Atlantic: Yakon is not commonly grown in this region.

Southeast/Gulf Coast: Set out tubers during April. Yacon is only successful in areas with minimal frost. The plants like filtered sun and average water. Although the plants will overwinter in the garden with no special care in some areas, it is best to mulch before frost. Seed production can be a problem in low ground or colder areas.

Upper Midwest: Yakon is not commonly grown in this region.

Southwest: Yakon is not commonly grown in this region.

Central West Coast: The roots of yacon should be planted during April. The plants like partial sun and average water, and will overwinter in the garden with no special care. To keep the roots from rotting during wet winters, always plant in high well-drained areas.

Maritime Northwest: Yacon cannot be grown in this region.

The Cucurbitaceae family in its many and varied forms has been feeding the world since the beginning of recorded history. The remains of cucumbers and gourds have been found in archaeological excavations dating two centuries before Christ. Various members of Cucurbitaceae can be found in every country of the world and in every culture both past and present.

Members of the Cucurbitaceae family have origins in many different regions of the world. They are some of the first plants used by mankind and have been widely dispersed throughout the world. Only the *Cucurbita* genus (squash) is thought to have originated in the warm regions of North, Central and South America. Cucurbits provided an important part of the diets of the Inca and Maya civilizations.

FAMILY TAXONOMY

Cucurbitaceae have easily identified tendril-bearing vines and alternate leaves. Most of the cultivated members of the Cucurbitaceae family are tender, heat-loving annuals. The perennial exceptions are *Sechium edule, Cucurbita ficifolia* and *Cucurbita foetidissima*.

POLLINATION CHARACTERISTICS AND TECHNIQUES

All members of the Cucurbitaceae family rely on insects for pollination. Each plant produces both male and female flowers. Insects, especially honeybees, randomly move pollen from flower to flower and from plant to plant. All members of the Cucurbitaceae fam-

Cucurbitaceae in the Garden		
Genus	Species	Common Name
Benincasa	*hispida*	wax gourd (winter melon)
Citrullus	*lanatus*	watermelon, citron
Cucumis	*anguria*	West Indian gherkin (burr cucumber)
	melo	muskmelon, cantaloupe, honeydew, casaba, Armenian cucumber (snake melon), Asian pickling melon, pocket melon (vine pomegranate), vine peach (mango melon)
	metuliferus	jelly melon (African horned cucumber)
	sativus	cucumbers (except Armenian cucumber, burr cucumber and African horned cucumber)
Cucurbita	*ficifolia*	Malabar gourd (chilacayote)
	foetidissima	calabazilla
	maxima	squash (vars. - banana, buttercup, hubbard, turban)
	mixta	squash (vars. - green striped cushaw, white cushaw, wild Seroria squashes, silver seeded gourds)
	moschata	squash (vars. - butternut, cheese, golden cushaw)
	pepo	squash (vars. - acorn, crookneck, scallop, small striped and warted gourds, spaghetti, zucchini)
Cyclanthera	*pedata*	caihua (achoecha)
Lagenaria	*siceraria*	hard shelled gourd
Luffa	*acutangula*	angled luffa
	aegyptiaca	smooth luffa
Momordica	*balsamina*	balsam apple
	charantia	balsam pear (bitter melon)
Sechium	*edule*	chayote (vegetable pear)
Sicana	*odorifera*	cassabanana
Trichosanthes	*anguina*	serpent gourd

Facing Page: Squash collection (*Cucurbita spp.*) spilling from an oxcart at Heritage Farm, Seed Savers' headquarters near Decorah, Iowa. (Photo by Larsh Bristol)

Left: Male squash blossoms, taped to prevent insect contamination and then stripped of petals for use in hand-pollinations. Right: Immature fruit (ovary) at the base of a taped female squash blossom.

ily will accept pollen from other varieties within the same species. In other words, any two (or more) varieties within the same species must be prevented from crossing in order to save pure seed. The progeny of any uncontrolled crosses produces plants and fruits that are widely varied and bear little resemblance to their parents. To prevent such random pollinations, insects must be kept from visiting the flowers selected for seed saving and the pollen must then be transferred by hand.

During the process of hand-pollination, pollen from a male flower is transferred to a female flower of the same variety. If male and female flowers from the same plant are used for hand-pollination, the process is known as "selfing." Plants are generally "selfed" whenever seed purity is in question or when

specific plant characteristics are being selected. When male and female flowers are taken from different plants of the same variety, the process is referred to as "sibing" and results in a greater degree of genetic diversity.

Seed savers must first be able to differentiate between male and female blossoms in order to hand-pollinate a member of the Cucurbitaceae family . Female blossoms sit atop a small, immature fruit (ovary), while male blossoms are attached only to a straight stem. This structural difference is most easily seen in squash which have large, easily manipulated flowers. Watermelons, muskmelons, cucumbers and chayote have very small flowers whose sex is more difficult to identify.

A morning and evening inspection of the plants

Left: Tape and tips of female blossom are gently removed. Right: Pollen-covered anthers of the petal-less male flower are used as a brush to transfer pollen onto the stigma of the female flower.

and their blossoms will be required each day. Seed savers must learn to identify blossoms that are still green (immature), or are about to open, or have already opened. Blossoms that are almost ready to open will begin to show some color along their seams and the tip of the blossom may begin to break apart. Flowers that have already opened will be wilted and are of no use for making pollinations.

Male and female blossoms that will open the next morning must be taped shut in the evening and then relocated the following morning. The only exception to this evening/morning schedule is *Lagenaria siceraria*, the hard-shelled gourds, whose white blossoms open in the evening and bloom during the night. Male and female blossoms of *L. siceraria* must be located and taped shut in the morning and hand-pol-

linated during the evening of the same day.

Sometimes blossoms that were taped shut 10-12 hours earlier are difficult to relocate. Brightly painted stakes or surveyor's flags are often used to mark the row and can even be placed next to the taped flowers. Another trick is to stick a piece of masking tape on the leaf above the taped flower. Also, always try to walk in the same pattern each evening and morning. If the flowers were seen while walking east to west in the evening, walk in that same direction in the morning. The taped flowers are less likely to be hidden from view by leaves if the orientation is the same.

The next morning after the dew has dried, pick the male flower and several inches of its stem. Remove the tape from the male blossom and carefully tear off all of the flower petals. Next, gently remove

Cucurbitaceae

Left: Female blossom is retaped to prevent insect contamination. Right: Hand-pollinated fruit is marked with surveyor's tape and covered with the used male flower that melts down as an additional insect barrier.

the tape from the female flower, which will slowly open. When untaping flowers, be sure to work quickly. Bees have been known to fly into an untaped flower that has just been pollinated, before it can be taped shut again. If that occurs, the flower cannot be used for seed saving.

Hold the petal-less male flower by its stem like a brush and gently rub pollen onto each section of the stigma of the female flower. Pollination will be more successful if several male flowers are used to pollinate each female flower. Now retape the female flower and tie a brightly colored marker around its stem, possibly a piece of yarn or plastic surveyor's ribbon. Markers must be strong and durable enough to withstand water, heat, sunlight and birds looking for nesting materials. If the markers get lost, at har-

vest time there will be no way to tell which fruits were hand-pollinated and contain pure seed. Poultry bands, available from hatcheries and animal feed stores, work well as markers and come in many colors and sizes. The brightly colored plastic bands expand, stay put and are reusable.

Each species within the Cucurbitaceae family has slightly different physical characteristics and requires slight variations in the hand-pollination technique, which are detailed in the following sections. Any plant, no matter what species, is attempting to produce only a limited number of fruits. Although the plant will continue to produce flowers after those fruits are set, the later blossoms will be aborted unless those fruits are damaged or removed. Hand-pollination is most successful early in the season during the formation of the "crown fruit" (first fruit to be set) and the few additional fruits that follow. If the plant has already set numerous fruits that were not hand-pollinated, those fruits can be removed. The plant will then begin producing new flowers, which provides another chance for hand-pollination. This technique only works, of course, if the new fruits still have time to mature before frost.

PLANT SELECTION

Genetic diversity within a population is best preserved by growing as many plants of a variety as possible. Twenty four plants is the recommended population size at government facilities for all Cucurbita species.

GENERAL PRODUCTION
AND PROCESSING TECHNIQUES

Cucurbitaceae must be grown to full maturity before being harvested. A study at Arizona State University determined that the point at which the greatest number of fertile seeds occurs is 20 days after the fruit is fully mature. During the 20 days after the fruit is picked, the seeds continue to increase in size and to gain strength. If the fruit is picked when immature, its seeds gain some weight during that period, but will never gain the full strength displayed by mature seeds. The study was repeated using several different species and seemed to hold true for all cucurbits. Seed savers should always remember to take advantage of this 20-day period during which the seeds actually improve in the fruit after harvest.

After this post-harvest ripening period, the fruits are cut open and the seeds are removed. The flesh and seed attachments are cleaned off, either by washing the seeds in a strainer or by putting the seeds through a fermentation process. Fermentation is recommended for cucumbers and can be used with other genera as well. Some studies indicate that fermented Cucurbitaceae seeds have a slightly higher germination rate. The fermentation process probably destroys a germination inhibitor or fungi that are present. (Fermentation techniques are explained in detail in the section on cucumbers.)

The seeds are then rinsed and dried on a rigid surface away from direct sunlight. Seeds should never be dried in an oven, since damage begins to occur at temperatures above 95° F. Avoid drying seeds on napkins, paper towels or other paper products, because the paper sticks to the dry seed and is difficult to remove. Seeds are easily dried on plastic or glass plates and on cookie sheets.

Cucurbitaceae seeds that will break in half are dry enough for storage. If the seeds bend instead of breaking, continue the drying process. Place the completely dry seeds in an airtight container which should be stored in a cool, dry, dark area or frozen for long-term storage.

Citrullus lanatus - Watermelon and Citron

With hybridization, watermelons have become nearly rindless and uniformly sweet. The old-fashioned watermelons our great-grandparents grew had plenty of seeds for spitting, a thick protective rind that was used for watermelon pickles, and were just as sweet and delicious as modern varieties.

Citron is practically unknown to the home gardener. While just as easy to grow as watermelon, citron is not eaten fresh. Its flesh is made into preserves, sweet pickles and candied fruit.

Both watermelon and citron are indigenous to South Central Africa. In times of extreme drought, watermelons have been used by man and beast as a source of uncontaminated water. Immature watermelons can also be prepared like summer squash, and watermelon wine is common in some areas of Africa.

BOTANICAL CLASSIFICATION

Watermelons and citron belong to the genus *Citrullus* and the species *lanatus*. *C. lanatus* are frost tender, vining annual fruits that require warm temperatures and a long growing season.

Watermelon flesh can range in color from white to ivory, light yellow to dark orange, and light pink to blood red. The seeds can be white, yellow, reddish, brown, black, or mottled with brown and black. The colors and patterns of the rinds are too varied and numerous to mention.

The rind of citron is usually green with either white or greenish white flesh. The seeds are bright green, red, or dull gray. Citron fruits keep for six months and can be processed after summer canning chores have slowed.

POLLINATION, CROSSING AND ISOLATION

Watermelon is an outbreeding plant. All varieties of watermelon will cross with each other and with citron. Isolation of 1/2 mile is recommended to prevent cross-pollination by insects, usually honeybees. When more than one variety is grown in close proximity, hand-pollination is necessary.

General techniques for hand-pollination are described in the introductory pages of the Cucurbitaceae family. Hand-pollination of watermelons is relatively easy, even though the flowers are rather small. Watermelon and citron pollinations are usually successful 50-75% of the time, if conditions are favorable and the plants are not under stress. In early maturing watermelons, this percentage can be increased if the very first female flowers are selected for hand-pollination. The number of fruits set by late maturing varieties, which drop nearly 90% of their first flowers, is much higher if the second flush of flowers is hand-pollinated. The success rate can also be increased if each female flower is pollinated with two or more male flowers, because in some varieties the males don't produce very much pollen.

Sometimes it is difficult to tell which watermelon flowers are going to open the next morning. Go ahead and tape any flowers that appear to be ready. When the tape is removed the next morning, the flowers that are ready will pop open. When a female flower is located that is ready to open, usually the second flower back along that vine is a male flower that will also open the next morning. The tiny, circular, ridged, pollen-bearing structures in the center of the male flower are its anthers, which look like a tiny fuzzy yellow ball once the pollen starts to shed. Male flowers which lack that appearance are not mature enough to be used for pollination purposes.

SEED PRODUCTION, HARVEST AND PROCESSING

Many gardeners have trouble determining just when a watermelon is ripe. Counting the number of days from planting works only in those rare seasons when the weather is fairly normal. The plink, plank, plunk method of thumping is popular, but seldom reliable. Watching for the light-colored patch, where the watermelon touches the ground, to change to the next darker shade works with some varieties. Probably the most reliable sign of ripening occurs when the small tendril directly opposite the fruit's "peduncle" (stem attachment) changes from green to brown and becomes dry. Commercially, watermelons are plugged and their juice is checked against a refractive index. Good quality watermelons that are ready for harvest should have a soluble solids reading of 10.5% at the center or core of the fruit.

Children are great at saving watermelon seeds.

When the watermelon is ready to eat, the seeds are also mature. Try donating watermelons to a teacher at a local elementary school with the following instructions. Gather a large group of children on the lawn, provide each child with a cup for the seeds, and make everyone promise to spit the seeds into their cup. When tummies and cups are full, collect the seeds in a bowl, add a squirt of mild dishwashing soap and wash the seeds gently. Washing will remove the sugar and saliva that remain on the seeds. Then pour the seeds into a strainer and rinse thoroughly.

Citron has hard flesh and the seeds must be picked out by hand. If the melon is also to be used for processing, remove the center of the melon with the greatest seed concentration. The remainder of the flesh will be nearly seedless. Pick the seeds out one by one and rinse thoroughly. It is also possible to leave the citron melons out to rot. After the flesh and rind are soft, put the fruits in a wheelbarrow or large container and chop them up with a shovel or hoe. The seeds will sink when water is added, and the debris is then poured off. Repeat the process until most of the seeds are clean. Put the seeds in a strainer and rinse. Drain the seeds and dry as with other members of the Cucurbitaceae family.

SEED STATISTICS

Watermelon and citron seeds will remain viable for six years when stored in cool, dry, dark conditions. Members of the Seed Savers Exchange annually offer about 94 varieties of watermelon, and the *Garden Seed Inventory* lists sources for 148 varieties that are available from commercial seed companies. There are approximately 315 seeds per ounce (11 per gram or 5,040 per pound), depending on the variety. Federal Germination Standard for commercially sold watermelon seed is 70%.

GROWING WATERMELON AND CITRON FROM SEED

Watermelon and citron are annual, heat-loving plants. Most watermelon varieties require a long, warm growing season, although some short season (70 day) varieties are available. Watermelon seed is mature when the fruits are ripe and ready to eat. The seed germinates at temperatures ranging from 85-95° F. with germination usually occurring in 3-5 days. Watermelon and citron are usually direct seeded, covering the seeds .75" deep. Plant in full sun in fully warmed soil. The plants should be thinned to 12-24" for food and seed production.

REGIONAL GROWING RECOMMENDATIONS

Northeast: Watermelons should be started in a greenhouse from late April to early May and transplant into the garden about June 1. The plants like full sun and average water. We use floating row covers until flowering to protect against striped melon beetles. Only early varieties mature here, and it's risky at that.

Mid-Atlantic: Watermelons can be direct seeded from April 15 to May 15, or started in a greenhouse about March 1 and transplanted into the garden April 15 to May 15. The plants like full sun and average water. Mulch helps in hot dry weather (compost, rotted manure or rotted leaves).

Southeast/Gulf Coast: Watermelons can be direct seeded from April 15 to May 20. The plants like full sun and are drought tolerant.

Upper Midwest: Watermelon and citron can be direct seeded from May 15 to June 15. The plants like full sun.

Southwest: Watermelon can be direct seeded from March 15 to July 1. The plants like full sun and average water.

Central West Coast: Watermelon can be direct seeded from April 15 to June 15. The plants like full sun and average water.

Maritime Northwest: Watermelon can be direct seeded about June 1-10. The plants like full sun and average water. In much of the Maritime Northwest the early part of June is still wet and cool, hence make sure you direct seed when it looks like you will get several days of warm weather, even if you must wait until June 10. This is better than having watermelon seed rot in cool weather.

Cucumis melo - Melons

Melons are thought to have originated in tropical West Africa, where more than 40 wild species have been found. A secondary center of origin occurs in the areas surrounding Iran, south central Russia and some regions of Southeast Asia.

In the United States only the sweet varieties of *Cucumis melo* are referred to as melons. Throughout Asia, however, numerous other melon varieties are grown for pickling. After the seed cavity is emptied, the thin flesh and rind are brined or made into fresh condiments. The fruits are also used like summer squash in various ethnic dishes.

In addition to Asian pickling melons, a now neglected small group of melons was also once grown for the fragrance of the fruits. Before daily bathing became popular, European ladies carried Queen Anne's pocket melons in the pockets of their gowns. The sweet fragrance emitted from the melons helped mask less desirable odors.

BOTANICAL CLASSIFICATION

Melons belong to the genus *Cucumis* and the species *melo*. All varieties of *C. melo* will cross with one another, but do not cross with watermelons or any other members of the Cucurbitaceae family.

There are seven recognized groups or subspecies within *Cucumis melo*. Cantalupensis Group includes medium-sized fruits with hard, rough or scaled rinds. These are the true cantaloupes whose mature fruits do not slip from the vine and do not have netted skin. True cantaloupes are commonly grown in Europe, but are seldom seen in the United States. Members of the Cantalupensis Group should not be confused with the netted muskmelons that are common throughout the United States.

Chito Group includes mango melon, orange melon, garden lemon, melon apple and vine peach. Members of this group all have small leaves, yellow or orange fruits about the size of a lemon or orange, and are primarily used in Asia for making pickles.

Members of the Conomon Group have smooth, oblong or club-shaped fruits and are widely grown in Asia. This group includes all of the Asian pickling melons which are prized for their crisp flesh and usually made into pickles.

Queen Anne's pocket melon, also known as vine pomegranate or plum granny, belongs to the Dudaim Group. Their fruits are about the size of oranges and are very fragrant.

Armenian cucumbers, also called snake melons, belong to the Flexuosus Group and can be eaten or processed like cucumbers. Most gardeners mistakenly think that this group is related to cucumbers, but they are melons and will cross only with *Cucumis melo*.

Christmas melons, honeydew melons, crenshaw melons and casaba melons comprise the Inodorus Group. Their rinds may be smooth or wrinkled, with flesh that is either green or white.

Muskmelons and Persian melons belong to the Reticulatus Group. The common muskmelon with its netted rind and firm orange flesh is characteristic of the Reticulatus Group, which will often slip from their stems when ripe.

It is important to remember that these groups,

Armenian cucumber (*Cucumis melo*, Flexuosus Group), although grown and used like a cucumber, is botanically a melon and will cross with all other varieties of *C. melo*, regardless of group.

which are sometimes called subspecies, are used only to describe plants within a species that have similar characteristics. All of the varieties within all of the groups mentioned above belong to *Cucumis melo*, and will therefore all cross with one another.

POLLINATION, CROSSING AND ISOLATION

Melons, which are outbreeding plants, can be the most frustrating species of Cucurbitaceae for seed savers. Melon plants rely on bees and small flies for pollination. Despite multiple insect visits to each flower, melons will abort about 80% of the female blossoms, plus hand-pollination is even less effective than insect pollination. There is no way to tell which flowers the plant is going to abort, so only about 10-15% of the hand-pollinated blossoms will develop into fruits.

Melon seed can be successfully saved using one of three methods. The easiest way, although not al-ways practical, is to use isolation, with 1/2 mile recommended between varieties. Caging with introduced pollinators is commonly used at research stations and universities, which often employ a beekeeper who maintains small, specially constructed hives built into the sides of the cages. Such techniques are complex and can be quite expensive, and are seldom used by home gardeners. The third option is to pollinate the fruits by hand.

Hand-pollination is not difficult, but is very time-consuming. The flowers are tiny and require a delicate touch. Careful observation is required to identify male and female blossoms that are ready to open. Using small pieces of masking tape about 1/4" wide and 1.5" long, tape flowers closed in the early evening. When wrapping the narrow strips of tape around the tips of the female flowers, pinch the tape together beside the flower but leave the two tip ends of the tape apart. That will make it much easier to untape the female flower the next morning. Always be careful to not break the tiny stem off of the male flower when tearing off its leaves. That happens very easily and makes the blossom awkward to manipulate, but a piece of masking tape can be used in place of the stem.

The following morning after the dew has dried, gently remove the tape from the female flower. Pick the male flower and remove the tape and its petals, then gently rub the pollen from the anthers of the male flower onto the stigma of the female flower. Retape the female flower and mark the stem with colored yarn, plastic ribbon or a poultry band. If the melon's stem attachment is still green after three days and the tiny fruit has slightly enlarged, chances are good that the pollination was successful.

The success rate with hand-pollinated melons can be slightly improved if pollinations are made using the first female flowers that bloom, which are the most likely to set fruit. Each time that the plant sets a fruit, more of the subsequent flowers are going to abort. Fruits that are not hand-pollinated should be removed, which will keep the plant blooming and improve the chances for successful hand-pollinations.

SEED PRODUCTION, HARVEST AND PROCESSING

Melon seeds are mature when the fruits are ready to eat. Slightly overripe fruits have 2-10% more mature seeds, but are not very palatable. Most home gardeners appreciate being able to eat the fruits as well as save the seeds.

Melons should be cut open carefully. The seeds of many varieties will simply fall out, while others are attached to the cavity of the melon or to a soft core and will need to be scooped out. In any case, have a bowl ready. Work the seeds between your fingers to free them of any attachments and pulp. Add enough water to allow the hollow seeds and the attachment fibers to float. Pour off the water and debris, repeating the process until only clean seeds remain. Pour the seeds into a strainer and rinse thoroughly under a stream of cool water to remove any traces of sugar. Dry the bottom of the strainer on a dish towel to remove as much moisture as possible. Then dump the cleaned seeds onto a glass or plastic plate or onto a cookie sheet to dry.

SEED STATISTICS

Melon seeds will remain viable for five years when stored in cool, dry, dark conditions. Members of the Seed Savers Exchange annually offer about 136 varieties of melons, and the *Garden Seed Inventory* lists

sources for 185 varieties of melons that are available from commercial seed companies in the United States and Canada. There are approximately 1,260 seeds per ounce (45 per gram or 20,160 per pound), depending on the variety. Federal Germination Standard for commercially sold melon seed is 75%.

GROWING MELONS FROM SEED

Melons are annual, heat-loving vines. Melon seed is mature when the melons are ready to eat. Melons are usually direct seeded, covering the seeds .5-.75" deep. The seed germinates at temperatures ranging from 80-90° F. with germination usually occurring in 3-5 days. Plant in full sun. The plants should be thinned to 12-18" for both food and seed production.

REGIONAL GROWING RECOMMENDATIONS

Northeast: Melons can be started in a greenhouse from late April to early May and transplanted into the garden about June 1. We use floating row covers until flowering to protect against striped melon beetles. Only earlier-maturing varieties can be relied on here.

Mid-Atlantic: Melons can be direct seeded from April 15 to June 1, or started in a greenhouse March 1 to April 15 and transplanted into the garden April 15 to June 1. The plants like full sun and average water. Mulching helps in hot dry weather (compost or rotted manure). Cucumber beetles, squash borers and squash bugs are sometimes a problem.

Southeast/Gulf Coast: Melons can be direct seeded from April 1 to May 1. The plants like full sun and average water. We use floating row covers until flowers appear, for protection from cucumber beetles.

Upper Midwest: Melons can be direct seeded from May 1 to June 20. The plants like full sun and average water. Many insects cause problems.

Southwest: Melons can be direct seeded from March 15 to June 15. The plants like full sun and average water.

Central West Coast: Melons can be direct seeded from April 15 to June 15. The plants like full sun and average water.

Maritime Northwest: Melons can be direct seeded about June 1-10. The plants like full sun and average water. In much of the Maritime Northwest late May and early June are still wet and cool, hence make sure you direct seed this species when it looks like you'll get several days of warm weather, even if you must wait until June 10. It's better to wait than to have your seed rot.

Jelly melon, an obscure exotic fruit, was recently rediscovered in New Zealand where it is now being grown as an export crop. The oval fruits, which are beginning to appear in American supermarkets as tropical oddities, usually grow to 3" x 5" and are covered with sharp horns or projections. Jelly melon's eye-catching orange rind contrasts strikingly with its chartreuse green flesh. The fruits can be juiced like oranges or eaten fresh like melons, with a flavor that is often likened to a mixture of bananas and limes.

BOTANICAL CLASSIFICATION

Jelly melon, which belongs to the genus *Cucumis* and the species *metuliferous*, is also sometimes known as African horned cucumber, kiwano or hedgehog gourd. At this time only one variety of jelly melon is available in the United States; however, other varieties are likely to exist. *C. metuliferous* does not cross with any other Cucurbitaceae.

Jelly melon is best grown on trellises to save garden space and prevent fruit rot. The vines resemble cucumbers, but are more rampant and spiny. Jelly melons will grow to maturity anywhere cucumbers can be grown for seed. Fully mature fruits will keep at room temperature for up to six months and contain four times the vitamin C of an orange.

A few words of caution about jelly melon might be appropriate. Some authorities are concerned about the potential for jelly melon to escape and become a noxious weed. Jelly melon plants are definitely killed by frost, but might be able to self-sow. Anyone who has seen the fruit's sharp spines and rampant vines can appreciate this concern.

POLLINATION, CROSSING AND ISOLATION

Jelly melon is an outbreeding plant. The vines of jelly melon produce both male and female flowers that are insect-pollinated. The isolation distances used for cucumbers, 1/2 to 1 mile, should ensure complete seed purity if more than one variety is grown. Hand-pollination, described in the introductory pages of the Cucurbitaceae family, is also possible.

SEED PRODUCTION, HARVEST AND PROCESSING

Jelly melons are mature and ready for harvest when the fruits turn bright orange. Undamaged fruits keep up to six months, and seed cleaning can be initiated at any time. Carefully cut the melon open and scoop the jelly capsules into a blender or food processor. Process briefly at low speed, just until the

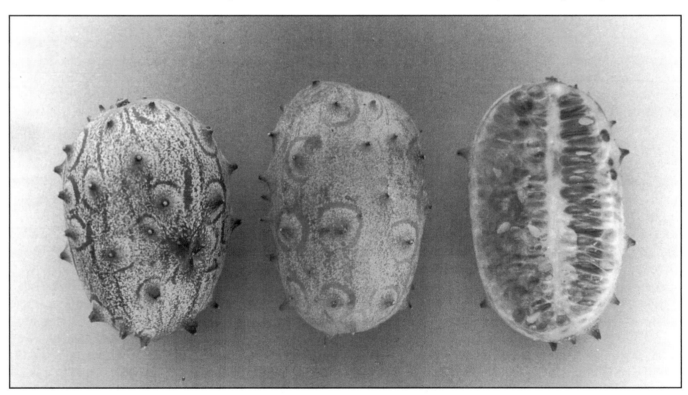

Jelly melon, sometimes known as African horned cucumber (*Cucumis metuliferus*).

capsules are broken. Each capsule will yield one tiny seed.

The seed capsules can also be fermented to free the seeds. Depending on the temperature, the fermentation process will take from two to five days to break down the seed capsules. During this time the aromas emanating from the bowl will grow increasingly worse and some mold may form over the top of the mixture. Stir the mass twice each day. The fermentation process should be stopped when most of the seeds have settled to the bottom of the bowl and the seed cases are floating on the top of the mixture.

After either blending or fermenting, add as much water as possible, stir the mixture and allow the good, clean seeds to settle to the bottom. Gently pour off the debris and hollow seeds. Add more water and repeat the process until only clean seeds remain. Pour the seeds into a strainer and rinse thoroughly under running water. Wipe the bottom of the strainer on a towel to remove as much moisture as possible, and dump the seeds onto a cookie sheet or dish to dry.

Stir the seeds twice daily to ensure even drying. Never dry seeds in direct sunlight or in an oven, because damage begins to occur at temperatures above 95° F. The seeds are dry enough for storage when they break or snap in half. If the seeds bend instead of breaking, more drying is needed. Store the completely dried seeds in an airtight container in a cool, dry, dark area or freeze them for long-term storage.

SEED STATISTICS

Information on seed longevity for jelly melon is not available. Jelly melon is offered by members of the Seed Savers Exchange, and is also available from commercial sources listed in the *Garden Seed Inventory*. There are approximately 845 seeds per ounce (30 per gram or 13,520 per pound), depending on the variety. Federal Germination Standard should be the same as for cucumbers, which is 80%.

GROWING JELLY MELON FROM SEED

Jelly melon is a heat-loving, annual vine. The plants exhibit some daylength sensitivity and, when grown in short season climates, may not produce mature fruit. Jelly melons are direct seeded, because the plants do not transplant well. Cover the seeds with .5" of soil. The seed germinates at temperatures ranging from 85-95° F. with germination usually occurring in 5-7 days. Plant or set out in full sun, and provide a trellis for the rampant vines. The leaves are irritating, so plant away from frequently traveled garden areas. The plants should be thinned to 18" for both food and seed production.

REGIONAL GROWING RECOMMENDATIONS

Northeast: Jelly melon cannot be grown in this region.

Mid-Atlantic: Jelly melon can be direct seeded about April 15, or started in a greenhouse about March 1 and transplanted into the garden about April 15.

Southeast/Gulf Coast: Jelly melon can be direct seeded from April 1 to May 1. The plants like full sun and average water.

Upper Midwest: Jelly melon can be direct seeded May 15. Plants like full sun and are drought tolerant.

Southwest: Jelly melon can be direct seeded from March 15 to June 15. The plants like full sun and average water.

Central West Coast: Jelly melon can be direct seeded from April 15 to May 15. The plants like full sun and are drought tolerant.

Maritime Northwest: Jelly melon cannot be grown in this region.

Cucumis sativus - Cucumber

Botanists believe that cucumbers are descendants of a wild cucurbita found in the Himalayas. Cucumbers in various forms are found in pictures and carvings from India dating about two centuries before Christ. Today the largest and most widely varied populations of indigenous cucumbers are still found growing in India.

Cultural preferences for various shapes, colors and sizes strongly govern the agricultural production of cucumbers. Round cucumbers are prized in Asia, as are very long varieties. Americans generally favor 8" dark green types. The cornichon, a tiny cucumber grown for pickling, is a favorite in France. Specially bred varieties that do not require pollination to produce fruits are commonly grown in European greenhouses. Such fruits are referred to as parthenocarpic and are seedless. Of the choices available to seed savers, there is a color, texture and shape to suit every need and preference.

Cucumber bitterness is a subject that generates much speculation among home gardeners. Bitterness is caused by compounds called cucurbitacins, and the amount of the compound found in the fruit is genetically controlled. Some gardeners believe that bitter-

Some of the myriad shapes, colors and sizes exhibited by cucumbers (*Cucumis sativus*).

ness is the result of a lack of water and can be corrected by watering the plant more often. While it is true that the concentration of this compound can be slightly influenced by the amount of water the plants receive, bitterness is not caused by a lack of water. Bitterness is also not caused by crossing with melons or squash, which is not botanically possible. Cucurbitacins are toxic to humans, but bitter fruits are not palatable and are rarely eaten. Plants that produce bitter fruits should not be used for seed saving.

BOTANICAL CLASSIFICATION

Cucumbers belong to the genus *Cucumis* and the species *sativus*. West Indian gherkins, Armenian cucumbers, snake melons and serpent gourds are all commonly referred to as cucumbers because of similar usage, but do not belong to *C. sativus* and will not cross with cucumbers.

Although shapes and sizes vary considerably, varieties grown for commercial pickling have an ideal length-to-diameter ratio of three-to-one. Slicing varieties have usually been selected for a longer length. All varieties can be used for both pickling and slicing, but many home gardeners feel that the best pickles are made from drier-fleshed cucumbers. Varieties with crisp, juicy flesh are usually chosen for slicing.

Cucumber vines vary in size and suitability for trellising. In general, smaller vines with lighter colored fruits do better on the ground. Trellised cucumbers often sunburn in hot summer climates, but in very humid regions, trellising is often preferred because it reduces some mildew problems.

The cucumber varieties commonly grown in the United States are moderately daylength sensitive. Studies indicate that the greatest number of female blossoms are produced on days with 11 hours of daylight. This occurs in the early and late summer and helps explain why some gardeners complain of a midsummer cucumber shortage.

POLLINATION, CROSSING AND ISOLATION

Cucumbers are outbreeding plants. All cucumbers, *Cucumis sativus*, will cross with one another. Armenian cucumbers, also known as snake melons, are used like cucumbers but are really melons, *Cucumis melo*, and will cross with muskmelons and cantaloupes. West Indian gherkin, *Cucumis anguria*, and serpent gourd, *Trichosanthes anguina*, are both used similarly, but will not cross with cucumbers.

Cucumber varieties must be isolated by 1/2 mile. Many gardeners prefer to grow several different varieties of cucumbers, which poses no problem for the seed saver who is adept at hand-pollination. The success rate for hand-pollinated cucumbers is usually about 85%. Slightly higher rates are possible if two or more male flowers are used to pollinate each female blossom. Cucumber flowers are .5-1" in diameter. Each female blossom sits atop a tiny immature cucumber, while the male blossom is just attached to a straight stem. After a bit of practice, blossoms that will open the next morning become easy to identify. The hand-pollinating technique, described in the introductory pages of the Cucurbitaceae family, works well without any special modifications.

Hand-pollination has the best chance of being successful during 11-hour days when the vines produce the greatest number of female flowers. Cucumber plants will abort their fruits during periods of drought and excessively high temperature, so hand-pollination should not be attempted during those times.

SEED PRODUCTION, HARVEST AND PROCESSING

Cucumbers that are being saved for seed must be grown to full maturity and allowed to ripen past the edible stage. The fruits will be large and beginning to soften. Depending on the variety, the fruits will change from green to white or deep yellow or orange.

Each cucumber that is successfully hand-pollinated will yield hundreds of seeds. Fully mature cucumbers, when cut from the vine and kept for about two weeks, have a slightly greater number of viable seeds. Sometimes hand-pollinated cucumbers will mature but have few if any seeds when cut open. Such blossoms either received an inadequate amount of pollen, or that variety may have a parthenocarpic tendency and is capable of developing fruit without fertilization.

After harvest, carefully cut open the cucumbers and scoop the seeds into a large bowl. Each cucumber seed is encased in a gelatinous sack that is most easily removed by fermenting the seeds. Add about as much water as seeds but not too much or fermentation will be slowed. Then set the bowl away from direct sunlight in a protected location to ferment. Depending on the temperature, fermentation will take from one to three days. At 90+° F., 24-36 hours should be sufficient. During this period, the aromas from the bowl will be less than pleasing and some mold may form over the top of the mixture. Stir the mass

twice a day. Fermentation is complete when most of the seeds have settled to the bottom of the bowl and the seedcases are floating on top of the mixture.

Now stir the mass while adding as much water as possible, which allows the clean seeds to settle to the bottom. The debris and hollow seeds will float and can be gently poured off with the excess water. Repeat this process until only clean seeds remain. Then pour the seeds into a strainer, wipe the bottom of the strainer on a towel to remove as much moisture as possible, and dump the seeds out to dry on a cookie sheet or other non-stick surface.

SEED STATISTICS

Cucumber seeds will remain viable for ten years when stored under ideal conditions. Members of the Seed Savers Exchange annually offer about 111 varieties of cucumber, and the *Garden Seed Inventory* lists sources for 124 varieties that are available from commercial seed companies. There are approximately 985 seeds per ounce (35 per gram or 15,760), depending on the variety. Federal Germination Standard for commercially sold seed is 80%.

GROWING CUCUMBER FROM SEED

Cucumbers are annual, heat-loving vines that exhibit some daylength sensitivity. Cucumbers are usually direct seeded, covering the seeds with .25-.5" of soil. The seed germinates at temperatures ranging from 75-95° F. with germination usually occurring in 5-7 days. Cucumbers should be planted in full sun. The plants should be thinned to 18-24" for both food and seed production.

REGIONAL GROWING RECOMMENDATIONS

Northeast: Cucumbers can be direct seeded after May 25. The plants like full sun and average water. We use floating row covers until flowering commences, to protect against striped melon beetles. Some late-maturing types must be started indoors like melons.

Mid-Atlantic: Cucumbers can be direct seeded about April 15, or started in a greenhouse about March 1 and transplanted into the garden about April 15. The plants like full sun and average water.

Southeast/Gulf Coast: Cucumbers can be direct seeded from April 1 to May 10. The plants like full sun.

Upper Midwest: Cucumbers can be direct seeded from May 1 to June 20. The plants like full sun and average water.

Southwest: Cucumbers can be direct seeded from

March 15 to June 15. The plants like full sun and average water.

Central West Coast: Cucumbers can be direct seeded from April 15 to June 15. The plants like full sun and average water.

Maritime Northwest: Cucumbers can be direct seeded about May 20. The plants like full sun and average water.

———— *Cucurbita spp.* - Squash, Malabar Gourd and Calabazilla ————

Cucurbita maxima - Squash
C. mixta - Squash
C. moschata - Squash
C. pepo - Squash
C. ficifolia - Malabar Gourd (Chilacayote)
C. foetidissima - Calabazilla

Various members of the genus *Cucurbita*, known collectively as squash, have been used for many centuries by Native Americans throughout the North and South American continents. The number, sizes, shapes and colors of the varieties once grown are astounding. Many Native American varieties have been overlooked by home gardeners who are often interested only in meal-sized winter squashes. Our ancestors, prized larger squash for their ability to feed large numbers of people. Squash were also used as edible mixing bowls, water containers, and for livestock feed.

Summer squash, winter squash and pumpkins are three commonly used terms that have left more than a few people confused. All squash and pumpkins can be eaten when young and tender, and also when mature. Varieties that have been selected for outstanding keeping qualities and dry flesh are known as winter squash. Others that have young, tender skin and few seeds are referred to as summer squash. The difference between pumpkins and winter squash can be even more confusing. In the United States, small, round, orange squash used for pies and jack-o'-lanterns are commonly referred to as pumpkins. However, the term pumpkin is also a frequently used name for certain types of large, orange, field pumpkins. Actually, all pumpkins are squash. Pumpkins are not even a "subspecies" (group).

BOTANICAL CLASSIFICATION

Squash belong to the genus *Cucurbita* and to one of six different species. Each of the six species has specific stem, leaf, flower and seed characteristics which are described below. The following are extensive lists of all of the known squash varieties within each species, so that gardeners can make an isolated planting that includes one variety from each of the species without having to resort to hand-pollination. Also, "Regional Planting Recommendations" have

been included for each of the six species, following each of the lists of variety names.

Cucurbita maxima

Squash varieties that belong to *C. maxima* have very long vines, huge, hairy leaves and soft, round, spongy, hairy stems. The thick seeds are white or tan or brown with cream-colored margins and thin cellophane coatings.

The following varieties all belong to the species *C. maxima* and will cross with each other: All Gold, Alligator, American Indian, Amish Pie Pumpkin, Araucana, Argentine, Argentine Primitive Pumpkin, Argentine Summer, Arikara, Asuncion, Atlantic Giant, Atlas, Australian Butter Pumpkin, Autumn Pride, all varieties of **BANANA (Blue, Chinese, Giant, Guatemalan Blue, Hartman, Orange, Pink, Pink Jumbo)**, Banquet, Bay State, Belaya Medovaya, Belgium Pumpkin, Big Max, Big Moon, Big Red, Black Forest, Blaugrauer Kuerbis Staatz, Blue Ballet, Blue Hungarian, Bluebell, Bulgarina, Burgess Giant Pumpkin, all varieties of **BUTTERCUP (Bitterroot, Blue, Branscomb, Branscomb White, Burgess, Bush, Discus Bush, Golden Bush, Hard Shell, Kindred, Russian, Sweet, Verda's)**, California White Pumpkin, Candy Roaster, Cherokee Indian Pumpkin, Chersonskaya, Chestnut, Cinderella (the renamed Rouge Vif d'Etampes), Courge Olive Verte, Criolo, Crown Prince, Doe, Emerald, Equadonantian, Essex, Essex Hybrid, Estampes, Flat White Boer, Forragero, Fortna White, Francis Bellew's Candy Roaster, Galeux d'Eysines, Genuine Mammoth, Georgia Roaster, German, German Green Pumpkin, German Sweet Potato, Gilmore, Ginny's Large, Gold Mountain, Gold Nugget, Golden Delicious, Goldkeeper, Goldpak, Golzar, Great Pumpkin, Greek Small Orange Pumpkin, Green Delicious, Greengold, Guatemalan Blue, Harvest Moon, Herman's Delight, Hillbilly, Hokkaido Green, Hokkaido Orange, Hopi Groie, Hopi Orange, Hopi Pale Grey, all varieties of **HUBBARD (Anna Swartz, Azure, Baby, Baby Blue, Baby Green, Black, Blue, Blue Special, Chicago, Chicago Warted, Golden, Green, Green Delicious, Green Improved, Kitchenette, Large Blue, Little Gem, Mini Green, Minnesota, NK580, Sugar, True, Warted, Warted**

Green, Warted Improved), Hungarian Mammoth, Hungarian Mammoth (Cornell Strain), Hungarian Winter, Iran, Iron Pot, Ironclad, Japanese, Jarrahdale, Jattepumpa, Kabocha, Kabule, Kara Kabak, Kentucky, Kindred, Kuri Blue, Kuri Red, La Calabaza (Philippine), La Kalabaza, Lakota, Large Mammoth, Large Moroccan, Large Yellow Paris, Large White Manteca, Leningrad Giant, Lower Salmon River, Lumina, Mammoth Chile, Mammoth Gold, Mammoth King, Mammoth Orange Gold, Mammoth Whale, Mantecca Large White, Marblehead, Marina di Chioggia, all varieties of **winter MARROW (Autumnal, Boston, Orange, Prolific, Warted**), Mayo Blusher, Mexican Indian, Mexigold, Mooregold, Mohawk, Mountaineer, My Best Pie, Nanicoke Indian, Ni-es-pah Long, Nightfire, Old Blue, Old English, Old Humbolt, Old Winter, Orange Giant, Orange New Guinea, Pikes Peak Pumpkin, Pink Giant Pumpkin, Plymouth Rock, Quality, Quality Winter Squash, Queensland Blue, Rainbow, Red Chestnut, Red Estampes, Red Gold, Red Skin, Redondo di Tronco, Riesenkuerbis Oestereicher, Riesen-melonenkuerbis, Roaster, Rouge Vif d'Etampes, Shanghai, Show King, Sibley, Silver Bell, Siva Stambolka, Smooth Green Pie, South American, Stambolka, Sweetbush, Sweetkeeper, Sweetmeat, Taos Pueblo, Tiny Turk, Tokyo, TriStar, Triamble, all varieties of **TURBAN (American, Golden, Lakota Sioux, Red Warren, Turk's, Warren, Windsor Black**), Uchiki Kuri, Umatilla Marblehead, Valenciano, Verruquex du Portugal, Victor Watten, Vojicka, Vounicheo Blue, Vounicheo Orange, Week's North Carolina Giant, West Virginia Big, Whanga Crown, Whangaparoa, White African, White Pumpkin, Wickersham Sweet Potato, Winnebago, Yakima Marblehead, Yugoslavian Pie Pumpkin, Zapallo Macre, Zapallo Poloma, Zipinki Campana, Zucca Quintale, Zucca Marina di Chioggia.

REGIONAL GROWING RECOMMENDATIONS

Northeast: *Cucurbita maxima* can be direct seeded from May 20 to June 10. The plants like full sun and average water. We use floating row covers until the vines run, to guard against damage by striped melon beetles.

Mid-Atlantic: *C. maxima* can be direct seeded from April 15 to June 1, or started in a greenhouse March 1 to April 15 and transplanted April 15 to June 1.

Southeast/Gulf Coast: *C. maxima* can be direct seeded from April 15 to May 1, or started in a greenhouse about July 1 and transplanted into the garden about July 21-30. The plants like full sun and average water. Squash vine borers are a serious problem for varieties that mature slowly.

Upper Midwest: *C. maxima* can be direct seeded May 1 until June 15. The plants like full sun and average water. Many insects can cause problems.

Southwest: *C. maxima* can be direct seeded March 15 to June 10. Plants like full sun and average water.

Central West Coast: *C. maxima* can be direct seeded from April 15 to May 30. The plants like full sun and average water.

Maritime Northwest: *C. maxima* can be direct seeded about May 20. The plants like full sun and average water.

Cucurbita mixta

Varieties that belong to *C. mixta* have spreading vines and large, hairy leaves. The fruit's stem, which flares out only slightly where it attaches to the fruit, is hard, hairy and slightly angular. The leaves of *C. mixta* are slightly lighter green than those of *C. moschata,* and have a rounded leaf tip and hardly any indentations along their sides. The white or tan seeds have a pale margin and cracks in the skin coat on the flat sides of the seeds which are covered with a thin cellophane coating.

The following varieties belong to the species *C. mixta* and will cross readily with each other: Big White Crookneck, Black Sweet Potato, Calabaza de las Aguas, Campeche, Chompa, Cochita Pueblo, most of the varietes of **CUSHAW (Albino Hopi, Albino Pepita, Australian, Cochiti Puebla, Gila, Gila Cliff Dweller, Gold Striped, Green Striped, Hopi, Hopi Black Green, Longneck, Magdalena Striped, Neckless, Old Fashioned, Papalote Ranch, Parral, Pure White, Santa Domingo, Solid Green, Tri-Color, White, White Crookneck or White Jonathan and Winter**) [the exceptions are Golden Cushaw, Orange Cushaw and Orange Striped Cushaw which are all *C. moschata*], Gila Cliff Dweller, Hindu, Hopi Black Green, Hopi Taos, Hopi Teardrop, Indian Vining Zucchini, Japanese Pie, Jonathan, Large White New Mexico Cliff Dweller, Mayo Arrote, Mexican Xtop, Mixta Gold, Mrs. Morris' Potato Pumpkin, Papago, Papalote, Pennsylvania Crookneck, Pepita Guatemala, San Barnardo, all of the wild **SERORIA SQUASH**, all of the **SILVER SEEDED GOURDS**, Striped Belize, Tamala, Tamala de Carne, Tamala de Hueso, Tennessee Sweet Potato, Tohona O'odham, Winter Vining, Woodrey Sweet Potato, Zapotec.

REGIONAL GROWING RECOMMENDATIONS

Northeast: *Cucurbita mixta* can be direct seeded about June 1. The plants like full sun and average water. We use floating row covers until the vines run, to guard against striped cucumber/melon beetles. Only certain varieties produce mature seed here.

Mid-Atlantic: *C. mixta* can be direct seeded from April 15 to May 1, or started in a greenhouse March 1 to April 1 and transplanted into the garden April 15 to May 1. The plants like full sun and average water.

Southeast/Gulf Coast: *C. mixta* can be direct seeded from April 15 to May 15. The plants like full sun and average water.

Upper Midwest: *C. mixta* can be direct seeded from May 1 to June 15. The plants like full sun and average water. Many insect problems must be addressed.

Southwest: *C. mixta* can be direct seeded from March 15 to June 15. The plants like full sun and average water.

Central West Coast: *C. mixta* can be direct seeded from April 15 to June 1. The plants like full sun and average water.

Maritime Northwest: *C. mixta* cannot be grown in this region; not enough heat units to mature it.

Cucurbita moschata

C. moschata varieties have spreading vines and large hairy leaves. The fruit's stem, which flares out quite noticeably where it attaches to the fruit, is hard, hairy and slightly angular. The flower has large, leafy, green sepals at its base. The leaves of *C. moschata* are slightly darker green than *C. mixta*, and have a pointed leaf tip and slight indentations along their sides. Each of the small, beige, oblong seeds has a dark beige margin.

The following varieties all belong to the species *C. moschata* and cross readily: African, African Bell, Aizu Gokwuase, Alagold, Borinquen, Butterbush, all varieties of **BUTTERNUT (Baby, Big Neck, Bush, Early, Eastern, Hercules, Improved, Mexican, Ponca, Puritan, Waltham, Western)**, Calabaza (or Cuban Squash), Calhoun, Canadai Mezoides, Cangold, Carrizo, all varieties of **CHEESE (Cutchoque Flat, Flat Warty, Large, Long Island, Magdalena Big, Showell Ovoid, Small Flat Cheese Pumpkin, Tan, Wisconsin)**, Chirimen, Choctaw

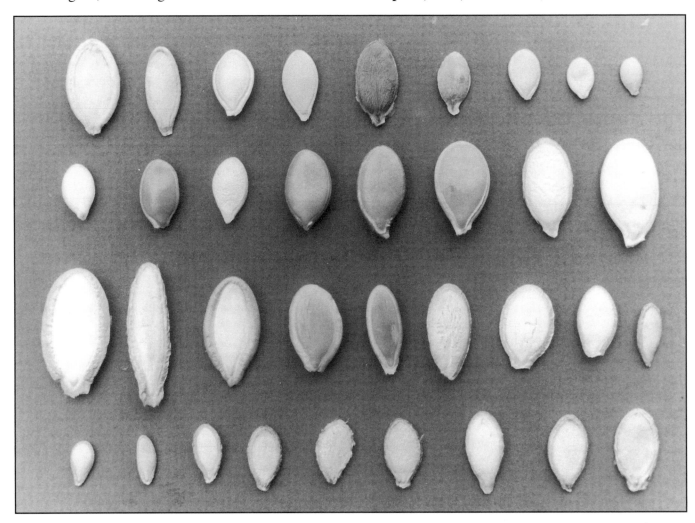

Typical seeds of the four squash species. Top to bottom: *C. pepo, C. maxima, C. mixta and C. moschata.*

Sweet Potato, Courge Longue de Nice, Cow Pumpkin, Creole, Citrouille d'Eysines, Cuban, Dickinson, Dulce de Horno, East India Big Red, Fairytale, Field Pumpkin, Flat Tan Field, Florida Buff Pie, Fortuna, Futtsu Black, Futtsu Early Black, Futtsu Kurokawa, **Golden Cushaw**, Gomez Farias Milpa, Gray, Guinea, Hawaiian, Hercules, Honduran, Hopi Tan, Hyuga Black, Kentucky Field, Kikuza, La Primera, Landreth, Long Island, Long Keeper, Longfellow, Lunga di Napoli, Magdalena Big, Mamuzo, Maryland Pie Pumpkin, Mayo Segualca, Mediterranean, Melon Squash (or Tahitian Squash), Mexican, Neck, Milk Pumpkin, Mrs. Amerson's Pumpkin, Musque de Provance, Neck Pumpkin, New Jersey, Old-Fashioned Tennessee Vining, Old Time Tennessee, **Orange Cushaw**, **Orange Striped Cushaw**, Papaya, Patriot, Paw Paw, Peraora, Piena di Napoli, Pima Bajo, Ponca, Priester Crookneck, Quaker Pie Squash, Rampicante Zucchetta, Rio Fuerte Mayo Arrote, Rio Fuerte Mayo Segualca, Seminole Acorn, Seminole Pumpkin, Sequalca, Showell Sweet Potato, Shumway's Tennessee Sweet Potato, Sicilian, Sweet Red, Tahitian Squash (or Melon Squash), Tamala, Thai, Tromboncino, Trombone, Trombone Rampicante, Upper Ground Sweet Potato, Virginia Mammoth, Whanga Crown, White Rind Sugar, Wisconsin Canner, Zaug's Pumpkin, Zucca Piena di Napoli, Zucchetta Rampicante.

REGIONAL GROWING RECOMMENDATIONS

<u>Northeast</u>: *Cucurbita moschata* can be direct seeded about June 1. We use floating row covers until vines start to run, to guard against striped cucumber/melon beetles. Many varieties are hard to mature here; probably should be started indoors.

<u>Mid-Atlantic</u>: *C. moschata* can be direct seeded April 15 to June 1, or started in a greenhouse March 1 to April 15 and transplanted April 15 to June 1.

<u>Southeast/Gulf Coast</u>: *C. moschata* can be direct seeded from April 15 to May 1, or started in a greenhouse about July 1 and transplanted into the garden about July 21. We use floating row covers to protect fall crops from squash bugs. This crop is ignored by squash vine borers in our region.

<u>Upper Midwest</u>: *C. moschata* can be direct seeded May 1 to June 15. The plants like full sun and average water. Many insect problems need to be addressed.

<u>Southwest</u>: *C. moschata* can be direct seeded from March 15 to June 10.

<u>Central West Coast</u>: *C. moschata* can be direct seeded from April 15 to June 1.

<u>Maritime Northwest</u>: *C. moschata* can be direct seeded about May 20.

Cucurbita pepo

Varieties belonging to *C. pepo* have prickly leaves and stems, especially when mature. The fruit's stem is hard and has five sharply angular sides. The seeds are cream colored and each has a white margin. Included within this species are the soft-shelled striped and warted decorative gourds found in grocery stores at Thanksgiving and nearly all of the commonly grown summer squashes.

The following varieties belong to the species *C. pepo*: Acoma, Acoma Pumpkin, all varieties of **ACORN (Des Moines, Ebony, Ebony Bush, Fisher's, Fordhook, Golden, Jersey Golden, Paydon Heirloom, Royal, Snow White, Swan White, Table Gold, Table King, Table King Bush, Table Queen, Table Queen Bush, Table Queen Ebony, Table Queen Mammoth, Tuffy, White)**, Alabama Sweet Potato, Alagold, Algonquin Pumpkin, Amish Field Pie Pumpkin, Ancestors, Arlesa, Austrian Bush Summer, Baby Bear, Baby Boo, Baby Pam Pumpkin, Bahce, Bakery's, Bela Sakaska, Big Red California Sugar, Big Tom, Black Beauty, Bloomfield Pumpkin, Bulgarian Summer, Buscholkurbis Naked Seed, Bushkin, Caserta, Casper, Chestnut, Cheyenne Bush, Chiefini, Chinese Miniature, Chinese Miniature White, Cinderella (a yellow halloween pumpkin that predates and is <u>not</u> Rouge Vif d'Etampes), Citrouille de Touraine, all varieties of **COCOZELLE (Green, Green Striped, Long, Vining),** Connecticut Field, Connecticut Sweet Pie, Cornfield Pumpkin, Cou-Tors Hatif, Cozini, Cow Pumpkin, all varieties of **CROOKNECK (Dwarf Summer, Dixie, Early Summer Golden, Early Summer Yellow, Giant Summer, Golden, White Summer, Yellow Summer Improved)**, Crystal Bell, Cupid, Dancing Gourd, Delicata, Disc Narancs, Dumpling, Early Cheyenne Pie, Early Prolific, Early Prolific Straightneck, Eat-All, Englisher Gelber, Erken, Eskandarany, Fairytale, Fat Boy, Fordhook, Fordhook Bush, Fort Berthold, French White Bush, Gem, Ghost Rider, Gills Golden Pippin, Gold Rush, Golden Centennial, Golden Custard, Golden Oblong, Golden Scallopini Bush, any of the **small, decorative, striped and warted GOURDS (Bicolor Spoon, Dancing Gourd, Nest Egg, Sweet Dumpling or Vegetable Gourd)** Gourmet Globe, Gririt, Half Moon, Halloween, Happy Jack, Hmong, Hondo Small Sugar Pumpkin, Honeyboat, Hopi White Jack-O'-Lantern, Howden, Howden Biggie, Huicha, Hyuga Black, Ichabod, Idaho Gem, Ingot, Jack Be Little, Jack-B-Quik, Jack-O'-Lantern, Jack-o-Lite, Japanese Pie, Jumpin Jack (May), Kahcona, King of Giants, King of Mammoths, Kline Pumpkin, Kumi

Kumi, Lady Godiva, Lady Godiva Bush, Lakota, Large Yellow Paris, Lebanese, Lebanese Light Green, Lebanese Pumpkin, Lemon, Little Boo, Little Gem, Little Lantern, Long Pie Pumpkin, Lubnani, Lunghissimo Bianco di Palermo, Mammoth Gold, Mandan, Mandan Green, Mandan Strain No. 1, Mandan Yellow, Manteca Large White, Marego, Maryland Pie Pumpkin, Mayeras, Melonette de St. Julien de Concelles, Menominee, Midwest Sweet Potato, Mihoacan, Mini-Jack Pumpkin, Miniature Pumpkin, Minnesota Sweet, Montana Jack, Mt. Pima Vavuli, Munchkin, Naked Seeded, New England Pie Pumpkin, Northern Bush, Northern Gold, Oaxacan, Oaxacan Bicolor, Oaxacan White, Odessa, Oland, Old Timey Flat Pumpkin, Omaha, Omaha Pumpkin, Panama, Pankow's Field, Patisson Golden Marbre, Patisson Orange, Patisson Panache Jaune et Vert, Patisson Panache Vert et Blanc, Pepinos, Perfect Gem, Pie Pumpkin, Potimarron, Potiron Panache Jaune et Verte, Precoce Re Maraiche, Prilepska, Primitive Argentine, Prostate, Puschino, Ranger, Rocky Mountain Pie, Rondo de Nice, Royal Bush, Sakiz, Saffron Prolific Straightneck, San Felipe del Agua, all varieties of **SCALLOP (Benning's Green Tint, Early White Bush, Early Yellow Bush, Golden Bush, Long Island White Bush, Mammoth White Bush, Patty Pan, St. Pat, Summer Bush, White Bush, Yellow Bush, Yellow Custard, Yellow Golden)**, Scarchuk's Supreme, Showell, Small Sugar Pie, Small Sugar Pumpkin, Snack 'R Jack, Sonoran Hulless, Southern Miner, Spaghetti Squash, Speckled Hmong, Spookie, Stickler, Storage, Straightneck, Streaker, Styrian Hulless, Sucrette du Berry, Sugar Baby, Sugar Loaf, Sugar Pie, Sweet Potato, Sweetie Pie, Sweetnut, Table Dainty, Table Gold, Tahitian Small, Tallman, Tarahumara Indian Pumpkin, Tatume, Tepehuan, Thelma Sanders Sweet Potato, Thomas Halloween, Todo el Ano, Tom Fox, Tondo di Nizza, Tricky Jack, Triple Treat, Tuckernuck, Turner Family, Tweet-ee-oo Bakers, Uconn, Uncle Herman, all varieties of **VEGETABLE MARROW (Bush, Danish Strain, English, Green Bush Improved, Italian, Lebanese, Long White, Long Yellow, Mammoth White Bush, Tender and True, Trailing Green, Vegetable, White Bush, White Vining Vegetable)**, Vegetable Spaghetti, White Syrian Coussa, Wilbur Field Pumpkin, Winter Luxury, Winter Luxury Pie, Winter Nut, Woods Prolific, Woods Earliest Prolific, Xochitlan Pueblo, Youngs Beauty, Yugoslavian Finger Fruit, Yumarta, Zapallito del Tronco, all varieties of **ZUCCHINI (Black, Black Beauty, Black Magic, Black Shelled, Burpee's Fordhook, Burpee's Golden, Cereberus Bush, Costata Romanesca, Dark Green, French White Bush, Gialla Nostrale, Gold Rush, Gold Satin, Golden, Green, Green Satin, Grey, Karin, Lebanese, Lungo Florentino, Mezza Lungo Bianco di Trieste, Midnight, Nano Bolognese, Nano Verde di Milano, Nimba, Nizza, Odessa, Oestereicher, Ronde de Nice, Round, Siciliano, Small Green Algerian, Small Tree of Sarzana, Striato d'Italia, Tondo di Firenze, Whitaker, White, White Egyptian, White Gila, Yellow, Zuboda)**, Zikusa.

REGIONAL GROWING RECOMMENDATIONS

<u>Northeast</u>: *Cucurbita pepo* can be direct seeded about June 1. The plants like full sun and average water. We use floating row covers until vines start to run, to guard against striped melon beetles. Some varieties are difficult to mature in this region.

<u>Mid-Atlantic</u>: *C. pepo* can be direct seeded from April 15 to June 1, or started in a greenhouse March 1 to April 15 and transplanted into the garden April 15 to June 1. Squash borers are always a problem; watch also for squash bugs and cucumber beetles.

<u>Southeast/Gulf Coast</u>: *C. pepo* can be direct seeded April 15 to May 1, or started in a greenhouse about August 1 and transplanted into the garden about August 21. Early sowings often have fewer pest problems.

<u>Upper Midwest</u>: *C. pepo* can be direct seeded May 1 to June 15. The plants like full sun and average water. Many insect problems need to be addressed.

<u>Southwest</u>: *C. pepo* can be direct seeded from March 15 to June 10. The plants like full sun and average water.

<u>Central West Coast</u>: *C. pepo* can be direct seeded from April 1 to July 15.

<u>Maritime Northwest</u>: *C. pepo* can be direct seeded May 20. The plants like full sun and average water.

Note: The general rule of interspecies incompatibility in squash has worked well for most seed savers for many years. A recent study, however, has proven that some crossing can occur between *C. moschata* and *C. mixta* (which some researchers have suggested be renamed *C. argyrosperma*), when *C. mixta* is the female parent and *C. moschata* provides the pollen. The study focused on certain Mexican cushaws and wild squash, however, and the possible extent of such crossing in garden varieties is not clear. Hand-pollination should probably be used to ensure absolute purity when *C. mixta* and *C. moschata* are grown in close proximity.

Cucurbita ficifolia

C. ficifolia is also known as Malabar Gourd, Chilacayote or Fig-Leaved Gourd. Varieties that belong to *C. ficifolia* have very flat, black or gray seeds. The plant produces an abundant number of female flowers before any males, and takes a very long season to produce fruit. The fruits have greenish cream mottled skin and keep for three years. The fruit's flesh is crisp and used in Mexico for making candy. *C. ficifolia* is best grown as a perennial in frost free regions.

REGIONAL GROWING RECOMMENDATIONS

Northeast: *Cucurbita ficifolia* cannot be grown in this region.

Mid-Atlantic: *C. ficifolia* can be direct seeded from April 15 to May 1, or started in a greenhouse about March 1-15 and transplanted into the garden about April 15 to May 1.

Southeast/Gulf Coast: *C. ficifolia* can be direct seeded from April 15 to May 10. The plants like full sun and are drought tolerant.

Upper Midwest: *C. ficifolia* can be started in a greenhouse about April 15 and transplanted May 10. In this region, it is very marginal to get mature fruits.

Southwest: *C. ficifolia* can be direct seeded from March 15 to May 15.

Central West Coast: *C. ficifolia* can be direct seeded from April 15 to May 15.

Maritime Northwest: *C. ficifolia* cannot be grown in this region.

Cucurbita foetidissima

C. foetidissima is also known as Calabazilla or Buffalo Gourd. Varieties of *C. foetidissima* have light gray, arrowhead-shaped leaves that emit a disagreeable odor when brushed. The 4" diameter fruits are not eaten, but the seeds are pressed as a source for oil. *C. foetidissima* is best grown as a perennial in frost free regions.

REGIONAL GROWING RECOMMENDATIONS

Northeast: *Cucurbita foetidissima* cannot be grown in this region.

Mid-Atlantic: *C. foetidissima* can be direct seeded from about April 15 to May 1, or started in a greenhouse March 1-15 and transplanted into the garden April 15 to May 1. The plants like full sun and average water.

Southeast/Gulf Coast: *C. foetidissima* can be direct seeded from April 15 to May 10. The plants like full sun. We always grow this crop on a fence or trellis.

Upper Midwest: *C. foetidissima* should be started in a greenhouse about April 1 and transplant into the garden about May 1. The plants like full sun and are drought tolerant. Marginal seed production in this region.

Southwest: *C. foetidissima* can be direct seeded from March 15 to June 15. The plants like full sun and are drought tolerant.

Central West Coast: *C. foetidissima* can be direct seeded from April 15 to May 15 (can become perennial, resprouting each spring). The plants like full sun, are drought tolerant, and overwinter in the garden with no special care.

Maritime Northwest: *C. foetidissima* cannot be grown in this region.

POLLINATION, CROSSING AND ISOLATION

All squash varieties are outbreeding, insect-pollinated plants (see the discussion of Population Sizes in Section I). Squashes are divided into six different species: *Cucurbita maxima*, *C. mixta*, *C. moschata*, *C. pepo*, *C. ficifolia* and *C. foetidissima*. Different varieties within the same species will cross easily, but crossing does not occur between the different species. Therefore, one variety from each of the six different species (one from each group listed above) can be grown together without cross-pollination problems. Different varieties within the same species must be separated by 1/2 mile or must be hand-pollinated, so be sure to check neighbors' gardens for varieties that could ruin your isolated plantings.

Squash is easy to hand-pollinate even for the beginner, because the blossoms are large and easy to identify. The female blossom sits atop a tiny immature squash, while the male blossom is just attached to a long, straight stem. In the early evening, identify male and female flowers that will open the following morning unless sealed shut. Such blossoms will begin to show a yellow flush of color, especially along their seams, and the different sections of the flower may start to just barely break open at the tip. Use 3/4" masking tape to securely tape the tips of the blossoms shut. Morning dew will sometimes cause cheap brands of tape to burst open, so be sure to select an extra sticky brand.

To ensure a greater amount of genetic diversity, choose male and female blossoms from different plants of the same variety. If there is any question about the seed's purity, however, male and female blossoms on the same plant should be used.

Wait until after the dew dries the next morning, because the female flower will need to be retaped after being hand-pollinated, and the wet tape doesn't stick very well. Locate the male and female flowers that were taped shut the previous evening. Pick the male flower including a good-sized chunk of its stem which will be used as a handle. Remove the tape from the male flower and carefully tear off all of its petals. Some gardeners hold the male flower between their teeth, so that both hands are free to untape the female flower. Next, carefully tear off just the tip of the female flower including the tape. Then, as if in slow motion, the female flower will open wide.

Holding the petal-less male flower by its stem like a brush, swab the pollen-covered anthers of the male flower onto each of the sections of the stigma of the female flower. The success rate of hand-pollinations can be increased by using two or more male flowers on each female flower. If more than one male flower is to be used, however, be sure to prepare all of the male flowers before removing the tape from the female flower. That way there will be less chance of bees contaminating the female flower while it is exposed.

After the pollination process is complete, retape the female flower and mark the fruit's stem with a marker. Sometimes an especially brittle flower will split along one of the large seams that run from the tip of the flower to the tiny fruit. If that should happen, keep taping closer and closer to the fruit until the hole along the seam is covered. The entire blossom can be covered with tape and the technique will still work. Be careful, however, not to damage the small, sensitive neck between the tiny fruit and the base of the flower, which will cause the fruit to abort.

In some areas of the United States, bumblebees and some solitary bees will chew through the sides of taped flowers to gain access to the pollen, which causes crossing even though the flower was hand-pollinated. If this becomes a recurring problem, female flowers can be covered with 2" wide masking tape. The tape should form a band around the entire flower. Petals from the male flowers used during the pollination process can also be draped over the top of the taped female blossoms. The petals will wilt down quickly over the female flowers, forming a double or triple layer that is more difficult for the bees to chew through.

SEED PRODUCTION, HARVEST AND PROCESSING

Winter squash or pumpkins used for seed saving must be grown until fully mature. Hand-pollinated summer squashes must be left to grow until quite large

with hard-shelled rinds that cannot be dented by a fingernail. Squash have a greater number of viable seeds when cut from the vine and left to sit for three weeks or longer. This is easily accomplished with winter squash, which are usually stored for 3-6 months before being used. When hand-pollinated squash are stored along with the main crop which are to be eaten, the rinds of ones being saved for seed can be clearly marked with an indelible marking pen. Most summer squash will not keep beyond two months. Their seed should be removed three weeks or longer after harvest.

Winter squash are often cut or chopped open to remove the seeds and prepare the flesh for eating. Summer squash that are ready for seed saving can be smashed open with an ax or shovel. Be sure to exercise caution, however, because the squash can easily roll out from under the smashing implement. Gather any scattered seeds and pick out those seeds still attached to the flesh. Rinse the seeds in a colander under a stream of water and remove any debris. If squash flesh remains attached to the seeds, rub the seeds in a wire strainer under running water to loosen it. Drain the seeds and dry as with other Cucurbitaceae.

GROWING SQUASH FROM SEED

Squash species are heat-loving vines, usually grown as annuals. *Cucurbita pepo* varieties, used as either summer or winter squash, produce fruits in the shortest amount of time. *Cucurbita maxima* varieties tend to be the most susceptible to insects, especially squash bugs. *C. mixta* and *C. moschata* need longer and hotter seasons than either *C. pepo* or *C. maxima*. Some *C. mixta* varieties exhibit daylength sensitivity, setting fruits after days shorten. *C. ficifolia* produces an abundant number of female flowers before any male flowers appear, and takes a very long season to produce fruit. *C. ficifolia* and *C. foetidissima* are best grown as perennial plants in frost free regions.

Most squash plants are direct seeded, covering the seeds with 1" of soil. The optimum seed germination temperature is 70° F. with germination usually occurring in 5-10 days. Plants may be started in greenhouses, but care must be taken to set the plants out as soon as 1-2 sets of true leaves have developed. Plants allowed to become pot bound do not set out well. Plant or set out in full sun when the ground is thoroughly warmed. The plants should be thinned to 18-30" for food production or breeding purposes.

SEED STATISTICS

Squash seeds will remain viable for six years when

stored in cool, dry, dark conditions. Members of the Seed Savers Exchange annually offer about 289 varieties of squash, and the *Garden Seed Inventory* lists sources for 343 varieties that are available from commercial seed companies. There are approximately 176-300 seeds per ounce (6-10 per gram or 2,800-4,800 per pound), depending on the variety. Federal Germination Standard for commercially seed is 75%.

Lagenaria siceraria - Hard-Shelled Gourd

Gourds have played a major role in the daily life of many cultures around the world. Although eaten in their immature stages, gourds have more importantly been made into bottles, bowls, ladles, churns, spoons, pipes, musical instruments, penis sheaths and planting tools. Since modern cultures seldom grow their own bowls, many of the hard-shelled gourds are becoming endangered.

Few American seed companies offer varieties of hard-shelled gourds. Members of the Seed Savers Exchange, however, do make available a rich assortment of gourds. The names of just a few varieties currently being offered include African Warty, African Kettle, Alligator, Bali Sugar Trough, Bushel Basket, Cannon Ball, Hawaiian Mask, Indonesian Water Bottle, Long Handled Dipper, Peyote Ceremonial, Tobacco, Box, Trough, Water Jug, and the ancient-looking Dinosaur gourd.

BOTANICAL CLASSIFICATION

Hard-shelled gourds belong to the genus *Lagenaria* and the species *siceraria*. Different varieties of *L. siceraria* do not cross with any other Cucurbitaceae. The small, multicolored, striped and warted gourds seen in grocery stores around Halloween and Thanksgiving belong to *Cucurbita pepo* and are discussed in the section on squash.

L. siceraria vines are rampant growers and are often trellised or tied along a fence to save space. The long-necked bottle or dipper gourds develop perfectly straight necks when hanging from a trellis. The necks of such gourds often curve or curl when the plants are grown on the ground.

Some *L. siceraria* varieties are eaten like summer squash when very young. Various Italian varieties of Cucuzzi, also known as Longissima, are prized for their flavor and texture when immature. Most varieties of *L. siceraria*, however, are grown for their mature shell. Many hard-shelled gourds contain toxic amounts of bitter compounds called cucurbitacins that must be leached from the dry shells before the gourds are used for food storage containers. The American Gourd Society (P.O. Box 274, Mt. Gilead, OH 43338, website www.americangourdsociety.org) offers pamphlets on gourd curing, carving, preservation and use, as well as information about additional seed sources.

POLLINATION, CROSSING AND ISOLATION

Hard-shelled gourds are outbreeding plants (see also the discussion of Population Size in Section I). *Lagenaria siceraria* flowers are large, white and as thin as tissue paper. The female blossoms are attached to a tiny, immature gourd and are easily identified. Male blossoms have only a straight stem. The flowers open in the late afternoon or early evening, remain open during the night, and are pollinated primarily by crepuscular insects in the tropics. In more temperate zones, cucumber beetles and honeybees visit the flowers repeatedly while they are open in the late afternoon.

Although *L. siceraria* will not cross with any other Cucurbitaceae, different varieties within the species can easily be crossed by insects. An isolation distance of 1/4 to 1/2 mile is recommended. When more than one variety is grown in close proximity, hand-pollination is necessary. During the morning, male and female flowers that will open that evening are located and taped shut. The hand-pollination process takes place that same evening, when the blossoms would normally be opening.

Except for the reversal of the sessions, the hand-pollination technique for *L. siceraria* is the same as for squash. Carefully pick the male flower and remove the tape and white flower petals. Gently untape the female flower and rub the pollen from the anthers of the male flower onto the stigma of the female flower. Retape the female flower and mark its stem.

SEED PRODUCTION, HARVEST AND PROCESSING

All hard-shelled gourds must be grown to full maturity, which is best determined by examining the stem of the fruit. A gourd is ready for harvest when the fruit's stem changes from green to brown or yellow. Although mature, gourds at this stage still contain large amounts of water and should be placed in a cool, dry location with good ventilation until completely dry. During this drying period, the shell and the contents of the gourd dry so completely that the seeds will rattle when the gourd is shaken vigorously.

The seeds can be removed from mature gourds

that are not completely dry, if the gourd's shell is not going to be used for other purposes. Fermentation is not necessary, and the seeds only need to be separated from the pulp and air-dried. The pulp of *L. siceraria* can be quite irritating. Wet pulp can cause minor cuts to become swollen and painful, and the dust from dry pulp can irritate the nose and respiratory tract.

To preserve the gourd for use or display, drill or cut a small opening in the stem or blossom end and remove the seeds through that opening. Gourds that will be made into bowls or storage vessels can be cut in half around the middle, or a lid can be cut from the top portion. Shake the seeds out of the gourd and pull them free of any fiber or dry flesh. Seeds that snap in half when folded are sufficiently dry for storage. Seeds that bend instead of breaking need further drying.

SEED STATISTICS

Gourd seeds do not require any further treatment and will remain viable for six years when stored in cool, dry, dark conditions. Members of the Seed Savers Exchange annually offer about 89 varieties of gourds, and the *Garden Seed Inventory* lists sources for 24 varieties that are available from commercial seed companies. There are approximately 140 seeds per ounce (5 per gram or 2,240 per pound), depending on the variety. Federal Germination Standard for commercially sold gourd seed is 75%.

GROWING HARD-SHELLED GOURDS FROM SEED

Hard-shelled gourds are heat-loving, rampant vines, requiring a very long growing season. Gourds are usually direct seeded. Plants may be started in greenhouses, but care must be taken to set the plants out as soon as 1-2 sets of true leaves have developed. Plants that are allowed to become pot bound do not transplant well. Either plant or set out in full sun, covering the seeds with 1" of soil. Gourd seed germinates at temperatures ranging from 75-90° F. with germination usually occurring in 10-15 days. "Scarifying" (nicking the seeds just prior to planting) will improve germination. Plant or set out in full sun. The plants should be thinned to 36-72", depending on the variety. Small-fruited varieties may be trellised to conserve garden space.

REGIONAL GROWING RECOMMENDATIONS

Northeast: Hard-shelled gourds cannot be grown in this region.

Mid-Atlantic: Hard-shelled gourds can be direct seeded from April 15 to June 1, or started in a greenhouse March 1 to April 15 and transplanted into the garden April 15 to June 1. The plants like full sun and average water.

Southeast/Gulf Coast: Hard-shelled gourds can be direct seeded from April 15 to May 15. The plants like full sun and average water.

Upper Midwest: Hard-shelled gourds can be direct seeded up to June 1, but are best started in a greenhouse about May 10 and transplanted into the garden about May 30. The plants like full sun.

Southwest: Hard-shelled gourds can be direct seeded from March 15 to June 10. The plants like full sun and average water.

Central West Coast: Hard-shelled gourds can be direct seeded about April 15, or started in a greenhouse about March 1 and transplanted into the garden about April 15. The plants like full sun and average water.

Maritime Northwest: Hard-shelled gourds cannot be grown in this region.

Sechium edule - Chayote (Vegetable Pear)

Chayote is grown in many tropical regions throughout the world. The first green shoots are harvested in the spring when 6-8" long and are eaten like asparagus. The leaves are used for animal fodder, the vines are woven into rope, and the mature roots are prepared like potatoes. Chayote fruits are seasoned, spiced or sweetened and are eaten in soups, salads, main courses, breakfast foods, custards and desserts.

In 1901 the USDA printed a bulletin entitled *The Chayote. A Tropical Vegetable* by O. F. Cook, Special Agent for Tropical Agriculture. The bulletin included black and white pictures of twelve different varieties of chayote that were being grown in Mexico, Central America and on various tropical islands. Mr. Cook recommended chayote as a useful and desirable crop for farmers in the southern United States. The bulletin also states that chayotes were in great demand in France in 1888 as a substitute for artichoke hearts, and that hats made from chayote vines were fashionable in Paris during the summer of 1900.

Chayote is an excellent perennial plant for large home gardens in regions of the United States where the ground does not freeze. Although frost will kill the plants to the ground, the roots will resprout each spring. Chayote can be grown as an annual in northern climates when started in a greenhouse 2-3 months before the last frost date. The roots can also be dug after the first frost and stored over the winter in moist sawdust at temperatures slightly above freezing.

BOTANICAL CLASSIFICATION

Chayote belongs to the genus *Sechium* and the species *edule*. *S. edule* does not cross with any other Cucurbitaceae. Of the varieties listed in Mr. Cook's article, only the one with spineless, green, pear-shaped fruits is available in the United States. Other documented varieties include fruits that were round, pear-shaped, spineless, spiny, white, and green. The white varieties were described as more tender than the thicker skinned green types, but did not store as long and were easily bruised. The spines on some wild varieties are capable of inflicting serious cuts during harvest. Chayote fruits are also known by such names as christophine, chuchu, mirliton and vegetable pear.

POLLINATION, CROSSING AND ISOLATION

Chayote, an outbreeding plant, produces both male and female flowers on the same plant and is pollinated by insects. Some books suggest that two plants must be grown to provide for adequate pollination, but neither reduced set nor self-incompatibility was observed in solitary plantings of the pear-shaped, spineless, green variety.

Chayote varieties can be cross-pollinated by insects. Bees are strongly attracted to the flowers, which yield abundant nectar and appear late in the season. If more than one variety of chayote is grown, isolation of one mile is necessary to ensure absolute purity. Hand-pollination is possible, but the flowers are very small and difficult to identify and to tape.

SEED PRODUCTION, HARVEST AND PROCESSING

Each chayote contains a single seed that is enclosed within the fruit and cannot be separated from the flesh. Fully mature fruits, which can be recognized by their tough-looking skins, should be harvested for future plantings. The fruit should be wrapped individually in newspaper and stored in boxes, but never more than three fruits deep. A dark, cool area with a constant temperature of 35-40° F. will provide the best storage conditions. Less mature fruits are stored the same way and can be eaten throughout the fall and winter. The entire sprouted fruit is planted out the next spring with the large end buried just below the soil's surface.

SEED STATISTICS

Members of the Seed Savers Exchange are not currently offering chayote, but the *Garden Seed Inventory* lists four commercial sources.

GROWING CHAYOTE

Chayote is a perennial vine that requires a 9-10 month frost free season. The rampant vines require trellising and frequent pruning. Flowering occurs in the fall when days reach 12 hours in length. Fruits set quickly thereafter and may be eaten at any size. Fruits used for sprouting take a full 10 months to develop. The roots do not tolerate freezing ground, but may be dug, stored and set out in the spring. (However convenient this sounds, I have yet to find anyone who has successfully accomplished the task.) Plant fruits or set out roots in full sun on a very large and substantial trellis. Cover fruits used for seed just below the soil level. Sprouts should remain above ground. Vines are capable of covering 160 square feet of trellis in a season. Pruning does reduce yields. The plants should be spaced 48-60" apart.

REGIONAL GROWING RECOMMENDATIONS

Northeast: Chayote cannot be grown in this region.

Mid-Atlantic: Chayote can be direct seeded about April 15, or started in a greenhouse about February 1 and transplanted into the garden about April 15. Likes full sun and average water. Cut the plants back after harvest and mulch to protect from frost damage.

Southeast/Gulf Coast: The whole fruit of chayote can be planted from April 1 to May 15. Trellising improves production.

Upper Midwest: Chayote cannot be grown in this region.

Southwest: Chayote should be mulched during summer heat in low desert areas.

Central West Coast: Chayote should be started in a greenhouse from January to March and transplanted into the garden April to May. The plants become perennial, getting bigger and bigger each year, and like full sun and average water. Chayote plants overwinter in the garden with no special care, but in some areas the plants require mulching after harvest to protect new shoots in the spring.

Maritime Northwest: Chayote cannot be grown in this region.

Cucurbitaceae

Benincasa hispida
Wax Gourd (Winter Melon)

Wax gourd, also known as winter melon, is an important food crop in India and China. Seed is available in the United States under a variety of names including ash gourd, Chinese preserving melon, Chinese watermelon, gourd melon, tallow gourd and white pumpkin. At full maturity the fruits can weigh 100 pounds with a diameter of 10" and will keep for 12-18 months. The dark green skin is thin, hard and waxy. The flesh is very bland and releases a lot of water when cooked. Wax gourd is most famous as the main ingredient in winter melon pond soup, or dong gwa jong. The soup, which includes spiced meats, mushrooms, chunks of seeded winter melon and many spices, is traditionally served in the carved rind of the melon. In India, the fruits of wax gourd are cooked with sugar and made into a sweetmeat called heshim.

Fresh juice collected from the vines of the plants is said to be a beneficial treatment for nervous disorders and to expel tapeworms. Wax scraped from the melon skin has been used to make candles.

Fuzzy melon, a smaller variety of *Benincasa hispida*, is slightly larger than a cucumber and is covered with short white hairs. Fuzzy melon, which is also known as tseet gwa, has firmer flesh than wax gourd. Tseet gwa is used by Cantonese cooks to make a family-size version of winter melon soup, and is often used as a squash-like vegetable in stir-fry dishes. The fruits can also be used in place of summer squash in any recipe.

POLLINATION, CROSSING AND ISOLATION

Wax gourd (winter melon) is an outbreeding plant. All varieties of fuzzy melon and wax gourd will cross with one another, but will not cross with any other Cucurbitaceae. Isolation of 1/2 mile or hand-pollination will maintain seed purity.

SEED STATISTICS

Members of the Seed Savers Exchange offer two types of winter melon (wax gourd), but the *Garden Seed Inventory* does not list any commercial sources. There are 300 seeds per ounce (10 per gram or 4,800 per pound), depending on the variety. Federal Germination Standard for commercially sold wax gourd seed is 70%.

GROWING WAX GOURD FROM SEED

Wax gourd (winter melon) is an annual, heat-loving vine that can be grown wherever winter squash is successful. Winter melon is usually direct seeded, covering the seeds .5" deep. The seeds germinate at temperatures from 70-85° F. with germination occurring in 6-10 days. Plant in full sun. The plants should be thinned to 24-36" for both food and seed production.

REGIONAL GROWING RECOMMENDATIONS

Northeast: *Benincasa hispida* is not commonly grown in this region.

Mid-Atlantic: *B. hispida* can be direct seeded from April 15 to May 15, or started in a greenhouse March 1 and transplanted into the garden from April 15 to May 15. The plants like full sun and average water.

Southeast/Gulf Coast: *B. hispida* can be direct seeded from April 15 to May 20. The plants like full sun and are drought tolerant.

Upper Midwest: *B. hispida* can be started in a greenhouse April 1 and transplanted May 15. Plants need a very long season. This is a marginal crop here.

Southwest: Direct seeded March 15 to May 15.

Central West Coast: *B. hispida* can be direct seeded from April 15 to May 30.

Maritime Northwest: *B. hispida* can be direct seeded about June 1, or started in a greenhouse May 1 and transplanted into the garden June 1. It is too cool for this crop in some areas of the Maritime Northwest.

Cucumis anguria
West Indian Gherkin (Burr Cucumber)

Many gardeners have planted West Indian gherkin mistakenly thinking it was a cucumber used for pickle making. Gherkin pickles are made from many different varieties of immature cucumbers processed in a brine and sweet syrup. Despite their name, gherkin pickles have nothing to do with West Indian gherkin.

The decorative vines of West Indian gherkin produce spiny, green, seedy, 1-2" diameter fruits. The plant is also referred to as gooseberry gourd, goarseberry gourd and burr cucumber. Seeds are very difficult to secure and are not available from commercial seed companies in the United States.

Very young fruits of *Cucumis anguria* are edible when the spines are soft and the seeds are immature. Fully ripe fruits of West Indian gherkin will split open exposing the seeds.

POLLINATION, CROSSING AND ISOLATION

West Indian gherkin is an outbreeding plant that relies on insects for pollination and will not cross with any other members of the Cucurbitaceae family. Isolation of 1/4 mile or hand-pollination will prevent crossing between varieties.

SEED STATISTICS

Several members of the Seed Savers Exchange offer West Indian gherkin, but the *Garden Seed Inventory* does not list any commercial sources. Federal Germination Standard for commercially sold seed is 80%.

GROWING WEST INDIAN GHERKIN FROM SEED

West Indian gherkin is an annual vine crop that can be grown to seed anywhere cucumbers are successful. West Indian gherkin is usually direct seeded, covering the seeds .25" deep. The seed germinates at temperatures ranging from 72-85° F. with germination usually occurring in 7-10 days. The plants like full sun, may be trellised, and should be thinned to 12" for both food and seed production.

REGIONAL GROWING RECOMMENDATIONS

Northeast: West Indian gherkin is not commonly grown in this region.

Mid-Atlantic: West Indian gherkin isdirect seeded April 15 or August 1, or started in a greenhouse March 1 or June 15 and transplanted April 15 or August 1.

Southeast/Gulf Coast: West Indian gherkin can be direct seeded April 1 to May 15. We use floating row covers to protect against cucumber beetles.

Upper Midwest: West Indian gherkin can be direct seeded from May 15 to July 1.

Southwest: West Indian gherkin can be direct seeded from March 15 to June 15.

Central West Coast: West Indian gherkin can be direct seeded from April 15 to June 15.

Maritime Northwest: West Indian gherkin is not commonly grown in this region.

—————— *Cyclanthera pedata* ——————
Caihua (Achoecha)

Caihua is a perennial, daylength sensitive vine that grows in cool, frost free areas of the Andes. Caihua fruits are eaten in Peru and Bolivia where the plants are grown as cultivated weeds. The 10' plants have small yellow or white flowers and produce 2" fruits with scattered prickles. Caihua is not well adapted to culture in any region of the United States. The plant can be greenhouse grown, but has not produced fruits. Caihua is offered by members of Seed Savers Exchange. *C. pedata* does not cross with any other Cucurbitaceae species.

REGIONAL GROWING RECOMMENDATIONS

Northeast: Caihua cannot be grown in this region.

Mid-Atlantic: Caihua is not commonly grown in this region.

Southeast/Gulf Coast: Caihua is not commonly grown in this region.

Upper Midwest: Caihua can be started in a greenhouse about April 10 and transplanted into the garden about May 15. The plants like full sun and average water. It is difficult but possible to produce mature seed in this region.

Southwest: Caihua is not commonly grown in this region.

Central West Coast: Caihua can be started in a greenhouse about February 1 and transplanted into gallon buckets about April 15. The plants like full sun and average water. The plants are daylength sensitive, so try to get blooming during short spring days in order to produce mature seed. However, full blooming may not result in mature seed.

Maritime Northwest: Caihua cannot be grown in this region.

—————— *Luffa acutangula* ——————
Angled Luffa

Angled luffa, grown extensively in Asia, is sometimes referred to as Chinese okra or ridged gourd. The vine is delicate and has night-blooming yellow flowers. The seeds are black with a pitted surface and lack a rim on the margin. A single generic variety is sold in the United States, although several varieties are available in Asia. The immature fruits are eaten in curries throughout India and are used like summer squash in Asia. Mature dry fruits can be prepared for use like sponges. Although the ridges make it more difficult to scrape the dry flesh off of the fibrous core, the sponges are softer than those from *L. aegyptiaca*.

Luffa is an outbreeding plant and it has generally been thought that *L. acutangula* does not cross with *L. aegyptiaca*. However, Charles Heiser, a noted authority on gourds, reports that a hybrid can be obtained when the pollen of *L. aegyptiaca* is applied to the stigmas of *L. acutangula*. The resulting seed will produce vigorous hybrid plants with good fruit set, but the fruits do not contain viable seed. Luffa seeds are saved like those of hard-shelled gourds.

Luffa aegyptiaca
Smooth Luffa

The immature fruits of smooth luffa can be eaten but are most often grown for the fibrous core inside the mature gourds. Different varieties of smooth luffa sponge are available in the United States and will cross with one another. Hand-pollination or isolation of 1/2 mile is recommended for complete seed purity. Black (or occasionally white) *L. aegyptiaca* seed is smooth with a distinctive rim or groove around the margin and lacks the pitting of *L. acutangula.* Smooth luffa preparation is discussed in a pamphlet from The Gourd Society (see *Lagenaria siceraria* for the organization's address). Luffa seeds are saved like hard-shelled gourds.

SEED STATISTICS

Members of the Seed Savers Exchange annually offer 8 varieties of luffa, and the *Garden Seed Inventory* lists sources for 5 varieties available from commercial seed companies. There are approximately 300 seeds per ounce (10 per gram or 4,800 per pound), depending on the variety. Federal Germination Standard is 75% for both angled luffa and smooth luffa.

GROWING ANGLED LUFFA
AND SMOOTH LUFFA FROM SEED

Luffa is an annual, heat-loving vine that can be grown wherever melons are successful. Luffa plants are usually direct seeded. The seedlings are weak and may be greenhouse started and set out when there are two sets of true leaves. The seed germinates from 70-80° F. with germination occurring in 10-12 days. Either plant or set out in full sun and in thoroughly warmed soil. The plants should be thinned to 18" for both food and seed production, and are usually trellised.

REGIONAL GROWING RECOMMENDATIONS

Northeast: Angled luffa and smooth luffa are not commonly grown in this region.

Mid-Atlantic: Both angled luffa and smooth luffa can be direct seeded from April 15 to June 1, or started in a greenhouse March 1 to April 15 and transplanted into the garden April 15 to June 1. The plants like full sun and average water.

Southeast/Gulf Coast: Angled luffa and smooth luffa can be direct seeded from April 15 to May 15. Trellising is needed for straight fruits.

Upper Midwest: Angled luffa and smooth luffa can be started in a greenhouse about May 1 and transplant into the garden about May 25. The plants likes full sun and average water. Trellis after germination.

Southwest: Angled luffa and smooth luffa can be direct seeded from March 15 to June 15. The plants like full sun and average water.

Central West Coast: Angled luffa and smooth luffa can be direct seeded about April 15.

Maritime Northwest: Angled luffa and smooth luffa can be direct seeded about June 1, or started in a greenhouse about May 1 and transplanted about June 1.

Momordica balsamina
Balsam Apple

Balsam apple is not usually used for food, but is probably edible if prepared like balsam pear. Historically, the fruits have been used to make a salve said to cure skin rashes. At maturity the fruits split open exposing red, fleshy seed capsules. Balsam apple does not cross with balsam pear or with any other Cucurbitaceae family member. Both balsam apple and balsam pear (bitter melon) are outbreeding plants.

Momordica charantia
Balsam Pear (Bitter Melon)

Balsam pear is also known as bitter melon in the United States and by the Cantonese name foo gwa or fu kwa. The fruits are used in Asia for Indian curry, Ceylonese pickles, Indonesian salads and Cantonese stir-fry dishes. The melons have warty skins, grow 4-10" long, and are quite bitter and firm in their immature stages. Fully ripe melons turn orange and soft. Cantonese cooks parboil immature balsam pears in several changes of water before using in recipes, which removes much of the bitterness. Balsam pear shoots and leaves can be eaten as greens. Insects can cross-pollinate different varieties of balsam pear, so isolation or hand-pollination is required to ensure seed purity. Balsam pear does not cross with balsam apple or any Cucurbitaceae species.

SEED STATISTICS

Several kinds of balsam apple and balsam pear (bitter melon) are offered by members of the Seed Savers Exchange, and are available in the *Garden Seed Inventory*. There are 224 seeds per ounce (8 per gram or 3,600 per pound), depending on the variety. Federal Germination Standard for commercial seed is 75%.

GROWING BALSAM APPLE AND BALSAM PEAR (BITTER MELON) FROM SEED

Balsam apple and bitter melon are heat-loving, annual vines that can be grown to maturity anywhere melons are successful. "Scarifying" (gently nicking the seedcoats) will greatly enhance both the rate and speed of germination. Balsam apple and bitter melon are usually direct seeded. They may be greenhouse started, but care needs to be given to setting them out as soon as they have two sets of true leaves. The seeds should be covered .5" deep. The seed germinates at temperatures ranging from 75-85° F. with germination usually occurring in 7-10 days. Plant or set out in full sun. Trellis or cage support will produce clean, easy-to-find fruits. The plants should be thinned to 12" apart for both food and seed production.

REGIONAL GROWING RECOMMENDATIONS

Northeast: Balsam apple and balsam pear (bitter melon) cannot be grown in this region.

Mid-Atlantic: Balsam apple and balsam pear can both be direct seeded from April 15 to June 1, or started in a greenhouse March 1 to April 15 and transplanted into the garden April 15 to June 1. The plants like full sun and average water.

Southeast/Gulf Coast: Balsam apple and balsam pear can be direct seeded April 15 to May 15. The plants like full sun and average water. We trellis both.

Upper Midwest: Balsam apple and balsam pear can both be started in a greenhouse about May 1 and transplanted about May 20. The plants likes full sun and should be trellised when just beginning to vine.

Southwest: Balsam apple and balsam pear can both be direct seeded from March 15 to June 15. The plants like full sun and average water.

Central West Coast: Balsam apple and balsam pear can both be direct seeded from about April 15 to May 30. Both plants like full sun and average water.

Maritime Northwest: Balsam apple and balsam pear can be direct seeded about June 1, or started in a greenhouse about May 1 and transplanted about June 1. The plants like full sun and average water.

Sicana odorifera
Cassabanana

Cassabanana is a perennial vine commonly found growing wild in the Gulf States of America. The orange cylindrical 24" fruits have a pleasing odor and are edible and somewhat sweet. The seeds are not commercially available, and different varieties are not documented. The plants produce flowers in response to shortening days and are very frost-sensitive. The large vines are inappropriate in greenhouses and will not produce fruit in areas with winter temperatures below 35° F. Try starting the plants in a greenhouse in February, then transplant into gallon containers about April 15. Because of problems with daylength sensitivity, try to get plants large enough to flower in spring for seed. Successful outdoor production of cassabanana seed is limited to parts of Florida and other totally frost free, tropical climates.

Trichosanthes anguina
Serpent Gourd

Serpent gourd, also known as club gourd or snake cucumber or viper gourd, is about 36" long and 4" in diameter. The fruits are commonly grown in India and eaten in curries. The plants are also found in Central America where the fruits are used like squash. Serpent gourd requires a long growing season and is successful in climates where hard-shelled gourds will mature. Serpent gourd is an outbreeding plant. *T. anguina* will not cross with members of the *Lagenaria* genera or with any other members of the Cucurbitaceae family. Different varieties of serpent gourd will cross, so hand-pollination or 1/4 mile isolation is required to ensure purity.

SOURCES

Members of the Seed Savers Exchange offer serpent gourd, and it is available from four commercial companies listed in the *Garden Seed Inventory*. There are 14,430 seeds per ounce (510 per gram or 230,000 per pound), depending on the variety. Federal Germination Standard for commercially sold seed is 70%.

GROWING SERPENT GOURD FROM SEED

Serpent gourd is a perennial, heat-loving vine that can be grown as an annual. The plants exhibit daylength sensitivity, require a long growing season and are successful where hard shelled gourds or very long season winter squash can be grown to maturity. The plants are usually direct seeded, covering the seeds .75" deep, but can be started in a greenhouse from February 1 to March 15 and transplanted into the garden about April 15. The seed germinates at temperatures from 80-85° F. with germination occurring in 7-10 days. Plant in full sun when the ground is thoroughly warmed and the weather is settled. The plants should be thinned to 24" for both food and seed production. Trellis support is necessary for the long fruits.

Vegetables in the Leguminosae family rank second only to grains as the most important source of food for mankind. Leguminosae have been cultivated for over 6,000 years. Various species are thought to have originated in Africa, China, India, Indochina, Europe and South America. Grains and legumes, when eaten together, provide all of the essential amino acids needed by man. In addition to their value as food crops, species within the Leguminosae family provide forage crops, timber, fiber, dyes, tannins, gum resins, insecticides, flavorings and flowers.

FAMILY TAXONOMY

The Leguminosae family includes more than 600 genera and 12,000 species. Only about 25 species are commonly used for food in the developed world. Pisum (peas) and Phaseolus (beans) are important both as green vegetables and as dry food crops. Many other Leguminosae species are grown primarily for their dry seeds. The leaves, shoots and roots of some species also are used as minor vegetables.

The Leguminosae family has been reclassified many times by various taxonomists. Faboideae, Caesalpinioideae and Mimosoideae are now considered subfamily names of no botanical standing. Between the time that *Hortus Second* and *Hortus Third* were published, substantial changes in classification occurred. Some of the genus and species names included here will definitely conflict with taxonomical texts published before *Hortus Third*.

Leguminosae in the Garden

Genus	Species	Common Name
Arachis	*hypogaea*	peanut
Cajanus	*cajun*	pigeon pea
Canavalia	*ensiformis*	jack bean
	gladiata	sword bean
Cicer	*arietinum*	garbanzo (chick pea)
Cyamopsis	*tetragonolobus*	cluster bean
Dolichos	*lablab*	hyacinth bean
Glycine	*max*	soybean
Lens	*culinaris*	lentil
Lupinus	*mutabilis*	tarwi
Pachyrhizus	*ahipa*	ahipa
	erosus	jicama (yam bean)
	tuberosus	potato bean
Phaseolus	*acutifolius var. latifolius*	tepary bean
	coccineus	runner bean
	lunatus	lima bean (butter bean)
	vulgaris	common bean
	vulgaris subsp. nunas	nunas (popping bean)
Pisum	*sativum*	garden pea, edible podded pea
Psophocarpus	*tetragonolobus*	winged bean, asparagus pea
Vicia	*faba*	fava bean (broad bean)
Vigna	*aconitifolia*	moth bean
	angularis	adzuki bean
	mungo	black gram
	radiata	mung bean (green gram)
	umbellata	rice bean
	unguiculata	cowpea
	unguiculata var. sesquipedalis	yard long bean (asparagus bean)

Facing Page: Various varieties of common beans (*Phaseolus vulgaris*), runner beans (*P. coccineus)* and lima beans (*P. lunatus).* (Photo by Ian Adams)

Some taxonomists classify legumes according to the position of the "cotyledons" (seed halves) during germination. "Hypogeal" refers to cotyledons that remain under the surface of the earth when the seedlings emerge. Peas, fava beans and runner beans all have hypogeal cotyledons. "Epigeal" cotyledons are pushed above the surface during emergence. *Phaseolus vulgaris*, common beans, have epigeal cotyledons.

POLLINATION CHARACTERISTICS AND TECHNIQUES

Leguminosae flowers are perfect, usually butterfly shaped and quite pretty. Leguminosae flowers are self-pollinating, but are occasionally crossed by honeybees and other insects. The flowers usually open between 7 a.m. and 8 a.m. and never close. The anthers "dehisce" (shed pollen) the evening before the flowers open. The pollen does not usually get transferred to the stigma until the flower is disturbed or tripped, usually by the wind. Insects, especially bees, also visit the flowers and can cause some amount of cross-pollination.

The extent of insect cross-pollination is hotly debated. The percentage of crossing is dependent upon the type of flower, the number of bees and other pollen carrying insects that are present, and whether or not there are other pollen and nectar sources in the area. Thus, it is possible to have considerable crossing in some populations in some areas, while other populations may show little or no crossing.

The distinctive seed coat patterns and the shapes of various Leguminosae seeds are sometimes used in attempts to prove the presence or absence of crossing. Leguminosae species also possess a wide variety of genetic characteristics that are not visible in their seeds, so statements about seed purity based solely on seed coat characteristics are not valid. Changes in seed coat color are an indication of crossed seed.

Always remember, even if crossing has occurred that is capable of showing up visibly, the crossed seeds that are harvested will look exactly like the parent seeds. After a flower is crossed, the seeds that are produced will carry that cross unseen within them. Evidence of crossing only becomes visibly apparent when another generation is grown out from those crossed seeds, first appearing as variations within the population of plants and then in the seeds that are harvested. Therefore, always save and label seeds from each year's crop in separate containers. If crossing becomes visible in the seeds, remember that the previous generation of seeds is not pure either, even though it appears to be. Throw away the generation

of seed that is visibly crossed, throw away the previous generation that is carrying the cross, and start over with seed from the generation before that, which should be pure.

Saving Leguminosae seed may require isolation, bagging or caging depending on the following factors. The larger the flower, the more likely it is to be visited by bumblebees and honeybees. When more desirable sources of pollen are available, bees are less likely to bother with legumes. Insects with smooth bodies are extremely inefficient at carrying pollen and are unlikely to cause crossing. Finally, insects that chew through the side of a blossom to extract nectar, do not usually come in contact with pollen and are very unlikely to cross-pollinate flowers.

In areas where other pollen sources are abundant, growers often claim that beans and other Leguminosae do not cross at all. However, growers in desert and mountain areas, where other pollen sources are scarce, have sometimes demonstrated up to 25% crossing. Many researchers claim that legumes are rarely visited by bees, but other studies have shown that various crops can be frequently visited by bees. Depending on the site and other available pollen sources, crossing can be rare or commonplace.

When attempting to prevent crossing, consider cages for bush plants and blossom bags for the taller varieties. Cages are easily made from spun polyester or window screen and need to be in place from first blossom until last. Blossom bagging, using spun polyester or a similar material, is more time-consuming. The bag must not block too much light or the flowers will not develop properly. Paper bags exclude far too much light and plastic bags trap too much heat and humidity.

Blossom bags must be tied carefully into place when the flowers begin to form along the "raceme" (flower cluster). The flowers can be examined through the bag, and the bag can be removed when the tiny pods begin to show. As the bags are removed, tag the racemes that were bagged so that those pods can be harvested separately for seed saving. String, tape or poultry bands all make good markers.

PLANT SELECTION

Always save seeds from healthy plants that appear true-to-type and bear heavily. Legumes should be rogued after the plants emerge, and during both flowering and pod formation. When the plants are about 6" tall, remove any that show off-type foliage or that are of an unusual height. Later, when the flowers appear, remove any plants with flowers that are not true-to-type for color, shape and number of flowers per node. Finally, remove any plants with newly formed pods that are not the typical shape, size and color. Seed should never be collected from plants that do not exhibit the characteristics of the variety.

GENERAL PRODUCTION AND PROCESSING TECHNIQUES

Legume seeds are usually left on the plant to dry, however sometimes fully mature but still green pods can be picked and then allowed to dry until crisp. Timing for green seed harvest is critical and should only be used as a last resort. A better method for green harvest, sometimes used when a nearly mature crop is about to be ruined by frost, is to pull the entire plant and hang it upside down in a warm area until the pods are dry. This method allows the seeds to continue to draw energy from the plant for several days, which results in higher quality seed. Depending on the climate, however, there can be some problems with pod damage from either extreme heat, freezing temperatures or molds.

Leguminosae seeds are enclosed in pods that split along both sides. Pods that are crispy dry can be broken open and the seeds will fall free. Although that sounds relatively simple, the actual process can be quite frustrating at times. The I-Tech Seed Winnower (see Section I) does an excellent job on many Leguminosae seeds, but its success depends on having the right-sized screen. If I-Tech or another seed cleaning device is unavailable, any of the following methods can be used.

Feed Sack Method - Place the dry pods in a feed sack or pillow case, and tape or tie the opening shut. Then either place the sack on the floor and jog in place on top of it, place the sack on a work bench and roll with a rolling pin, or hang the sack in a tree and beat it with a baseball bat or stick.

Tarp Method - Dump the dry pods onto a tarp and jog in place or beat with a flail.

Hand Method - Splitting the pods by hand and letting the seeds fall into a container is rather slow, but makes it easy to grade the seed quality and keep the seeds clean.

If the seeds need additional cleaning, place them in baskets or bowls. The seeds can be winnowed by pouring them from one basket to another during a stiff breeze. Vary the distance between the baskets according to the wind velocity. The chaff will be blown away as the seeds in the baskets become progressively cleaner. Sometimes unexpected wind gusts can blow seeds right out of the baskets. If the area is covered with a clean tarp or sheet, the seeds can be easily retrieved. Always be careful to avoid mixing, however, by flipping the tarp each time that a new variety is started. It is also possible to use a hair dryer or fan in place of the wind. Small fans from old vacuum cleaners or computers are very handy.

Leguminosae seeds are very susceptible to bean weevils, which can totally destroy stored seeds in a very short time. The adults lay eggs in the flowers or young pods. The larvae hatch inside the seeds and slowly eat their way out, leaving tiny round holes in the seed coat. The weevils usually emerge in the spring, mate and lay eggs in a new crop of blossoms. Weevils are almost always present in home-saved seeds and can destroy the seed if left unchecked.

To prevent weevil damage, freeze the dry seeds when they are ready for storage. If it isn't possible to get to threshing and winnowing right away, put the pods into an airtight container and freeze them. Weevil eggs are killed by three days at 0° F. Leguminosae seeds should be left in the freezer for five days, since all portions of the home freezer may not reach 0° F. When the seeds are removed from the freezer, let the airtight container set out overnight to reach room temperature. If the container is opened too soon, condensation will form on the cold seeds causing them to take on moisture. It is possible for the seeds to be recontaminated if left in an open container where weevils are present. If whole pods were frozen because you couldn't get to them right away, the seeds should be refrozen after being cleaned and winnowed.

Seeds that are not totally dry may be damaged by freezing, but a quick check can be made with a hammer. Put several seeds on a hard surface such as concrete and hit each one with the hammer. Seeds that shatter are dry enough for storage. Seeds that mash instead of shattering need further drying.

Most Leguminosae seeds maintain high germination rates over relatively long periods of time when stored under ideal conditions.

Arachis hypogaea - Peanut

Gardeners have long been intrigued by the peanut's unusual growth habit. The flower stalk produces a fertilized ovary called a "peg." The peg grows downward penetrating 1-2" into the soil where seedpods form.

A native of South America, the peanut is now grown throughout the temperate world. In the United States peanuts will grow to maturity as far north as New York State.

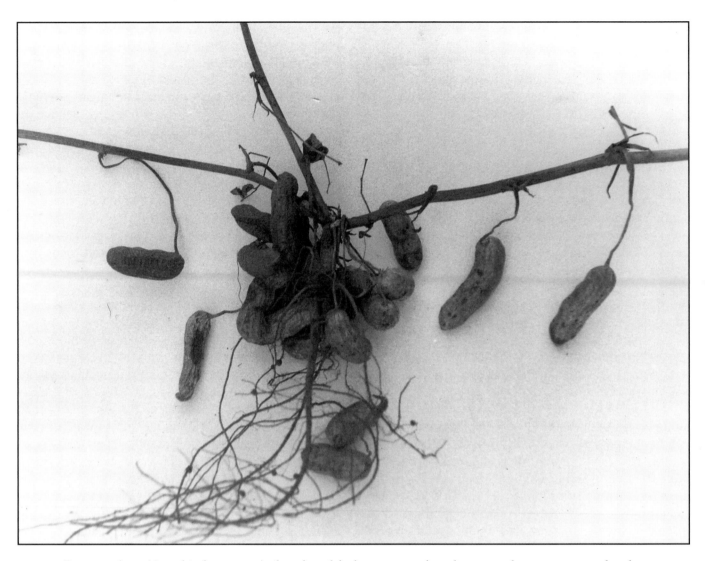

Peanut plant (*Arachis hypogaea*) showing dried pegs growing downward to mature seedpods.

In June 1925, George Washington Carver published "How to Grow the Peanut and 105 Ways of Preparing It for Human Consumption." His recipes included mock veal peanut cutlets, baked peanuts and rice, peanut stuffing, peanut salad, peanut bisque, peanut bread and even peanut confections. Dr. Carver did, however, leave out one item. The tender shoots and leaves of the peanut can be used as a green vegetable.

BOTANICAL CLASSIFICATION

Peanuts belong to the genus *Arachis* and the species *hypogaea*. We refer to *A. hypogaea* as nuts, but that is botanically incorrect. Peanuts are seeds which grow in seedpods under the ground.

There are two distinct types of peanuts grown in the United States. The Virginia types have true runners, require a long growing season, and usually have two seeds per pod. Their seeds require a long rest period between harvest and germination. The Span-

ish and Valencia types are more erect plants, need a shorter growing season, and require no rest period between harvest and germination. Spanish peanuts usually contain two seeds per pod, while Valencia types have three to four.

POLLINATION, CROSSING AND ISOLATION

Peanuts are inbreeding plants. Peanut flowers are perfect and self-pollinating. The flowers are very attractive to bees and other insects, which can cause up to 35% crossing between varieties. Several researchers have noted that the percentage of cross-pollination relates directly to the protrusion of the stigma out of the "keel" (lower petals of the flower). A few of the very old varieties have flowers which impede self-pollinating and require insect-pollination. Peanut varieties should be isolated by one mile to ensure seed purity. Varieties grown in closer proximity to one another should be caged to prevent any crossing.

SEED PRODUCTION, HARVEST AND PROCESSING

Peanuts are harvested when the plants turn yellow at the end of the season. The whole plant is pulled out of the ground with the peanuts still hanging on the pegs. The plants are left to cure in the garden or in a frost-protected enclosure for 2-3 weeks. After this drying period, the pods are stripped from the vines. Pods kept for seed should be thoroughly dry, but do not need any further treatment.

SEED STATISTICS

Peanuts remain viable for four years when stored at 35° F. and 5% moisture. When stored in gunny sacks in outbuildings, however, peanuts lose 50% germination over a period of 12 months. If also exposed to sunlight during storage, peanuts lose the power to germinate even more quickly. Members of the Seed Savers Exchange annually offer about 14 varieties of peanuts, and the *Garden Seed Inventory* lists sources for 20 varieties that are available from commercial seed companies. There are approximately 28-56 seed peanuts, weighed in the shell, per ounce (1-2 per gram or 450-900 per pound), depending on the variety. Federal Germination Standard for commercially sold peanut seed is 70%.

GROWING PEANUTS FROM SEED

Peanuts are annual, heat loving vines. Varieties are adapted to regions with at least 120 days of hot weather. Peanuts are usually direct seeded, covering the seeds 2" deep. They may also be greenhouse started to extend the season. The plants grow quickly, so take care not to start them indoors too early. Peanut seed germinates at 70-80° F. with germination usually occurring in 7-10 days. Plant or set out in full sun in fully warmed soil. Plants should be thinned to 10-12" for both food and seed production. Hilling is often used to provide a loose textured soil for successful penetration of the pegs.

REGIONAL GROWING RECOMMENDATIONS

Northeast: Peanuts can be direct seeded about May 20. The plants like full sun and average water. Only a very few varieties mature in this region.

Mid-Atlantic: Peanuts can be direct seeded from April 15 to May 15. The plants like full sun and average water, and prefer sandy soil. Dig the plants in September and air-dry. Rodents are always an issue, digging up seed.

Southeast/Gulf Coast: Peanuts can be direct seeded from April 15 to May 10. The plants like full sun and are drought tolerant.

Upper Midwest: Peanuts can be direct seeded about May 15. The plants like full sun and are drought tolerant.

Southwest: Peanuts can be direct seeded from March 15 to April 15. The plants like full sun and average water.

Central West Coast: Peanuts can be direct seeded about April 15. The plants like full sun and are drought tolerant.

Maritime Northwest: Peanuts cannot be grown in this region; we don't have enough heat units.

Cajanus cajun - Pigeon Peas

Pigeon peas are probably native to Africa and are commonly grown in India. Although not yet widely known in the United States, pigeon peas are very drought tolerant and adapt easily to a variety of climates. The plants are perennials, but are sensitive to frost.

Pigeon peas have a distinctively pleasant flavor. The young green pods are eaten like green peas and the immature shelled seeds are used like shelly beans. The entire plant is used for food in India, where it also provides forage and fodder for animals, firewood, thatching, and dry material for basket making.

BOTANICAL CLASSIFICATION

Pigeon peas belong to the genus *Cajanus* and the species *cajun*. *C. cajun* are branched, free-standing plants that grow 3-4' tall. The plants are very attractive and are often used as borders in flower gardens.

Pigeon pea varieties available in India are grouped by pod color. Flavus or tur varieties mature very early and have green, three-seeded pods. Bicolor or arhar varieties have purplish green pods which contain four to five seeds. Arhar varieties are daylength sensitive and mature during short, warm days.

POLLINATION, CROSSING AND ISOLATION

Pigeon peas are outbreeding, self-pollinating plants. The plant's flowers are small and seem to be difficult for insects to enter. Research indicates, however, that small bees are attracted to the flowers and can effectively cross-pollinate different varieties grown within 1/2 mile of each other. Blossom bagging or caging will ensure seed purity when two or more varieties are grown in close proximity. Pigeon peas do not cross with any other species.

SEED PRODUCTION, HARVEST AND PROCESSING

Pigeon pea pods are easily collected and are not difficult to shell. General information on shelling techniques is given in the introductory pages of the Leguminosae family. Pigeon peas are occasionally available from Indian and Hindi food stores in larger cities across the United States.

SEED STATISTICS

Information on the decline of germination rates during storage was not available for pigeon peas. Members of the Seed Savers Exchange occasionally offer pigeon peas, and it is also listed by three commercial seed companies in the *Garden Seed Inventory*. There are approximately 145-200 seeds per ounce (5-7 per gram or 2,320-3,200 per pound), depending on the variety. Federal Germination Standard for commercially sold seed is 80%.

GROWING PIGEON PEAS FROM SEED

Pigeon peas are perennial, frost intolerant, heat-loving vines. Daylength sensitive varieties are inappropriate for most regions of the Unites States. Flavus or tur varieties will mature in regions where lima beans are successful. Pigeon peas are usually direct seeded, covering the seeds .5" deep. Pigeon pea seeds germinate best at 80° F. with germination usually occurring in 5-7 days. Plant or set out in full sun in thoroughly warmed soil, and providing a trellis or other support is recommended. The plants should be thinned to 10" apart for both food and seed production.

REGIONAL GROWING RECOMMENDATIONS

Northeast: Pigeon peas cannot be grown in this region.

Mid-Atlantic: Pigeon peas can be direct seeded from April 15 to May 15. The plants like full sun and average water.

Southeast/Gulf Coast: Pigeon peas can be direct seeded from April 15 to May 15. The plants like full sun and are drought tolerant.

Upper Midwest: Pigeon peas cannot be grown in this region due to daylength and frost sensitivity.

Southwest: Pigeon peas can be direct seeded from March 15 to June 10. The plants like full sun and average water.

Central West Coast: Pigeon peas can be direct seeded about April 15. The plants like full sun and average water.

Maritime Northwest: Pigeon peas cannot be grown in this region.

―――――――― *Cicer arietinum* - Garbanzo (Chick Pea) ――――――――

Garbanzo is often referred to as chick pea in Europe and the United States. The plants are grown throughout the temperate world and are an important source of protein in many countries. Whole dried seeds are used like dry peas or beans, and the green pods and tender leaves are eaten as a green vegetable. In the United States the mature seeds are canned in brine and used in salads.

BOTANICAL CLASSIFICATION

Garbanzo is a member of the genus *Cicer* and the species *arietinum*. *C. arietinum* is also known as Indian bean, Egyptian pea and Bengal gram. The plants are bushy, upright annuals that grow up to 2' tall. Each of the short, oblong, 1" pods contains one or two angular seeds.

The leaves and stems of the plants are covered with "glabular" (sticky) hairs. The hairs exude malic acid that is widely collected in India and used like vinegar or for medicine. In remote rural villages, Indian women wrap the plants in fabric each evening. The fabric is removed the following morning and the liquid exuded by the plants is wrung out and collected in containers.

Garbanzos are attractive plants in any vegetable garden. Whenever the plants are touched, however, malic acid is deposited on clothing and skin. Some persons are bothered by rashes after contact with the plant.

POLLINATION, CROSSING AND ISOLATION

Garbanzo beans are inbreeding plants. Garbanzo flowers are perfect and self-pollinating. Several research reports indicate that honeybees frequent the flowers and cross-pollination is common. Different varieties should be isolated by 1/2 mile or caged to ensure seed purity.

SEED PRODUCTION, HARVEST AND PROCESSING

Water should be withheld from garbanzo plants after the seeds have set and flowering ceases. In regions with summer rains during harvest, the plants can be pulled and allowed to dry under cover. The dry plants are then threshed to free the seeds, which helps prevent skin irritations that might result from trying to pick the pods individually. The Leguminosae family pages describe various threshing and winnowing techniques.

SEED STATISTICS

Garbanzos maintain 60% germination for three years when stored in a cool, dry, dark location. Members of the Seed Savers Exchange annually offer about 22 varieties of garbanzos, and the *Garden Seed Inventory* lists sources for 13 varieties that are available from commercial seed companies. Federal Germination Standard for commercially sold seed is 70%.

GROWING GARBANZO BEAN FROM SEED

Garbanzo beans produce annual, heat loving, twining bushes. Varieties are adapted to many regions and are worth trying, even in the Northern parts of the United States. Garbanzo beans are usually direct seeded, covering the seeds .75" deep. Garbanzo seed germinates best at temperatures from 70-85° F. with germination usually occurring in about 10 days. Plant in full sun, and thin the plants to 12-18" apart.

REGIONAL GROWING RECOMMENDATIONS

Northeast: Garbanzos can be direct seeded about May 10. The plants like full sun and average water. I lost lots of seed to chipmunks and red squirrels when the seed was planted within 100' of a stone wall or hedgerow.
Mid-Atlantic: Garbanzo beans can be direct

Garbanzo (*Cicer arietinum*) foliage and seedpods.

seeded from April 15 to May 15. The plants like full sun and average water.
Southeast/Gulf Coast: Garbanzos can be direct seeded from April 15 to May 15. The plants like full sun and are drought tolerant.
Upper Midwest: Garbanzos can be direct seeded about May 1. The plants like full sun and are drought tolerant.
Southwest: Garbanzos can be direct seeded from September 15 to February 15. The plants like full sun and average water.
Central West Coast: Garbanzos can be direct seeded about April 15. The plants like full sun and are drought tolerant.
Maritime Northwest: Garbanzos can be direct seeded from April 1-15 or November 1-15. The plants like full sun and are drought tolerant.

Dolichos lablab - Hyacinth Bean

Hyacinth bean plants in full bloom are covered with beautiful flowers that spread perfume throughout the garden. The plants are relatively unknown in the United States and deserve a great deal more attention. Hyacinth beans are short-lived perennials in frost free areas, and will tolerate both drought and poor soil.

Hyacinth bean pods have a distinctive, strong bean-like taste that is much appreciated in Southeast Asia and India. The flavor is sometimes a bit overwhelming when the pods are cooked alone, but is quite pleasant in combination with other vegetables. Unfortunately, the "anthazion" (colored layer) in the purple podded varieties is quite thin and disappears no matter how briefly the beans are cooked.

Full-sized immature seeds are sometimes used like

Immature pods, dried pods and dry seeds of hyacinth bean (*Dolichos lablab*) with light green podded variety, left, and purple podded variety, middle and right.

shelly beans. The dry beans with colored seed coats contain cyanogenic glucosides in toxic amounts. Some references indicate that soaking dry seeds in several changes of water renders them edible, while other texts caution against eating the dry beans at all.

BOTANICAL CLASSIFICATION

Hyacinth beans belong to the genus *Dolichos* and the species *lablab*. *D. lablab* are also known as Bonavista beans, Lubia beans, Bovanist beans, Seim beans, Indian beans and Egyptian beans. Available varieties include those with white flowers and large light green pods, pink flowers and light green pods, pink flowers and dark green pods, purple flowers and green pods, and purple flowers and purple pods.

POLLINATION, CROSSING AND ISOLATION

Hyacinth beans are inbreeding plants that have large, perfect flowers and are very attractive to a wide variety of insects. The blossoms are certainly large enough for bees to work with ease, but are not really significant sources of pollen or nectar. Isolation or bagging should be used to ensure seed purity.

SEED PRODUCTION, HARVEST AND PROCESSING

Hyacinth bean pods are very difficult to shell. The large "hilum" (seed scar) is firmly attached to the pod, and the pod also shrinks tightly around the individual seeds as it dries. For large amounts of seeds, a mechanical seed thresher is highly recommended.

SEED STATISTICS

Information on the decline of germination rates during storage was not available for hyacinth beans. Members of the Seed Savers Exchange annually offer about 5 varieties of hyacinth beans, and the *Garden Seed Inventory* lists sources for 2 varieties that are available from commercial seed companies. There are approximately 85-140 seeds per ounce (3-5 per gram or 1,360-2,240 per pound), depending on the variety. Federal Germination Standard for commercially sold seed is 70%.

GROWING HYACINTH BEAN FROM SEED

Hyacinth beans are short lived perennials in frost free areas, and can be grown in regions where lima beans are successful. Hyacinth beans are direct seeded, covering the seeds .5" deep. Optimum germination temperatures range from 70-80° F. with germination usually occurring in 5-7 days. Plant in full sun, thinning the plants to 12" apart. Trellis or fence support is necessary for the large vines.

REGIONAL GROWING RECOMMENDATIONS

Northeast: Hyacinth beans cannot be grown in this region.

Mid-Atlantic: Hyacinth beans can be direct seeded from April 15 to May 15. The plants like full sun and average water.

Southeast/Gulf Coast: Hyacinth beans can be direct seeded from about April 15 to May 15. The plants like full sun and average water. We trellis prior to planting.

Upper Midwest: Hyacinth beans can be direct seeded about May 10. The plants like full sun and average water, but are disease-prone and difficult to grow to maturity in this region.

Southwest: Hyacinth beans can be direct seeded about March 15 or August 10. The plants like full sun and average water.

Central West Coast: Hyacinth beans can be direct seeded from March 15 to May 1. The plants like full sun and are drought tolerant.

Maritime Northwest: Hyacinth beans can be direct seeded from about May 20 to June 10. The plants like full sun and average water. Mildew can sometimes be a problem.

Phaseolus coccineus - Runner Bean

Runner beans are native to Central America. Some runner bean varieties are daylength sensitive and may not flower during the first year of growth in northern regions. Immature runner bean pods are used like snap beans. The mature dry seeds are mealy and are used in some areas of Central America. Runner beans appear frequently in English gardens where the flowers, edible pods and green shelly beans are much appreciated.

Runner bean varieties are often included in the flower sections of seed catalogs because of their striking ornamental blossoms. Scarlet Runners have red flowers and light burgundy seeds with black blotches. Black Runners have more intense red flowers and seeds that are completely black. The variety known as Painted Lady has beautiful bicolored blossoms that are half white and half light red, with seeds that are similar to Scarlet Runners. White Runners have white flowers and white seeds.

BOTANICAL CLASSIFICATION

Runner beans belong to the genus *Phaseolus* and the species *coccineus*. Varieties of *P. coccineus* do not cross with any other bean species.

Runner beans are easily distinguished from other bean species by their unique growth habit. The plant's "cotyledons" (seed halves) remain underground as the vine emerges. The first growth that appears above the ground is the stem and first set of true leaves. To assist the rather weak, unprotected seedlings, the soil should be well prepared.

Runner beans also climb differently from most other species. Most beans twine counterclockwise when viewed from above, but runner beans twine clockwise. Be sure to take this into consideration when assisting the young plants on poles. The vines will either break or literally fall off of the pole if twined in the wrong direction.

POLLINATION, CROSSING AND ISOLATION

Runner beans are cited by some references as inbreeding plants, and by other references as outbreeding. The flowers of runner beans are very large and open, and are quite attractive to honeybees, bumblebees and hummingbirds. There is often considerable crossing between different varieties of runner beans. Isolation of 1/2 mile will maintain seed purity. Two or more runner bean varieties grown in close proximity will require blossom bagging or caging for seed purity. Runner bean flowers are perfect but are unable to self-pollinate without being tripped by insects. To simulate insect tripping and ensure seed set, remove the blossom bag or cage and depress the bottom portion of each of the new flowers. Continue tripping the flowers each day until the desired number of seedpods are set. Blossom bagging techniques are discussed in the introductory pages of the Leguminosae family.

SEED PRODUCTION, HARVEST AND PROCESSING

Runner bean plants are perennial, but light frost will kill their foliage to the ground. Each spring the plant sprouts from tuberous roots that are poisonous if eaten. In areas where the ground freezes, the roots must be dug in the fall, stored over winter in slightly damp sand, and replanted in the spring. Vines that grow from the tuberous roots produce flowers much earlier in the season than those started from seeds.

In short season climates, runner bean pods often do not have enough time to dry on the vine. The pods can be harvested when fully mature and just beginning to change color, and then should be spread out and left to dry away from direct sunlight. The large pods are not difficult to shell by hand. When using other shelling methods, take extra care to avoid breaking the large seeds.

SEED STATISTICS

Runner bean seeds will retain 50% germination for three years when stored in a cool, dry, dark location. Members of the Seed Savers Exchange annually offer about 35 varieties of runner beans, and the *Garden Seed Inventory* lists sources for 38 varieties that are available from commercial seed companies. There are approximately 75 seeds per ounce (2-3 per gram or 1,200 per pound), depending on the variety. Federal Germination Standard for commercially sold runner bean seed is 80%.

GROWING RUNNER BEANS FROM SEED

Runner bean is a frost intolerant, vining perennial, but the plants are usually grown as annuals. The roots may be overwintered indoors and set back out for very early flower and pod production. (As easy as that sounds, I do not know anyone who successfully completes this garden task.) Runner beans are direct seeded, covering the seeds 1" deep. A loose soil is necessary for successful plant emergence. The seed germinates at temperatures ranging from 65-85° F. with germination usually occurring in 8-12 days. Plant or set out in full sun, and thin the plants to 6-12" apart. Trellis support is needed for the large vines.

REGIONAL GROWING RECOMMENDATIONS

Northeast: Runner beans can be direct seeded about June 1, although many varieties are marginal for maturity here unless started in pots. The plants like full sun and average water. We trellis, with 5-6 bean seeds per pole, and deter deer with hex-wire cylinders 6-8' tall and 3-4' in diameter. Deer can sometimes be a problem, and so are Mexican bean beetles occasionally.

Mid-Atlantic: Runner beans can be direct seeded from April 15 to May 1. The plants like average water and full sun, but partial sun is all right. They also prefer cool summer temperatures, so plant as early in the season as possible. Spider mites are sometimes a difficult pest, and also bean beetles can cause problems later in season.

Southeast/Gulf Coast: Runner beans can be direct seeded about April 10-30. Partial sun is okay. We trellis when planting. Runner beans are most successful in the upper South; deep South and coastal areas are too hot.

Upper Midwest: Runner beans can be direct seeded about May 10. The plants like partial sun and average water, and will not set seed during hot humid weather. The plants grow rapidly until late June, do nothing during July, and regrow in August.

Southwest: Runner beans can be direct seeded from April 15 to June 15. The plants like full sun and average water.

Central West Coast: Runner beans can be direct seeded from March 15 to April 30. The plants like full sun and average water, and require mulching with straw; roots may overwinter in some years.

Maritime Northwest: Runner beans can be direct seeded about May 20. The plants like full sun and average water. We put trellises for runner beans into place around May 1.

Phaseolus lunatus - Lima Bean (Butter Bean)

Large-seeded lima beans have been traced back to 5000-6000 B.C. in Huaca Prieta, Peru. Small-seeded varieties, also called sieva beans, date back to 300-500 B.C. in Guatemala and Mexico. Wild varieties of limas can still be found in many regions throughout Central and South America. Some of the wild types contain toxic amounts of cyanogenic glucosides and are considered to be poisonous, but can be rendered edible with repeated "leaching" (repeatedly adding and discarding water during cooking). Lima varieties available in the United States contain variable amounts of cyanogenic glucoside, but do not require leaching to be used as food. Some people cannot eat limas, however, and report being very sensitive to the compound.

BOTANICAL CLASSIFICATION

Limas are members of the genus *Phaseolus* and the species *lunatus* and will not cross with any other beans. Both bush and pole varieties are available in the United States. Baby limas or sieva limas are annuals and are sometimes classified as *Phaseolus lunatus var. lunonanus*. The large-seeded perennial limas, that are also referred to as potato limas, are sometimes classified as *Phaseolus limensis var. limenanus*. Neither the plant nor the root of the large-seeded varieties can tolerate frost. These taxonomic classifications are simply attempts to group the members of the species by flowering times and by their annual or perennial tendencies.

POLLINATION, CROSSING AND ISOLATION

Limas are inbreeding plants. All varieties of both small-seeded and large-seeded limas will cross with one another. Limas have self-pollinating flowers that are filled with high quality nectar. Honeybees work the flowers intensely when the blossoms first open. In some areas beehives are moved into lima fields, not to benefit the beans, but to produce a fine, light-colored honey.

Different varieties of limas must be isolated by at least one mile to ensure seed purity. If two or more varieties are to be grown in close proximity, blossom bagging or plant caging is necessary. Bagging and caging techniques are discussed in the Leguminosae family pages and also in Section I.

SEED PRODUCTION, HARVEST AND PROCESSING

Lima pods that are left to dry on the vine shatter very easily and must be picked carefully. Close your hand around each seedpod before picking the pod off the vine. The dry pod will usually crack open in your hand. If bean weevils are a problem, the pods can be picked when fully mature but not yet dry. Spread the pods out and allow them to dry as quickly as possible before shelling. Continue drying the shelled beans until the seeds shatter when struck with a hammer. Then freeze the seeds for 48 hours to kill the weevil eggs that are under the seed coat.

SEED STATISTICS

Lima beans will maintain 50% germination for three years when stored in cool, dry, dark conditions. Members of the Seed Savers Exchange annually offer about 86 varieties of lima beans, and the *Garden Seed Inventory* lists sources for 70 varieties that are available from commercial seed companies in the U. S. and Canada. There are approximately 20-30 lima bean seeds per ounce (1 per gram or 220-480 per pound), depending on the variety. Federal Germination Standard for commercially sold lima bean seed is 70%.

GROWING LIMA BEANS FROM SEED

Some of the large seeded limas are heat-loving, perennial vines, usually grown as annuals. Small seeded limas are heat loving, annual vines. Varieties are available that will produce in many climatic regions. Limas can usually be grown where long season pole beans are successful. Lima beans are usually direct seeded, covering the seeds .5-1" deep, depending on the seed size. The seeds germinate at temperatures ranging from 75-90° F. with germination usually occurring in 5-10 days. Plant in full sun in thoroughly warmed soil, thinning the plants to 4-6" apart. Trellis support is needed for the large pole varieties.

REGIONAL GROWING RECOMMENDATIONS

Northeast: Limas cannot be grown in this region.

Mid-Atlantic: Limas can be direct seeded about April 15. The plants like full sun and average water. Bean beetles can be a problem.

Southeast/Gulf Coast: Limas can be direct seeded from April 15 to June 15, or July 20 to August 1. The plants like full sun and are drought tolerant. We trellis at planting.

Upper Midwest: Lima beans can be direct seeded about May 20. The plants like full sun and average water.

Southwest: Limas can be direct seeded from March 15 to June 10. The plants like full sun and average water.

Central West Coast: Limas can be direct seeded from April 15 to June 15. The plants like full sun and are drought tolerant.

Maritime Northwest: Limas can be direct seeded about May 20. The plants like full sun and average water. We put lima bean trellises into place around May 1.

Leguminosae

The easiest way to turn gardeners into seed savers is to show them a large assortment of beans. The beautiful shapes, colors and patterns of the seeds are enough to entice almost any gardener. Especially popular are the numerous bush and pole varieties of *Phaseolus vulgaris*, which include snap beans, string beans, wax beans, shelly beans, kidney beans and all kinds of dry beans. The immature pods of the most tender varieties are eaten as snap beans or green beans. When the beans swell to their maximum size but have not yet started to dry, the seeds are often shelled out and eaten as shelly beans. When left to dry on the vine, the seeds are commonly known as dry beans or soup beans.

Many old-timers prefer bean varieties with strings, which they claim are more highly flavored and taste beanier than the modern stringless types. While this may be true, stringless varieties have brought beans to the forefront of the processed green vegetables. About $250 million of fresh, canned and frozen green beans are sold each year in the United States. Increased consumption has also meant increased monotony, as breeders and producers strive to develop the perfect processing bean. Consumers nationwide are all purchasing nearly identical strains of Blue Lake or Kentucky Wonder at the grocery store.

BOTANICAL CLASSIFICATION

Common beans are members of the genus *Phaseolus* and the species *vulgaris*. Members of the Seed Savers Exchange are maintaining more than 2,200 varieties of snap and dry beans. Many are heirloom varieties maintained by many generations of gardeners for their flavor, productivity and climatic adaptability.

POLLINATION, CROSSING AND ISOLATION

Common beans are inbreeding plants. All *P. vulgaris* flowers are perfect and self-pollinating. After reading the information on crossing in the Leguminosae family pages, decide what precautions will be needed to save seed in your area. Other local seed savers may prove to be good sources of information on bean crossing.

At the very least, do not grow different varieties of *P. vulgaris* side by side if you intend to save seed. Also, never grow two white-seeded varieties next to each other, which would destroy any possibility of noticing possible crossing. For a more complete discussion of visible signs of crossing in beans, see the Leguminosae family pages.

SEED PRODUCTION, HARVEST AND PROCESSING

Most *P. vulgaris* varieties are easily harvested from the dry vines. The pods are also easy to clean using the methods described in the Leguminosae family pages.

SEED STATISTICS

Bean seeds will maintain 50% germination for four years when stored in cool, dry, dark conditions. Members of Seed Savers offer about 1,413 varieties of common beans, and the *Garden Seed Inventory* lists sources for 704 varieties that are available from commercial seed companies. There are approximately 30-65 seeds per ounce (1-2 per gram or 480-1,040 per pound), depending on the variety. Federal Germination Standard for commercially sold seed is 70%.

GROWING COMMON BEANS FROM SEED

The thousands of varieties of common beans are all annuals. Varieties are adapted to nearly every climatic condition and grower preference. Common beans are direct seeded, covering the seeds with 1" of soil. Germination temperatures range from 60-85° F. with germination usually occurring in 3-7 days. Plant in full sun. Some afternoon shade in very hot, dry climates is well tolerated. Trellis support is needed for pole varieties. The plants should be thinned to 3" for both food and seed production.

REGIONAL GROWING RECOMMENDATIONS

Northeast: Common beans can be direct seeded from May 20 to June 10. The plants like full sun and average water. Deer or other animals are problems.

Mid-Atlantic: Common beans can be direct seeded from April 15 to July 1. Fungus diseases and bean beetles are sometimes problems.

Southeast/Gulf Coast: Common beans are direct seeded April 10-20 (pole or bush), or August 1-15 (bush). The plants like partial sun and average water. We trellis half-runners and pole beans at planting. Sometimes there are heat checks in the July-August heat.

Upper Midwest: Common beans can be direct seeded from May 1 to June 15. The plants like full sun and average water. Watch out for bean beetles destroying the developing seed crop.

    Southwest: Common beans can be direct seeded from March 15 to June 10. The plants like full sun and average water.

    Central West Coast: Common beans can be direct seeded from March 15 to July 15. The plants like full sun and average water.

    Maritime Northwest: Common beans can be direct seeded about May 20. The plants like full sun and average water. We trellis in place by May 1.

Pisum sativum - Garden Pea and Edible Podded Pea

Peas originated in the eastern Mediterranean. Carbonized seeds have been discovered in Switzerland that date back to about 7000 B.C. During this lengthy period of cultivation, a gradual separation of varieties occurred. Succulent sweeter varieties were selected for vegetable use, while starchy varieties were grown for dry use and fodder. In Asia, peas were further selected for succulent edible pods and tender shoots. Varieties with edible young leaves and vines have also been long prized in some Asian cuisines.

With the introduction in the late 1970s of Sugar Snap and its related varieties, peas have received a great deal of new attention. Their fat, sweet, edible pods do not require stringing or shelling. These peas are easily grown and have tempted many gardeners into trying other types of peas for the first time. Sugar Snap varieties are not new, however, and were quite popular in France in the 1800s. Vilmorin's 1885 edition of *The Vegetable Garden* documents seven distinct varieties of the edible podded peas.

BOTANICAL CLASSIFICATION

Peas belong to the genus *Pisum* and the species *sativum*. *P. sativum* does not cross with any other species of peas or beans.

Most of the peas that are grown as green vegetables have green or white seeds, white flowers and wrinkled seed coats. The smooth-seeded varieties, *Pisum sativum var. arvense*, are starchy and better adapted to cool weather than the wrinkled-seeded types. These varieties have violet flowers, angular seeds which are often a grayish color, and are grown for forage, meal and silage.

POLLINATION, CROSSING AND ISOLATION

Peas are inbreeding plants. Pea flowers are perfect and self-pollinating. Most references indicate that the flowers are pollinated before opening and that crossing is very minimal. In European countries, the required isolation distance for commercially grown seed stock is 100 meters.

Any crossing in peas that does occur would be very hard to notice, because of the similarities in varieties. Whenever there is little else to feed on, bees will visit pea flowers, which greatly increases the chances that crossing will occur. Pea varieties should be separated by a minimum of 50'. Blossom bagging or caging can be used to assure seed purity when it is necessary to grow different varieties side by side.

SEED PRODUCTION, HARVEST AND PROCESSING

Peas mature rather early in the summer and are usually allowed to dry on the vines. Both harvest and shelling are fairly easy. Suggestions for threshing are discussed in the Leguminosae family pages.

SEED STATISTICS

Pea seeds will retain 50% viability for three years when stored in cool, dry, dark conditions. Members of the Seed Savers Exchange annually offer about 719 varieties of peas, and the *Garden Seed Inventory* lists sources for 230 varieties that are available from commercial seed companies. There are approximately 115-140 seeds per ounce (4-5 per gram or 1,840-2,240 per pound), depending on the variety. Federal Germination Standard for commercially sold seed is 80%.

GROWING PEAS FROM SEED

Peas are annual, twining vines. The plants tolerate a range of climates, but production is enhanced by cool weather. Peas are usually direct seeded, covering the seeds .5-1" deep. Pea seeds will germinate at a wide range of temperatures from 45-75° F. with germination usually occurring in 5-7 days. Plant in full sun or partial shade, depending on the climate and time of planting. The plants should be thinned to 1-2" apart. Trellis support makes the harvest easier.

REGIONAL GROWING RECOMMENDATIONS

Northeast: Peas should be direct seeded before May 20. The plants like full sun and average water. We trellis with 3-5' hex-wire on poles 6' apart, set in place before sowing. Deer are a problem.

Mid-Atlantic: Peas can be direct seeded from February 15 to March 15. The plants like full sun and average water. When the plants are 2-4" high, stake with flat brush or 4' high peach or apple prunings.

Southeast/Gulf Coast: Peas can be direct seeded from February 1 to March 1. The plants like full sun and average water. We trellis at planting.

Upper Midwest: Peas should be direct seed as early as possible. The plants like partial sun. Plant very early, as hot dry winds will terminate late-planted crops.

Southwest: Peas can be direct seeded from February 1 to April 15, or August 1 to October 15.

Central West Coast: Peas can be direct seeded from February 15 to March 15, or September 15 to October 15. The plants like partial sun and average water. Peas are difficult to grow in the heat of this region, and harvest can be very limited.

Maritime Northwest: Peas can be direct seeded from March 20 to April 10. The plants like full sun and average water. We trellis in place by May 1.

Vicia faba - Fava Bean (Broad Bean)

Fava beans are one of the oldest legumes under cultivation and have been an important crop since the Stone Age. Favas were well known in the ancient cultures of Egypt, Greece, Italy and many Middle Eastern countries.

In some people, especially males of southern European ancestry, eating fava beans or inhaling fava pollen causes a potentially deadly reaction called favism. The symptoms include muscle weakness, paralysis and, in extreme cases, death. Favism is an inherited disorder usually associated with eating large quantities of fresh fava beans.

BOTANICAL CLASSIFICATION

Fava beans belong to the genus *Vicia* and the species *faba*. *V. faba* are also known as broad beans, horse beans, English beans, European beans, Windsor beans, field beans and tick beans.

Fava plants have rigid stems and an upright growth habit. Varieties range from 2-6' tall and have white flowers with dark purple or violet blotches. The pods vary from 2-12" in length and contain from one to several large seeds.

POLLINATION, CROSSING AND ISOLATION

Favas are both an inbreeding and outbreeding plant. Fava beans are self-pollinating, but bees are attracted to the large flowers and can cause a good deal of cross-pollination. An isolation distance of one mile is necessary to ensure seed purity. When varieties are grown in closer proximity, caging or bagging is required.

SEED PRODUCTION, HARVEST AND PROCESSING

Fava beans are usually picked from dry vines. The pods are moderately difficult to thresh. The seed's "hilum" (scar where the seed was attached) is firmly fastened to the inside of the seedpod. Hand shelling is only recommended for small amounts of seeds.

SEED STATISTICS

Fava beans will maintain 50% germination for six years when stored in cool, dry, dark conditions. Members of the Seed Savers Exchange annually offer about 116 varieties of fava beans, and the *Garden Seed Inventory* lists sources for 58 varieties available from commercial seed companies. There are approximately 15-20 seeds per ounce (.5-1 per gram or 240-320 per pound), depending on the variety. Federal Germination Standard for commercially sold seed is 75%.

GROWING FAVAS FROM SEED

Fava beans are hardy annuals, tolerating frost but not prolonged freezes. In mild winter climates, favas are fall planted for spring harvest. The plants do not tolerate heat well. Favas are direct seeded, covering the seeds with 1" of soil. Fava seeds will germinate at temperatures ranging from 55-75° F. with germination usually occurring in 5-10 days. Plant in full sun or partial shade, depending on the time of planting. The plants should be thinned to 4-6" for both food and seed production.

REGIONAL GROWING RECOMMENDATIONS

Northeast: Favas should be direct seeded by May 15, or as soon as possible. The plants like full sun and average water. Because I grow over 50 varieties each year under row cover (Elmer Plantex cotton gauze) for pollination control, there are aphid buildup problems, for which I use ladybugs. However, anyone growing just one variety would not have to deal with this. Deer damage is often a problem where the crop is uncovered.

Mid-Atlantic: Favas can be direct seeded from

February 15 to March 15, or started in a greenhouse about January 15 and transplanted into the garden about March 1. The plants like full sun and average water. Plants overwinter in the garden with no special care sometimes; light mulch with loose straw or hay or asparagus leaves might help in moderate winters. Aphids are a universal pest.

Southeast/Gulf Coast: No real experience with favas, having only grown it as a fall cover crop.

Upper Midwest: Favas can be direct seeded as early as possible. The plants like partial sun, and quickly die when temperatures heat up after late June.

Southwest: Favas can be direct seeded from September 15 to February 15. The plants like full sun and average water.

Central West Coast: Favas can be direct seeded from September 15 to October 15. The plants like full sun and average water, and overwinter in the garden with no special care.

Maritime Northwest: Favas can be direct seeded from March 20 to April 10. The plants like full sun and average water.

Vigna unguiculata - Cowpea

Cowpeas migrated from Asia into Africa, and from there to Jamaica and the southern United States carried by slaves. Cowpeas are eaten as immature pods, shelled green peas and dry peas. Most varieties have well-developed spots or eyes surrounding the "hilum" (seed scar). Varieties that have a black spot or eye around the hilum are commonly called blackeyed peas. Other varieties have eyes that are dark purple, brown or maroon.

BOTANICAL CLASSIFICATION

Cowpeas belong to the genus *Vigna* and the species *unguiculata*. The pods of *V. unguiculata* vary from 4-12" long. Cowpeas do not cross with any other Leguminosae species.

POLLINATION, CROSSING AND ISOLATION

Cowpeas are inbreeding plants. Cowpea flowers are self-pollinating and the process is generally complete before the flower opens. The flower's receptivity to pollen is limited to the tip of the stigma and only for a short time. Pollen rubbed on the style will not induce fertilization.

Cowpea flowers are attractive to honeybees and bumblebees. The flowers are fairly tight and require a heavy insect to depress the flower's wings and expose the stigma. Honeybees do visit the flowers, but are probably not heavy enough to accomplish any fertilization. Bumblebees, however, are definitely capable of crossing the flowers. Caging or blossom bagging might be used to ensure absolute purity when different varieties are grown side by side.

SEED PRODUCTION, HARVEST AND PROCESSING

Cowpea seeds are allowed to dry on the vines before harvest. The pods are easily shelled using any of the methods discussed in the Leguminosae family pages.

SEED STATISTICS

Cowpea seeds will maintain 80% germination for four years (and 50% for seven years) when stored in cool, dry, dark conditions. Members of the Seed Savers Exchange annually offer about 120 varieties of cowpeas, and the *Garden Seed Inventory* lists sources for 104 varieties that are available from commercial seed companies. There are approximately 250 seeds per ounce (9 per gram or 4,000 per pound), depending on the variety. Federal Germination Standard for commercially sold cowpea seed is 80%.

GROWING COWPEAS FROM SEED

Cowpeas are annual, heat-loving, self-supporting vines. Cowpeas are direct seeded, covering the seeds 1" deep. Cowpea seeds germinate at temperatures from 75-85° F. with germination usually occurring in 5-7 days. Plant in full sun in fully warmed soil and settled warm weather. The plants should be thinned to 3-6" for both food and seed production.

REGIONAL GROWING RECOMMENDATIONS

Northeast: Cowpeas cannot be grown in this region.

Mid-Atlantic: Cowpeas can be direct seeded from April 15 to July 15. The plants like full sun and are drought tolerant.

Southeast/Gulf Coast: Cowpeas can be direct seeded from May 1 to June 30. The plants like full sun and are drought tolerant.

Upper Midwest: Cowpeas can be direct seeded about June 1. The plants like full sun and average water.

Southwest: Cowpeas can be direct seeded from

April 15 to July 15. The plants like full sun and are drought tolerant.

Central West Coast: Cowpeas can be direct seeded from April 15 to May 15. The plants like full sun and average water.

Maritime Northwest: Cowpeas can be direct seeded about May 20, although in some areas of the Maritime Northwest there aren't enough heat units to mature this crop. The plants like full sun and average water.

Lesser Grown Leguminosae

Canavalia ensiformis
Jack Bean

Jack beans are an annual bushy plant from Central America. The pods grow 3" wide by about 10" long and contain 3-18 white seeds. Both the young pods and the immature seeds are reportedly used for food. Young pods grown in central California were very tough and not very savory, while the immature seeds were bland with a texture not unlike a very large fava. Mature jack bean seeds are poisonous.

POLLINATION AND CROSSING

Jack beans are inbreeding plants. Jack bean flowers are large and attractive to bees. Different varieties grown in close proximity would most likely be crossed by insects.

SEED STATISTICS

Jack bean is not available from members of the Seed Savers Exchange, but are being offered by two commercial seed companies listed in the *Garden Seed Inventory*.

GROWING JACK BEAN FROM SEED

Jack beans are annual, heat-loving bushes that need a long season of hot weather to reach seed saving maturity. Growers should try jack beans where long season, pole limas are successful. Jack beans are usually direct seeded, covering the seeds with 2" of soil. The seeds germinate at temperatures ranging from 75-90° F. with germination usually occurring in about 7 days. Plant or set out in full sun. The plants should be thinned to 10-12" apart.

REGIONAL GROWING RECOMMENDATIONS

Northeast: Jack bean cannot be grown in this region.

Mid-Atlantic: Jack bean can be direct seeded from about April 15 to May 15. The plants like full sun and average water.

Southeast/Gulf Coast: Jack bean can be direct seeded from April 15 to May 15. The plants like full sun and average water.

Upper Midwest: Jack bean cannot be grown in this region, due to problems involving both day-length and frost sensitivity.

Southwest: Jack bean can be direct seeded anytime between March 15 to June 10. The plants like full sun and average water.

Central West Coast: Jack bean can be direct seeded about April 15. The plants like full sun and average water.

Maritime Northwest: Jack bean cannot be grown in this region.

Canavalia gladiata
Sword Bean

Sword bean is even larger than jack bean. The flat pods commonly grow 3" wide and 15" long. Each pod contains 5-10 dark red seeds. The shape of the slightly curved pod resembles a sword. Mature seeds rattle inside of the seedpods, which have been used as musical instruments.

Sword beans are inbreeding, vining perennials that are native to tropical Asia and Africa. The vines and roots are very sensitive to frost. The immature pods and immature green seeds are eaten as vegetables. The vine is sometimes grown for animal fodder. As with jack bean, the mature seeds are reported to be poisonous.

Information about possible different varieties of sword bean is unavailable. Only one member of the Seed Savers Exchange offers sword bean, and there are no commercial sources.

GROWING SWORD BEAN FROM SEED

Sword beans are perennial, heat-loving vines that need a long season of hot weather to reach seed saving maturity. Growers should try sword beans where long season, pole limas are successful. Sword beans are usually direct seeded, covering the seeds with 2" of soil. Sword bean seeds germinate from 75-90° F. with germination usually occurring in about 7 days.

Sword bean (*Canavalia gladiata*).

Plant or set out in full sun. The plants should be thinned to 10-12" apart and trellising is needed.

REGIONAL GROWING RECOMMENDATIONS

Northeast: Sword beans cannot be grown in this region.

Mid-Atlantic: Sword beans can be direct seeded from April 15 to May 15. The plants like full sun and average water.

Southeast/Gulf Coast: Sword beans can be direct seeded from about April 15 to May 15. The plants like full sun and average water. Trellising is recommended.

Upper Midwest: Sword beans cannot be grown in this region, due to daylength and frost sensitivity.

Southwest: Sword beans can be direct seeded about March 15. The plants like full sun and average water.

Central West Coast: Sword beans can be direct seeded about April 15, or started in a greenhouse about February 1 and transplanted into the garden about April 1. The plants like full sun and average water, and are slow to flower.

Maritime Northwest: Sword beans cannot be grown in this region.

―――――― *Cyamopsis tetragonolobus* ――――――
Cluster Bean

Cluster bean, which is native to India and also found throughout Southeast Asia, is an inbreeding annual which forms an attractive bush that grows about 3' tall. The pods contain 5-12 oval seeds that can be harvested usually about 120 days after planting. The immature pods are eaten and the plants are also used for animal feed. The seeds are very "mucilaginous" (slimy) when cooked.

In central California the plants produced tasty pods late in the season with little attention. The flowers are small in size and do not seem attractive to bees. Information on possible crossing between varieties is unavailable, and there are no known sources of seed in the United States.

GROWING CLUSTER BEAN FROM SEED

Cluster bean is a long season, heat-loving annual. Some varieties may exhibit daylength sensitivity, but this cannot be confirmed. Growers should try growing cluster bean where long season pole limas are successful. Cluster bean can be direct seeded during April and May, covering the seeds 1" deep. Cluster bean seed germinates at 75-85° F. with germination usually occurring in 5-7 days. Plant in full sun, thinning to 6-8" apart. The plants like full sun and average water.

―――――― *Glycine max* ――――――
Soybean

The soybean, one of the world's oldest crops, has been grown in Asia for 5,000 years. An important source of plant protein, soybeans are also a valuable oil crop. Most soybeans are grown as large-scale agricultural crops for their dry seeds. However, the seeds of some varieties can be shelled when green and are used as a cooked green vegetable.

Soybeans are inbreeding, daylength sensitive plants, but varieties have been developed for both long day and short day areas. Soybean flowers are self-fertile. The anthers "dehisce" (shed pollen) before the flowers open. In other words, pollination and fertilization are completed even before the soybean flower opens.

Soybean pods are allowed to dry on the plants before being harvested. The pods are brittle and sharp, so shelling can be extremely hard on the hands. A seed cleaner (such as the I-Tech described in Section I) works well and is a necessity for large amounts of soybean seeds.

SEED SPECIFICS

Members of the Seed Savers Exchange annually offer about 41 varieties of vegetable soybeans, and the *Garden Seed Inventory* lists sources for 31 varieties that are available from commercial seed companies in the United States and Canada. There are approximately 100 soybean seeds per ounce (4 per gram or 1,600 per pound), depending on the variety. Federal Germination Standard for commercially sold soybean seed is 75%.

GROWING SOYBEANS FROM SEED

Soybeans are heat-loving annuals. Varieties are adapted to a wide range of climates and season lengths. Soybeans are direct seeded, covering the seeds .5" deep. Soybean seeds germinate at temperatures from 70-85° F. with germination usually occurring in 5-7 days. Plant in full sun, thinning the plants to 3-4" apart.

REGIONAL GROWING RECOMMENDATIONS

Northeast: Soybeans can be direct seeded about May 10-20. The plants like full sun. We use floating row covers or hex-wire for animal protection. Only type 00 or earlier varieties can be expected to mature here. Deer and woodchucks can cause devastating problems, and electric fencing is only partially successful. Live-trapping is most effective for woodchucks.
Mid-Atlantic: Soybeans can be direct seeded from April 15 to May 1. The plants like full sun and average water.
Southeast/Gulf Coast: Soybeans can be direct seeded from April 15 to May 15. The plants like full sun and are drought tolerant.
Upper Midwest: Soybeans can be direct seeded about May 10. The plants like full sun and average water.
Southwest: Soybeans can be direct seeded from March 15 to June 10. The plants like full sun and average water.
Central West Coast: Soybeans can be direct seeded from April 15 to August 1. The plants like full sun and average water.
Maritime Northwest: Soybeans can be direct seeded from May 20 to June 10. The plants like full sun and average water. With our wet late springs in the Maritime Northwest, we must wait for warm conditions in the late spring in order to plant this crop successfully.

———— *Lens culinaris* ————
Lentil

Lentil was probably one of the earliest domesticated crops. Both the immature pods and the dry seeds are used as staples in Indian cuisine. Lentils are inbreeding plants that are very delicate in appearance.

The plant's tiny flowers are self-pollinating and do not seem to be attractive to bees. The plants continue to produce pods over a long season, but do not tolerate long, hot days in full sun. The ripe pods shatter easily and need to be collected carefully in order to produce the amaximum harvest. Lentil seeds are easily shelled.

SEED STATISTICS

Members of the Seed Savers Exchange annually offer about 4 varieties of lentils, and the *Garden Seed Inventory* lists sources for 13 varieties that are available from commercial seed companies in the United States.

GROWING LENTIL FROM SEED

Lentils are annual, self-supporting vines. The plants benefit from some shade in very hot, dry climates. Varieties are available for a wide range of climates. Lentils are direct seeded, covering the seeds .5" deep. Lentil seeds germinate at temperatures ranging from 65-85° F. with germination usually occurring in 5-7 days. Plant in full sun or partial shade, depending on the climate. The plants should be thinned to 4-6".

REGIONAL GROWING RECOMMENDATIONS

Northeast: Lentils can be direct seeded about May 15 in this area. The plants like full sun and average water. Lentils are not a consistent success in this region.
Mid-Atlantic: Lentils can be direct seeded from April 15 to May 1. The plants like full sun and average water.
Southeast/Gulf Coast: Lentils can be direct seeded from April 15 to May 15. The plants like full sun and are drought tolerant.
Upper Midwest: Lentils can be direct seeded about April 15. The plants like full sun. Lentils do not grow well here; the plants succumb to disease 95% of the time.
Southwest: Lentils can be direct seeded from September 15 to February 15. The plants like full sun and average water.
Central West Coast: Lentils can be direct seeded from March 30 to June 1. The plants like full sun and average water.
Maritime Northwest: Lentils can be direct seeded from May 20 to June 10. The plants like full sun and average water.

─────── *Lupinus mutabilis* ───────
Tarwi

Tarwi is an inbreeding plant that produces brilliant blue blossoms and seeds that contain about 40% protein. Although the plant is widely grown in Peru, Bolivia and Ecuador, its importance as a world food crop has been restricted because of alkaloids in the seeds. Indians in the Andes highlands remove the bitter alkaloids by soaking the seeds in running water for several days. Tarwi requires a long growing season, but the plants are very frost and drought tolerant. Different varieties grown within half a mile of each other would be easily crossed by insects. Tarwi will also cross with some of the wild lupines found growing in the United States. Tarwi seeds are available from several commercial seed companies in the United States.

GROWING TARWI FROM SEED

Tarwi is a widely adapted annual. The plants are frost and drought tolerant. Tarwi is direct seeded, covering the seeds .25-.5" deep. Tarwi seeds germinate at temperatures from 65-75° F. with germination usually occurring in 5-7 days. Plant in full sun or partial shade in very hot, dry climates. The plants should be thinned to 8-10" apart.

─────── *Pachyrhizus ahipa* ───────
Ahipa

Ahipa, a relative of jicama, is a popular vegetable in Bolivia and Peru. The sweet, white tubers can be eaten raw and in fruit salads, or are fried like potatoes. The plant's leaves, stem, seedpods and seeds are toxic and thought to contain large amounts of rotenone. Ahipa plants do not appear to be daylength sensitive and will not tolerate any frost. Ahipa is an inbreeding plant that produces lavender or white blossoms and needs a six-month frost-free season to develop seeds. Information about different varieties and the possibilities of cross-pollination is unavailable. There are no known sources for ahipa seed in the United States.

GROWING AHIPA FROM SEED

Ahipa is a perennial vine that requires a six-month frost-free season at the minimum. Tubers do not achieve full size for 9-12 months. Start in a greenhouse about February 1 and transplant into the garden about March 15. Plants started from seed may

not bloom for 12 months or more. Germination usually occurs in about 7-10 days. Cuttings may be rooted and used to start new plants. Plant or set out in full sun. The plants should be thinned to 12" for food production. Growing ahipa is possible, but very difficult, in areas of the Central West Coast.

─────── *Pachyrhizus erosus* ───────
Jicama (Yam Bean)

Jicama, which grows wild in Mexico and Central America, has long climbing vines and large blue or white flowers. Each plant can yield up to seven turnip-shaped roots, but will only produce in the extreme southern regions of the United States. Jicama was grown successfully in central California, but only with a great deal of effort. The seeds were started in a greenhouse during January and the vines were set out on March 30 when all danger from frost had passed. The vines, which only covered a square yard per plant, were grown in full sun and were given plenty of water. Only one 4" root per plant was harvested in late October.

Jicama is an inbreeding plant and its flowers appeared late in the season, producing ripe but not dry seeds by harvest time. Both the seeds and seedpods are poisonous. Jicama seeds are available from several commercial seed companies in the United States. Information on pollination and varietal crossing is unavailable.

GROWING JICAMA

Jicama is a perennial vine that requires a six-month frost-free season at the minimum. Jicama tubers do not achieve full size for 9-12 months. Plants started from seed may not bloom for 12 months or more. Germination usually occurs in 7-10 days. Cuttings may be rooted and used to start new plants. Plant or set out in full sun. The plants should be thinned to 12" for food production.

REGIONAL GROWING RECOMMENDATIONS

Northeast: Jicama cannot be grown in this region.
Mid-Atlantic: Jicama can be started in a greenhouse about February 1 and transplanted into the garden April 15 to May 1. The plants like full sun and average water. Only very small roots are possible in this region.
Southeast/Gulf Coast: Jicama cannot be grown for seed in this region. When being grown as a food crop, start in a greenhouse about April 1, transplant

into the garden about May 1, and harvest about September 15. Jicama does best in the lower South where days are short.

Upper Midwest: Jicama cannot be grown for seed in this region. For a food crop, start in a greenhouse about March 1, transplant into the garden about May 20, and harvest in early October.

Southwest: In high desert, jicama is not commonly grown because of frost.

Central West Coast: Jicama should be started in a greenhouse about February 1 and then transplanted into the garden about March 30. The plants like full sun and are drought tolerant, and will produce flowers and mature seeds, but at the expense of a large root.

Maritime Northwest: Jicama cannot be grown in this region.

——— *Pachyrhizus tuberosus* ———
Potato Bean

Potato bean is native to South America, where it grows wild. The roots are collected and are similar to jicama. Potato bean is a perennial, long season, frost intolerant, root crop that is usually propagated from cuttings. Seeds are produced between 12-24 months after plants are started. The plants have irritating hairs that cause major skin rashes. Potato bean can be direct seeded about April 15 in areas of the Central West Coast. The plants like full sun and average water. Seeds of potato bean are unavailable in the United States.

——— *Phaseolus acutifolius var. latifolius* ———
Tepary Bean

Tepary bean is a traditional food crop of Native Americans in the desert areas of the United States Southwest and northern Mexico. Teparies can be substituted for green beans, shelly beans or dry beans in recipes. Tepary seeds often carry bean common mosaic virus (BCMV) and will infect other beans that are grown nearby. BCMV is most commonly spread by aphids, but can also be spread by splashing rain or irrigation, by people moving through wet plants, or by infected seed and crop debris.

Tepary beans are inbreeding plants. The extent of crossing between tepary bean varieties is dependent on the insect populations s in the area (see the discussion in the Leguminosae family pages). Teparies are drought tolerant and produce crops under extremely dry, hot weather conditions and on alkali soil. Seeds are saved similarly to other Phaseolus species.

SEED STATISTICS

Members of the Seed Savers Exchange annually offer about 19 varieties of tepary beans, and the *Garden Seed Inventory* lists sources for 36 varieties that are available from commercial seed companies. There are approximately 182 seeds per ounce (6 per gram or 2,900 per pound), depending on the variety. Federal Germination Standard for commercially sold tepary seed is 70%.

GROWING TEPARY BEAN FROM SEED

Tepary beans are annual vines, similar to common beans, but are more tolerant of hot, dry climates. They do not do well in cool or wet summer conditions. Tepary beans are direct seeded, covering the seeds .5" deep. Tepary seeds germinate at temperatures ranging between 60-85° F. with germination usually occurring in 3-7 days. Tepary beans should be planted in full sun, and trellis support is needed. The plants should be thinned to 3" for both food and seed production.

REGIONAL GROWING RECOMMENDATIONS

Northeast: Tepary beans cannot be grown in this region.

Mid-Atlantic: Tepary beans can be direct seeded from about April 15 to May 1. The plants like full sun and average water. Watch closely for bean beetle damage.

Southeast/Gulf Coast: Tepary beans can be direct seeded about April 10-20. The plants like full sun and are drought tolerant. We trellis the plants.

Upper Midwest: Tepary beans can be direct seeded about May 10. The plants like full sun and are drought tolerant. Tepary beans do poorly in wet years.

Southwest: Tepary beans can be direct seeded from March 15 to August 10. The plants like full sun and are drought tolerant.

Central West Coast: Tepary beans can be direct seeded from March 15 to June 1.

Maritime Northwest: Tepary beans cannot be grown in this region.

——— *Phaseolus vulgaris subsp. nunas* ———
Nunas (Popping Bean)

Nunas is a type of common green bean with one important difference - when heated the seeds pop like popcorn. Popped nunas taste slightly like roasted peanuts and are a favorite snack food in Ecuador and

Peru. Nunas are grown like other pole beans. The flowers are more open than most *Phaseolus vulgaris* and can be more easily cross-pollinated by bees. The plants must be isolated from other *P. vulgaris* varieties by half a mile or caged to ensure purity. Seed is saved like other *P. vulgaris* varieties.

Nunas are presumed to be inbreeding plants. Some nunas varieties are daylength sensitive and will not produce pods before frost in most areas of the United States.

SEED STATISTICS

Home garden trials of day-neutral nunas varieties are just starting, so seed should be available from U.S. seed companies within a few years. There are approximately 182 seeds per ounce (6 per gram or 2,900 per pound), depending on the variety. Federal Germination Standard for commercially sold seed is 70%.

GROWING NUNAS FROM SEED

Nunas are annual, frost intolerant, day-length sensitive vines. Some day-neutral varieties are documented, but not yet available. Nunas are direct seeded, covering the seeds .5" deep. Germination temperatures range from 60-85° F., usually occurring in 5-7 days. Plant in full sun; trellising will be needed. The plants should be thinned to 4-6" apart.

REGIONAL GROWING RECOMMENDATIONS

Northeast: Nunas (popping bean) can be direct seeded from May 20 to June 10. The plants like full sun and average water.

Mid-Atlantic: Nunas can be direct seeded from April 15 to May 1. The plants like full sun and average water.

Southeast/Gulf Coast: Nunas can be direct seeded about April 10-20. The plants like average water and full sun, but partial sun is okay.

Upper Midwest: Nunas can be direct seeded from May 1 to June 15. The plants like full sun and average water. Watch for bean beetles.

Southwest: Nunas can be direct seeded from about March 15 to June 10. The plants like full sun and average water.

Central West Coast: Nunas can be direct seeded from April 15 to May 15. The plants like full sun and average water.

Maritime Northwest: Nunas can be direct seeded about May 20. The plants like full sun and average water. We trellis.

Psophocarpus tetragonolobus
Winged Bean

Winged bean has been grown for centuries in Asia and India. Crops are quite successful in hot, humid regions where it is difficult to grow soybeans. The entire plant is used for food: immature pods are eaten like green beans; seeds are shelled and used like soybeans; tender shoots, flowers and leaves are eaten like pea vines; and the tuberous roots are used like potatoes. The plants are perennial, but frost kills the vines to the ground.

Winged bean does not grow well in hot, dry climates. The plants stayed alive in central California and managed to produce small amounts of foliage, pods and roots. Seed savers report excellent yields in Hawaii, where the plant is much better adapted.

POLLINATION AND CROSSING

Winged bean is an inbreeding plant. The flowers of winged bean are perfect and self-pollinating. Winged bean will not cross with any other vegetable species. Information was unavailable on possible insect cross-pollination between different varieties of winged bean.

SEED STATISTICS

Members of the Seed Savers Exchange occasionally offer winged bean, and it is available from three commercial seed companies listed in the *Garden Seed Inventory*.

GROWING WINGED BEAN FROM SEED

Winged beans are perennial plants, tolerating no frost and preferring a hot, humid, tropical climate. Winged beans are usually direct seeded, covering the seeds .5" deep. The seeds germinate at temperatures ranging from 70-85° F. with germination usually occurring in 7-10 days. Plant in full sun. Trellis support is needed for the pole varieties. Reference has been made to the plants as "herbs," possibly indicating a bush or self-supporting variety. The plants should be thinned to 6" when grown as an annual, perhaps up to 12" when grown as a perennial.

Psophocarpus tetragonolobus
Asparagus Pea

Asparagus pea, one of ten subspecies of *Psophocarpus tetragonolobus*, forms a ground cover that is 3" tall and 12" in diameter. The flowers are brilliant red and very decorative in the spring. The peas resemble miniature winged beans and are eaten as a green vegetable when very young. As the pods mature, a cellulose layer forms that is impossible to chew. Asparagus pea pods can be shelled, but the seeds are small and not usually considered worth the trouble.

POLLINATION AND CROSSING

Asparagus pea is an inbreeding, self-pollinating plant. The flowers are attractive to small insects and some crossing between varieties is possible. Within a period of 2-3 months in the very early spring, asparagus pea blooms, produces fruit, sets seeds and dies. The plants are unlikely to be blooming at the same time or in the same climate as winged bean. Information on possible crossing between these two subspecies is unavailable.

SEED STATISTICS

Members of the Seed Savers Exchange annually offer about 6 varieties of asparagus peas, and the *Garden Seed Inventory* lists sources for 10 varieties that are available from commercial seed companies.

GROWING ASPARAGUS PEA FROM SEED

Asparagus peas are frost tolerant, spreading annual plants that can be fall planted in temperate climates for early spring harvest. Asparagus peas are direct seeded, covering the seeds .25" deep. Asparagus pea seeds germinate at temperatures ranging from 65-80° F. with germination usually occurring in 5-7 days. Plant in full sun or afternoon shade. The plants should be thinned to 8" apart.

REGIONAL GROWING RECOMMENDATIONS FOR WINGED BEAN AND ASPARAGUS PEA

Northeast: Winged bean and asparagus pea cannot be grown in this region.

Mid-Atlantic: Winged bean and asparagus pea can be direct seeded from April 15 to May 1 in some areas, or September 1 for asparagus pea. The plants like partial sun and average water. Virus and mildew can be problems.

Southeast/Gulf Coast: Winged bean and asparagus pea can be direct seeded about April 1-15. The plants like full sun and are drought tolerant. We trellis at planting.

Upper Midwest: Winged bean and asparagus pea can be direct seeded about April 15-30. The plants like full sun and average water.

Southwest: Winged bean and asparagus pea can be direct seeded from February 1 to April 15, or August 1 to October 15. The plants like full sun and average water.

Central West Coast: Winged bean and asparagus pea can be direct seeded from February 1 to April 1, or September 1 to October 1. The plants like full sun and average water. Plants overwinter in the garden with no special care.

Maritime Northwest: Asparagus pea can be direct seeded from about May 20 to April 10. The plants like full sun and average water. We trellis the plants at planting time.

—————— *Vigna aconitifolia* ——————
Moth Bean

Moth bean, sometimes called mat bean, is widely grown in India. The green pods are used as a vegetable and the mature seeds are cooked like lentils. Moth bean is an inbreeding, short-day, warm season, drought tolerant plant.

SEED STATISTICS

Four members of the Seed Savers Exchange are offering moth bean (and mat bean), and the seed is also available from two commercial seed companies listed in the *Garden Seed Inventory*.

GROWING MOTH BEAN FROM SEED

Moth beans are very small, heat-loving, annual vines that are self-supporting. Usually moth beans are direct seeded in the spring, covering the seeds .25" deep. The seeds germinate at temperatures ranging from 70-85° F. with germination usually occurring in 3-5 days. Try planting moth beans in the beds where squash or other Cucurbitaceae are later planted, so that the small plants will mature seeds under the cover of the expanding squash vines. Plant in full sun or partial shade, thinning to 3" apart.

REGIONAL GROWING RECOMMENDATIONS

Northeast: Moth bean cannot be grown in this region.

Mid-Atlantic: Moth bean can be direct seeded from April 15 to June 15. The plants like full sun and average water.

Southeast/Gulf Coast: Moth bean can be direct seeded about April 1-15. The plants like average water and full sun, but partial sun is okay.

Upper Midwest: Moth bean can be direct seeded about May 15. The plants like full sun and average water.

Southwest: Moth bean can be direct seeded from April 15 to July 15. The plants like full sun and average water.

Central West Coast: Moth bean can be direct seeded from April 15 to May 15. The plants like full sun and average water.

Maritime Northwest: Moth bean can be direct seeded about May 20. The plants like full sun and average water.

--------- *Vigna angularis* ---------
Adzuki Bean

Adzuki bean is probably a native of Japan, where bush varieties are quite popular. Vining varieties of adzuki are widely grown in China and Taiwan. Adzuki beans are inbreeding plants that are "hypogeal" (develop with their seed halves underground) and flower during short, warm days. Adzuki bean seeds are usually red and have white hilums.

SEED STATISTICS

Members of the Seed Savers Exchange annually offer about 9 varieties of adzuki beans, and the *Garden Seed Inventory* lists sources for 4 varieties that are available from commercial seed companies. Seeds are also available from Japanese groceries and specialty stores.

GROWING ADZUKI BEAN FROM SEED

Adzuki beans are heat-loving, daylength sensitive, annual plants. Both bush and vining varieties are available. Varieties exhibiting strong daylength sensitivity are suited to long, hot growing seasons found in the southern portions of the United States. Adzuki beans are direct seeded, covering the seeds .5" deep. The seeds germinate at 70-85° F. with germination usually occurring in 3-5 days. Plant in full sun. Trellis support is necessary for vining varieties. The plants should be thinned to 3-5" apart.

REGIONAL GROWING RECOMMENDATIONS

Northeast: Adzuki beans can be direct seeded about May 20. The plants like full sun and average

water. Some varieties tend to shatter before the plants are mature. Only a few varieties mature in this region. Deer browsing is a problem.

Mid-Atlantic: Adzuki beans can be direct seeded from April 15 to June 15. The plants like full sun and average water.

Southeast/Gulf Coast: Adzuki beans can be direct seeded from April 10 to May 1. The plants like full sun and are drought tolerant.

Upper Midwest: Adzuki beans can be direct seeded about May 20. The plants like full sun and average water.

Southwest: Adzuki beans can be direct seeded from April 15 to July 15. The plants like full sun and average water.

Central West Coast: Adzuki beans can be direct seeded from April 15 to June 15. The plants like full sun and average water.

Maritime Northwest: Adzuki beans can be direct seeded about May 20, although in some areas of the Maritime Northwest there aren't enough heat units for this crop. The plants like full sun and average water.

--------- *Vigna mungo* ---------
Black Gram

Black gram is an important crop in India. The immature pods are used as a green vegetable and the mature seeds are used like dry beans. Seeds may be available from some Indian groceries here in the United States. Black gram is not currently available from any members of the Seed Savers Exchange, nor is it offered by any of the commercial seed companies listed in the *Garden Seed Inventory*.

GROWING BLACK GRAM FROM SEED

Black gram is an inbreeding, self-supporting, heat-loving annual. Varieties are adapted to a wide range of of climates, but do require warm days and nights to produce abundantly. Gardeners should try growing black gram where cowpeas are successful. Black gram is direct seeded, covering the seeds .25" deep. The seeds germinate at temperatures ranging from 65-80° F. with germination usually occurring in 3-5 days. Plant in full sun, and should be thinned to 5" apart.

REGIONAL GROWING RECOMMENDATIONS

Northeast: Black gram cannot be grown in this region.

Mid-Atlantic: Black gram can be direct seeded from April 15 to June 15. The plants like full sun and average water.

Southeast/Gulf Coast: Black gram can be direct seeded from April 10 to May 1. The plants like full sun and are drought tolerant.

Upper Midwest: Black gram can be direct seeded about June 1. The plants like full sun and average water.

Southwest: Black gram can be direct seeded from April 15 to July 15. The plants like full sun and average water.

Central West Coast: Black gram can be direct seeded from April 15 to June 15. The plants like full sun and average water.

Maritime Northwest: Black gram can be direct seeded about May 20. The plants like full sun and average water.

Vigna radiata
Mung Bean (Green Gram)

Mung bean, an ancient crop native to India, is used as both a green vegetable and a dry bean. In many parts of the world, mung bean seeds are sprouted and sold as bean sprouts. Mung beans are inbreeding plants. The small, self-pollinating flowers do not open before falling off the developing pods. Any chance of cross-pollination is very unlikely.

SEED STATISTICS

Members of the Seed Savers Exchange annually offer about 2 varieties of mung beans, and the *Garden Seed Inventory* lists sources for 4 varieties that are available from commercial seed companies.

GROWING MUNG BEAN FROM SEED

Mung beans are self-supporting, heat-loving annuals. Varieties are adapted to a wide variety of climates, but do require warm days and nights to produce abundantly. Gardeners should try mung beans where cowpeas are successful. Mung beans are direct seeded covering the seeds .25" deep. The seeds germinate at temperatures ranging from 65-80° F. with germination usually occurring in 3-5 days. Plant in full sun, and thin to 5" apart.

REGIONAL GROWING RECOMMENDATIONS

Northeast: Mung beans (green gram) cannot be grown in this region.

Mid-Atlantic: Mung beans can be direct seeded from April 15 to June 15. The plants like full sun and average water.

Southeast/Gulf Coast: Mung beans can be direct seeded about April 10-30. The plants like full sun and are drought tolerant.

Upper Midwest: Mung beans can be direct seeded aboput June 1. The plants like full sun and average water.

Southwest: Mung beans can be direct seeded from April 15 to July 15. The plants like full sun and average water.

Central West Coast: Mung beans can be direct seeded from April 15 to June 15. The plants like full sun and average water.

Maritime Northwest: Mung beans can be direct seeded about May 20, although in some areas of this region there aren't enough heat units for this crop. The plants like full sun and average water.

Vigna umbellata
Rice Bean

Rice bean is commonly grown in Southeast Asia, where the dry seeds are eaten as a rice substitute or in combination with rice. Rice beans are inbreeding plants that are very similar to cowpeas in growth habit. The immature bean pods and shelled green beans are eaten like cowpeas. The mature pods are slender, slightly curved and grow to about 3-5" in length. The seeds are white with a tiny black or dark brown eye around the hilum. Rice bean does not cross with any other Vigna species.

SEED STATISTICS

Members of the Seed Savers Exchange annually offer about 2 varieties of rice bean, and the *Garden Seed Inventory* lists sources for 2 varieties that are available from commercial seed companies in the United States. There are approximately 250 seeds per ounce (9 per gram or 4,000 per pound), depending on the variety. Federal Germination Standard for commercially sold seed is 80%.

GROWING RICE BEAN FROM SEED

Rice beans are annual, heat-loving, self-supporting vines that are successful wherever cowpeas are grown. Rice beans are direct seeded, covering the seeds 1" deep. The seeds germinate at temperatures ranging from 75-85° F. with germination usually occurring in about 5-7 days. Plant in full sun in fully warmed soil and settled warm weather. The plants should be thinned to about 3-6" for both food and seed production.

REGIONAL GROWING RECOMMENDATIONS

Northeast: Rice beans cannot be grown in this region.

Mid-Atlantic: Rice beans can be direct seeded from April 15 to June 15. The plants like full sun and average water.

Southeast/Gulf Coast: Rice beans can be direct seeded about April 10-30. The plants like full sun and average water.

Upper Midwest: Rice beans can be direct seeded about June 1. The plants like full sun and average water.

Southwest: Rice beans can be direct seeded about April 15 to July 15. The plants like full sun and average water.

Central West Coast: Rice beans can be direct seeded from April 15 to June 15. The plants like full sun and average water.

Maritime Northwest: Rice beans can be direct seeded about May 20. The plants like full sun and average water.

─── *Vigna unguiculata var. sesquipedalis* ───
Yard Long Bean (Asparagus Bean)

Yard long might be overstating the length of this Vigna species a bit, but the pods really do grow from 12-30" in length. Yard long beans are inbreeding plants that are fairly day-neutral and can be grown throughout the United States. Yard long beans are usually grown to produce the immature pods that are widely favored in Asian cuisines. The pods, when lightly cooked, can be twisted into pretzel shapes to make an impressive garnish. Children who will not eat green beans might be coaxed into eating yard long beans.

The flowers of yard long beans are not attractive to bees, because the pollen is shed before the blossoms open. Crossing rarely occurs even if varieties are grown in close proximity.

Yard long bean is sometimes referred to as asparagus bean. Varieties are available commercially that have white seeds in light green pods, black seeds in dark green pods, and black seeds in purple pods. The purple-podded variety, which has a very heavy layer of anthazion over the chlorophyll, remains purple if cooked for a short period of time in a small amount of water.

SEED STATISTICS

Members of the Seed Savers Exchange annually offer about 8 varieties of yard long beans (and asparagus beans), and the *Garden Seed Inventory* lists sources for 15 varieties of yard long beans (and asparagus beans)that are available from commercial seed companies in the United States. There are approximately 250 seeds per ounce (9 per gram or 4,000 per pound), depending on the variety. Federal Germination Standard for commercially sold seed of yard long bean is 80%.

GROWING YARD LONG BEAN FROM SEED

Yard long beans (asparagus beans) are annual, heat-loving vines that are successful wherever cowpeas are grown. Yard long beans are direct seeded, covering the seeds 1" deep. The seeds germinate at temperatures ranging from 75-85° F. with germination usually occurring in about 5-7 days. Plant in full sun after the soil has fully warmed and during settled warm weather. Trellis support is needed. The plants should be thinned to 3-6" for both food and seed production.

REGIONAL GROWING RECOMMENDATIONS

Northeast: Yard long beans (asparagus beans) cannot be grown for seed, but can be grown as a food crop in this region.

Mid-Atlantic: Yard long beans (asparagus beans) can be direct seeded from about April 15 to June 15. The plants like full sun and average water. Brush can be used to stake the plants. Peg sticks from pronged branches of apple or peach prunings work well when about 4' high and .5" diameter.

Southeast/Gulf Coast: Yard long beans can be direct seeded from about April 20 to May 30. The plants like full sun and are drought tolerant. We trellis the plants.

Upper Midwest: Yard long beans can be direct seeded about June 1. Must be trellised or the pods will rot.

Southwest: Yard long beans can be direct seeded from April 15 to July 15. The plants like full sun and average water.

Central West Coast: Yard long beans can be direct seeded from April 15 to June 15. The plants like full sun and average water.

Maritime Northwest: Yard long beans can be direct seeded about May 20. The plants like full sun and average water.

Throughout European history the Solanaceae family has been synonymous with nightshade, and nightshade with poison. Only witches and fairies dealt with tomatoes and sunberries. One bite of their deadly fruits was known to strike children dead. The Europeans didn't know that in other parts of the world, sunberry leaves were being sauteed as green vegetables and tomatoes were being made into salsa.

FAMILY TAXONOMY

Solanaceae family includes about 90 genera and 2,000 species that are mostly native to Central America and South America. Potatoes, tomatoes, peppers and eggplants are the most important culinary members of the family. Tobacco is the most significant inedible member.

Solanacea comes from the Latin word solamen which means quieting. The name refers to the sedative properties of some of the species. Many of the species produce significant amounts of alkaloids. While small amounts of alkaloids can be quieting, larger doses can cause death.

All members of the Solanaceae family have a flower shape that is easy to identify. Sizes and colors vary, but each flower has five united or partially united petals. The petals form a symmetrical, wheel-shaped corolla. The five stamens are attached near the base of the corolla.

Solanaceae in the Garden

Genus	Species	Common Name
Capsicum	annuum	sweet and chili peppers
	baccatum	kellu-uchu
	frutescens	tabasco, squash pepper
	pubescens	manzano
Cyphomandra	betacea	tree tomato (tamarillo)
Lycopersicon	lycopersicum	tomato
	pimpinellifolium	currant tomato
Physalis	alkekengi	Chinese lantern
	ixocarpa	tomatillo (Mexican husk tomato)
	peruviana	cape gooseberry (poha)
	philadelphica	wild tomatillo
	pruinosa	strawberry tomato (dwarf cape gooseberry)
	pubescens	downy ground cherry (yellow husk tomato)
	subglabrata	purple ground cherry
Solanum	Burbankii	sunberry (wonderberry)
	integrifolium	tomato-fruited eggplant
	melanocerasum	garden huckleberry
	melongena	eggplant
	muricatum	pepino (melon pear)
	nigrum	common nightshade
	quitoense	naranjilla
	tuberosum	potato

POLLINATION CHARACTERISTICS AND TECHNIQUES

The cultivated species of the Solanaceae family are self-pollinating. Honeybees are not especially fond of Solanaceae flowers, but many other insects are, and a good deal of crossing can result.

Isolation or caging will prevent crossing of different varieties within a Solanaceae species. Seeds should be saved from as many different plants as possible to ensure the greatest genetic diversity within the population.

GENERAL PRODUCTION AND PROCESSING TECHNIQUES

Seeds from the various Solanaceae species are always harvested from fully ripe fruits. Plastic buck-

Facing Page: Not all eggplants (*Solanum melongena*) are dark purple. Fruit colors include pure white, lime green, bright orange, and violet with white stripes.

ets are often used, because the acid in some of the fruits will pit or discolor metal surfaces. The fruits are sliced, chopped, crushed or squeezed to expose the seeds. The chopped fruits are placed in a bowl or bucket, water is added, and the mixture is stirred vigorously. The good seeds will sink, while the fruit particles and immature seeds will float and can be poured off. More water is added and the process is repeated as many times as is necessary, until all that remains are good clean seeds at the bottom of a bowl of clear water.

The seeds are then poured into a strainer, but always be sure that the seeds are not small enough to pass through the strainer holes. Wipe the bottom of the strainer on a towel to remove as much moisture as possible, and then dump the seeds out onto a glass or ceramic dish to dry. Do not attempt to dry the seeds on paper or other absorptive surfaces as it is extremely difficult to remove the seeds from these surfaces.

Stir the seeds twice daily as they are drying to prevent the seeds from bunching together and to ensure even drying. Never dry seeds in direct sunlight or in the oven.

The dry seeds should be placed in an airtight container and kept in a cool, dry, dark location or frozen for long-term storage.

Capsicum spp. - Peppers

Capsicum annum - Sweet and Chili Peppers
C. baccatum - Kellu-uchu
C. frutescens - Tabasco and Squash Pepper
C. pubescens - Manzano

Peppers were cultivated in Central America and South America centuries before the arrival of Columbus. Most wild peppers have high concentrations of capsaicin, the hot compound found in some types of peppers. The highest concentrations of capsaicin are found in the pepper's interior walls (placental walls). The outer wall and even the immature seeds are rather mild until the capsaicin matures and is shed internally.

Peppers are perennial in warm climates, but are quickly killed by frost. Gardeners in cold areas can dig pepper plants from the garden in the fall and transfer them to a greenhouse for the winter. When the soil warms in the spring, plants can be set back out in the garden for summer fruiting. In general the hotter the variety, the more tolerant it is to cool, wet weather.

Most pepper fruits are green during their immature stage and undergo color changes while ripening. In their ripe or mature state, peppers turn yellow, orange, red, purple or black. In most parts of the world, green peppers are considered unripe and are not commonly eaten. The widespread use of green peppers is unique to American cuisine.

BOTANICAL CLASSIFICATION

The genus *Capsicum* contains five cultivated species and 18 documented wild species. *Capsicum annuum* and *C. frutescens* are the species of peppers that are commonly grown in the United States. All of the bell peppers and hot peppers found in grocery stores are *C. annuum*.

Tabasco peppers, *C. frutescens*, are grown in tropical areas of the southeastern United States and are the key ingredient in Louisiana Tabasco Sauce. *C. frutescens* also includes several peppers native to the Amazon River Basin. The best known of these is the squash pepper, which is also known as rocotillo. Until recently squash peppers were considered to be members *of C. chinense*. Researchers were unable to find any morphological differences between *C. frutescens* and *C. chinense*, however, and are now recommending that the two species be combined into *C. frutescens*.

POLLINATION, CROSSING AND ISOLATION

Peppers are inbreeding plants. The flowers of all peppers are perfect and self-pollinating. Insect cross-pollination is common, especially by honeybees and tiny sweat bees. A research study at New Mexico State University showed up to 80% crossing in some populations. Some studies report fruit set in certain varieties is greatly improved if insects visit the flowers, while other studies show little increase in fruit set due to insect visitation.

The pungent or hot gene is dominant in peppers. Sweet peppers that were grown next to hot peppers and then allowed to self-sow, probably account for garden tales of bell pepper volunteers turning hot.

Isolation of 500' is considered sufficient to ensure seed purity. When varieties are grown in closer proximity, caging is required. Only one variety of pepper should be grown in each cage, because small ground-dwelling bees are capable of crossing all of the plants within a cage. In hot climates a cage covered with spun polyester acts as a shade cloth and helps reduce blossom drop, which is common in peppers when temperatures exceed 100° F.

Some varieties may need flower agitation or hand-pollination to induce fruit set. Remove the cage between 7-11 a.m. and gently rub or thump each flower. The rubbing simulates an insect visit and "trips" the flower, inducing pollination.

Pepper flowers can also be bagged to prevent crossing. In the evening identify ready-to-open flowers and place a tiny spun polyester bag over unopened blossoms. At the same time, place a marker on the flower stem. If a fruit forms, the marker will identify it for seed saving. The marker and bag will fall off with the aborted flower if the fruit fails to form. Always bag blossoms on as many different plants of that variety as possible and then mix the seeds from those fruits at harvest time, which will help retain some variation within the population.

SEED PRODUCTION, HARVEST AND PROCESSING

Peppers seeds are ready for harvest when the fruit is fully mature. Select peppers that are ripe, fully colored and show no signs of disease. When cleaning large-fruited bell peppers, break or cut the flesh off without damaging the internal core. The stem should be left attached to the core and will act as a handle. The blade of a small knife can be used to carefully scrape the seeds off of the core and into a bowl.

Peppers can also be cleaned in a blender or food processor, if the flesh is not going to be eaten. Cut the stems off of the fleshless seed cores, adding enough water to cover the cores. Blend at low speed until the cores disintegrate and the seeds are free. Gently stir the mixture, and the good seeds will sink to the bottom. The immature seeds and flesh fragments will float and can be poured off with part of the water. Add more water, blend the mixture again, pour off more debris, and repeat until clean.

Small hot peppers can also be cleaned using a blender or food processor. Cut off their stems and a little bit of their shoulders, before putting the pods and water into the blender. Always wear thick rubber gloves when working with hot chilies. Chili oil is very pungent and will remain on unprotected fingers even after washing. Touching any area of the face with hands that contain chili oil residue can cause extreme discomfort. Also, be sure to clean chili peppers in a well-ventilated room, because the fumes can cause severe respiratory distress.

After all of the debris has been poured off, dump the remaining water and clean seeds into a strainer. Wipe the bottom of the strainer on a towel and dump the seeds out onto a dish or cookie sheet to dry.

Pepper seeds should be dried away from direct

Squash pepper (*Capsicum frutescens*) was formerly classified as *C. chinense*.

sunlight, until the seeds break when folded. If the seeds bend instead of breaking, additional drying is necessary.

SEED STATISTICS

Pepper seeds will retain 50% germination for three years when stored in a cool, dry, dark area. Members of the Seed Savers Exchange annually offer about 886 varieties of peppers (several species), and the *Garden Seed Inventory* lists sources for 562 varieties that are available from commercial seed companies. There are approximately 3,920 seeds per ounce (138 per gram or 62,720 per pound), depending on the variety. Federal Germination Standard for commercially sold pepper seed is 55%.

GROWING PEPPERS FROM SEED

Peppers are perennial plants grown as annuals. The plants are typically greenhouse started 6-8 weeks before the last average frost date, in order to ensure a long enough season for mature fruits. Pepper seeds should be covered .25" deep. The seeds germinate at temperatures ranging from 75-95° F. with germination usually occurring in 7-10 days in greenhouse conditions. Germination is greatly enhanced by bottom heat. Pepper seedlings are not vigorous and are subject to several viral diseases. Use sterilized, soilless, seed starting mixes, and avoid wood flats to limit disease transmission. Seedlings are usually transplanted 2-3 times before being set out in the garden. Peppers do poorly in cold weather and should not be set out before the weather is stable and the soil is warm. Set out in full sun, or afternoon shade in very hot climates. Support is not needed, but is beneficial in windy areas and when fruit set is heavy, which can cause plant breakage. The plants should be set out 12-24" apart.

REGIONAL GROWING RECOMMENDATIONS

Northeast: Sweet peppers and chili peppers can be started in a greenhouse about April 20 and transplanted into the garden about June 1. The plants like full sun and average water. Not all varieties will mature in this region.

Mid-Atlantic: Peppers can be direct seeded from April 15 to June 1, or started in a greenhouse from March 1 to April 15 and transplanted into the garden April 15 to June 1. The plants like full sun and average water.

Southeast/Gulf Coast: Peppers can be started in a greenhouse about March 1 and transplanted into the garden about April 15-30. The plants like full sun and average water, and require mulching in early summer, with any organic mulch material. In this region, production of large-fruited varieties is modest until fall.

Upper Midwest: Peppers can be started in a greenhouse about April 1 and transplant into the garden about May 20. The plants like full sun and average water. We use floating row covers to prevent crossing.

Southwest: Peppers can be direct seeded from March 15 to May 15. The plants like full sun, but partial sun is okay. The plants like average water.

Central West Coast: Peppers can be started in a greenhouse about February 1 and transplanted into the garden about April 1. The plants like full sun and average water.

Maritime Northwest: Peppers can be started in a greenhouse from March 20 to April 1 and transplanted into the garden May 20 to June 1. The plants like full sun and average water. Long-season chilies may not ripen to full seed maturity.

Growers report mixed success growing *C. frutescens* in various regions around the U.S. In the Northeast and the Maritime Northwest, the species cannot be grown. In the Mid-Atlantic and Southeast/Gulf Coast regions, plants are started in a greenhouse about March 1, transplanted into the garden from April 15 to May 1, like full sun and require mulching in early summer. In the Upper Midwest, the plants are started in a greenhouse in early March and transplanted into the garden about mid-May, but reportedly take a very long season to mature seed. In the Southwest, *C. frutescens* can be direct seeded from about March 15 to May 15 and likes full sun, but also does well in partial sun. And in the Central West Coast the plants are started in a greenhouse about February 1, transplanted into the garden about April 1, potted in five-gallon pots before frost, and replanted about April 1.

C. baccatum varieties are available from members of the Seed Savers Exchange and include escabeche, kellu-uchu and puca-uchu. The plants have very large leaves and large, white flowers. Growers in the United States report that varieties of *C. baccatum* appear to be daylength sensitive. In frost free areas of the Central West Coast, *C. baccatum* may be grown as a perennial or as a potted plant in winter. The plants should be started in a greenhouse about February 1, transplanted into the garden about April 1, potted in five-gallon pots before frost, and replanted about April 1. The plants like full sun and average water.

Plants of *C. pubescens* are covered with a light fuzz, hence their name, and have purple flowers and dark brown or black seeds. Often called manzano, the plants are native to Mexico, Central America and high elevations in the Andes Mountains. *C. pubescens* can grow 6' tall with 8" diameter trunks. The plants need support in windy areas, but will tolerate excessive rains and cool climates. Both flowering and fruit set are triggered by short days. In some areas of the Central West Coast, *C. pubescens* can be started in a greenhouse about February 1 and transplanted into the garden about April 1. At the end of the season the plants are potted in 5 gallon containers, protected from frost and replanted the next April. In areas of the U.S. Southwest, *C. pubescens* can be started in a greenhouse from January 1 to March 15, and transplanted into the garden March 15 to May 15. The plants are difficult to grow to seed in low desert areas due to damaging heat, but will set fruit in a cooled greenhouse. Manzano, rocoto, locoto and caballo are available on a limited basis from members of the Seed Savers Exchange.

Lycopersicon lycopersicum - Tomato
L. pimpinellifolium - Currant Tomato

Tomatoes were domesticated from wild perennial species in Mexico, Central America and South America. When Columbus took tomatoes back to Spain, the plants quickly spread throughout Europe and were considered a poisonous garden oddity. On their way from poisonous to popular, the attitudes of gardeners concerning tomato consumption went through a gradual transformation. The following advice from Harriott Horry's *Receipt Book* in 1602 is typical: "It is alright, but not advisable, to eat the tomato, if it is thoroughly cooked. Tomatoes should never be eaten raw as death will be instantaneous."

Although a rich red color is standard for today's tomatoes, many other colors exist. Heirloom varieties include fruit colors of white, lime green, lemon yellow, yellow with red stripes, gold, persimmon, orange, pink, purple, mahogany and black.

BOTANICAL CLASSIFICATION

Garden tomatoes belong to the genus *Lycopersicon* and the species *lycopersicum* (formerly *L. esculentum*). Currant tomatoes, *L. pimpinellifolium*, have red fruits that are only .25" in diameter and grow in clusters. Crossing between different varieties of *L. pimpinellifolium* is common.

POLLINATION, CROSSING AND ISOLATION

The extent of cross-pollination in tomatoes has been a controversy among seed savers for a long time. Some say that crossing is rampant, while others have reportedly never seen crossing after years of growing different varieties next to one another. Charlie Rick, whose tomato breeding accomplishments are legendary, describes the evolution of the tomato *in Potential Genetic Resources in Tomato Species* (1952). "The ancestral tomato species could not reproduce by self-

Diversity abounds in the shapes, sizes and colors of tomatoes (*Lycopersicon spp.*).

Solanaceae

pollination. . . . .It had a long style, extending far beyond the anther tube, to facilitate cross-pollination by insects. . . . .As this ancestral species evolved into the wild predecessor of the cultivated tomato it developed the ability to self-pollinate. . . . .With this development, the style became shorter but still protruded beyond the anther tube. . . . .As the tomato migrated northward, the style continued to shorten and in some species totally retracted inside the anther tube, precluding any possibility of insect crossing. . . . ."

Tomatoes are inbreeding plants. Most modern tomato varieties have totally retracted styles. Such flower structure severely limits (and may totally preclude) any crossing between these varieties. Three groups of tomato varieties have been found to have protruding styles. however: currant tomatoes, *L. pimpinellifolium*; all of the potato-leaved varieties of *L. lycopersicum*; and any fruit formed from double blossoms on beefsteak types of *L. lycopersicum*. Potato-leaved tomatoes have rampant vines and smooth-edged leaves that resemble the leaves of a potato plant.

Although not all tomato varieties have been examined, most modern varieties available commercially will not cross with one another due to their retracted styles. Seed savers should therefore have no problem with cross-pollination when growing one currant tomato (or one potato-leaved variety) and any number of modern varieties with styles that are covered by their anther tubes. Caging can be used to prevent crossing when more than one variety of *L. pimpinellifolium* or more than one potato-leaved variety of *L. lycopersicum* are grown in close proximity. Double blossoms, commonly seen in amongst the early flowers of beefsteak tomatoes, often have exposed stigmas, making them more prone to insect cross-pollination. Seeds should not be saved from double fruits for this reason.

To determine the style position for any given tomato variety, choose 10-20 new blossoms from several different plants. Examine each blossom with a magnifying glass to see if the style is recessed or protruding. The anther tube will open as the fruit forms, so it is important to choose newly opened blossoms.

Most tomato varieties will set more fruit if the flowers are agitated or tripped. This increases the amount of pollen traveling down the anther tube. The wind usually provides sufficient agitation, but fans

Left: Seeds and gel are squeezed into a labeled deli tub. Right: After one to three days, a layer of fungus will have grown completely across the surface of the mixture.

are often used to simulate the wind in greenhouse situations. Daily shaking can be used to increase flower set in caged plants.

SEED PRODUCTION, HARVEST
AND PROCESSING

Tomatoes used for paste and slicing are particularly easy for seed saving. The seeds can be saved and the fruit can be eaten or processed without any waste. Pick and wash fully ripe tomatoes, and then cut the fruits across the middle, not through the stem and blossom ends. This exposes the large seed cavities and makes the seeds accessible without mashing the fruit. Now squeeze the seeds and surrounding gel into a bowl or bucket.

The same process can be used for cherry and currant tomatoes, however grinding the fruits is far easier. Place the clean, fully ripe fruits in a blender or a food processor fitted with a metal blade. Process at low speed until all of the fruits are mashed and the mixture is very thick. The small, hard seeds will not be damaged. To aid in seed separation, add one cup of water to each cup of mashed fruit and stir.

Each tomato seed is encased in a gelatinous sack. The gel in these sacks contains chemicals that inhibit seed germination, which prevents the seeds from sprouting inside the wet flesh of the tomato. In nature the ripe tomatoes fall from the plant and slowly rot. The rotting away of the fruits is a natural fermentation process during which the gel sacks are destroyed. Eventually the fruits totally rot away leaving the seeds on the surface of the soil, ready to germinate when conditions are right.

Artificially duplicating the tomato fruit's fermentation process is not difficult. In addition to removing the gel sack, fermentation also kills many seedborne tomato diseases. The container of tomato seeds and gel should be set aside to ferment for one to three days. Fermentation will proceed more quickly as the daytime temperatures increase.

During this period the container of seeds will begin to stink and will become covered with a layer of white or gray mold. Because of the horrible smell, do not keep the bowl in the house or where it might be tipped over by animals or children. The fermentation process should be stopped when the layer of mold completely covers its surface. Be sure to monitor the

Left: Seeds, liquid and fungus are poured into a strainer. Right: The seeds are washed until clean by rubbing the mixture against the strainer under running water.

Solanaceae

process closely because, if allowed to continue too long, the seeds will begin to germinate in the mixture.

Add enough water to double the mixture and then stir it vigorously. The good seeds will settle to the bottom of the container, allowing the mold and debris and hollow seeds to be poured off. Add more water and repeat the process until only clean seeds remain.

Some growers prefer to pour the entire contents of the container into a strainer, without adding any water, and then wash under running water. make a fist and use the fronts of your fingers to rub the mod and softened debris through the screen. Wipe the bottom of the strainer on a towel to remove as much moisture as possible and dump the seeds out on a glass or ceramic dish to dry. Do not attempt to dry the seeds on soft paper or cloth or non-rigid plastic, as it is extremely difficult to remove the seeds from these surfaces. Coffee filters, which are inexpensive to purchase, reportedly work well and tend to wick the moisture away from the seeds during drying.

To ensure even drying and to prevent the seeds from bunching together, stir at least twice a day. Never dry seeds in direct sunlight or in an oven. Tomato seeds will begin to germinate if not dried quickly. In hot humid weather, a fan will help speed the drying process.

SEED STATISTICS

Tomato seeds will remain viable for 4-10 years depending on the variety and storage conditions. Completely dried seeds should be sealed in an airtight container and stored in a cool, dry area or frozen for long-term storage. Members of the Seed Savers Exchange annually offer about 3,200 varieties of tomatoes, and the *Garden Seed Inventory* lists sources for 1,080 varieties that are available from commercial seed companies. There are approximately 8,400 seeds per ounce (300 per gram or 135,000 per pound), depending on the variety. Federal Germination Standard for commercially sold tomato seed is 75%.

GROWING TOMATOES FROM SEED

Tomatoes are short-lived perennial plants grown as annuals. Tomato plants are typically started in a greenhouse 6-8 weeks before the last average frost date, in order to ensure an early harvest. The plants are set out when the weather is stable and the soil is warmed. Tomatoes can also be direct seeded in long season climates, covering the seeds .25" deep. The seeds germinate at temperatures ranging from 75-95° F. with germination usually occurring in 5-7 days in greenhouse conditions. Germination is greatly en-

hanced by bottom heat. Use sterilized, soil-less, seed starting mixes and avoid wood flats to limit disease transmission. Seedlings are usually transplanted 2-3 times before being set out in the garden. Transplant or direct seed in full sun. The plants should be set out 12" apart for food and seed production. Larger spacing may be used for specimen plantings. Provide shade for developing fruits, if sun scald is a problem. Tomato plants are somewhat self-supporting, but spread over a large area, making fruit difficult to pick. Cages or other supports are usually provided.

REGIONAL GROWING RECOMMENDATIONS

Northeast: Tomatoes can be started in a greenhouse about April 20 and transplanted into the garden about June 1. We use floating row covers to protect against flea beetles, at least for a couple of weeks. Trellis with 4' stakes for indeterminate varieties.

Mid-Atlantic: Tomatoes can be direct seeded from April 15 to June 1, or started in a greenhouse March 1 to April 15 and transplanted into the garden April 15 to June 1. The plants like full sun and average water. Stake or cage plants soon after setting them out. Mulching helps moderate temperature variations; use compost, manure, straw or hay. Tomato diseases and early and late blight are often problems.

Southeast/Gulf Coast: Tomatoes can be started in a greenhouse about March 1 and transplanted into the garden April 15 to May 15. The plants like full sun. Cage by the time the plants are 12-14" tall. Plants require mulch in early summer; any organic mulch is fine. Fusarium wilt (yellows) is extremely common on susceptible heirloom varieties. *L. pimpinellifolium* often re-seeds in this region.

Upper Midwest: *L. lycopersicum* can be started in a greenhouse from April 1 to May 1 and transplanted into the garden May 15 to June 15. *L. pimpinellifolium* can be started in a greenhouse about April 1 and transplant into the garden about May 15. Both species like full sun and average water.

Southwest: Tomatoes can be direct seeded from about March 15 to May 10, or August 1 to September 15. The plants like full sun, but filtered sun is okay and some shade often helps. The plants like average water.

Central West Coast: Tomatoes can be direct seeded about April 15, or started in a greenhouse about February 1-15 and transplanted into the garden about April 1-15. The plants like full sun and average water.

Maritime Northwest: Tomatoes can be started in a greenhouse about April 1-20 and transplanted into the garden about May 20 to June 1.

Physalis spp. – Ground Cherries, Husk Tomatoes, Tomatillos, etc.

Physalis alkekengi - Chinese Lantern
P. ixocarpa - Tomatillo (Mexican Husk Tomato)
P. peruviana - Cape Gooseberry (Poha)
P. philadelphica - Wild Tomatillo
P. pruinosa - Strawberry Tomato
  (Dwarf Cape Gooseberry)
P. pubescens - Downy Ground Cherry
  (Yellow Husk Tomato)
P. subglabrata - Purple Ground Cherry

The genus *Physalis* includes several species that are little appreciated in the United States, but are widely grown in other parts of the world. Tomatillos, *P. ixocarpa* and *P. philadelphica*, are staples in Mexican cuisine. Translations of Mexican recipes often refer to tomatillos as green tomatoes, which can be confusing for the cook. Tomatillos have a distinctive flavor and texture. They resemble green tomatoes in color only. Tomatillos have small, hard, green fruits that are enclosed in tan, papery husks. As the fruit grows, the husk becomes increasingly filled until, at full maturity, the fruits actually split the husks open.

Chinese lantern, *P. alkekengi*, has very small, ed- ible fruits that are encased in bright red husks. Their small, lantern-like husks are often used in dry arrangements. *P. alkekengi* is sometimes called strawberry tomato.

The other species of Physalis are commonly known as ground cherry, husk tomato, poha, golden berry and cape gooseberry. All of their fruits are formed inside a tan husk and range from .25"-1" in diameter. The fruits do not split the husks open when mature, but simply fall off the plant. Gathering these fallen fruits is the easiest way to harvest. Ground cherries can be eaten out of hand, made into pies, jams, sauces, or dried for use in fruit cakes.

BOTANICAL CLASSIFICATION

Tomatillos belong to the genus *Physalis* and the species *ixocarpa*. *P. ixocarpa* are multibranched and usually sprawl on the ground. The plants can be grown in tomato cages to conserve garden space.

There is a good deal of confusion over the species characteristics, botanical classifications and common names for *P. peruviana, P. pruinosa* and *P.*

Zuni tomatillo (*Physalis philadelphica*), left, and Large Green tomatillo (*Physalis ixocarpa*), right.

159

Solanaceae

pubescens. While *P. peruviana* is a perennial and will tolerate some frost, *P. pruinosa* and *P. pubescens* are said to be annual plants. Another species, *P. subglabrata*, has sweet purple fruits which make identification a bit easier. Perennial species can grow 4-5' tall and take up a square yard of garden space, but pruning and staking reduces their sprawling nature.

Seed companies often incorrectly refer to tomatillo as ground cherry and rarely list the correct botanical names for various Physalis species. Confusion over the botanical classifications is unlikely to clear up until a definitive study of the genus is completed.

POLLINATION, CROSSING AND ISOLATION

All of the species of Physalis are inbreeding plants and have flowers that are perfect and self-pollinating. Tomatillo, *P. ixocarpa*, will not cross with any other Physalis species. There is widespread confusion about the classification of other Physalis species, however, so isolation or caging is recommended for seed purity.

SEED PRODUCTION, HARVEST AND PROCESSING

Fully ripe tomatillos and ground cherries are easy to save for seed. Select fruits from as many different plants as possible. The paper husks are removed and the berries are placed in a blender or food processor with enough water to cover them. The seeds, which are small and slippery, will not be harmed by the metal blades. When the fruits are totally blended, empty the contents into a large bowl. Add enough water to double the mixture, stir vigorously, and allow the good seeds to settle to the bottom. Gently pour off the debris and hollow seeds. Add more water and repeat the process until only clean seeds and water remain.

The clean seeds are poured into a strainer, but always be sure the seeds are not small enough to pass through the strainer's holes. Wipe the bottom of the strainer on a towel to remove as much moisture as possible and dump the seeds onto a glass or ceramic dish to dry.

SEED STATISTICS

Physalis seeds will remain viable for three years when stored in cool, dry, dark conditions. Members of the Seed Savers Exchange annually offer about 24 varieties of ground cherries and 24 varieties of tomatillos (other species are also listed), and the *Garden Seed Inventory* lists sources for 14 varieties of ground

cherries and 10 varieties of tomatillos that are available from commercial seed companies. There are approximately 33,600 seeds per ounce (1,185 per gram or 537,600 per pound), depending on the variety. Federal Germination Standard for commercially sold seed is 75%.

GROWING PHYSALIS SPECIES FROM SEED

Physalis species are short-lived perennial plants usually grown as annuals. The plants are typically greenhouse started 4-6 weeks before the last average frost date, but may be direct seeded in long season climates. In short season climates, use greenhouse starting to ensure a good harvest of mature fruits. Some tropical varieties may exhibit daylength sensitivity. The seeds are covered .25" deep and germinate at temperatures ranging from 75-90° F. with germination usually occurs in 5-7 days in greenhouse conditions. Set out in full sun, or afternoon shade in very hot climates. The plants are self-supporting, but sprawl over a large area. Cage or trellis the plants where space is limited. The plants should be thinned to 12-24" apart. (Use 12" if plants are trellised or caged.)

──────── *Physalis alkekengi* ────────
Chinese Lantern

REGIONAL GROWING RECOMMENDATIONS

Northeast: Chinese lantern can be direct seeded about April 20. The plants like full sun and average water. We use floating row covers. This is a risky crop in our region, because many pods may not be fully filled.

Mid-Atlantic: Chinese lantern can be direct seeded about April 15, or started in a greenhouse about March 1 and transplanted about April 15. The plants like partial sun and average water. This crop will re-seed.

Southeast/Gulf Coast: Chinese lantern can be direct seeded about May 1-15. The plants like full sun and are drought tolerant.

Upper Midwest: Chinese lantern can be started in a greenhouse about April 1 and transplanted into the garden about May 15.

Southwest: Chinese lantern is not commonly grown in this region.

Central West Coast: Chinese lantern can be started in a greenhouse about February 1 and transplanted into the garden about April 1. Perennial plants overwinter in the garden with no special care.

Maritime Northwest: Chinese lantern is not commonly grown in this region.

Physalis ixocarpa
Tomatillo (Mexican Husk Tomato)

Northeast: Tomatillo can be started in a greenhouse about April 20 and transplanted into the garden about June 1. The plants like full sun and average water. We use floating row covers to keep out flea beetles. I often after-ripen fruits (in the husk) for 1-2 weeks after picking before harvesting seed.

Mid-Atlantic: Tomatillo can be direct seeded about April 15, or started in a greenhouse about March 1 and transplanted into the garden about April 15. The plants like average water and full sun, but partial sun is okay.

Southeast/Gulf Coast: Tomatillo can be direct seeded from April 15 to May 15, or started in a greenhouse about March 1 and transplanted into the garden April 15 to May 15. We cage when the plants are 12-14" tall. This crop often re-seeds heavily.

Upper Midwest: Tomatillo can be started in a greenhouse about April 15 and transplanted into the garden about May 15. The plants like full sun and average water. We have many insects that live in the husk and eat the tomatillos, leaving a hollow husk.

Southwest: Tomatillo can be direct seeded from March 15 to June 10. The plants like full sun and are drought tolerant, but the plants like average water.

Central West Coast: Tomatillo can be direct seeded from April 1 to May 1, or started in a greenhouse about March 1 and transplanted into the garden about April 1. The plants like full sun and are drought tolerant.

Maritime Northwest: Tomatillo can be started in a greenhouse about April 1-20 and transplanted into the garden from May 20 to June 1. The plants like full sun and are drought tolerant.

Physalis peruviana
Cape Gooseberry (Poha)

Northeast: Cape gooseberry can be started in a greenhouse about April 20 and transplanted into the garden about June 1. The plants like full sun and average water, and are not at all drought tolerant. We use floating row covers to keep out flea beetles. Although one can get plenty of good seed, there will always be <u>lots</u> of the crop that gets hit by frost too early and won't mature.

Mid-Atlantic: Cape gooseberry can be direct seeded about April 15, or started in a greenhouse about March 1 and transplanted into the garden about April 15. The plants like full sun, but partial sun is okay. The plants like average water.

Southeast/Gulf Coast: Cape gooseberry can be direct seeded about May 1-15. The plants like full sun and are drought tolerant.

Upper Midwest: Poha can be started in a greenhouse about April 1 and transplant into the garden about May 15. The plants like full sun and average water. Poha is more difficult than other ground cherries in this region.

Southwest: Cape gooseberry can be direct seeded from March 15 to June 10. The plants like full sun and average water, but are drought tolerant. Some tropical varieties may have difficulty with the heat.

Central West Coast: Cape gooseberry can be direct seeded from April 1 to May 1, or started in a greenhouse about March 1 and transplanted into the garden about April 1. The plants like full sun and are drought tolerant. Plants overwinter in the garden with no special care.

Maritime Northwest: Cape gooseberry can be started in a greenhouse about April 1-20 and transplant into the garden about May 20 to June 1. The plants like full sun and are drought tolerant.

Physalis philadelphica
Wild Tomatillo

Northeast: Wild tomatillo can be started in a greenhouse about April 20 and transplant into the garden about June 1. The plants like full sun and average water. We use floating row covers.

Mid-Atlantic: Wild tomatillo can be direct seeded about April 15, or started in a greenhouse about March 1 and transplanted into the garden about April 15. The plants like full sun, but partial sun is okay. The plants like average water.

Southeast/Gulf Coast: Wild tomatillo can be direct seeded from April 15 to May 15, or started in a greenhouse about March 1 and transplanted into the garden April 15 to May 15.

Upper Midwest: Wild tomatillo can be started in a greenhouse about April 15 and transplanted into the garden about May 15. The plants like full sun and average water. Insects are a problem with this crop.

Southwest: Wild tomatillo can be direct seeded from March 15 to June 10. The plants like full sun and average water, but are drought tolerant.

Central West Coast: Wild tomatillo can be direct seeded April 1 to May 1, or started in a greenhouse about March 1 and transplanted about April 1. The plants like full sun and are drought tolerant.

Maritime Northwest: Wild tomatillo can be started in a greenhouse about April 1-20 and transplant into the garden about May 20 to June 1.

Physalis pruinosa
Strawberry Tomato (Dwarf Cape Gooseberry)

Northeast: Strawberry tomato can be started in a greenhouse about April 20 and transplanted into the garden about June 1. The plants like full sun and average water, and are not at all drought tolerant. We use floating row covers to protect against flea beetles. Although one can get plenty of good seed, there will always be lots of the crop that gets hit by frost too early and won't mature.

Mid-Atlantic: Strawberry tomato can be direct seeded about April 15, or started in a greenhouse about March 1 and transplanted into the garden about April 15. The plants like average water and full sun, but partial sun is okay.

Southeast/Gulf Coast: Strawberry tomato can be direct seeded about May 1-15. The plants like full sun and are drought tolerant.

Upper Midwest: Strawberry tomato can be started in a greenhouse about April 1 and transplanted into the garden about May 15. The plants like full sun and average water.

Southwest: Strawberry tomato can be direct seeded from March 15 to June 10. Partial sun is okay, but some shade is necessary. The plants like average water, and sometimes have trouble with the excessive heat in this region.

Central West Coast: Strawberry tomato can be direct seeded from April 1 to May 1, or started in a greenhouse about March 1 and transplanted into the garden about April 1. The plants like full sun and are drought tolerant.

Maritime Northwest: Strawberry tomato can be started in a greenhouse about April 1-20 and transplanted into the garden about May 20 to June 1. The plants like full sun and are drought tolerant.

Physalis pubescens
Downy Ground Cherry (Yellow Husk Tomato)

Northeast: Downy ground cherry can be started in a greenhouse about April 20 and transplanted into the garden about June 1. The plants like full sun and average water. We use floating row covers.

Mid-Atlantic: Downy ground cherry can be direct seeded about April 15, or started in a greenhouse about March 1 and transplanted into the garden about April 15. The plants like average water and full sun, but partial sun is okay.

Southeast/Gulf Coast: Downy ground cherry can be direct seeded about May 1-15. The plants like full sun and average water.

Upper Midwest: Downy ground cherry can be started in a greenhouse about April 1 and transplanted into the garden about May 15. The plants like full sun and average water.

Southwest: Downy ground cherry can be direct seeded from March 15 to June 10. Some shade is necessary. The plants like average water.

Central West Coast: Downy ground cherry can be direct seeded from April 1 to May 1, or started in a greenhouse about March 1 and transplanted into the garden about April 7. The plants like full sun and are drought tolerant.

Maritime Northwest: Downy ground cherry can be started in a greenhouse about April 1-20 and transplanted into the garden about May 20 to June 1. The plants like full sun and are drought tolerant.

Physalis subglabrata
Purple Ground Cherry

Northeast: Purple ground cherry can be started in a greenhouse about April 20 and transplanted into the garden about June 1. The plants like full sun and average water. We use floating row covers.

Mid-Atlantic: Purple ground cherry can be direct seeded about April 15, or started in a greenhouse about March 1 and transplanted into the garden about April 15. The plants like full sun, but partial sun is okay. The plants like average water.

Southeast/Gulf Coast: Purple ground cherry can be direct seeded May 1-15. The plants like full sun and are drought tolerant.

Upper Midwest: Purple ground cherry can be started in a greenhouse about April 1 and transplanted into the garden about May 15. The plants like filtered sun and average water.

Southwest: Purple ground cherry can be direct seeded from March 15 to June 10. Some shade is necessary. The plants like average water.

Central West Coast: Purple ground cherry can be direct seeded from April 1 to May 1, or started in a greenhouse about March 1 and transplanted into the garden about April 1. The plants like full sun and are drought tolerant.

Maritime Northwest: Purple ground cherry can be started in a greenhouse about April 1-20 and transplanted into the garden about May 20 to June 1. The plants like full sun and are drought tolerant.

Solanum melongena - Eggplant
S. integrifolium - Tomato-Fruited Eggplant

Eggplants originated in India from bitter-fruited, spiny plants. Centuries of selection and cultivation have produced fruits whose bitterness has been almost eliminated. Records in China show that a non-bitter variety appeared in the 5th century B.C. Eggplants then traveled to Spain, Africa and Italy, where further development resulted in the varieties known today.

The first eggplants grown in Europe were probably small, white, egg-shaped types. Such varieties may have been responsible for eggplant receiving its English name.

Eggplants are perennial, but do not tolerate frost. Cuttings can be rooted, overwintered in a greenhouse, and then set out when the weather warms up the following spring.

BOTANICAL CLASSIFICATION

Eggplants belong to the genus *Solanum* and the species *melongena*. The plants of various varieties of *S. melongena* range from 1-8' in height. The fruits vary from the size of pearls to huge sword-shaped fruits over 18" long. Fruit color is just as variable and includes varieties that are light green, white (maturing to yellow), pink, purple, and white with purple stripes.

Red-fruited and orange-fruited eggplants belong to the genus *Solanum* and the species *integrifolium*. Both bitter and non-bitter types of *S. integrifolium* are cultivated in Asia and Africa. Their fruits lack a solid interior and are sometimes referred to as tomato-fruited eggplants or gilos. The plants grow 2-3' tall with fruits that rarely exceed 2" in diameter. Some of the wild types have tiny, bitter, orange fruits that are the size of peas.

Bright orange, tomato-fruited eggplant (*Solanum integrifolium*).

Solanaceae

POLLINATION, CROSSING AND ISOLATION

Eggplants are inbreeding plants. Eggplant flowers are perfect and are primarily self-pollinated. Some studies indicate that eggplant pollination is enhanced by insects, while other studies have demonstrated that just as many fruits form on caged plants as form on uncaged plants. Eggplant flowers are not particularly attractive to honeybees, but bumblebees and some solitary bees will work the flowers.

Cross-pollination can be prevented by isolation of 50' or by caging. Bagging the individual flowers is possible, but tedious. Cages covered with spun polyester or screen wire should be in place very early in the season before the flea beetles appear. Any flea beetles that are trapped inside the cage will continue to seriously damage the plants.

SEED PRODUCTION, HARVEST AND PROCESSING

Always grow as many eggplants of each variety as possible to maintain the greatest amount of variation within a population. Six plants should be considered an absolute minimum. Depending on the variety and the length of the growing season, several eggplants can be harvested for eating before the fruits that will be saved for seed are allowed to mature.

To save seeds from eggplants, let the fruits grow far past the edible stage. All eggplants change color when fully ripe: purple varieties become a dull purplish brown; green fruits turn yellowish green; and white fruits turn golden. At their ripe, inedible stage, the fruits are dull, off-color and hard. Seeds saved from immature or ready-to-eat eggplants will not be viable.

Several references have described saving seeds from eggplant fruits that are fully ripe but not rotten. This would seem to contradict nature, as the fruits must rot in order for the seeds to reach the soil and germinate. In most varieties, seeds from partially rotten fruits have germinated well. Harvested fruits can be held at room temperature for several weeks before cleaning. The firm, brown seeds are usually located in the bottom portion of the fruit.

Anyone who has ever picked seeds one by one out of eggplant flesh will appreciate the following method. Grate or blend the bottom portion of the eggplant, which contains the greatest seed density, using a hand grater or food processor. The small brown seeds are firm and slippery, so there is very little damage. The grating exposes the maximum number of seeds to the surface of the flesh. Put all of the gratings in a bowl or bucket that can hold at least twice that capacity. Some of the seeds will have popped free of the flesh and should also be put into the bowl. Add water to within 2" of the rim, roll up your sleeves and begin squeezing the gratings vigorously. The good seeds will come free and will sink to the bottom, and the grated flesh will float. Continue squeezing until very few seeds are left in the flesh. The grated flesh is then lifted out of the bucket and can be fed to the chickens or composted.

Another seed cleaning method requires a food processor with a blunt plastic blade, or a blender. Cut the bottom portion of an eggplant into .5" squares. Turn on the food processor or blender and gradually add the eggplant cubes. Pour in a bit of water and continue adding the cubes. When the receptacle is full, dump the eggplant mash into a bowl. Repeat if more cubes remain. Add fresh water to the bowl, stir the mixture, let the good seeds settle, and pour off the debris. Repeat until only clean seeds remain in the bottom of the bowl. Add more water and pour through a strainer. Dry the bottom of the strainer on a towel and dump the seeds out onto a glass or ceramic plate. Spread the seeds evenly over the surface of the plate and stir twice daily to ensure even drying, which prevents the seeds from bunching together.

SEED STATISTICS

Eggplant seeds will maintain 50% germination for seven years when stored in a tightly sealed container in a cool, dry, dark location. Thoroughly dry seeds sealed in an airtight container can also be frozen for long-term storage. Members of the Seed Savers Exchange annually offer about 129 varieties of eggplant, and the *Garden Seed Inventory* lists sources for 71 varieties that are available from commercial seed companies. There are approximately 5,600 eggplant seeds per ounce (200 per gram or 89,600 per pound), depending on the variety. Federal Germination Standard for commercially sold eggplant seed is 60%.

GROWING EGGPLANT FROM SEED

Eggplants are perennial plants grown as annuals. The plants are typically greenhouse started 6-8 weeks before the last average frost date, in order to ensure a long enough season for mature fruits. The seeds should be planted .25" deep. Germination temperatures range from 75-95° F. with germination usually occurring in 10-15 days in greenhouse conditions. Germination is greatly enhanced by bottom heat. Eggplant seedlings are not vigorous and are subject to several viral diseases. Use sterilized, soil-less, seed starting mixes, and avoid wood flats to limit disease transmission. Seedlings are usually transplanted 2-3 times before being set out in the garden. Eggplants do poorly in cold weather and should not be set out before the weather is stable and the soil is warm. Set out in full sun or afternoon shade in very hot climates. The plants should be set out 12-18" apart. Support is not needed but is beneficial in windy areas and where fruit set is heavy, which causes plant breakage.

REGIONAL GROWING RECOMMENDATIONS FOR EGGPLANT

Northeast: Eggplant cannot be grown for seed in this region, but some very early varieties can be grown as a food crop. The plants are started in a greenhouse March 20 and transplanted into the garden June 1.

Mid-Atlantic: Eggplants can be direct seeded April 15 to May 15, or started in a greenhouse March 1 to April 1 and transplanted into the garden April 15 to May 15. The plants like full sun and average water. Mites, thrips and potato beetles are problems.

Southeast/Gulf Coast: Eggplants can be started in a greenhouse about March 10 and transplanted into the garden May 1-20. The plants like full sun and are drought tolerant.

Upper Midwest: Eggplants can be started in a greenhouse about April 1 and transplanted into the garden about May 20. The plants like full sun and average water. Care must be taken to control flea beetles.

Southwest: Eggplants can be direct seeded from January 15 to May 15. The plants like full sun and average water.

Central West Coast: Eggplants can be started in a greenhouse about February 1 and transplanted into the garden about April 1. The plants like full sun and average water.

Maritime Northwest: Eggplants can be started in a greenhouse about March 20 to April 1 and transplant into the garden about May 20 to June 1. The plants like full sun and average water. Some of the later-maturing eggplant varieties may have difficulty reaching seed maturity.

REGIONAL GROWING RECOMMENDATIONS FOR TOMATO-FRUITED EGGPLANT

Northeast: Tomato-fruited eggplant cannot be grown in this region.

Mid-Atlantic: Tomato-fruited eggplant can be direct seeded from April 15 to May 15, or started in a greenhouse March 1 to April 1 and transplanted into the garden April 15 to May 15. The plants like full sun and average water.

Southeast/Gulf Coast: Tomato-fruited eggplant can be started in a greenhouse about March 10 and transplanted into the garden May 1-20. The plants like full sun.

Upper Midwest: Tomato-fruited eggplant can be started in a greenhouse about April 1 and transplanted into the garden about May 15. The plants like full sun and average water.

Southwest: Tomato-fruited eggplant can be direct seeded from January 15 to May 15. The plants like full sun and average water. Some varieties may have difficulty maturing before excessive heat comes on.

Central West Coast: Tomato-fruited eggplant can be started in a greenhouse about February 1 and transplanted into the garden about April 1. The plants like full sun and average water.

Maritime Northwest: Tomato-fruited eggplant can be started in a greenhouse about March 20 to April 1 and transplanted into the garden about May 20 to June 1. The plants like full sun and average water. Only a few varieties will mature here; others are daylength sensitive and will not reach maturity before frost.

—— *Solanum spp.* - Sunberry, Garden Huckleberry and Common Nightshade ——

Solanum Burbankii - Sunberry (Wonderberry)
S. melanocerasum - Garden Huckleberry
S. nigrum - Common Nightshade (Poisonberry)

Sunberry was introduced by Luther Burbank and classified as *Solanum Burbankii*. Great controversy immediately arose about its origins, because many people claimed that Burbank had simply reintroduced *S. nigrum*, the common garden huckleberry, as a new plant. In 1957 Charles Heiser set out to put the matter to rest and reexamined the sunberry. Although

sunberry does resemble *S. nigrum* somewhat, its berries are blue and slightly sweet in flavor while common nightshade has dullish black, acrid fruits.

The berries of *S. Burbankii*, *S. melanocerasum* and *S. nigrum* have long suffered under the same misapprehensions once associated with tomatoes. Talk of poison invariably enters any discussion of huckleberries and usually scares off even the most adventurous. All three species, however, are eaten by various cultures around the world. Even the leaves are cooked for greens in Africa.

Although some varieties may have slightly toxic leaves, the toxicity is destroyed by cooking. Also, studies indicate that the fruits of these three species are not poisonous. This is not to suggest that all small black Solanum fruits picked in the wild are edible. It is best to obtain seeds of known varieties and to grow the plants intentionally. The berries from all three can be used in jams, pies and preserves.

BOTANICAL CLASSIFICATION

Sunberry, which is sometimes called wonderberry, belongs to the genus *Solanum* and the species *Burbankii*. *S. Burbankii* has .25" deep blue fruits that are covered with a white bloom.

Garden huckleberries, which belong to *S. melanocerasum*, are commonly grown in the tropics of western Africa. The 3-5' branched plants produce .5" shiny black berries.

Common nightshade, which is sometimes called poisonberry or schwartzbeeren, belongs to *S. nigrum*. The multibranched plants grow 18" tall and produce .25" dull black fruits that have a strong acrid taste.

POLLINATION, CROSSING AND ISOLATION

Sunberry, garden huckleberry and common nightshade are inbreeding plants that all have flowers that are perfect and self-pollinating. The three species do not cross with one another. If unique varieties were to become available, however, different varieties within each species could be insect-crossed and would require isolation of 50' or caging to maintain seed purity.

Volunteer seedlings usually provide more than enough plants for growing and trading. Seeds need only be collected for preservation and exchange purposes.

SEED PRODUCTION, HARVEST AND PROCESSING

Select fully ripe berries from as many different plants as possible. Grind the berries in a food processor or blender, or squeeze each berry by hand. The berries do not need to be washed or have their stems removed, and a small amount of water can be added during grinding. The blended mixture is poured into a bowl, more water is added, and the mixture is stirred to encourage separation. The good seeds sink to the bottom of the bowl, while the skins, stems and immature seeds will float. The floating debris should be poured off very slowly and carefully. Add more water, stir, pour off the floating matter, repeat this process until only clean seeds remain at the bottom of the bowl. Pour the seeds into a strainer, wipe the bottom of the strainer on a towel to remove moisture, and dump the seeds onto a glass or ceramic dish to dry.

SEED STATISTICS

There is no known germination study for sunberries, garden huckleberries, or common nightshade, but experience would suggest that at least 50% germination would be maintained for four years. Members of the Seed Savers Exchange annually offer about 4 varieties of garden huckleberries (plus wonderberry and *S. nigrum*), and the *Garden Seed Inventory* lists 3 varieties of garden huckleberry and also a source for wonderberry that are available from commercial seed companies. There are approximately 33,600 seeds per ounce (1,185 per gram or 537,600 per pound), depending on the variety.

GROWING SUNBERRIES, GARDEN HUCKLEBERRIES AND COMMON NIGHTSHADE FROM SEED

Sunberry, garden huckleberry and common nightshade are annual plants that tolerate a wide variety of climates and conditions, but do not tolerate frost. All three species may be greenhouse started or direct seeded, covering the seeds .25" deep. The seeds germinate at temperatures ranging from 65-90° F. with germination usually occurring in 5-7 days in greenhouse conditions. The plants should be thinned or set out 10-12" apart in full sun, or afternoon shade in very hot climates. The plants are self-supporting, but sprawl over a large area. Cage or trellis plants where space is limited.

REGIONAL GROWING RECOMMENDATIONS

Northeast: All three species can be started in a greenhouse about April 20 and transplanted June 1. The plants like full sun and average water.

Mid-Atlantic: Garden huckleberry can be direct seeded about April 15, or started in a greenhouse about March 1 and transplanted into the garden about April 15. Sunberry and common nightshade can both be direct seeded about April 15 to May 1. All like full sun and average water.

Southeast/Gulf Coast: Sunberry can be direct seeded about May 1-15, or started in a greenhouse about March 15 and transplanted into the garden about May 1. Garden huckleberry can be started in a greenhouse about March 15 and transplanted into the garden May 1-20. This crop often re-seeds. Common nightshade can be direct seeded about May 1-15. All three like full sun and average water.

Upper Midwest: All three species can be started in a greenhouse about April 1 and transplanted into the garden about May 15. All three like full sun and average water.

Southwest: All three species can be direct seeded from March 15 to June 10. All three like full sun and average water.

Central West Coast: All three species can be direct seeded from April 15 to June 15. All three like full sun and are drought tolerant. Harvest when the berries are dark purple/black. Can become a weed.

Maritime Northwest: Garden huckleberry and common nightshade can be started in a greenhouse April 1-20 and transplanted into the garden May 20 to June 1. Sunberry can be direct seeded about May 15-30. All three like full sun and average water.

Solanum tuberosum - Potato

Potatoes originated in the mountainous regions of Peru where Indian farmers once grew more than 3,000 varieties. The introduction of the potato into Europe is rather obscure. Various references describe the potato as first being grown in the Netherlands, France, Russia and Switzerland. Today the vast majority of the world's potatoes are produced in Europe. The Soviet Union leads all other nations in consuming the most potatoes per person.

Gardeners throughout the United States have recently been introduced to yellow, blue, purple, and striped potatoes. Purple-fleshed potatoes are just as savory as their white counterparts and are a real conversation piece at the dinner table. Yellow-fleshed potatoes appear to have already been buttered.

SEED PRODUCTION, HARVEST AND PROCESSING

Potatoes grown for food are usually planted from tuber cuttings, so those plants are clones of the parent plant. Potatoes, which are inbreeding plants, are also sometimes raised from true seeds, by either potato breeders or by amateur experimenters. Potato blossoms will occasionally produce a small, hard, green fruit. The seeds contained in these seed balls do not come true-to-type; every seed will produce a different variety.

Potato seed balls should be picked about two months after they form, when they are completely mature and a bit soft. At this stage they often fall off the plant. Squeeze the seeds from the fruits into a bowl and add enough water to cover. The good seeds will sink to the bottom of the bowl. Add more water, pour off the debris, drain and dry the seeds. Some research suggests that a fermentation period of two to three days may aid germination. Potato seeds germinate best at temperatures ranging from 65-80° F. and are treated like tomato seedlings.

Potatoes are almost always propagated vegetatively by planting whole or cut tubers. Unfortunately,

viral diseases and root knot nematodes are often carried in the tubers, and several states, including California and Florida, prohibit the importation of non-certified seed potatoes for this reason.

Tuber-transmitted diseases and pests can usually be eliminated by utilizing the following method. Plant the tubers in a large pot, using a sterile potting mix. Let the shoots grow 6-8" tall and then cut them off at least 2" above the soil mix. Do not allow the growing shoots to bend over and touch the potting mix, and never let the cut shoots come in contact with it. The shoots are then planted in a flat filled with previously unused sterile soil. The original tuber and the potting medium should be burned to prevent contamination or disease transmission. The sprouts will root in the flat in about 10 days and can be planted into the garden as soon as a good root system has formed.

Cuttings from potato plants can also be taken and rooted whenever weather or insects threaten the crop. Rooted plants can be maintained in a cool greenhouse for up to a year.

SEED STATISTICS

Late potato varieties are the best candidates for winter storage. After curing, pack the tubers in baskets or boxes. Avoid storing potatoes near apples. Potatoes will keep for 4-6 months when stored between 32-40° F. and 80-90% humidity.

Members of the Seed Savers Exchange annually offer about 564 varieties of potatoes, and the *Garden Seed Inventory* lists sources for 163 varieties that are available from commercial seed companies.

GROWING POTATOES FROM SEED

Seed for starting potato plants is commercially available. Plants started from seed are free from the potato diseases usually transmitted when plants are started from tubers. Potato seed is typically greenhouse started 4-6 weeks before the last average frost

A few of the 600 potato varieties (*Solanum tuberosum*) being maintained by the Seed Savers Exchange.

date, covering the seeds .25" deep. Potato seed germinates at temperatures ranging from 65-80° F. with germination usually occurs in 5-7 days in greenhouse conditions. Germination is greatly enhanced by bottom heat. Set out in full sun, about 12" apart for both food and seed production. Afternoon shade is beneficial in very hot climates.

REGIONAL GROWING RECOMMENDATIONS

Northeast: Potatoes can be direct seeded May 10 to July 15. The plants like full sun and average water.

Mid-Atlantic: Potatoes can be direct seeded about March 1. Dig the tubers about June 15 and store in a cool dry place. Potato beetles are a problem. Tubers usually rot before they can be replanted, and virus contamination is also a problem. New tubers from more northern areas are usually used.

Southeast/Gulf Coast: Plant cut tubers from February 15 to March 20. The plants like full sun and average water. Floating row covers can be used to prevent Colorado potato beetle damage. Mulch, preferably with straw, when plants are 6" tall and again

four weeks later. Dig the tubers in June and store indoors or in underground pits. Early-maturing cultivars are best. Scab is a common cosmetic disease.

Upper Midwest: Plant late types April 15 and early types June 30 to allow digging from late September on. The plants like full sun and average water.

Southwest: Potatoes can be direct seeded from February 15 to May 15. The plants like full sun and average water. Desert soils are not conducive to good potato growth. Amend soils according to cultural requirements, particularly adding organic matter.

Central West Coast: Potatoes can be direct seeded about March 1 or November 1, or started in a greenhouse about February 1 and transplanted into the garden about March 1. Some shade is necessary. The plants like average water. Dig the plants in June and store in dark conditions. Replant in November or March. This is not a good crop for this region. It is difficult to raise disease-free tubers due to pressures from tomato diseases.

Maritime Northwest: Potatoes can be direct seeded from March 20 to April 10; usually asexually reproduced. The plants like full sun and average water.

Cyphomandra betacea
Tree Tomato (Tamarillo)

Tree tomato, sometimes called tamarillo, is native to Mexico and grown commercially in Australia. The shrub-like plants can grow 10' tall, but are extremely frost tender and will not overwinter in most areas. Tree tomato plants take about 18 months to produce fruit when grown from seeds. The plants reach full production in 3-4 years. In mild winter areas, the fruits mature from October to December. Red and yellow fruited varieties are available from several seed companies in the United States.

Tree tomatoes are inbreeding plants. Tree tomato flowers are perfect, but must be tripped or agitated for pollination to occur. Different varieties can be insect-crossed, so the flowers must be bagged or taped to maintain seed purity if more than one variety is being grown in close proximity.

Harvest fully ripe fruits and squeeze or pick the seeds out of the fruit. Using a strainer, wash the seeds thoroughly and then dry and store using the techniques described for Solanum species.

SEED STATISTICS

Four mail-order nurseries listed in the *Fruit, Berry and Nut Inventory* offer the seeds of tree tomato.

GROWING TREE TOMATO FROM SEED

Tree tomatoes are not suited to most of the regions in the United States. The plants are frost intolerant, heat-loving, daylength sensitive perennials that typically require 18–24 months to produce fruits. Tree tomatoes may be greenhouse started 6-8 weeks before the last average frost date. The plants are set out when the weather is stable and the soil is warm, and may be grown until the weather just begins to cool in the fall. Then cuttings are taken and rooted in a greenhouse, and the plants are overwintered in warm, moist, very light greenhouse settings. The plants are then set back out, and may bloom and set fruit during the relatively short days of spring. The process is then repeated each fall. Tree tomato seeds are covered .25" deep and germinate at temperatures ranging from 75-95° F., usually in 7-10 days in greenhouse conditions. Germination is enhanced by bottom heat. Seedlings are usually transplanted 2-3 times before being set out in the garden. The plants are set out 24-48" apart in full sun or afternoon shade in hot climates.

REGIONAL GROWING RECOMMENDATIONS

Northeast: Tree tomato cannot be grown in this region.

Mid-Atlantic: Tree tomato can be started in a greenhouse about February 1 and transplanted into a large pot about May 1. The plants like full sun and average water. Plants must be brought in and protected from frost damage.

Southeast/Gulf Coast: Tree tomato is started in a greenhouse March 1 and transplanted to a large pot. Bring the pot into a frost-free area to overwinter. Some shade is necessary. The plants like average water.

Upper Midwest: Tree tomato cannot be grown in this region.

Southwest: Tree tomato is not commonly grown in this region.

Central West Coast: Tree tomato can be started in a greenhouse about February 1 and transplanted into the garden about April 1. The plants like average water and full sun, but partial sun is okay. Dig plants before frost and pot in five-gallon pails. Protect from frost and replant about April 1.

Maritime Northwest: Tree tomato cannot be grown in this region.

Solanum muricatum
Pepino

Pepino is an inbreeding plant that is native to Peru and grown commercially in Australia. The plants are easily started from seeds. The flowers are perfect, but require tripping for self-pollination to occur. Different varieties can be insect-crossed. The plants are perennial, multibranched, 2' shrublets.

Pepino fruits are often light greenish yellow, and some also have purple streaks or stripes. Pepino tastes like a cross between a cucumber and a sweet melon, and is eaten fresh or in fruit salads. Pepino plants are available from some nurseries specializing in tropicals.

SEED STATISTICS

Fruit, Berry and Nut Inventory lists sources for 5 varieties of pepino that are available from mail-order nurseries in the United States.

GROWING PEPINO FROM SEED

Pepino is not suited to most of the regions in the United States. The plants are frost intolerant, heat-loving, daylength sensitive perennials that typically require 18–24 months to produce fruits. Pepino may be greenhouse started 6-8 weeks before the last average frost date. The plants are set out when the weather is stable and the soil is warm, and may be grown until the weather just begins to cool in the fall. Then cuttings are taken and rooted in a greenhouse, and the plants are overwintered in warm, moist, very light greenhouse settings. The plants are then set back out and may bloom and set fruit during the relatively short days of spring. The process is then repeated each fall. Pepino seeds are covered .25" deep and germinate at temperatures ranging from 75-95° F., usually in 7-10 days in greenhouse conditions. Germination is greatly enhanced by bottom heat. Seedlings are usually transplanted 2-3 times before being set out in the garden. The plants are set out 24-48" apart in full sun or afternoon shade in hot climates.

REGIONAL GROWING RECOMMENDATIONS

Northeast: Pepino cannot be grown in this region.

Mid-Atlantic: Pepino can be started in a greenhouse about February 1 and transplanted into the garden about April 15. The plants like full sun and average water. Dig plants before frost, pot them and keep in a frost-free location, or take cuttings and root. Mildew can be a problem.

Southeast/Gulf Coast: Pepino is not commonly grown in this region.

Upper Midwest: Pepino cannot be grown in this region.

Southwest: No experience growing pepino.

Central West Coast: Pepino can be started in a greenhouse about February 1 and potted into one-gallon containers. Transplant into the garden about April 1. The plants like full sun and average water. Dig plants before frost, pot in five-gallon containers, and replant about April 1 to produce a seed crop. Pepino are daylength sensitive and only bloom during short days.

Maritime Northwest: Pepino cannot be grown in this region.

————— *Solanum quitoense* —————
Naranjilla

Naranjilla is widely grown in Ecuador for juice. The yellow 2" fruits are filled with a green, gelatinous pulp that is sieved to prepare drinks and sauces. The plants grow for about seven months before flowering and take six more months to produce mature fruits.

Naranjilla plants quickly die in cold, wet soil. The plants are also very susceptible to damage from several different nematodes and do not tolerate any frost.

The stems and leaves of naranjillas are covered with soft, purple hairs. Plants can grow to 5' during their commercial production period, that usually lasts four years. In Ecuador the plants are grown in frost-free valleys at 3,500-7,500'. Seeds and plants are both available commercially in the United States.

SEED STATISTICS

Three mail-order nurseries listed in the *Fruit, Berry and Nut Inventory* offer the seeds of naranjilla.

GROWING NARANJILLA FROM SEED

Naranjilla is not suited for growing in most regions in the United States. The plants are frost intolerant, heat-loving, daylength sensitive perennials that typically require 18–24 months to produce fruits. In areas of the Central West Coast, Naranjilla may be greenhouse started 6-8 weeks before the last average frost date, usually in January-February. The plants can be kept in large pots in a sunny frost-free area, but some shade is generally necessary. Set out when the weather is stable and the soil is warm, and then the plants can be grown until the weather just begins to cool in the fall. At that time, cuttings are taken and rooted in a greenhouse, and the plants are overwintered in warm, moist, very light greenhouse settings. The plants are then set back out and may bloom and set fruit during the relatively short days of spring. The process is then repeated each fall. Naranjilla seeds should be covered .25" deep and germinate at temperatures ranging from 75-95° F, usually in 7-10 days in greenhouse conditions. Germination is greatly enhanced by bottom heat. Seedlings are usually transplanted 2-3 times before being set out in the garden. The plants are set out 24-48" apart in full sun or afternoon shade in hot climates.

Facing Page: Cool-storage seed vault in the basement of Seed Savers' office complex at Heritage Farm, where the seeds of more than 20,000 endangered vegetable varieties are stored. (Photo by Ian Adams)

THE UMBELLIFERAE FAMILY

The Umbelliferae family includes those groups of plants that have umbrella-shaped flowers. The "pedicels" (individual stems of each flower) radiate from a common point on the stalk. The family is very large with over 200 species. Many are oily and aromatic, and some are poisonous. Carrots, celery, fennel and parsnips are among the most commonly grown vegetables. Dill, parsley and coriander, which are commonly grown as annuals in the vegetable garden, have also been included.

FAMILY TAXONOMY

All members of the Umbelliferae family have flowers that are referred to as umbels. The main seed stalk initially forms the primary umbel, which contains the highest quality seeds. Additional branches form lower on the seed stalk and produce secondary umbels, usually smaller than the primary umbels. Smaller still are the tertiary umbels that form on small branches along the stalks of the secondary umbels.

The umbels develop and mature over a period of 30-40 days. The primary umbels mature first, then the secondary umbels, and finally the tertiary umbels. The maturation process may not be complete until the hottest part of the summer, and the seeds can be damaged when temperatures exceed 100° F. Some growers harvest the seed crop when the primary and secondary umbels are mature, rather than risk damaging their high quality seeds while waiting for the tertiary umbels.

Umbelliferae family members are often divided into those that produce roots and those grown for their foliage. The root crops are biennial, and must be over-wintered before producing seeds during their second season.

Several Umbelliferae family members are poisonous. Never presume that all wild plants with umbels are edible.

POLLINATION CHARACTERISTICS AND TECHNIQUES

Umbelliferae flowers are perfect, but cannot self-pollinate. The anthers shed pollen before the stigma is receptive. The individual flowers on each flower head open over a long period and the stigmas are receptive for 5-7 days depending on the genus. Thus, some of the flowers on any umbel will be shedding pollen and some will be receptive at the same time.

Honeybees and other hairy insects move pollen from one flower to another. In experiments where all insects were prevented from visiting the plants, only about 10% of the flowers produced seeds. The pollination that did occur was attributed to the flower bags rubbing back and forth across the flower heads on windy days.

Three methods can be used to save pure seeds of

Umbelliferae in the Garden		
Genus	Species	Common Name
Apium	graveolens	celery, celeriac
Anethum	graveolens	dill
Anthriscus	cerefolium	chervil
Arracacia	xanthorriza	Peruvian carrot
Chaerophyllum	bulbosum	turnip-rooted chervil
Coriandrum	sativum	coriander
Daucus	carota	carrot
Foeniculum	vulgare	fennel
Pastinaca	sativa	parsnip
Petroselinum	crispum	parsley, parsley root
Sium	sisarum	skirret

Umbelliferae. The easiest method is isolation. Depending on the size of the crop and the local geography, three miles is usually considered sufficient. In some areas weeds will also have to be controlled. Queen Anne's lace (wild carrot) and wild fennel are examples of weeds that will contaminate a seed crop.

Hand-pollination is also possible with Umbelliferae crops. For good seed production, the flowers must be hand-pollinated every day for at least two weeks and preferably for 30 days. The immature umbels are bagged before any of their flowers open. At least 10 umbels of each variety should be covered using Reemay bags, corn tassel bags, paper sacks or cloth bags. Secure each bag with a removable string or plastic twist tie. Each morning between 7:00-11:00, debag as many flower heads as can be kept free of insects. Rub a camel hair brush over the open flowers, moving from head to head and back again. Cover

---

Facing Page: Harvesting dill (*Anethum graveolens*) seed.

each flower head twice in rotation. This will help ensure that some of the flowers receive pollen from another plant. Rebag the flowers and repeat the process daily. The bags can be removed when all of the seeds have set, but be sure to tag the hand-pollinated umbels.

Bagged umbels may also be pollinated using the palm of the hand. Although not as effective as using a brush, this technique may be useful with carrots or when using similar techniques for seed-producing onions. After unbagging the umbels (or onion seed heads), gently rub the palm of the hand over the umbel in a circular motion. This helps ensure that pollen will come in contact with receptive florets. Always be careful to just barely touch the umbel, so that the tiny styles will not be damaged. Check your palm for tiny streaks of yellow pollen before moving to the next umbel. Keep as much pollen on the palm as possible while moving from one flower head to the next, so that each umbel will receive pollen from several other plants. All of the umbels must be kept free of insects while you work. Rebag each of the umbels and thoroughly wash your hands, arms, and under your fingernails before working with the next variety.

Two caging methods can be used with umbels. Alternate day caging is the easier method and requires that a cage be constructed for each of the varieties. Each morning one cage is removed; each evening that cage is replaced and an alternate cage is removed the next morning. This method allows insects to pollinate each variety for one day and excludes insects the next. Of course, this method requires isolation from any plants of the same species and any wild relatives. Once all of the seeds have set and flowering has stopped, the cages are no longer needed. Remember to tag the plants that were caged.

Caging with introduced pollinators, a rather complicated and expensive method for the home seed saver, is discussed in Section I.

GENERAL PRODUCTION AND PROCESSING TECHNIQUES

Two different methods are used for growing biennial Umbelliferae. The most common is the seed-to-root-to-seed method. Seeds are planted in the spring and the crop grows to maturity. The roots are carefully dug in the fall, examined and sorted. Healthy roots that are true-to-type are stored through the winter months. In mild winter areas the roots can be replanted almost immediately. In colder climates the roots are replanted in the spring, and the plant that results eventually produces a seed stalk.

In mild winter areas it is also possible to grow biennial Umbelliferae using the seed-to-seed method. The crop is planted in the summer or early fall, grows throughout the winter and bolts to seed during the next spring. Although this method is much less time-consuming, the roots cannot be examined and sorted, so any off-type roots are not removed before cross-pollination occurs. If there is any question about the purity of seeds involved, always use the seed-to-root-to-seed method.

The umbels are cut from the plant when the seeds are fully formed. If further drying is necessary, the umbels can be dried in the sun below 95° F. and then covered at night to protect from the dew.

It is easiest to rub the umbels over a screen to remove the seeds and break up the seed heads. Cleaner seed can be harvested from fully mature, dry umbels attached to slightly green stems. Gently rub the umbels between the hands. Most of the chaff can be removed by screening. Winnowing is sometimes difficult because the seeds are very light.

Apium graveolens - Celery and Celeriac

Celery is 94% water, which makes it a great diet food. Some dieters claim that chewing celery uses more calories than the stalks contain. Despite its low food value, celery is the third most common salad ingredient in the United States.

Wild celery, sometimes called smallage, can be found growing in damp and marshy areas from Sweden to Algeria and also throughout Asia. The wild varieties are rather bitter and were first used by the Greeks as a medicine. Not until the 16th century does the literature indicate that celery was being used as food. At that time the plants were probably very bitter and strong tasting. The stalks were covered with earth and blanched to make them more palatable. Through consistent selection, the stalks became larger and more commonly used as a vegetable, rather than as a medicine or seasoning.

Celeriac, which is also known as celery root or knob celery, was selected specifically for its roots rather than for its foliage. Celeriac roots are usually harvested when about the size of a baseball after one full season of growth. The roots taste somewhat like celery, and are used both cooked and raw. Celeriac is much less particular about growing conditions than celery and is easily grown throughout the United States.

BOTANICAL CLASSIFICATION

Celery and celeriac are biennials and belong to the genus *Apium* and the species *graveolens*. Self-blanching celery varieties are usually grown and sold through grocery stores in the United States. In Europe the stalks are still earthed up or wrapped with paper to produce blanched or white celery. Yellow, golden and pink celery varieties have garnered popularity at various times, but are rarely grown commercially.

POLLINATION, CROSSING AND ISOLATION

Celery and celariac are outbreeding plants. Celery flowers, like the flowers of other members of the Umbelliferae family, shed pollen before the stigma is receptive. Therefore, the crop relies on insects for pollination. All celery varieties will cross with one another as well as with smallage and celeriac. Celery does not cross with lovage. Isolation, bagging or caging are necessary to prevent cross-pollination between varieties. Pollination techniques are described in the introductory pages of the Umbelliferae family.

SEED PRODUCTION, HARVEST AND PROCESSING

Some gardeners harvest a few outer stalks of celery without pulling the plant out of the ground. This practice can increase the chances of plant injury and disease. If only a few stalks are carefully removed and the plant is not damaged, however, seed production should not be harmed. Celeriac leaves can also be lightly harvested during the growing season without diminishing the seed crop.

In mild climates, both types of *A. graveolens* can be overwintered in the ground. Where winters are severe, the plants must be dug and stored in a root cellar. Celery plants should be trimmed back rather severely and stored in damp earth or sand with the crowns exposed. Celeriac roots should be carefully dug, all side roots trimmed, and tops trimmed to 2". Celeriac will keep for 3-4 months when stored in slightly damp sawdust, leaves or sand at 32-40° F. and 90% humidity.

After being replanted in the garden the following spring, the plants will develop flower stalks that must be prevented from crossing, as was already discussed. Celery's primary umbels mature first and often shatter before the secondary umbels are dry. It is best to hand harvest the umbels as they mature. The seeds can be separated easily as the umbels are harvested

and will be fairly clean. Any remaining dust and debris can be removed by screening or winnowing.

SEED STATISTICS

Celery and celeriac seeds will maintain 50% germination for at least eight years when stored under cool, dry, dark conditions. Members of the Seed Savers Exchange annually offer about 11 varieties of celery and 6 celeriacs, and the *Garden Seed Inventory* lists sources for 68 varieties of celery and 19 celeriacs that are available from commercial seed companies. There are approximately 56,000 seeds per ounce (1,975 per gram or 896,000 per pound), depending on the variety. Federal Germination Standard for commercially sold seed is 55%.

GROWING CELERY (AND CELERIAC) FROM SEED

Celery and celeriac are biennials which are grown as annuals for food production. Celeriac, or root celery, can be grown wherever other root crops are successful. Celery requires a frost free, cool weather climate with plenty of nutrients and water, and is not adapted to the temperature ranges and season length in many parts of the United States. Celery may be direct seeded but is usually greenhouse started, covering the seeds very lightly. The seed germinates at temperatures ranging from 55-75° F. with germination usually occurring in 10-20 days. Plant or set out in full sun or partial shade, when the soil temperature is above 55° F. The plants should be thinned to 10-12" for celery and 6-8" inches for celeriac. Trenching or wrapping the mature plants may be used to lighten the color of the celery stalks, but also invites insect and disease problems.

REGIONAL GROWING RECOMMENDATIONS

Northeast: Celery (and celeriac) can be started in a greenhouse about mid-April (1st year) and transplanted into the garden after May 20. The plants like full sun and average water. Dig the plants in early to mid-October and store heeled in sand or soil or sawdust in buckets in a cool damp cellar. Celeriac foliage should be trimmed off and roots stored in tight barrels, with a minimum of root trimming and earth removal. Overwintering (both types) is very dicey here. I'm undecided whether celery tops are best left on or trimmed. Celeriac roots are hard to keep from drying out (spreens). I have very inconsistent luck with this crop.

Mid-Atlantic: Celeriac can be direct seeded from March 1 to April 1. The plants like full sun and average water. Celeriac plants overwinter in the garden with no special care. Humidity, rain and mildew make celery nearly impossible to grow to seed in this region.

Southeast/Gulf Coast: Celeriac can be direct seeded about March 15. Celeriac plants like filtered sun and average water, and overwinter with no special care. Celery winterkills, but celeriac often survives winter and produces flowers and seeds in spring. Celery, used as a food crop, can be started in a greenhouse about January 30, transplanted into the garden about March 15 and harvested for food about June 1-15.

Upper Midwest: Celery can be started in a greenhouse about March 1 and transplanted into the garden about April 25. The plants like full sun and average water. Dig the plants in early November, store in moist sand and replant in early April.

Southwest: Not commonly grown in this region.

Central West Coast: Celeriac can be direct seeded about August 1. Celeriac plants like full sun and average water, and overwinter in the garden with no special care. Celeriac is easy here, but celery usually can't stand the heat. Celery, being used as a food crop, can be started in a greenhouse about February 1, transplanted into the garden about March 15 and harvested for food before the heat of June-July.

Maritime Northwest: Celery and celeriac can be started in a greenhouse January 20 to February 10 and transplanted into the garden April 1-10. The plants like full sun and average water, and overwinter in the garden with no special care.

Daucus carota - Carrot

Carrots are the most important commercial member of the Umbelliferae family. Wild carrots are found throughout Asia, Africa, Europe and the Americas. Carrot roots were first used as medicine, but gradually gained importance as a food crop. Records indicate that carrots were first cultivated in Europe about the 10th century. By the 1600s carrots had become such an important crop that early American settlers are known to have brought several varieties from Europe.

BOTANICAL CLASSIFICATION

Carrots are biennial and belong to the genus *Daucus* and the species *carota*. Orange-colored carrot varieties are by far the most common, but white, yellow, red, purple, and black varieties are also available. Yellow and orange carrot varieties are high in provitamin A, while white carrots contain very little. The anthocyanin pigment in red, purple and black va-

Carrot plants (*Daucus carota*) in full bloom.

rieties does not contribute to their vitamin content.

Carrots range from 2-36" in length. The shorter varieties have been developed for heavy clay soils. Varieties are usually referred to as round, stubby, triangular or tapered.

POLLINATION, CROSSING AND ISOLATION

Carrots are outbreeding plants that are insect-pollinated and attract a wide variety of insects. All carrot varieties will cross with one another as well as with Queen Anne's lace, which is a wild carrot. Carrot varieties being grown for seed must be isolated by 1/2 mile. Techniques for hand-pollination and caging are described in the introductory pages of the Umbelliferae family.

Wild carrots can be a significant source of seed contamination. In areas where Queen Anne's lace is a common weed, isolation is nearly impossible. Even the carrot umbels inside cages made of window screen must be staked, because bees will cross any flowers that touch the sides of the cage. White root color is dominant in carrots, so crossing with the white-rooted Queen Anne's lace will eventually become visible. Such crossing in carrots often becomes apparent in a change in root color during the following generations. Extra care must be taken when growing white carrot varieties in areas where Queen Anne's lace is growing, because a change in root color will not be obvious.

SEED PRODUCTION, CROSSING AND ISOLATION

Carrots are best grown using the seed-to-root-to-seed method described in the general production techniques in the introductory pages of the Umbelliferae family. If this is impractical for gardeners in mild winter areas, at least dig down around each root to make sure it is the right color and right shape before letting the crop go to seed. Gardeners in northern areas should dig carrot roots before a hard freeze. Clip the tops to 1" above the root and store in sawdust, sand or leaves. Carrots will store for 6-8 months at 32-40° F. and 90% humidity.

The carrot umbels produced during the second season can be left to dry in the garden, or can be cut when fully mature and air dried for an additional two to three weeks. Many growers harvest the entire crop when the primary and secondary umbels are beginning to dry, since those umbels produce the best seeds. Home gardeners can gather the seeds as each of the umbels dries to a brown color. Some seed savers harvest, clean and save all seeds from the primary um-

Left and center: Carrot (*Daucus carota*). Right: Queen Anne's lace or wild carrot (also *D. carota*).

bels separately.

All carrot seeds have a beard or hairs on the seed coat. That may come as a surprise, if you have never seen home-saved carrot seeds. When commercial carrot seeds are cleaned, the beard is removed to make the seeds easier to package. Debearding is not necessary and does not affect germination.

Carrot seeds can be easily cleaned by rubbing the umbels over a 22 mesh (1/22") screen. The seeds will fall through such a screen and be partially debearded in the process. A second screening using a much smaller screen will remove any remaining dust and loose hairs. Carrot seeds are very light and should be winnowed with care.

SEED STATISTICS

Carrot seeds will maintain a high rate of germination for three years, after which the rate falls off very quickly. Members of the Seed Savers Exchange annually offer about 57 varieties of carrots, and the *Garden Seed Inventory* lists sources for 145 varieties that are available from commercial seed companies. There are approximately 19,600 seeds per ounce (690 per gram or 313,600 per pound), depending on the variety. Federal Germination Standard for commercially sold carrot seed is 55%.

GROWING CARROTS FROM SEED

Carrots are biennials that are grown as annuals for food. Carrot varieties are adapted to nearly every region and climatic condition. In mild winter areas, carrots may be planted in the late summer through the following spring for a continual harvest. Carrots are spring planted for fresh eating and storage in cold winter climates. Carrots are direct seeded, covering the seeds very lightly. The seeds germinate at temperatures ranging from 50-75° F. with germination usually occurring in 6-21 days. Plant in full sun, or partial shade in very hot climates. The plants should be thinned to 1-1.5" for food production.

REGIONAL GROWING RECOMMENDATIONS

Northeast: Carrots can be direct seeded in early July. The plants like full sun and average water. We use hex-wire caging to foil deer and other animals. Dig the plants in late October and store in tight barrels in a cold damp cellar, using leaves to cushion layers. Replant as soon as possible (early May). Alternaria blight often ruins seed heads, especially late ones. Due to our long winter, it is important to remove roots from the cellar as early in the spring as possible. As the cellar warms up, the spreen may either rot (too wet) or shrivel (too dry). Planting soon is the best prevention. Newly-replanted roots need lots of animal protection (hex-wire). Also, tarnished plant-bug can ruin the seed, even though it looks perfectly fine. Since my isolation plots are bordered by Queen Anne's lace, I must rely increasingly on caging.

Mid-Atlantic: Carrots can be direct seeded from March 1 to April 1. The plants like full sun and average water. Sometimes the plants overwinter in the garden with no special care, but mulching might help with overwintering.

Southeast/Gulf Coast: Carrots can be direct seeded March 1-30, or July 20 to September 1. The plants like full sun. Plants overwinter in the garden with no special care. Spring crops are for food only. Fall food crops need to be harvested by early December or they lose quality. Copious flowers are produced in mid-spring from any overwintered carrot.

Upper Midwest: Carrots can be direct seeded in early May. Dig the plants in early November, store in moist sand and replant in early April. Watch for crossing with wild carrot.

Southwest: Carrots are grown for a food crop in this region, but rarely withstand the heat to produce seed.

Central West Coast: Carrots can be direct seeded March 1, or from August 15 to September 15. The plants like full sun and average water, and overwinter in the garden with no special care.

Maritime Northwest: Carrots can be direct seeded from June 15 to July 15 (for a seed crop you want to plant later than for a food crop). The plants like full sun and average water. Dig the plants about October 1 and store in a root cellar or in punctured plastic bags with wood shavings in a cooler. Due to the freeze/thaw cycle in the Maritime Northwest, it is important to dig and store sound roots in a cooler or root cellar at 32-40° F. until late March to early April. Put the roots in a punctured plastic bag with wood shavings.

Petroselinum crispum – Parsley and Parsley Root

Curly leaf varieties of parsley are the most commonly used garnish in the world. Flat leaf varieties are usually processed into dried parsley flakes that are widely used for flavoring. Hamburg parsley, also known as parsley root or turnip rooted parsley, is savored in Europe but not often grown in the United States. The leaves of parsley root are flat and can be used as either a garnish or an herb. The roots are harvested after a full season of growth and have a mild parsley flavor when used like parsnips in soups and stews.

BOTANICAL CLASSIFICATION

All types and varieties of parsley belong to the genus *Petroselinum* and the species *crispum*. Parsley is a biennial and does not cross with any other vegetable species.

POLLINATION, CROSSING AND ISOLATION

Parsley is an outbreeding plant, which produces umbels that rely on insects for pollination. Like other Umbelliferae family members, a large variety of insects visit parsley flowers. A wild parsley exists that is native to Europe where it crosses with cultivated parsley, but the plant is not common in the United States. Isolation of one mile is commonly recommended for commercial crops. When more than one variety of parsley is grown in close proximity, use the hand-pollination or caging techniques described in the introductory pages of the Umbelliferae family.

SEED PRODUCTION, HARVEST AND PROCESSING

Parsley varieties can be lightly picked during the first year without harming the quantity or quality of the seed harvest. All varieties can be overwintered in the ground where winters are mild. Leaf parsley varieties store best when cut back and actually planted in earth or sand with their crowns exposed in a storage area where a temperatures from 32-40° F. can be maintained all winter. Although somewhat cold-tender, parsley will tolerate below zero temperatures in the ground when covered with 2-3' of straw or leaves. Parsley root should be carefully dug, and then tops are trimmed to 2" and all side roots are removed. The roots will keep 3-4 months when stored in sawdust, leaves or sand at 32-40° F. and 90% humidity.

Parsley seedheads, produced after replanting the next spring, will shatter easily and are usually harvested individually as each one becomes dry. The primary and secondary umbels will produce the highest quality seeds. The seeds that are dry can be rubbed off of the umbel during harvest. If the seeds are fully formed but not completely dry, the umbel can be cut and dried further. Small stems and other debris can be removed by winnowing or reverse screening. A very fine mesh screen will remove dust and small debris, while leaving the seeds on top of the screen.

SEED STATISTICS

Parsley seeds will retain 50% germination for three years when stored under optimum conditions. Members of the Seed Savers Exchange annually offer about 27 varieties of parsley, and the *Garden Seed Inventory* lists sources for 52 varieties that are available from commercial seed companies. There are 9,800 seeds per ounce (345 per gram or 156,800 per pound), depending on the variety. Federal Germination Standard for commercial seed is 60%.

GROWING PARSLEY FROM SEED

Parsley is a biennial, grown as an annual for food production. The plants are adapted to many climatic conditions, and often are grown as winter greens in mild winter climates. Parsley may be direct seeded or greenhouse started, covering the seeds very lightly. The seeds germinate at temperatures ranging from 50-75° F. with germination usually occurring in 12-28 days. Plant or set out in full sun or partial shade. The plants should be thinned to 8-10" for food production, 4-6" for breeding purposes.

REGIONAL GROWING RECOMMENDATIONS

Northeast: Parsley (and parsley root) should be direct seeded before July 10, preferably in early spring. The plants like full sun and average water, and require mulching in mid-October with leaves or straw (loosely caged, so the leaves don't blow away and for protection from deer and other animals). Dig the plants in late October, store heeled in soil or sand in a cellar, and replant in early May. Deer, woodchucks and rabbits are all problems, but covering the plants with hex-wire helps.

Mid-Atlantic: Parsley can be started in a greenhouse about January 15 or July 1, and transplanted into the garden about March 1 or August 15. The plants overwinter in the garden with no special care, but a compost or manure mulch helps in winter.

Southeast/Gulf Coast: Parsley can be direct seeded from February 15 to March 15, or September 1-30. The plants overwinter in the garden with no special care. Very early spring sowings (subjected to a good chilling) often bloom their first spring, when quite young. Overwintered plants bloom in late spring.

Upper Midwest: Parsley can be direct seeded about April 15. Mulching in early November (with straw, etc.) works about 50% of the time, but it is best to dig the plants in early November, store in moist sand and replant in early April.

Southwest: Parsley is not commonly grown in this region.

Central West Coast: Parsley can be direct seeded about February 1 or September 1. The plants like average water and full sun (but some shade is necessary for early plantings), and will overwinter in the garden with no special care. Fall planting is best, as early planting can result in some plants burning back.

Maritime Northwest: Parsley can be direct seeded from May 15 to June 15 (for a seed crop plant later than for a food crop). The plants like full sun and average water, and overwinter in the garden with no special care.

Umbelliferae

Anethum graveolens
Dill

A seed head of dill is an essential ingredient in most cucumber pickle recipes. Dry dill seeds are also used to flavor breads, pickles and stews. Several shorter varieties of dill have recently been developed.

Dill is an outbreeding plant that will not cross with any other vegetables or herbs. Different varieties of dill can be crossed by insects. Dill is an annual and goes quickly to seed. Time isolation is often used when attempting to save seeds from two varieties of dill. Plant the first variety early, and then sow the second variety when the first variety is beginning to flower. The first variety should set seeds before the second begins to flower.

Each dill plant produces several umbels that are usually allowed to dry in the garden. The seeds shatter from the heads very easily during cleaning. To avoid losing seed, select fully mature, dry umbels whose stems are slightly green. Rub the umbels gently to free the seed. Any small stem pieces or other debris can be winnowed or screened. Dill seeds do not need any further treatment.

SEED STATISTICS

Dill seeds will maintain 50% germination for five years when stored in a dry, cool, dark location. Members of The Flower and Herb Exchange annually offer about 7 varieties of dill. There are approximately 13,630 seeds per ounce (480 per gram or 218,000 per pound), depending on the variety. There are no Federal Germination Standards for commercially sold herb (or flower) seeds.

GROWING DILL FROM SEED

Dill is an annual, adapted to many climatic conditions. The plants are often grown for winter greens in mild winter climates. Dill is usually direct seeded, covering the seeds very lightly. The seeds germinate at temperatures ranging from 50-75° F. with germination usually occurring in 7-10 days. Plant or set out in full sun or partial shade. The plants should be thinned to 3-4" for food production, and 2-3" for breeding purposes.

REGIONAL GROWING RECOMMENDATIONS

Heads of dill (*Anethum graveolens*) ripen unevenly and shatter easily. Individual umbels are harvested as they mature.

Northeast: Dill can be direct seeded about May 1-15. The plants like full sun and average water.

Mid-Atlantic: Dill can be direct seeded about April 1. The plants like full sun and average water.

Southeast/Gulf Coast: Dill can be direct seeded April 15-30 or August 15-30. The plants like full or filtered sun and average water, and exhibit very fast seed-to-seed production.

Upper Midwest: Dill can be direct seeded about April 15. The plants like full sun and average water.

Southwest: Dill can be direct seeded from September 15 to March 15. The plants like full sun and average water.

Central West Coast: Dill can be direct seeded anytime. The plants like full sun and average water, and overwinter in the garden with no special care.

Maritime Northwest: Dill can be direct seeded from March 20 to April 10. The plants like full sun and average water.

Anthriscus cerefolium
Chervil

Chervil has feathery leaves that impart a delicate anise flavor to foods. The leaves are usually chopped like parsley and included in salads and vegetable dishes. Chervil is also an important ingredient in French *fines herbes* mixtures.

In mild winter climates where the plants can be mulched or protected with frames, chervil seeds are often sown in the fall for winter harvest. Chervil does not do well in the heat of the summer and often bolts before producing much useful foliage. Abundant water and a shaded location may be useful in delaying seed production.

Chervil is an outbreeding annual that produces an umbel with small, white flowers. Seed catalogs rarely list different varieties of chervil, but various insects, including bees, are attracted to the flowers and could easily cross-pollinate any separate varieties grown near one another. Chervil will not cross with turnip-rooted chervil, *Chaerophyllum bulbosum*. Isolation distances are unavailable.

Chervil plants produce small, oval seeds that shatter easily. Consequently the plants are noted for reseeding themselves, and daily harvest is necessary for maximum seed yield. Chervil seeds are easily separated from the umbels, and winnowing will remove any debris.

SEED STATISTICS

Chervil seeds will retain 50% germination for three years when stored in coo, dry, dark conditions. Members of The Flower and Herb Exchange annually offer about 4 varieties of chervil. There are approximately 12,320 seeds per ounce (435 per gram or 197,120 per pound), depending on the variety. There are no Federal Germination Standards for commercially sold herb seeds.

GROWING CHERVIL FROM SEED

Chervil is a perennial, usually grown as an annual in the North, that is successful in cool, mild climates. The plants are often grown for winter greens in mild winter climates. Chervil is usually direct seeded, and the seeds germinate best uncovered. Germination temperatures range from 50-65° F. with germination usually occurring in 7-12 days. Plant in partial shade. The plants should be thinned to 3-4" apart for food production, and 2-3" for breeding purposes.

REGIONAL GROWING RECOMMENDATIONS

Northeast: Not commonly grown in this region.

Mid-Atlantic: Chervil can be direct seeded about April 1. Some shade is necessary. The plants like average water.

Southeast/Gulf Coast: Chervil can be direct seeded about March 1-15, or September 1-10. Some shade is necessary; The plants like average water. Spring sowings flower in about 60 days; fall sowings don't bloom before being winter-killed.

Upper Midwest: Chervil can be direct seeded about April 15-20. Some shade is necessary; needs very wet conditions.

Southwest: Not commonly grown in this region.

Central West Coast: Chervil can be direct seeded from February 1 to March 1. Some shade is necessary. The plants like average water.

Maritime Northwest: Not commonly grown in this region.

Arracacia xanthorrhiza
Peruvian Carrot

Peruvian carrot is native to the highlands of the Andes Mountains, where it is a very important crop for several Indian populations. The roots taste like a cross between carrot and celeriac. Documented varieties include roots that are white, cream, yellow, orange, and purple.

Peruvian carrots are usually grown from crown cuttings and are adapted to short day, frost free, cool climates. Each plant produces about 10 carrot-sized roots during the 10-month growing season. The plants grow well during cool temperatures, but do not tolerate any frost and require short days for root production. There are no known commercial sources of Peruvian carrot seeds in the United States.

Chaerophyllum bulbosum
Turnip-Rooted Chervil

Turnip-rooted chervil, native to southern Europe, is a biennial plant with divided leaves and violet-colored leaf stalks. The 3" roots look like stubby carrots with gray or black skin and yellow or cream-colored flesh. Seeds are produced on umbels from roots left to overwinter in the ground. The seeds shatter easily, and care must be taken to harvest mature seeds on a daily basis.

Turnip-rooted chervil is an outbreeding plant. If different varieties of turnip-rooted chervil still exist, they would be cross-pollinated by insects if grown in close proximity. Isolation distances are unavailable. Turnip-rooted chervil does not cross with salad chervil, *Anthriscus cerefolium*.

The seeds of turnip-rooted chervil have very difficult germination requirements and only remain viable for six months to one year. Seeds can be sown in a prepared bed in the fall, barely covered with sand. A straw mulch should be applied before snow cover. Germination will occur in the early spring. Alternatively, seeds can be harvested and immediately stored in a cool place folded in a cloth between layers of sand in a box or jar. The seeds can then be sown the following spring.

SEED STATISTICS

The seeds of turnip-rooted chervil will remain viable for only six months to one year. A few members of the Seed Savers Exchange are offering turnip-rooted chervil. There are approximately 12,320 seeds per ounce (435 per gram or 197,120 per pound), depending on the variety.

GROWING TURNIP-ROOTED
CHERVIL FROM SEED

Turnip-rooted chervil is a biennial, usually grown as an annual. The plants can be successfully grown for winter greens only in cool, mild climates. The seeds germinate at temperatures ranging from 50-65° F. with germination usually occurring in 7-12 days. In the Central West Coast, turnip-rooted chervil is usually direct seeded (February 1 to March 1), and the seeds germinate best uncovered. The plants require some shade, like average water, and will overwinter in the garden with no special care. The plants should be thinned to 3-4" for food production, and 2-3" for breeding purposes. This is a difficult crop. The plants often die from heat and sun.

───────────── *Coriandrum sativum* ─────────────
Coriander

Grown nearly worldwide, this plant is known as coriander to Americans, cilantro to Mexicans, har dhania to Indians and uen sai to the Cantonese. The plant's green leaves are either hated or craved depending on personal tastes. Coriander's flavor is considered to be an absolute necessity in Southeast Asian cuisine, where it is used extensively. In ancient times coriander was used as a medicine in European countries, but has gradually found its way into the kitchen as a seasoning.

Coriander is an outbreeding plant that is easily grown, bolts quickly to seed and will not cross with any other vegetable or herb. Most seed companies that sell coriander do not identify any distinct varieties. Different varieties would be insect-crossed, if grown within 1/2 mile of each other. The time isolation technique described for dill would also be well suited for coriander.

SEED STATISTICS

Members of the Seed Savers Exchange annually offer about 4 varieties of coriander and cilantro, and the *Garden Seed Inventory* lists sources for 9 varieties that are available from commercial seed companies. There are approximately 2,100 seeds per ounce (74 per gram or 33,600 per pound), depending on the variety. There is no Federal Germination Standard for commercially sold herb seed.

GROWING CORIANDER
(CILANTRO) FROM SEED

Coriander is an annual that is adapted to many climatic conditions. Plants are often grown for winter greens in mild winter climates. Coriander is usually direct seeded, covering the seeds .25" deep. The seeds germinate at temperatures ranging from 50-85° F. with germination usually occurring in 7-10 days. Plant or set out in full sun or partial shade. The plants should be thinned to 3-4" for food production, and 2-3" for breeding purposes.

REGIONAL GROWING RECOMMENDATIONS

Northeast: Coriander (cilantro) can be direct seeded anytime before May 25. The plants like full sun and average water.

Mid-Atlantic: Coriander can be direct seeded from February 15 to March 15, or started in a greenhouse January 15 and transplanted into the garden March 1. The plants like average water and full sun (but partial sun is okay), and overwinter in the garden with no special care. We often allow this crop to re-seed naturally. Coriander grows in cool seasons only, and can be harvested for food in spring and fall.

Southeast/Gulf Coast: Coriander can be direct seeded February 15, March 15, April 15 and September 1-30 (succession sowing). Spring sowings are very fast seed-to-seed. Fall sowings often overwinter, but benefit from hoop houses in the Upper South. Plants often re-seed.

Upper Midwest: Coriander can be direct seeded

about April 20. The plants like average water and partial sun.

Southwest: Coriander can be direct seeded from September 15 to March 15. The plants like full sun and average water, but are drought tolerant.

Central West Coast: Coriander can be direct seeded anytime, but early spring or late fall are best. Does well with either sun or shade. The plants like average water.

Maritime Northwest: Coriander can be direct seeded from March 20 to April 10. The plants like full sun and average water.

Foeniculum vulgare
Fennel

Fennel holds an interesting and important place in vegetable history. The ancient Greeks grew it for use as a medicine, food and insect repellent. Fennel tea was also served just before important battles to instill courage in Greek warriors.

Fennel is available in three different forms. In many parts of the United States, fennel grows wild as a leafy herb. Fennel leaves and seeds are used in baked goods, teas and as a flavoring in candy. Sicilian fennel, which grows in southern Italy, has tender stems that are eaten like celery. Florence fennel, also called finocchio, is grown for its thick leaf stalks that form a bulb at the base of the plant. Sicilian fennel and Florence fennel are both biennials.

All types and varieties of fennel are outbreeding plants that can all be crossed by insects. Different varieties should be isolated by 1/2 mile. When more than one variety is grown in close proximity, hand-pollination or caging can be used to ensure purity. Fennel seeds are easily harvested from the dry umbels.

SEED STATISTICS

Fennel seeds will retain 50% germination for four years when stored in cool, dry, dark conditions. Members of The Flower and Herb Exchange annually offer about 6 varieties of fennel. There are approximately 6,860 seeds per ounce (242 per gram or 109,760 per pound), depending on the variety. There is no Federal Germination Standard for commercially sold fennel seeds.

GROWING FENNEL FROM SEED

Fennel can be an annual (the common herb), biennial (Sicilian fennel) or perennial (Florence fennel or finocchio), and is adapted to many climatic condi-

tions. Plants are often sown in the late summer and harvested during winter and spring in mild climates. In colder winter climates, sow the seed in the spring. Fennel is usually direct seeded, covering the seeds .25" deep. The seeds germinate at temperatures ranging from 50-75° F. with germination usually occurring in 7-10 days. Plant or set out in full sun or partial shade. The plants should be thinned to 4-6" for food production.

REGIONAL GROWING RECOMMENDATIONS

Northeast: Fennel cannot be grown for seed in this region, but can be grown as a food crop. Direct seed between May 1 and July 15 (bulb-Florence type). Harvest late June through mid-October (Florence types). Both types probably can be grown to seed here, but I have had little success yet.

Mid-Atlantic: Fennel can be direct seeded from March 1 to April 1. The plants like average water and full sun (partial sun is okay) and overwinter in the garden with no special care, but require mulching before frost in some areas.

Southeast/Gulf Coast: Fennel can be direct seeded from March 1 to April 15. The plants like average water and full sun (partial sun is okay), and overwinter in the garden with no special care.

Upper Midwest: Fennel can be direct seeded from April 15 to June 15. The plants like full sun and average water.

Southwest: Not commonly grown in this region.

Central West Coast: Fennel can be direct seeded from September 15 to October 1. The plants like full sun and average water, and overwinter in the garden with no special care.

Maritime Northwest: Fennel can be direct seeded about June 15. The plants like full sun and average water, and overwinter in the garden with no special care. Perennial species overwinter easily in this region, although finocchio will freeze and die in some areas.

Pastinaca sativa
Parsnip

Parsnip is a favorite vegetable in northern Europe. The plant is a biennial and its seeds are very difficult to germinate. In mild winter areas parsnip seeds can be sown in the fall, but will not form large roots before bolting to seed during the next spring. Parsnip grows best when sown in the early spring in cold winter climates. Parsnip roots keep very well in the ground in nearly all parts of the country and develop

Left: Cultivated parsnip (*Pastinaca sativa*).
Right: Wild parsnip (also *P. sativa*).

a sweet, delicate flavor after exposure to freezing temperatures. In areas that have extremely cold winters, the roots should be carefully dug and the tops trimmed back to 2-3". Parsnips will keep 4-6 months when stored in sawdust, leaves or sand between 32-40° F. and at 90% humidity.

Some books claim that parsnips left in the ground during the winter become poisonous. Such statements are not true. USDA has investigated many such claims and found that in all cases the poisonings can be traced to cicuta, the water hemlock that closely resembles parsnip in appearance.

Parsnip is an outbreeding plant that is insect cross-pollinated. Different varieties should be separated by at least one mile depending on the number of plants and the geography of the region. Parsnip can be grown either seed-to-seed or seed-to-root-to-seed. In many regions of the United States, parsnips have escaped from cultivation and become weeds. These weedy types will cross with cultivated varieties.

Juice exuded from the stem and leaves of parsnips can cause serious skin rashes. Gardeners should never touch their faces if there might be any parsnip juice on their hands. Workers in commercial fields wear special overalls, long-sleeved shirts, hats, goggles and gloves.

Parsnips are very similar to carrots in seed development, pollination, crossing and harvest. Unlike carrots, however, parsnips are totally hardy and will overwinter in the ground without protection in all but the coldest climates.

SEED STATISTICS

Parsnip seeds are extremely short lived, remaining viable for only one year even when stored well. Members of the Seed Savers Exchange annually offer about 52 varieties of parsnip, and the *Garden Seed Inventory* lists sources for 18 varieties that are available from commercial seed companies. There are approximately 4,900 parsnip seeds per ounce (172 per gram or 78,400 per pound), depending on the variety. Federal Germination Standard for commercially sold parsnip seed is 60%.

GROWING PARSNIP FROM SEED

Parsnips are biennials, grown as annuals for food. Varieties are adapted to a wide variety of climatic conditions. In mild winter areas, parsnips may be planted in the late summer through the following spring for continual harvest. In cold winter climates, parsnips are spring planted for fresh eating and storage during winter. Parsnips are direct seeded, covering the seeds .5" deep. The seeds germinate at temperatures ranging from 50-75° F. with germination usually occurring in 5-28 days. Plant in full sun, or partial shade in very hot climates. The plants should be thinned to 2-3" for food production.

REGIONAL GROWING RECOMMENDATIONS

Northeast: Parsnip should be direct seeded byJune 1. The seeds germinate and grow best in cool, wet soil. The plants like full sun and average water, and overwinter in the garden with no special care. Even though parsnips will overwinter in the garden, theyshould still be replanted at a greater spacing (2' x 2') in order to cull and select the crop. Untimely weather shifts can cause shattering, which is not usually serious. Parsnip worm makes a web in the flower-unbel, but frequent search-and-destroy inspections (once or twice a week) can control this.

Mid-Atlantic: Parsnip can be direct seeded from about March 1 to April 15, or from about August 15 to September 15. The plants like full sun and average water, and overwinter in the garden with no special care.

Southeast/Gulf Coast: Parsnip can be direct

seeded from March 1-30. The plants overwinter in the garden with no special care. When used as a food crop, dig from October 15 to November 30. Overwintered plants bloom in the spring.

Upper Midwest: Parsnip can be direct seeded in early April. The plants like full sun and average water, and overwinter in the garden with no special care. Crossing with wild parsnip must be controlled, which is abundant here.

Southwest: Parsnip is not commonly grown in this region.

Central West Coast: Parsnip can be direct seeded from August 1 to September 15. The plants like full sun and average water, and overwinter in the garden with no special care.

Maritime Northwest: Parsnip can be direct seeded from June 15 to July 15 (plant later for a seed crop then for a food crop). The plants like full sun and average water, and overwinter in the garden with no special care.

Sium sisarum
Skirret

Skirret is a hardy perennial that produces several wrinkled, grayish brown roots from the center of its crown. Like many other root vegetables, skirret's flavor is better after frost. The roots can be braised, stewed, baked or creamed and are often mixed with potatoes or salsify. Skirret often has a central core that cannot be chewed, which should be removed after the root is boiled.

In mild winter areas, skirret can be grown as a perennial. The plant's new roots can be removed for eating as desired. Skirret plants will produce seeds each summer after the second year. In climates where the ground freezes, skirret can be left in the ground if mulched with straw or leaves.

Skirret is an outbreeding plant. If different skirret varieties exist and were grown near one another, they would be crossed by insects. The plant's seeds are formed and harvested much like carrots.

SEED STATISTICS

Skirret seeds will germinate well for 10 years when stored in cool, dry, dark conditions. Skirret seeds are difficult to find in the United States, but are available from a few members of the Seed Savers Exchange and from members of the The Flower and Herb Exchange, and also are available from three commercial seed companies listed in the current edition of the *Garden Seed Inventory*.

GROWING SKIRRET FROM SEED

Skirret is a perennial, grown as an annual for its roots, which are harvested after frost. Skirret is direct seeded, covering the seeds very lightly. The seeds germinate at temperatures ranging from 50-75° F. with germination usually occurring in 6-21 days. Plant in full sun or partial shade in very hot climates. The plants should be thinned to 3-5" for food production.

REGIONAL GROWING RECOMMENDATIONS

Northeast: Skirret is not commonly grown in this region.

Mid-Atlantic: Skirret can be direct seeded about March 1. Some shade is necessary, and the plants like average water. Skirret plants are perennial and overwinter in the garden with no special care.

Southeast/Gulf Coast: Skirret can be direct seeded from February 15 to March 1, or September 1-30.

Upper Midwest: Skirret cannot be grown in this region, as insect problems are severe.

Southwest: Not commonly grown in this region.

Central West Coast: Skirret can be direct seeded about April 15 or September 1. Skirret is a perennial and seed is produced each spring. The plants like partial sun and average water, and overwinter in the garden with no special care.

Maritime Northwest: Skirret is not commonly grown in this region.

SECTION III

OTHER FAMILIES
WITH
VEGETABLE MEMBERS

Much of the Amaranthaceae family, particularly the genus *Amaranthus*, is in botanical disarray. In other words, the family's botanical classifications are a mess. Some researchers believe that all grain amaranth originated from a single species in Mexico and Guatemala, and then spread to Africa, India and North America perhaps 400-500 years ago through established trade routes. These scientists think that the various grain amaranths known today evolved as this single species adapted to its new environments and was subjected to human selection. Other researchers believe that several distinct species of grain amaranth originated in different parts of the world.

The definitive study of amaranths, resulting in a reclassification of *Amaranthus* genus, has yet to be made. As a result, it is extremely difficult to make conclusive seed saving recommendations. After consulting with amaranth researchers all over the country, however, a few general guidelines are available. Research is continuing, and more classification changes will undoubtedly be made. For the moment, the following seed saving guidelines should result in the maintenance of pure varieties.

One other genus in the Amaranthaceae family is edible. *Celosia cristata* or cockscomb has edible leaves and flowers, and *C. argentea* or quail grass has edible leaves. All varieties of *C. cristata* and *C. argentea* have tiny, perfect flowers that are generally self-pollinated. Celosia leaves are served raw in salads or cooked like spinach. Very young celosia flowers can be included in salads or vegetable dishes, but become rather coarse and hard to chew as they mature.

------------ *Amaranthus spp.* ------------
Amaranth

Amaranth was a sacred food of the Aztecs. During sacrificial ceremonies, amaranth seed was mixed with human blood and offered to the gods. Red seed heads were often associated with blood in Aztec legends that explain the origins of the plants. When the Spanish Christians invaded Central America and Mexico, they forbade the growing of amaranth because of its association with pagan rituals. As a result the crop nearly became extinct in Mexico.

In Asia, varieties of *Amaranthus tricolor* have been grown as a green vegetable since the beginning of recorded history. The leaves of all amaranth species are high in calcium and iron, but have a high oxalic acid content that diminishes nutritionally available calcium. Amaranth seeds are high in lysine, an important amino acid that is missing in most grain crops. This means that amaranth, when combined with another grain, provides a complete protein.

BOTANICAL CLASSIFICATION

All amaranths belong to the genus *Amaranthus* and one of several different species. Various studies have documented crossing between *Amaranthus retroflexus* (also called pigweed or redroot), *A. hybridus* (grain amaranth from India that has become a North American weed), *A. hypochondriacus* (grain amaranth), *A. cruentus* (grain amaranth) and *A. caudatus* (Love-Lies-Bleeding). Some of the crosses are extremely rare and result in sterile offspring. Crosses between *A. retroflexus* and some grain species do produce viable seed, but it is very weak. The research on crossing between the various amaranth species has not been completed. Eventually the five species mentioned above may possibly be combined into a single species known as *A. hybridus*.

Many of the names used for amaranth species in seed catalogs are botanically incorrect, or are outdated and no longer in use. *A. gangeticus* and *A. salicifolius* have been reclassified as *A. tricolor*, and *A. paniculatus* has become *A. cruentus*.

Several other amaranth species names also appear. *A. blitum*, a North American Indian species, is not known to cross with other species. Also two weedy species, *A. powelli and A. viridis*, are not known to cross with each other or with any other species.

A. caudatus, commonly called Love-Lies-Bleeding, was once thought to be incapable of crossing with other grain species. Recent studies have demonstrated, however, that *A. caudatus* will cross with *A. hypochondriacus*. Other crosses may possibly occur, but are not known at this time.

A. tricolor includes the vegetable amaranths, that are sometimes called tampala. All members of *A. tricolor* have black seeds, but not all black-seeded amaranths are *A. tricolor*. Varieties of *A. tricolor* also bear flowers in clusters along the stems of the plant. Varieties within the species will cross with each other, but not with any other amaranth species.

Grain amaranth plants can grow 9' tall and 3' wide.

Facing Page: Seed head of grain amaranth (*Amaranthus spp.*) shatters easily.

The golden or burgundy colored seed heads are very attractive in the flower garden as background plants. Leaf amaranth varieties usually grow about 3' tall, but frequent pickings can result in even smaller plants.

POLLINATION, CROSSING AND ISOLATION

Grain amaranths and leaf amaranths are both wind-pollinated and produce male and female flowers on the same plant. Insects are also capable of cross-pollinating different varieties within the same species, but amaranth flowers are so small that such crossing is rare. Honeybees will visit amaranth if other pollen is not available.

Amaranth pollen is very small and light. Some research suggests that amaranth pollen has limited viability and is not carried great distances. The minimum isolation distance between two leaf amaranth varieties is 500' if there is a tall crop in between to help prevent pollen drift. The isolation distance between two varieties within a grain amaranth species may need to be as great as two miles, if absolute seed purity is to be ensured.

Amaranth flower heads can also be covered with corn tassel bags to prevent crossing. Inbreeding depression, which often results from self-pollination, can be avoided by growing five plants closely together in a hill, possibly surrounded by a round, funnel-shaped wire tomato cage. The crowded plants will grow a bit smaller than usual. When the flower heads have formed but before any individual flowers open, make a bag that will protect all five heads. Spun polyester is the easiest material to use. Insects can be excluded from the bag by stuffing cotton batting around the five stalks where the bottom of the bag is taped or tied. The wind should do an adequate job of moving the flower heads within the bag. A vigorous shake each morning will also help move pollen from the male to the female flowers.

The bag should be left in place until the seeds are harvested, since each flower head will continue to produce flowers at its tip even after the seeds at the bottom of the head are mature. Larger groups of plants can be grown in greenhouse-sized cages and with wind produced by fans.

SEED PRODUCTION, HARVEST AND PROCESSING

Amaranth leaves can be lightly harvested from both grain and leaf varieties without damaging the seed crops. Plants that are weak or not true-to-type should not be used for seed production.

Amaranth seeds mature unevenly along the seed stalks from bottom to top. To produce the maximum amount of seed, the heads can be harvested as the seeds mature by shaking into a bag each day. It is much more convenient, however, to harvest the entire crop of seed heads when most of the seeds are ripe. The seed heads should be placed on a covered surface to finish drying, but the heads should not be dried in the direct sun, especially in hot summer areas.

Always wear gloves when handling dry amaranth seed heads, because their flowers can be very stiff and sharp. Leaf amaranths and small amounts of the grain types can be rubbed by hand to free the seeds. Wearing gloves, rub the seed heads and allow the seeds to fall into a bowl. Amaranth seeds are very small, so baskets are not recommended.

For larger amounts of seeds, place the seed heads on a tarp, cover with a second tarp and jog in place on top of both. Turn the seed heads several times and continue to jog until most of the seeds are free. Beating the seed heads together is also an effective threshing method. Holding the stalk of a seed head in each hand, beat the heads together while standing over a tarp.

Some people cut the mature seed heads while still moist and remove the seeds by rubbing before the heads have dried. This method is much easier on the hands, but the moist chaff and seeds should be dried quickly or mold may possibly develop.

Dry seeds that have been threshed can be placed in a bowl and swirled around several times. Large pieces of flowers will rise to the top and are easy to remove. Most of the cleaning can be completed by just tipping the bowl and raking out the chaff. Small particles of dirt and other material can then be removed with a fine mesh screen. Regular window screen is the perfect-sized mesh, once the seeds have dried. Winnowing in a light breeze will remove the remaining papery seed caps, but the seeds are very light so be careful.

SEED STATISTICS

Germination rates for the various species are not available, but amaranth is a long-lived seed. Members of the Seed Savers Exchange annually offer about 78 varieties of amaranth, and the *Garden Seed Inventory* lists sources for 68 varieties that are available from commercial seed companies. There are approximately 44,000 amaranth seeds per ounce (1,550 per gram or 704,000 per pound), depending on the variety. Federal Germination Standard for commercially sold amaranth seed is 70%.

GROWING AMARANTH FROM SEED

Both grain and leaf amaranth varieties are tender annuals that tolerate no frost. Varieties adapted to a wide variety of conditions are available. Grain varieties set seed over a 100-120 day period. Leaf varieties set seed somewhat faster. Direct seeding in an area receiving full sun is very successful. Cover the seeds very lightly, or not at all, in either greenhouse or direct seeding situations. The seeds germinate best at 70-75° F., usually within 8-10 days, but will tolerate higher temperatures. Germination rates decrease dramatically at lower temperatures. Set out the plants in full sun. Plants being grown for display and food production should be thinned to 18-24" apart, but should be left as close as 3" for breeding purposes.

REGIONAL GROWING RECOMMENDATIONS

Northeast: Amaranth can be direct seeded about mid-May. The plants like full sun and average water. Only some varieties will mature here. Seed heads are cut and after-ripened/cured in a dry, airy place with a tarp beneath them.

Mid-Atlantic: Amaranth can be direct seeded from April 15 to June 1. The plants like full sun and average water.

Southeast/Gulf Coast: Amaranth can be direct seeded from April 10 to May 10. The plants like full sun and are drought tolerant. This is an easy crop for seed production.

Upper Midwest: Amaranth can be direct seeded from April 15 to June 15. The plants like full sun and are drought tolerant.

Southwest: Amaranth can be direct seeded from March 15 to June 10. The plants like full sun and average water, but are drought tolerant.

Central West Coast: Amaranth can be direct seeded from April 1 to June 1. The plants like full sun and average water.

Maritime Northwest: Amaranth can be direct seeded from March 20 to April 10.

THE BASELLACEAE FAMILY

The Basellaceae family includes two rarely grown vegetables, basella and ulluco. *Basella alba* and *B. rubra*, commonly called Malabar spinach, are discussed below. Ulluco is a native of the central Andes Mountains of South America and thrives in cool, moist conditions with bright sunlight. The plants are very frost resistant and produce tubers which are eaten fresh like potatoes. The crop is also dehydrated by placing the tubers out to freeze at night. In the morning the tubers are stomped on to release their moisture and then left in the sun to dry. This process is repeated for several days until the tubers are totally dry. Prepared in this way, ulluco is called chuno and has been known to store for five years. Ulluco rarely sets seed and is usually propagated from stem cuttings or tubers. There is no known commercial source for ulluco tubers in the United States.

Basella alba
Malabar Spinach

Malabar spinach is a beautiful, frost sensitive, perennial vine. The plant is native to Africa and Southeast Asia, and prefers hot, humid weather which produces fast, luxuriant growth. Each seed is encased in a berry-like seed coat. The dark red juice from the seed coat is a potent dye and has been used as an ink substitute in India.

The thick leaves of Malabar spinach are not bitter and are used in salads in place of spinach. The leaves are somewhat "mucilaginous" (slimy), which can be easily overcome with salad dressings that include vinegar.

BOTANICAL CLASSIFICATION

Malabar spinach belongs to the genus *Basella* and the species *alba*. *Hortus Third* lists *B. rubra* as a variety of *B. alba*, while some references consider *B. rubra* to be a separate species. *B. alba* has a light green vine with dark green leaves. *B. rubra* has a red vine with greenish red leaves. Both species are available from several seed companies in the United States.

POLLINATION, CROSSING AND ISOLATION

Malabar spinach is an inbreeding plant with flowers that are perfect and self-pollinating. The flowers are covered by perianth segments and never open to expose the stamens. Malabar spinach varieties, including *B. alba* and *B. rubra*, do not cross with each other or with any other garden vegetables.

SEED PRODUCTION, HARVEST
AND PROCESSING

A continuous light harvest of Malabar spinach leaves does not appear to reduce the quality or quantity of the seeds. Malabar spinach is easy to grow

Malabar spinach: *Basella rubra*, left, and *B. alba*, right.

and nearly pest-free, but is one of the messiest plants for seed savers. Each fully ripe seed is encased in a black fruit that is firmly attached to the branch of the plant. When subjected to frost, Malabar spinach plants literally melt into a black slime, depositing their seeds on the ground. In its native climate, birds and small animals eat the berries and excrete the seeds.

In long season climates, some of the fruits will dry around the seeds. These can be harvested without any further cleaning. It is very important that the seeds be thoroughly dry, however, or mold can form on the moist seed coats.

In most areas of the United States, the purplish black fruits must be picked individually. Always be sure to collect fruits from as many different plants as possible. The fruits are then placed in a metal strainer that is partially submerged in a bowl of soapy water. When rubbed against the sides of the strainer, the fruits disintegrate, exposing the seeds.

A food processor can also be used instead of a strainer. Insert the blunt plastic dough blade and process the fruits with an equal amount of water for 30 seconds. This method will crack some of the seeds, however, and the plastic bowl of the processor will have to be bleached to remove the purple stains.

Rinse the seeds in clear water and dry the bottom of the strainer on a towel to remove as much water as possible. The seeds are then placed on a glass or ceramic plate to dry. Seeds should never be dried in direct sun or in an oven. Stir the seeds twice daily to ensure even drying. The seeds will turn light tan when completely dry.

SEED STATISTICS

Malabar spinach seeds will remain viable for five years if stored in an airtight container in a cool, dry, dark location. Members of the Seed Savers Exchange annually offer about 4 varieties of malabar spinach, and the *Garden Seed Inventory* lists sources for 2 varieties that are available from commercial seed companies. There is no Federal Germination Standard for malabar spinach.

GROWING MALABAR SPINACH FROM SEED

Malabar spinach is a heat-loving annual that tolerates no frost and is best adapted to hot, long season climates. Seed production begins at about 100 days, but viability is low at that time. A frost-free season of 150 days or more is recommended for quality seed production. The seeds may be greenhouse started to extend the season. Direct seeding is easy in beds receiving full sun, covering the seeds .5" deep. The seeds germinate best at temperatures of 80° F. and above. Germination is poor below 75° F. Germination is variable, but usually occurs in 10-12 days. The plants need to be trellised or tied to grow upright for ease of harvest. Locations in full sun will produce the strongest plants, which should be thinned to 12-18" apart for adequate growth prior to seed set.

REGIONAL GROWING RECOMMENDATIONS

Northeast: Malabar spinach cannot be grown in this region.

Mid-Atlantic: Malabar spinach can be direct seeded from April 30 to June 1, or started in a greenhouse about March 15 and transplanted into the garden about April 30. The plants like full sun, but partial sun and some shade are okay.

Southeast/Gulf Coast: Malabar spinach can be direct seeded about April 10-30. The plants like average water and full sun, but partial sun is okay. We trellis at planting.

Upper Midwest: Malabar spinach cannot be grown for seed, but can be grown as a food crop in this region. The plants like full sun and average water. Used for a food crop, it can be direct seeded about May 30 and harvested from August until frost.

Southwest: Not commonly grown in this region.

Central West Coast: Malabar spinach can be direct seeded from April 1 to May 15. The plants like full sun and average water.

Maritime Northwest: Not commonly grown in this region.

THE CONVOLVULACEAE FAMILY

The Convolvulaceae family includes sweet potatoes, one of the world's most important food crops. Another member of the family, water spinach or swamp cabbage, is a significant vegetable in Asia.

Ipomoea aquatica
Water Spinach (Water Convolvus)

Water spinach has a long history in China, where reference was made to its use about 300 A.D. The plant are tradionally grown in shallow water or muddy areas. Water spinach can become an extremely serious perennial weed in frost-free regions, if allowed to escape into waterways. For this reason, the seeds and plants cannot be sent to Florida, Louisiana or California. The plants can be started from either seeds or cuttings.

BOTANICAL CLASSIFICATION

Water spinach belongs to the genus *Ipomoea* and the species *aquatica*. The plants have hollow stems which allow the vines to float on top of the water. Two distinct types of water spinach exist. Ching quat is best adapted to mud culture and pak quat prefers aquatic culture.

POLLINATION, CROSSING AND ISOLATION

Water spinach flowers are perfect and self-pollinating. Different varieties grown in close proximity would probably be cross-pollinated by insects. Isolation distances are not available.

Mature seeds often drop into the mud or water and can be quite difficult to find. Daily collection of the mature seeds will result in the greatest harvest. In Asia the shoots are harvested until the plants begin to flower. The fields are drained when the seeds begin to mature, so that the pods can be harvested and dried. Workers walk or run over the seedpods to free the seeds.

SEED PRODUCTION, HARVEST AND PROCESSING

Water spinach leaves and shoots can be harvested prior to the blooming period with little decrease in seed quantity or quality.

Place the harvested pods in a warm place to finish drying. The dry pods are put into a pillowcase or feed sack with the open end taped or tied shut. Roll a rolling pin over the sack until the majority of the pods are broken open and the seeds are free. The seeds should then be dried for several additional days away from direct sunlight.

SEED STATISTICS

Water spinach seeds should remain viable for three years when stored in cool, dry, dark conditions. The seeds are available from two commercial seed companies in the *Garden Seed Inventory*.

GROWING WATER SPINACH FROM SEED

Water spinach is a perennial, aquatic vine that grows in bogs, ponds, or flooded fields. The plants require a long, warm season to produce abundantly, and do not tolerate frost. Water spinach is direct seeded or started from rooted cuttings. Plant or set out in full sun in wet or boggy areas.

REGIONAL GROWING RECOMMENDATIONS

Northeast: Water spinach cannot be grown in this region.

Mid-Atlantic: Water spinach can be direct seeded about May 1. Some shade is necessary; needs very wet conditions.

Southeast/Gulf Coast: Water spinach can be direct seeded from April 15 to May 15. Filtered or partial sun is okay. The plants require very wet conditions, or an aquatic bog.

Upper Midwest: Water spinach can be started in a greenhouse about April 1 and transplanted June 1. The plants like full sun and need very wet conditions.

Southwest: Not commonly grown in this region.

Central West Coast: Water spinach can be direct seeded about April 15. The plants like full sun and need very wet conditions.

Maritime Northwest: Not commonly grown in this region.

Ipomoea batatas
Sweet Potato

Sweet potatoes have been cultivated since prehistoric times and are thought to have originated in tropical America. The tubers come in an assortment of colors that include white, yellow, orange, red, and purple. The vines are used as a cooked vegetable in Asia.

BOTANICAL CLASSIFICATION

Sweet potatoes are members of the genus *Ipomoea* and the species *batatas*. Some varieties of *I. batatas* are incorrectly referred to as yams. True yams belong to a different botanical family, Dioscoreaceae, and are not related to sweet potatoes.

SEED PRODUCTION, HARVEST AND PROCESSING

Sweet potatoes are perennial vines that are propagated vegetatively, either by shoots or from the tubers. When placed in a warm, moist medium, shoots form along the sides of each tuber and take root, and can then be broken off and rooted in a seed flat. Unfortunately, serious diseases and pests, including root knot nematodes, reside in sweet potatoes and can be transmitted from garden to garden when the tubers or shoots are planted. Several states, including California and

Sweet potato (*Ipomoea batatas*) vines and flowers.

Florida, prohibit the importation of sweet potatoes.

The following method may eliminate some of these problems. Place each tuber in a pot filled with sterile potting mix, covering half of the tuber with mix. Allow new shoots to grow 6-8" long without touching the potting mix. Cut the shoots off several inches above the tuber and re-root them in a new flat. The original tuber and the potting soil should be burned to prevent contamination or disease transmission.

Sweet potatoes are adapted to many regions of the United States, but do require a warm, frost free season. The tubers store well in a root cellar. After several days of curing to harden their skins, unblemished roots are wrapped in newspapers or packed in baskets of sawdust, making sure that the roots do not touch. Sweet potatoes will keep 3-5 months when stored at 50-60° F. and 60-70% humidity.

REGIONAL GROWING RECOMMENDATIONS

Northeast: Sweet potatoes cannot be grown in this region.

Mid-Atlantic: Plant sets about May 1. The plants like full sun and average water. Dig the tubers from September to October.

Southeast/Gulf Coast: Set out slips from May 1-30. The plants like full sun and are drought tolerant. Use floating row covers, if needed, for protection from deer. Dig the tubers in September and cure at high temperatures before storage.

Upper Midwest: Sweet potatoes can be started in a greenhouse about April 1 to get slips, and then set out the slips in the garden about June 1. The plants like full sun and are drought tolerant.

Southwest: Sweet potatoes are not commonly grown in this region.

Central West Coast: Plant sets about April 15-30. The plants like full sun and average water. Dig the plants about October 15 and store in a dry, dark, cool but frost-free location.

Maritime Northwest: Sweet potatoes cannot be grown in this region.

THE GRAMINEAE FAMILY

Gramineae is an extremely large botanical family that contains nearly all of the grains and grasses. Only two genera and species, *Zea mays* and *Sorghum bicolor*, are commonly grown in the vegetable garden.

Sorghum bicolor
Sorghum and Broom Corn

Sorghum is an important source of sugar syrup in areas where sugar cane is not grown and maple syrup is not produced. In the fall, sorghum stalks are stripped of their leaves and cut into workable lengths. Then the stalks are ground up and pressed, and the sweet, green juice is cooked down like maple syrup. Different sorghum varieties produce subtle flavor variations in the syrup, which is used like honey.

Broomcorn is grown specifically for the plant's stiff tassels that are made into brooms and brushes. Broom making can be a unique and enjoyable craft experience. Without good instructions or a helpful neighbor with old-time knowledge, the process can also be very frustrating. The *Foxfire* series and other craft books offer excellent broom-making guides.

BOTANICAL CLASSIFICATION

All sorghums and broomcorns belong to the genus *Sorghum* and the species *bicolor*. Three types of sorghums have been developed and refined over several hundred years: sweet sorghums, broom corns and grain sorghums. Broom corn is usually considered to be a variety of sweet sorghum. Grain sorghum, referred to as milo and kafir corn in some regions, is primarily used as a relatively low-quality livestock feed in the United States.

POLLINATION, CROSSING AND ISOLATION

Sorghums are inbreeding plants. Sorghum flowers have perfect florets that are self-fertile and are generally self-pollinated. The wind is probably sufficient to trip the flowers and increase their pollination. A small amount of crossing may occur between all types and varieties of *S. bicolor*, but is easily prevented by bagging the plant's tassel as soon as it begins to emerge. Weather resistant corn tassel bags work well, but paper or spun polyester bags can be used in dry climates. The bags should remain in place until all of the seeds have formed. Seed should be saved from as many plants as possible.

SEED PRODUCTION, HARVEST AND PROCESSING

The seed tassels can be cut when the stalks begin to dry. Sorghum seeds are easily rubbed off by hand and can then be winnowed in a moderate wind or with a fan. Continue drying the seeds for several days, but

Mature seed head of broom corn
(*Sorghum bicolor*).

germinate at temperatures ranging from 65-90° F. with germination usually occurring in 4-10 days. Plant in full sun, thinning to 4-6" apart.

REGIONAL GROWING RECOMMENDATIONS

Northeast: Sorghum can be direct seeded from May 15 to June 1. The plants like full sun and average water.

Mid-Atlantic: Sorghum can be direct seeded from April 15 to June 1. The plants like full sun and average water.

Southeast/Gulf Coast: Sorghum can be direct seeded from April 15 to May 10. The plants like full sun and average water.

Upper Midwest: Sorghum can be direct seeded from May 15 to June 10. The plants like full sun and are drought tolerant.

Southwest: Sorghum can be direct seeded from March 15 to June 10. The plants like full sun and average water, but are drought tolerant.

Central West Coast: Sorghum can be direct seeded from April 1 to May 1. The plants like full sun and are drought tolerant.

Maritime Northwest: Sorghum can be direct seeded about May 10-20. This crop frequently does not mature here.

Zea mays
Corn

Corn is one of the three most important cereal crops in the world. The corn plant first evolved in tropical America and has grown there since pre-Columbian times. Trading between Indian tribes gradually spread corn from the South American Andes to southern Canada. Many tribes hold a special reverence for corn as a gift from the gods. The first white settlers on this continent received corn as a gift from the Indians, a gift that allowed their new settlements to survive. Today more acreage is planted to corn than any other crop in North America.

Hybrid sweet corns have nearly taken over the home garden market. Many gardeners find these hybrids, especially the new super-sweets, hard to resist. Other gardeners think the super-sweets are too sugary and prefer open-pollinated varieties for their old-fashioned flavor. Even many of the older dent and flint varieties can be eaten like sweet corn in a very immature state.

Popcorn is a must for every child's vegetable garden. Many of the tiny, multi-colored popping ears that are beginning to show up in trendy supermarkets

not in direct sun. Several of the seeds can be hit with a hammer to test for dryness. If the seeds shatter, the crop is ready for storage. If the seeds are mashed instead of shattering, continue drying.

SEED STATISTICS

Sorghum seeds remain viable for at least four years when stored in cool, dry, dark conditions. Members of the Seed Savers Exchange annually offer about 44 total varieties of sorghum (sweet, grain and broomcorn), and the *Garden Seed Inventory* lists sources for 38 varieties that are available from commercial seed companies. There are approximately 1,400 seeds per ounce (50 per gram or 22,400 per pound), depending on the variety. Federal Germination Standard for commercially sold sorghum seed is 75%.

GROWING SORGHUM FROM SEED

Sorghum is an annual that grows 8-12' tall. Sorghum varieties are adapted to a wide range of climates, and should be successful in areas where long season field corns are grown. Sorghum is direct seeded, covering the seeds .5-.75" deep. The seeds aren't really new. Some are as old as the Indian tribes who selected and isolated their characteristics over several centuries.

The tiny immature ears of corn being served by many fancy restaurants are also not really a new vegetable item. Originally these tiny ears were harvested in the Orient from suckers and the small secondary ears which formed after the main harvest. Their use was simply an attempt to harvest as much food as possible from each planting, not as a delicacy. When the royal families of China developed a taste for the tiny ears, Chinese farmers began planting corn very close together and harvesting the tiny immature ears. Then, over time, varieties that produced an abundance of smaller ears were bred especially for that purpose.

BOTANICAL CLASSIFICATION

All corn varieties belong to the genus *Zea* and the species *mays*. Teosinte, a wild ancestor of corn, has historically been referred to as *Z. mexicana*. In the 1970s a perennial teosinte was discovered in Mexico and has subsequently been named *Z. diploperennis*. Since that discovery, *Z. mexicana* has been increasingly referred to as *Z. mays subsp. mexicana*. Teosintes will cross with *Z. mays* varieties, however the tetraploid teosintes do so with difficulty.

POLLINATION, CROSSING AND ISOLATION

All corn varieties are outcrossing plants that are wind-pollinated and will cross readily with each other. Pollen is produced by the tassel that forms at the top of each stalk of corn, which is the plant's male flower. As the tassel ripens, tiny structures called anthers emerge along the branches of the tassel and start to shed pollen. Healthy corn plants produce one or more ears along their stalk. The ears and the silks that emerge from them are the female parts of the plant. The wind blows grains of pollen from the tassel onto the silks. Each silk that is pollinated results in a kernel of corn developing on that ear. Corn pollen is light and can be carried for long distances by the wind. Isolating a variety of corn by two miles will ensure

The incredible diversity displayed by traditional Native American corns (*Zea mays*).

Gramineae

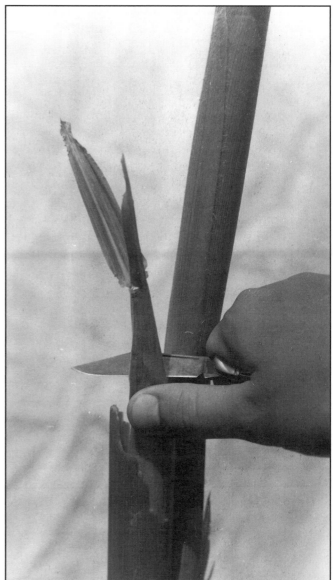

Left: In one smooth, downward motion, the leaf covering the ear is torn completely from the plant.
Right: The tips of the husk leaves are cut off to expose the emerging silks.

seed purity.

To provide maximum pollination in isolated patches, corns should always be grown in blocks rather than in long, single rows. If you choose to grow just one corn variety in isolation, grow at least 200 plants and break off the tassels of any off-type plants. Time isolation is also possible, which sometimes allows a gardener to save seeds from two varieties without having to hand-pollinate. Seed can be saved from both an early and a late variety that are planted near each other, if the tassels of the early variety finish shedding pollen before the silks of the late variety begin to emerge, and if the silks of the early variety dry up before the late variety starts to shed pollen. Time isolation sounds logical but variations in weather and maturity dates can be quite tricky, so the technique

should probably not to be counted on when working with rare varieties.

Most corn varieties are highly susceptible to inbreeding depression. If seeds are saved from too few plants for even one year, the loss of genetic diversity within the population is immediately noticeable and irreversible. Undesirable traits will begin to appear, such as the plants getting progressively shorter, yielding fewer ears and developing later in the season.

Inbreeding depression can usually be avoided by growing a population of 200 plants of each variety, which should maintain adequate genetic variability and diversity within the population. Out of those 200, always pull out and discard any plants that are not true-to-type. (Maintaining a highly variable land race would, of course, require a much larger population.)

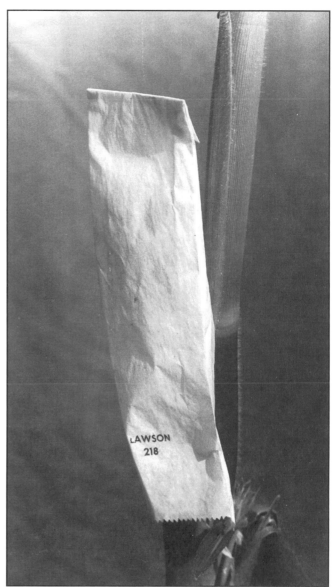

Left: Be careful not to damage the tip of the developing ear by cutting too deeply; remove just enough to expose a pea-size circle of silks. Right: A white shoot bag is wedged tightly between ear and stalk.

Inbreeding depression can also be minimized by never working with both the tassels and the ears on the same plants. Always try to bag the tassels of 100 plants and the ears of 100 other plants (50 of each is an absolute minimum). And be sure to make a mixture of equal amounts of seed taken from as many ears as possible, each from a different hand-pollinated plant within that population.

HAND-POLLINATION OF CORN

Hand-pollination, which is time-consuming but not difficult, is the only alternative for persons wanting to maintain the purity of two or more varieties of corn that are tasseling nearby at the same time. Uncontaminated pollen must be collected from the tas-

sels and sprinkled onto the silks of their ears. Bags must be placed around the ears before the silks appear and also around the tassels when the first anthers are beginning to emerge and shed pollen, in order to successfully control the pollination of the corn plant and to produce pure seed. This process was refined in Midwestern states where the air is saturated with corn pollen each summer when pollination is occurring, so the process does succeed in an atmosphere that is highly contaminated with foreign pollen.

Tools and materials needed to hand-pollinate corn include a pocketknife and a hand-held stapler, as well as shoot bags and tassel bags purchased from the Lawson Bag Company (PO Box 8577, Northfield, IL 60093, phone 847-446-8812). Lawson's bags are made from tough materials that will not decompose

Left: Tassels should be bagged when the anthers emerge and begin to shed pollen. Right: A brown tassel bag is stapled tightly around the stalk to prevent the pollen from falling out of the bag.

in the rain. Their #217 shoot bags are good for a wide range of ear sizes, and the #402 tassel bags are a good all-around size. Lawson Bag Company has agreed to sell these two styles of bags to home gardeners in lots of 1,000. (See "Supplies for Seed Savers" at the end of Section I.)

The process for hand-pollination of corn usually lasts two or three days, and possibly even longer if drought is slowing the rate of growth. (Sometimes an extremely diverse population can take more than a week, because the plants are not all at the same stage of development.) As an example, the two-day process would involve bagging ears on the first day, bagging tassels on the morning of the second day, and making the pollinations around noon on the second day. The three-day process would involve two days

of bagging ears at the beginning.

The hand-pollination process begins just before the silks start to emerge from the tiny ears. The first indication of that happening will be the appearance of husk leaves along the nodes of the stalk. Sometimes, however, the silks emerge almost before the tips of the ears become apparent. Many popcorns are difficult to work with for that very reason. Any silks that emerge before the ear is bagged will be contaminated with foreign pollen, which ruins that ear for seed saving purposes. If silks are already visible, the process should have been started sooner.

When it becomes apparent that the silks will soon emerge on a lot of the plants, bag as many ears as are ready that first day. Always bag the top ear, because the plant feeds that ear first and also aborts it last dur-

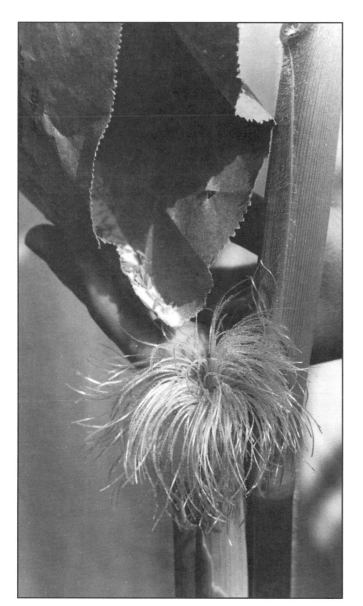 

Left: A portion of the pollen mix is shaken evenly onto the silks. Right: A used tassel bag is stapled loosely around the ear to prevent contamination and allow for further growth.

ing drought. Find an ear with husk leaves that are protruding, but from which no silks have yet emerged. Grab the leaf that is covering the ear and, in one smooth downward motion, tear that leaf completely off the plant.

Cut the tip off of the husk leaves with a pocket-knife, cutting off enough of the husk to expose the silks, which will look like a pea-sized circle in the center of the cut. Be careful not to cut too far down or the tip of the developing cob may be damaged, and that can encourage smut. More of the tip of the husks can be cut off than first imagined, but be careful with ears of popcorn which often have cobs that grow high inside the ear. How far to cut can be estimated by tearing open and examining a couple of ears on off-type plants that would not be used anyway.

The ear is then covered with a small white "shoot bag" that covers the whole ear and is wedged next to the stalk. If the shoot bag cannot be wedged behind the ear, make a small vertical cut with the knife down-ward between the ear and the stalk. The cut is often tricky to make. Try to just barely slit the base of the leaf that wraps around the stem. Be careful, because the ear can easily be cut off completely. It is always hard to wedge the bag into place if the leaf that cov-ers the emerging ear is not torn off. The number of ears that can be bagged the first day will depend on how many have silks that are about ready to emerge. More ears can also be bagged on the second day (and possibly the third, and the fourth, etc., depending upon the synchrony of the variety), especially if the tassels are still not shedding pollen.

Gramineae

The next objective is to staple a brown "tassel bag" around each tassel just as it begins to shed pollen. Close observation of the developing plants will reveal a green tassel emerging from the whorl of leaves at the top of each plant. As each tassel ripens, its lateral branches gradually droop away from the main vertical stalk of the tassel and eventually become horizontal. Tassels that are bagged when still too green will stop developing and not shed pollen at all, and green tassels can actually cook inside the bag in the hot sun. The perfect time to bag the tassel is when the "anthers" (tiny pollen-bearing structures) start to emerge along the tips of both the lateral branches and main vertical branch of the tassel.

Grab the stalk just below the tassel and give the tassel a vigorous shake. That will usually get rid of any foreign pollen that may have floated in and contaminated the tassel. Then pull all of the lateral branches upward and place the "tassel bag" over the tassel. The stalk of the plant should be placed in the corner of the tassel bag. Fold the opening of the bag back toward the stalk and then away again, before stapling the bag shut right beside the stalk. There are several folding techniques, but their common objective is to fasten the bag tightly enough around the stalk to keep the powdery pollen from falling down and out of the bag.

Avoid the large amount of pollen that collects in the whorl of leaves just below the tassel, which is usually old and contaminated. Staple the tassel bag well above that point, or tear off those leaves to clear that area.

Most pollen is shed from midmorning until noon, as the dew dries off and the tassel bags begin to heat up. The intense heat of the afternoon sun can kill the pollen inside the bags. If the tassel bags are left in place throughout an afternoon, the pollen collected will only be of fair quality and much larger amounts will be needed to get a decent set of seeds. A much better method is to put on tassel bags in the evening or the next morning after the dew dries, and then make the pollinations late that same morning or in the early afternoon.

In the late morning or early afternoon, pollen is collected from all of the tassels that were bagged. Bend each brown tassel bag over at a slight downward angle, but not enough to break the tassel or the plant. Give the tassel bag a couple of sharp whacks or vigorous shakes to dislodge as much pollen as possible. Unfasten the staple and, with the bag still held at a slightly downward angle, gently shake the tassel while pulling it out of the bag to dislodge even more pollen.

To help maintain as much genetic variability as possible, make a pollen mix by pouring the contents of all the tassel bags together into one of the bags and then shake the bag vigorously. The mix will contain pollen, a lot of dead anthers and quite a few live bugs. Pour the contents from the large brown tassel bag into the small white shoot bag taken from the first ear that will be pollinated. Gently shake the mixture along a seam of the brown tassel bag. The anthers will reach the lip of the bag first and can be carefully poured off and discarded. Then pour the pollen, which is the bright yellow, very fine powder, into the shoot bag. It is much easier to make the pollinations by shaking the pollen from the smaller shoot bag than from the large, clumsy, brown tassel bag.

Although the shoot bags are made out of white paper, the emerging silks can actually be seen through the sides of the bags. Each white shoot bag should be left in place until just before time to sprinkle the pollen onto that ear's silks. Too much pollen may be floating in the air to risk exposing the silks for any longer than necessary. Pollinations are easiest to make on a short 1" brush of silks that form a fairly even surface. If the silks are a lot longer than that or are ragged and different lengths, just cut back the silks to a 1" brush. That won't cause any damage or problems, because the pollen doesn't enter on the tips of the silks. Each strand of silk is receptive along its entire length, so the pollen can enter anywhere.

Try to estimate the amount of available pollen to be divided among the bagged ears that need pollinating. At first, it is difficult to guess how far the pollen will go, so be conservative. With a little gentle shaking, the pollen will settle to the bottom of the white shoot bag and any remaining anthers will float to the top. Make a small cut in one of the bottom corners of the shoot bag and shake pollen from that hole onto the silks. Shake on just enough so that the pollen is visible on the silks, probably about half a level teaspoon if there is that much for each ear. Sprinkle the pollen around uniformly, trying not to dump all of it in just one spot on the silks.

Now cover the pollinated ear with one of the brown tassel bags that was used to collect the pollen. Wedge the back of the bag between the ear and the stalk, into the old cut, and then pull the bag's bottom corners around *behind* the stalk and staple them a couple of times. The bag should be fastened rather loosely around the stalk to give the ear room to develop, but tight enough so the wind cannot blow it off. The bags can be left on until harvest to mark the ears that have been hand-pollinated. Also an indelible pen can be used to write the pollination date and other varietal data right on the bag, which will stay with the ear.

There are several potential sources of contamination that must be avoided. Always make sure that the tassel bags used to re-cover the ears are ones that were used on that same variety, or use new ones. Bags that were used in an adjacent block of corn will contain traces of other pollen. An easy way to make sure that tassel bags stay in the right block is to do only one population at a time, and throw away any extra tassel bags when you finish that population. The white shoot bags can be reused once or twice, but always wait at least a week to make sure that any remaining traces of pollen are dead. There is also a good possibility that pollen can be carried on a person's body or hands from one variety to the next. Avoid touching the insides of tassel bags, and always brush off clothing and wash hands thoroughly between varieties, concentrating on the fingernails.

HARVEST AND PROCESSING

Ears of corn are usually left on the stalks until completely dry. If insect or animal damage or weather conditions make that impossible, mature cobs can be removed, husked and dried under shelter. The drying should be done at a moderate temperature (less than 95° F.). To prevent damage, corn kernels should not be removed until both the cob and the kernels are dry. Electric and hand-cranked corn shellers work well when processing large quantities. For smaller amounts, simply rub two cobs together to remove the seeds from both. Any silk or cob debris mixed in with the seeds should be winnowed out. Kernels that are not completely formed should also be discarded. In a final attempt to minimize inbreeding depression, always make a mixture of seeds from 25-50 ears taken from different plants, taking more or less equal numbers of seeds from each ear.

SEED STATISTICS

Corn kernels should be completely dry before being stored. Sweet corn varieties will maintain 50% germination for three years when stored in cool, dry, dark conditions. Flint corns, dent corns and popcorns will retain high germination rates for 5-10 years (and sometimes much longer), depending on the variety and storage conditions. Members of the Seed Savers Exchange annually offer about 263 varieties of all types of corns, and the *Garden Seed Inventory* lists sources for 310 varieties that are available from commercial seed companies. There are approximately 156 seeds per ounce (5-6 per gram or 2,500 per pound), depending on the variety. Federal Germination Standard for commercially sold seed is 75%.

GROWING CORN FROM SEED

Corn is a warm to hot season annual, and should not be direct seeded when soil temperatures are below 65-70° F. The seeds are covered 1-2" deep and germinate at temperatures ranging from 65-85° F., usually within 4-10 days. Always plant in full sun, thinning to 6-8" apart.

REGIONAL GROWING RECOMMENDATIONS

Northeast: Corn can be direct seeded from May 15 to June 1. The plants like full sun and average water. The ears must be after-ripened before shelling for best quality. All corns must be electric-wired to deter raccoons. Sweet corn seed crops are sometimes ruined by late rains/mold.

Mid-Atlantic: Corn can be direct seeded from April 15 to June 1. The plants like full sun and average water, and prefer rich, fertile soil. Corn borers are a problem.

Southeast/Gulf Coast: Corn can be direct seeded from April 15 to May 10. The plants like full sun and average water.

Upper Midwest: Corn can be direct seeded from May 1 to June 15. The plants like full sun.

Southwest: Corn can be direct seeded from March 15 to July 15. The plants like full sun and average water. In the low desert, don't plant corn from May 1 to July 1.

Central West Coast: Corn can be direct seeded from April 1 to June 1. The plants like full sun and average water.

Maritime Northwest: Corn can be direct seeded about May 10-20. The plants like full sun and average water.

Gramineae

THE LABIATAE FAMILY

The Labiatae family includes about 180 genera and 3,500 species of herbs and small shrubs. Basil, the most renowned member of the family, has been included here because it is so commonly grown in vegetable gardens. Perilla and Chinese artichokes are both commonly grown vegetables in Asia, but are little known in the United States.

Ocimum basilicum
Basil

Numerous varieties of basil are native to India and have become important culinary additions to many cuisines around the world. Italian dishes are just not the same without basil. Holy basil grown near the doorstep keeps bad spirits from entering Pakistani homes. Anise and cinnamon basil fill a kitchen with lovely aromas that are said to stimulate the appetite. Lemon basil adds an unmistakable tang to salad dressings. Bush basil and purple basil make lovely additions to any edible flower garden.

Basil is an Old-World plant with an interesting but sometimes marred history. Chrysippus, who lived 200 years before Christ, condemned its use as "an enemy to sight and a robber of wits." The ancient Greeks, however, extolled its virtues and recommended basil for its medicinal properties as well as general culinary use. Roman gardeners believed that the tiny seed would not germinate unless they cursed the crop as it was being planted. Italian gardeners found that basil combined with olive oil and Parmesan cheese made the perfect pasta sauce and dubbed the concoction pesto.

BOTANICAL CLASSIFICATION

Basil belongs to the genus *Ocimum* and the species *basilicum*. The plants form small, multiple-branched bushes that, depending on the variety, can grow anywhere from 8-48" tall.

Left to right: Lemon, bush and sweet basil (*Ocimum basilicum*) in seed.

POLLINATION, CROSSING AND ISOLATION

Basil is an inbreeding plant. Basil flowers require insects for pollination and are frequently visited by thrips and small bees. Different varieties can be cross-pollinated by insects, but isolation of 150' will maintain seed purity. Alternate day caging can also be used, which would allow two or possibly more varieties to be grown simultaneously.

SEED PRODUCTION, HARVEST AND PROCESSING

Flower racemes mature progressively from the bottom of the stem to the top. When the bottom seed capsules start to turn brown, the stem can be cut and allowed to dry away from the direct sun in a well-ventilated area. Basil plants will continue to produce leaves and flowers even after the flower raceme is cut.

Each flower contains four seeds that are difficult to extract from the dried seedpod. When processing small quantities, rub each raceme over a fine wire mesh and winnow off the chaff. A seed thresher is recommended for larger quantities. Place the chaff and seeds in a bowl and very carefully swirl the contents around in the bottom of the bowl. The seeds will gather in the bottom of the bowl and the chaff will be on top. Tip the bowl until the chaff can be raked off and discarded. Then blow the rest of the chaff out of the bowl very carefully, because the light seeds can be blown away quite easily.

SEED STATISTICS

Basil seeds will remain viable for five years when stored in a cool, dry, dark location. Members of The Flower and Herb Exchange annually offer about 16 varieties of basil. There are approximately 22,400 basil seeds per ounce (790 per gram or 358,400 per pound), depending on the variety. There are no Federal Germination Standards for commercially sold herb seeds.

GROWING BASIL FROM SEED

Basil is a heat-loving, annual herb that may be either direct seeded or greenhouse started, covering the seeds .25" deep. The seeds germinate at temperatures ranging from 70-85° F. with germination usually occurring in 7-14 days. Plant or set out in full sun, thinning to 10" for food production and 6-8" for breeding purposes. Support may be beneficial for the very large varieties.

REGIONAL GROWING RECOMMENDATIONS

Northeast: Basil is not commonly grown for seed in this region.

Mid-Atlantic: Basil can be direct seeded from April 15 to June 1, or started in a greenhouse March 1 to May 1 and transplanted into the garden April 15 to June 15. The plants like full sun and average water.

Southeast/Gulf Coast: Basil can be started in a greenhouse about March 30 and transplanted into the garden about May 10, then continue monthly plantings until August 15. The plants like full sun and average water. Start new seedlings 2-3 times for a steady supply. Fusarium wilt is a common problem, so it is wise to plant extra.

Upper Midwest: Basil can be started in a greenhouse about April 1 and transplanted into the garden about May 15. The plants like full sun and average water.

Southwest: Basil can be direct seeded from March 15 to June 10. The plants like full sun and average water.

Central West Coast: Basil can be direct seeded from April 1 to June 1. The plants like average water and full sun, but partial sun is okay.

Maritime Northwest: Basil can be started in a greenhouse about April 1-20 and transplanted into the garden about May 20 to June 1. The plants like full sun and average water.

————— *Perilla frutescens* —————
Perilla

Perilla, a native of the Himalayas, is widely grown and much appreciated in Asia. Although closely related to basil, perilla leaves are not as fragrant. The leaves are widely used in pickling and as a condiment, and are highly valued for the beautiful red color that they impart to other vegetables. Turnips or white daikon radishes cooked with perilla turn a bright pink.

A leaf of perilla is often included in pickle jars in Asia. Like grape leaves in the United States, the pickles are thought to be crisper when the leaf is included. Ume boshi, a salt-cured plum, is wrapped in perilla leaves in Japan. Historically, the leaves have also been used as a seaweed replacement by Japanese Americans when seaweed was difficult to obtain in the United States.

BOTANICAL CLASSIFICATION

Perilla is a member of the genus *Perilla* and the species *frutescens*. The plants, which resemble an ornamental coleus, sometimes grow 6' tall but can be kept smaller by frequent picking. Both a green and a purple leafed variety are available in the United States.

POLLINATION, CROSSING AND ISOLATION

Perilla is an inbreeding plant. Perilla flowers require insects for pollination and are frequently visited by thrips and small bees. Different varieties can be cross-pollinated by insects, but isolation of 150' will ensure seed purity. Alternate day caging can also be used. Perilla seeds are harvested and cleaned like basil.

SEED STATISTICS

Perilla seeds will remain viable for five years when stored in cool, dry, dark conditions. Members of the Seed Savers Exchange annually offer about 4 varieties of perilla, and the *Garden Seed Inventory* lists sources for 4 varieties that are available from commercial seed companies. There are approximately 22,400 seeds per ounce (790 per gram or 358,400 per pound), depending on the variety.

GROWING PERILLA FROM SEED

Perilla is a heat-loving, annual herb that can either be direct seeded or greenhouse started, covering the seeds .25" deep. The seeds germinate at temperatures ranging from 70-85° F. with germination usually occurring in 7-14 days. Plant or set out in full sun, thinning to 10" for food production, and 6-8" for breeding purposes. Support may be beneficial, as the plants can attain 6' heights.

REGIONAL GROWING RECOMMENDATIONS

Northeast: Perilla is not commonly grown in this region.

Mid-Atlantic: Perilla can be direct seeded from April 15 to June 1, or started in a greenhouse March 1 to May 1 and transplanted into the garden April 15 to June 15. The plants like full sun and average water.

Southeast/Gulf Coast: Perilla can be direct seeded from April 15 to May 10. The plants can be invasive if allowed to re-seed.

Upper Midwest: Perilla can be started in a greenhouse about April 1 and transplanted into the garden about May 15. The plants like full sun and average water.

Southwest: Perilla is not commonly grown in this region.

Central West Coast: Perilla can be direct seeded from April 1 to May 15, or started in a greenhouse about March 1 and transplanted into the garden about April 1. The plants like full sun and average water.

Maritime Northwest: Perilla can be started in a greenhouse about April 1-20 and transplanted into the garden from May 20 to June 1. The plants like full sun and average water.

Stachys affinis
Chinese Artichoke

Chinese artichoke produces 2" pearly white tubers that are slightly pointed toward one end and are segmented like beads, like the rattles on a rattlesnake. *Stachys affinis* grows 10" tall and has square mint-like stems. The plants produce pegs like peanuts, with each peg producing a tuber. Any tubers left in the ground will resprout and can become a nuisance.

Stachys affinis is little known in the United States, but is grown throughout Asia and has been cultivated in China since the 14th century. Chinese artichoke is known as choro-gi in Japan, where it is an esteemed vegetable crop. French gardeners refer to the vegetable as *crosnes du Japon*, while English gardeners call the plant knotroot.

BOTANICAL CLASSIFICATION

Chinese artichokes belong to the genus *Stachys* and the species *affinis*. Both a white-flowered and a red-flowered variety are cultivated in Asia. A full season of growth and ample amounts of water will produce numerous tubers 3-6" below the surface of the soil. In most areas, the tubers can be left in the ground to overwinter.

SEED PRODUCTION, HARVEST AND STORAGE

Chinese artichokes are cultivated by tuber division. If the plants are grown without interruption for several seasons, white or red flowers will occasionally be produced and also possibly seed. Chinese artichoke tubers are dug in the fall or as needed throughout the winter in mild climates. Unwashed tubers also store well in plastic food containers in the refrigerator.

SEED STATISTICS

A few members of the Seed Savers Exchange offer Chinese artichoke, and four commercial seed companies are listed as sources in the *Garden Seed Inventory*.

GROWING CHINESE ARTICHOKE

Chinese artichokes are perennial, mild climate plants. Set out in full sun, or partial shade in hot summer climates, after the danger of frost has passed, spacing the tubers 6-8" apart and covering 2-3" deep. Sprouting usually occurs in 14-21 days.

REGIONAL GROWING RECOMMENDATIONS

Northeast: Chinese artichoke can be direct seeded by May 20. The plants like full sun and average water, and overwinter in the garden with no special care (but it's better to mulch them).

Mid-Atlantic: Set out tubers. The plants like filtered sun. Overwinter in the garden with no special care, but in very wet areas, dig and store tubers to prevent rotting in the ground.

Southeast/Gulf Coast: Chinese artichoke is not commonly grown in this region.

Upper Midwest: Chinese artichoke can be direct seeded (tuber propagated) May 15 to June 1, or started in a greenhouse April 1 and transplanted into the garden May 15 to June 1. The plants like filtered or partial sun and average water. Dig the plants before frost and store in moist sawdust or peat moss in a root cellar. Replant May 15 to June 1 to produce a seed crop.

Southwest: Chinese artichoke is not commonly grown in this region.

Central West Coast: Chinese artichoke can be direct seeded about April 1. Some shade is necessary; likes average water. The plants overwinter in the garden with no special care. Establishes perennial colonies and can become invasive.

Maritime Northwest: Chinese artichoke is not commonly grown in this region.

THE LILIACEAE FAMILY

The Liliaceae family includes asparagus and day lilies, two common garden edibles. Liliaceae does not include onions, which are now classified as members of the Amaryllidaceae family. Day lilies make a nice addition to any vegetable garden. Their blossoms are edible at all stages and make a beautiful garnish on plates and buffet trays. In China dried day lily blossoms are used in soups and vegetable dishes.

Asparagus officinalis
Asparagus

There are 240 genera within the Liliaceae family, but only asparagus is cultivated primarily as a food crop. Asparagus plants produce tender, edible spears early each spring. When asparagus plants are started from seeds, there is a three to five year wait for edible stalks. Step-by-step growing instructions are available in most garden books.

BOTANICAL CLASSIFICATION

Asparagus belongs to the genus *Asparagus* and the species *officinalis*.

POLLINATION, CROSSING AND ISOLATION

Asparagus is an outbreeding plant. Each asparagus flower develops with two sets of sexual organs. One set of organs aborts as the flowers mature, leaving all male or all female flowers on the plant. The flowers rely on insects, usually honeybees, for pollination. Wind is not considered a factor in asparagus pollination.

Asparagus varieties being grown for seed are easily crossed and should be separated by two miles. Alternate day caging has not been tried on a garden scale, but should work well.

SEED PRODUCTION, HARVEST AND PROCESSING

Asparagus can be eaten and also saved for seed, but seed quality and quantity will decline with each harvested stalk. Female asparagus flowers produce round, reddish, 3/8" berries containing six seeds. Birds find the berries tasty and often damage crops that are not caged or covered in some way. The ripe berries should be harvested before they drop from the plants. The fruits can be rubbed over a screen to free the seeds, which are then washed in several changes of water. Dry the seeds away from direct sunlight for several days before storing.

SEED STATISTICS

Asparagus seeds will maintain 50% germination for five years when stored under ideal conditions. Members of the Seed Savers Exchange annually offer about 6 varieties of asparagus, and the *Garden Seed Inventory* lists sources for 17 varieties available from commercial seed companies. There are approximately

1,400 seeds per ounce (50 per gram or 22,400 per pound), depending on the variety. Federal Germination Standard for commercially sold asparagus seed is 75%.

GROWING ASPARAGUS FROM SEED

Asparagus is a perennial plant that is best adapted to sandy soils in moderate climates. Asparagus seed can either be direct seeded or greenhouse started, covering .25" deep. The seeds germinate at temperatures ranging from 70-80° F. with germination usually occurring in 14-18 days. Plant or set out in full sun, or partial shade in hot, dry climates, and thin to 10-24" apart.

REGIONAL GROWING RECOMMENDATIONS

Northeast: Plant the perennial roots in May. The plants like full sun and average water, and overwinter in the garden with no special care.

Mid-Atlantic: Asparagus can be direct seeded about January 15, or started in a greenhouse from March 15 to May 15. For seed production, do not harvest the spears.

Southeast/Gulf Coast: Asparagus cannot be grown for seed, but can be grown as a food crop in this region. Set out crowns in late winter, as seedlings compete very poorly with weeds. Harvest from February 20 to April 1.

Upper Midwest: Asparagus can be direct seeded anytime. The plants overwinter in the garden with no special care.

Southwest: Asparagus is not commonly grown in this region.

Central West Coast: Asparagus can be direct seeded anytime. Grow the plants in pots for one year and set out from October to January of the second season in a permanent location. Asparagus is a perennial plant and will set seed each fall before dying back in the late fall. The plants like full sun and average water, and overwinter in the garden with no special care.

Maritime Northwest: Asparagus is not commonly grown in this region.

THE MALVACEAE FAMILY

Many members of the Malvaceae family are cultivated for their beautiful flowers. A number of species are edible, but only roselle and okra are grown as food crops.

Roselle, *Hibiscus sabdariffa*, is grown for its slightly acid-tasting red flowers which are steeped in sugar water and used for a refreshing beverage or as a base for jelly. The beautiful plants, that are also known as Jamaica sorrel and jelly plant, are often grown in flower gardens.

Roselle's flowers are perfect and do not cross with okra, cotton or hibiscus. If more than one variety of roselle is grown, isolate crops by 1/2 mile or bag individual blossoms to prevent cross-pollination by insects.

Abelmoschus esculentus
Okra

Okra's origins are obscure at best. Some European references cite Central and South America, but the species probably originated in Ethiopia and the Upper Nile where numerous wild varieties have been found. Several perennial varieties have also been found in West Africa. The presence of okra in the Americas can probably be traced to African slaves who most likely brought along seeds of the cherished plants.

BOTANICAL CLASSIFICATION

Okra belongs to the genus *Abelmoschus* and the species *esculentus*. Prior to the release of *Hortus Third*, *A. esculentus* was sometimes referred to as *Hibiscus esculentus*.

POLLINATION, CROSSING AND ISOLATION

Okra is an inbreeding plant. Okra flowers are perfect and self-pollinating, but are also large, showy, full of pollen and very attractive to bees. Different varieties are easily cross-pollinated by insects and must be isolated by one mile. Okra does not cross with roselle, cotton or hibiscus. To prevent crossing, entire plants can be caged or individual blossoms can be bagged. Muslin 4" x 6" drawstring bags make ideal individual blossom bags. Pieces of nylon hosiery or spun polyester are also easily adaptable.

Healthy, true-to-type plants should be selected for seed saving. In the late afternoon or evening put a bag over each okra blossom that is ready to open the next morning. The flowers will be fat, will have a light green striped appearance, and may also be starting to show some color. Each bag must be secured using a drawstring, rubber band or masking tape, making sure that insects are unable to wiggle in and

Unripe, ready-to-eat okra pods (*Abelmoschus esculentus*).

pollinate the blossom. Self-pollination takes place shortly after the blossoms open, and the flowers are completely unreceptive to pollen by noon. Leave the bags on during the next full day after the blossom opens, and then remove the bags the following day. At the same time that the bags are being removed, tag those blossoms with poultry bands, yarn, string or plastic ribbon. Okra pollen can remain viable for up to 24 hours, especially on cool days, so the bags should not be reused on other blossoms for at least 48 hours.

SEED PRODUCTION, HARVEST AND PROCESSING

Okra plants that are harvested consistently will continue to produce pods over a long period of time. A light harvest early in the season will have a very minimal effect on the number of pods available for seed production.

Green okra plants often cause skin irritations, but the dry pods are downright nasty. Always wear gloves when harvesting and cleaning okra pods. Still green but fully mature pods can be picked and left to finish drying away from direct sun until they split open.

Wearing gloves, break each pod open and let the seeds fall into a bowl or tightly woven basket. Dry pods can also be secured inside a feed sack or pillowcase. Place the sack on a hard surface and jog in place on it, which will break the pods open and free the seeds. Remove any crushed pieces of pods and dirt by using a hair dryer or fan to winnow the seeds.

SEED STATISTICS

Okra seeds will maintain 50% germination for five years when stored under ideal conditions. Members of the Seed Savers Exchange annually offer about 59 varieties of okra, and the *Garden Seed Inventory* lists sources for 43 varieties that are available from commercial seed companies in the United States and Canada. There are approximately 560 okra seeds per ounce (20 per gram or 8,960 per pound), depending on the variety. Federal Germination Standard for commercially sold okra seed is 50%.

Malvaceae

GROWING OKRA FROM SEED

Okra is a heat-loving annual that is usually direct seeded, but may be greenhouse started in short season climates. Okra seed should be planted .5-.75" deep and will germinate at temperatures ranging from 70-95° F., usually within 7-12 days. Plant or set out in full sun, thinning to 12-18" apart.

REGIONAL GROWING RECOMMENDATIONS

Northeast: Okra cannot be grown in this region.
Mid-Atlantic: Okra can be direct seeded from April 15 to June 15. The plants like full sun and average water.
Southeast/Gulf Coast: Okra can be direct seeded May 1-30. The plants like full sun and are drought tolerant.
Upper Midwest: Okra can be direct seeded about May 15. The plants like full sun and average water.
Southwest: Okra can be direct seeded March 15 to June 10. The plants like full sun and average water.
Central West Coast: Okra can be direct seeded from April 1 to June 1.
Maritime Northwest: There are not enough heat units in the Maritime Northwest to grow okra.

THE MARTYNIACEAE FAMILY

All three genera of the Martyniaceae family have sticky, hairy leaves, orchid-like flowers and woody, beak-shaped pods. The seeds of the yellow-flowered *Ibicella lutea*, which is native to South America, are not commercially available in the United States, although the species occurs as an occasional weed in California's Central Valley. Introduced members of the *Martynia* and *Proboscidea* genera are often found growing as weeds in the southwestern United States.

Martynia and *Proboscidea spp.*
Devil's Claw (Unicorn Plant)

Martynia annua - Devil's Claw
Proboscidea fragrans - Devil's Claw
P. louisianica - Devil's Claw

Devil's claw is a rather attractive plant with fragrant, orchid-like flowers. The green pods are edible when immature and can be cooked like okra with tomatoes and onions. Many farmers spray the wild plants with herbicides, so never eat pods from plants found growing near cultivated fields. Martynia pickles are a favorite in some parts of Mexico. The seeds can be opened and eaten like sunflower seeds or pressed to produce oil. American Indian tribes in the desert Southwest soaked the black pods in water and used the fibers in basket weaving.

BOTANICAL CLASSIFICATION

There is very little difference between the *Martynia* and *Proboscidea* genera. Martynia flowers have a calyx with five separate sepals and two fertile stamens. Proboscidea flowers have four fertile stamens.
Proboscidea fragrans, a dark purple-flowered species native to Brazil, is often found growing wild in the southwestern United States. *P. louisianica*, which has white flowers with violet and red spots, is most often seen in Gulf Coast states. *Martynia annua*, which has creamy violet flowers, is found throughout the United States and is classified as a noxious weed in some states.

POLLINATION, CROSSING AND ISOLATION

The three devil's claw species are all inbreeding plants that do not cross with one another, however different varieties within each of the species can be cross-pollinated by insects. When two or more varieties within the same species are grown in close proximity, seed purity can be ensured with isolation of 1/2 mile or by using alternate day caging.

SEED PRODUCTION, HARVEST AND PROCESSING

When devil's claw pods begin to dry, the green outer husk falls away, exposing the black, woody, beak-like pods. Completely dry pods split open, exposing the seeds. The curved tips of the pods are very sharp and can cause serious injury if lodged in the legs or feet of pets or farm animals. Care must be taken during seed cleaning to avoid puncturing or lacerating fingers and arms.

SEED STATISTICS

Various reports state that devil's claw seeds germinate well for only two years, but personal experience indicates that the seeds will maintain 75% germination for five years or longer. Members of the

Foliage, flowers, immature pods and dry pods of South American devil's claw (*Martynia spp.*).

Seed Savers Exchange annually offer about 2 varieties of devil's claw, and the *Garden Seed Inventory* lists sources for 8 varieties that are available from commercial seed companies.

GROWING DEVIL'S CLAW FROM SEED

Devil's claw is a heat-loving annual with a bad reputation as a weed. Usually it is direct seeded, but may be greenhouse started in short or cool summer climates. The seeds are planted .5" deep and germinate at temperatures ranging from 75-90° F., usually in 7-10 days. Plant or set out in full sun, or afternoon shade, thinning to 12-18" apart. The plants sprawl and may benefit from some support where space is at a premium.

REGIONAL GROWING RECOMMENDATIONS

Northeast: Devil's claw (unicorn plant) cannot be grown in this region.

Mid-Atlantic: Devil's claw can be direct seeded from April 15 to May 15. The plants like full sun and are drought tolerant.

Southeast/Gulf Coast: Devil's claw can be direct seeded from about May 1-30. The plants like full sun and are drought tolerant. Care is needed when handling the pods of devil's claw. The seed is difficult to germinate.

Upper Midwest: Devil's claw can be direct seeded anytime up to June 15. The plants like full sun and are drought tolerant.

Southwest: Devil's claw can be direct seeded from April 15 to June 10. The plants like full sun and are drought tolerant.

Central West Coast: Devil's claw can be direct seeded from April 1 to May 1. The plants like full sun and are drought tolerant.

Maritime Northwest: Devil's claw cannot be grown in this region.

Martyniaceae

Two members of the Polygonaceae family commonly appear in the vegetable garden. Both rhubarb and sorrel have been used as vegetables and medicines since before the time of Christ. Dioscorides, a Roman doctor, used rhubarb to treat Anthony and Cleopatra for weakness of the stomach. Dioscorides also used preparations made from rhubarb to treat ringworm and diseases of the liver.

Rheum rhabarbarum
Rhubarb

Rhubarb plants produce both flowers and seed stalks, however rhubarb seeds do not produce plants that are true-to-type. When rhubarb seeds are planted, a wide variety of plant types will result that may or may not look anything like the parent plants. If it is impossible to transport cuttings of a favorite rhubarb plant to a new garden, seeds can be used. Start 20 or more plants from seeds and select those that most resemble the desired variety.

SEED STATISTICS

Members of the Seed Savers Exchange annually offer about 4 varieties of rhubarb, and the *Fruit, Berry and Nut Inventory* lists sources for 13 varieties that are available from commercial seed companies.

REGIONAL GROWING RECOMMENDATIONS

Northeast: Set out perennial roots in May. Rhubarb plants like full sun and average water, and overwinter in the garden with no special care. If the plants are expected to mature a "true" seed crop, no rhubarb should be harvested that spring to promote early flower-stalk inception. Of course, rhubarb is usually increased by vegetative crown divisions.

Mid-Atlantic: Rhubarb cannot be grown for seed, but can be grown as a food crop in this region. Set out the plants when dormant, about March 1, and harvest in June. Rhubarb is difficult to grow here.

Southeast/Gulf Coast: Rhubarb cannot be grown in this region. Occasionally gardeners have success with rhubarb in a northern exposure and partial shade, especially in the Upper South, but it really resents summer heat.

Upper Midwest: Rhubarb is vegetatively propagated. The plants overwinter in the garden with no special care.

Southwest: Rhubarb is not commonly grown in this region.

Central West Coast: Rhubarb cannot be grown for seed in this region. Plants overwinter in the garden with no special care, but never flower. Rhubarb is not well adapted to hot summers.

Maritime Northwest: Rhubarb is not commonly grown in this region.

Rumex spp.
Sorrel

Rumex acetosa - Garden Sorrel
R. alpinus - Mountain Sorrel
R. scutatus - French Sorrel

Sorrel is the common name for three different species with acid-tasting green leaves. Common garden sorrel or sour dock belongs to *Rumex acetosa*. *Rumex alpinus* is often called maiden sorrel, monk's sorrel or mountain sorrel. *Rumex scutatus* is referred to as French sorrel, white sorrel, lettuce sorrel or blonde sorrel. All three species have been collected in the wild and cultivated in gardens for centuries. The plants are easily divided, so vegetative propagation is common. The plants produce both male and female flowers, requiring insects for pollination. If more than one variety of the same species is grown in close proximity, alternate day caging will prevent crossing.

SEED STATISTICS

Members of the Seed Savers Exchange annually offer about 7 varieties of sorrel.

GROWING SORREL FROM SEED

Sorrel is a perennial adapted to many climatic situations. The plants are usually produced from division and rarely from seed; some varieties do not even produce viable seed. Sorrel seed is either direct seeded or started in a greenhouse, covering the seeds lightly or not at all. Germination usually occurs in 14-21 days. Set out in full sun, or partial shade in hot summer climates. The plants should be thinned to about 12" apart.

REGIONAL GROWING RECOMMENDATIONS

Northeast: Garden sorrel, mountain sorrel and

French sorrel can all direct seeded in May. All three species like full sun and average water, and overwinter in the garden with no special care. The seed stalks of garden sorrel and French sorrel tend to bend over easily and are best staked.

Mid-Atlantic: Garden sorrel can be direct seeded about March 1. Mountain sorrel can be direct seeded about March 1, but is very difficult in hotter areas, or can be started in a greenhouse about January 15 or June 1. Some shade is necessary. French sorrel can be direct seeded about March 1, or started in a greenhouse about January 15 or June 1 and transplanted into the garden about March 1 or July 15. All three species like average water and full sun (partial sun is okay), and overwinter in the garden with no special care. Mulching with compost will help them survive hot dry summers.

Southeast/Gulf Coast: Garden sorrel and French sorrel can be direct seeded from February 20 to March 15, or September 1-10. Both plants like filtered or partial sun and average water. Mountain sorrel cannot be grown in this region.

Upper Midwest: Garden sorrel can be direct seeded as early as ground can be worked. French sorrel can be direct seeded in early April. Both plants like full sun and average water. Mountain sorrel cannot be grown in this region.

Southwest: All three species are not commonly grown in this region.

Central West Coast: Garden sorrel, mountain sorrel and French sorrel can all be direct seeded in the spring about March 15, or in the fall about September 15. Some shade is necessary for all three. The plants like average water and overwinter in the garden with no special care.

Maritime Northwest: Garden sorrel, mountain sorrel and French sorrel are not commonly grown in this region.

THE PORTULACACEAE FAMILY

Edible members of the Portulacaceae family are considered by various persons to be either noxious weeds or succulent salad greens. Miner's lettuce grows in the winter and early spring, while purslane grows during the summer months. Other Portulacaceae family members are grown as ornamental flowers in the warmer regions of the world.

Claytonia parvifolia
Miner's Lettuce

Miner's lettuce is commonly referred to as winter purslane in Europe. The delicate leaves appear in moist, shady, wooded areas in the early spring. The self-sowing plants are rarely planted and are most often foraged for like fiddlehead ferns.

Plants of miner's lettuce develop two types of leaves during their short life. The first leaves appear on 4-6" stems, are kidney-shaped and very succulent. Pretty round leaves appear later, encircling the flower stalks. The leaves are much sought after by restaurants and deserve a place in more gardens. Miner's lettuce produces early, rarely interferes with other crops and is easily intercropped between later vegetables.

BOTANICAL CLASSIFICATION

Miner's lettuce belongs to the genus *Claytonia* and the species *parvifolia*. Different varieties of miner's lettuce have been mentioned in literature, but may only be variations in growth caused by differences in altitude, climate, shade, etc.

POLLINATION, CROSSING AND ISOLATION

Miner's lettuce is an inbreeding plant that produces flowers that are perfect and self-pollinating. The flowers do not seem to be attractive to insects, but that may be due to their early spring emergence. There is no information available on different varieties or crossing between varieties. If true varieties do exist and were grown in close proximity, caging would prevent any possible cross-pollination by insects. Miner's lettuce does not cross with purslane.

SEED PRODUCTION, HARVEST AND PROCESSING

Miner's lettuce can be lightly picked for eating and still grown for seed. Tiny white blossoms emerge from the center of the round leaves and quickly form small seedpods. The top portion of the seedpods falls off and tiny, shiny black seeds fall out before the plant has started to dry. The seeds shatter easily and are hard to collect.

Entire plants are sometimes collected and put in pillowcases to dry, however that can be risky. The plants are very succulent and with damp, early spring weather a moldy mess is likely to result, rather than a tablespoon of black seeds. It is easier to dig miner's lettuce plants and set them out to mature and drop seeds where the plants are to grow. Collected seeds can be air-dried away from direct sun for several days before being stored.

SEED STATISTICS

Miner's lettuce seeds will remain viable for five years when stored in cool, dry, dark conditions. Some of the Seed Savers Exchange offer miner's lettuce, and the *Garden Seed Inventory* lists sources for 3 varieties that are available from commercial seed companies. There are approximately 78,400 seeds per ounce (2,765 per gram or 1,255,000 per pound).

GROWING MINER'S LETTUCE FROM SEED

Miner's lettuce is a cool season annual that is usually direct seeded. Do not cover the tiny seeds, which germinate at temperatures ranging from 50-65° F. Plant in partial shade in a cool, moist location, such as under deciduous trees, which works well. The plants self-sow easily in undisturbed soil, and should be thinned to 4-6" apart.

REGIONAL GROWING RECOMMENDATIONS

Northeast: Miners lettuce is not commonly grown in this region.

Mid-Atlantic: Miners lettuce is not commonly grown in this region.

Southeast/Gulf Coast: Miners lettuce is not commonly grown in this region.

Upper Midwest: Miner's lettuce can be direct seeded as early as the ground can be worked. The plants like full sun and average water.

Southwest: Miner's lettuce can be direct seeded about November 15. The plants like full sun and average water.

Central West Coast: Miner's lettuce can be direct seeded about October 30. Partial sun is okay, but some shade is necessary. The plants like average water and overwinter in the garden with no special care.

Maritime Northwest: Miner's lettuce can be direct seeded about October 15-30. Full sun, filtered or partial sun, or some shade are all okay. The plants like average water and overwinter in the garden with no special care.

──────── *Portulaca oleracea* ────────
Purslane

Purslane may be indigenous to the Himalayas, southern Russia and Greece. The plant was origi-

nally thought to have been brought to America from Europe, but current research suggests it may be indigenous to the Americas as well. Improved varieties of purslane are cultivated for market in Egypt and also in some parts of Central and South America.

Purslane, which is usually considered a weed, appears in the early summer when warm nights and moist conditions coincide. Recent nutritional studies have discovered that purslane contains omega-3 fatty acids, compounds found in certain seafoods that are thought to lower blood pressure and reduce the incidence of heart disease. Thus, an annoying garden weed has been added to the growing arsenal of foods that may combat disease.

Purslane does have some negative nutritional qualities. Like spinach, the plant's leaves can accumulate nitrates and contain oxalic acid that prevents calcium absorption. Too much of a good thing may actually be harmful. Eating excessive amounts of purslane to lower blood pressure could lead to calcium deprivation and weak bones.

BOTANICAL CLASSIFICATION

Purslane belongs to the genus *Portulaca* and the species *oleracea*. Wild varieties form a mat on the surface of the ground with individual plants reaching 12" in diameter. Improved garden varieties with large leaves can grow 10" in height. Both the golden and large leaf varieties produce upright, slow to bolt plants with large, tender leaves. Seeds for garden varieties are offered by seed companies specializing in herbs.

POLLINATION, CROSSING AND ISOLATION

Purslane is an inbreeding plant. Purslane flowers are perfect and self-pollinating, but they are also visited by many bees, small flies and butterflies Studies have not yet determined when pollination occurs. If the flowers self-pollinate before opening, cross-pollination by insects is probably not possible. If, however, the flowers open before the pollen is ripe, various improved varieties and the wild type probably can be crossed. Since improved varieties of purslane are not grown commercially in the United States, no information on crossing is available. If more than one variety were being grown, isolation or caging would ensure purity.

SEED PRODUCTION, HARVEST AND PROCESSING

Purslane can be lightly picked for eating with almost no decrease in the amount of seeds produced by each plant. Yellow blossoms appear on the tips of each branch of the plant and quickly develop into capped seedpods. The top portion or lid of each cap falls off as the seeds mature. The seedpods mature and release their seeds while the plants are green and continuing to grow. The pods shatter very easily, so seeds must be collected on a regular basis.

SEED STATISTICS

Purslane seeds will remain viable for seven years when stored in cool, dry, dark conditions. Members of the Seed Savers Exchange annually offer about 4 varieties of purslane, and the *Garden Seed Inventory: Fifth Edition* lists sources for 9 varieties that are available from commercial seed companies. There are approximately 78,400 seeds per ounce (2,765 per gram or 1,255,000 per pound), depending on the variety.

GROWING PURSLANE FROM SEED

Purslane is a heat-loving annual with a reputation as a noxious weed. Purslane is direct seeded, cover-ing the seeds lightly or not at all. The seeds germinate at temperatures ranging from 70-95° F. usually within 3-7 days. Plant in full sun, thinning to 8-10" apart.

REGIONAL GROWING RECOMMENDATIONS

Northeast: Purslane is not commonly grown in this region.
Mid-Atlantic: Purslane can be direct seeded from April 15 to June 15. The plants like full sun and are drought tolerant.
Southeast/Gulf Coast: Purslane is not commonly grown in this region.
Upper Midwest: Purslane is not commonly grown in this region.
Southwest: Purslane can be direct seeded June 1. The plants like full sun and are drought tolerant.
Central West Coast: Purslane can be direct seeded from April 1 to July 1. The plants like full sun and are drought tolerant.
Maritime Northwest: Purslane can be direct seeded from March 20 to April 10. The plants like full sun and average water.

THE TETRAGONIACEAE FAMILY

The Tetragoniaceae family includes only one vegetable species, New Zealand spinach. Sir Joseph Banks discovered the plant in New Zealand in 1770 and sent specimens to the Kew Gardens in England. From Kew, New Zealand spinach found its way into seed catalogs around the world. G. Don discovered three distinct varieties in Chile in 1834, which included a variety with smooth leaves, one with leaves that are smooth on top and hairy beneath, and a third with very small, glabrous leaves.

Tetragonia tetragonioides
New Zealand Spinach

New Zealand spinach is grown in many of the hot summer regions of the world. While not a true spinach, the plant's leaves are often used as a substitute for spinach in cooked vegetable dishes. The leaves are high in oxalic acid which some people find disagreeable.

The plants form vines with attractive spear-shaped leaves and inconspicuous greenish yellow flowers. New Zealand spinach will not tolerate any frost and does not begin growing until the soil is very warm and air temperatures are well into the 80s.

BOTANICAL CLASSIFICATION

New Zealand spinach belongs to the genus *Tetragonia* and the species *tetragonioides*. Although three varieties of *T. tetragonioides* are known to exist, American seed companies offer only generic New Zealand spinach. Until recently the species was included in the Aizoaceae family and was formerly classified as *Tetragoniaceae expansa*.

POLLINATION, CROSSING AND ISOLATION

New Zealand spinach is an inbreeding plant with flowers that are small and not showy. Two flowers usually grow tightly together in each leaf apex and may be mistaken for a single unit. The flowers are perfect and self-pollinating. Insect crossing might be possible if two varieties were grown together. In such cases, isolation or caging would ensure seed purity.

SEED PRODUCTION, HARVEST AND PROCESSING

New Zealand spinach seeds ripen progressively along the length of the vine. Its hard fruits each contain several seed capsules and change from green to brown at full maturity. The mature fruits often fall off the plant and are difficult to see on the ground. Full-sized green fruits can also be picked and allowed to dry until brown. Although picking the individual seedpods off of the vine is time-consuming, no further treatment of the seeds is necessary.

SEED STATISTICS

New Zealand spinach seeds will maintain 50% germination for five years when stored in cool, dry, dark conditions. Four members of the Seed Savers Exchange annually make New Zealand spinach seeds available, and it is being offered in the *Garden Seed Inventory* by 85 commercial seed companies. There are approximately 375 seeds per ounce (13 per gram or 6,000 per pound), depending on the variety.

GROWING NEW ZEALAND SPINACH FROM SEED

New Zealand spinach is a short lived, frost intolerant, heat loving, perennial plant that is usually direct seeded. The seeds are planted .5" deep and usually germinate within 7-10 days. Plant in full sun, thinning to 12-20" apart. New Zealand spinach plants sprawl and may be trellised to conserve garden space.

REGIONAL GROWING RECOMMENDATIONS

Northeast: New Zealand spinach cannot be grown in this region.

Mid-Atlantic: New Zealand spinach can be direct seeded from April 15 to May 15, or started in a greenhouse March 15 and transplanted April 15 to May 15. The plants like full sun and average water.

Southeast/Gulf Coast: New Zealand spinach can be direct seeded from April 15 to May 1, or August 15 to September 10.

Upper Midwest: New Zealand spinach can be direct seeded from May 15 to June 1. The plants like full sun and average water, but are drought tolerant.

Southwest: New Zealand spinach can be direct seeded from May 1 to June 15. The plants like full sun and average water.

Central West Coast: New Zealand spinach can be direct seeded from April 1 to May 15. The plants like full sun and are drought tolerant. This plant self-sows, and produces seed very easily.

Maritime Northwest: New Zealand spinach can be direct seeded from May 20 to April 10. The plants like full sun and average water.

THE VALERIANACEAE FAMILY

The Valerianaceae family includes about 10 genera and 400 species of herbs and small shrubs. Valerianella is the only genus that is grown in the garden as a vegetable.

--- *Valerianella spp.* ---
Corn Salad

Valerianella eriocarpa - Italian Corn Salad
V. locusta - Common Corn Salad

Like Portulaca, corn salad is a common weed in many parts of North America, Europe, North Africa and Asia. For centuries the delicate rosettes of leaves have been collected in early spring for sale in European markets, especially in France where the corn salad plant is called mache. Until recently corn salad was considered a weed in the United States, where the plant is sometimes called lamb's lettuce. With the current surge of interest in both gardening and cuisine, however, corn salad is becoming a fashionable food sought after by restaurants and greengrocers.

BOTANICAL CLASSIFICATION

Corn salad belongs to the genus *Valerianella* and to two distinct species. Italian corn salad, *V. eriocarpa*, grows 16" tall and has 5" leaves that are somewhat hairy. Common corn salad, *V. locusta*, forms rosettes that are 3-6" high with either smooth or crinkled leaves.

POLLINATION, CROSSING AND ISOLATION

Corn salads are outbreeding plants. Italian corn salad, *V. eriocarpa*, will not cross with common corn salad, *V. locusta*. Different varieties within each of the species, however, will cross with one another. Corn salad growing in the wild can also cross with the cultivated varieties.

Corn salad plants rely on insects for pollination. No information on isolation distances is available. Alternate day caging (described in Section I) would ensure purity if more than one variety of a species is grown for seed.

SEED PRODUCTION, HARVEST AND PROCESSING

Corn salad plants form bluish white flowers with the onset of warm weather. The flowers quickly form seeds which drop when mature and self-sow. The plants are so small and go to seed so early that warm season crops can be planted among the maturing corn salad plants without difficulty.

When the plants are beginning to dry, carefully collect the entire plant in a pillowcase. Shake the plants to free as many seeds as possible and then remove the seeds from the bag. The plants can be left in the bag to dry a bit further and the process can be repeated. Dry the seeds out of direct sunlight for several days and winnow to remove small pieces of debris.

SEED STATISTICS

Corn salad seeds will maintain 50% germination for five years when stored in cool, dry, dark conditions. Members of the Seed Savers Exchange annually offer about 7 varieties of corn salad, and the *Garden Seed Inventory: Fifth Edition* lists sources for 22 varieties that are available from commercial seed companies. There are approximately 11,200 seeds per ounce (395 per gram or 179,200 per pound), depending on the variety.

GROWING CORN SALAD FROM SEED

Corn salad is a cool season annual with a reputation as a weed in the United States. Corn salad is direct seeded, covering the seeds .25-.5" deep. The seeds germinate at temperatures ranging from 50-70° F. with germination usually occurring in 7-10 days. Plant in full sun or partial shade. The plants should be thinned to 4-9" for food production, and 2-4" for breeding purposes.

REGIONAL GROWING RECOMMENDATIONS

Northeast: Common corn and Italian corn salad can be direct seeded about April 15. The plants like full sun. These are easy spring annuals in this region.

Mid-Atlantic: Common corn and Italian corn salad can be direct seeded from February 1 to March 15, or started in a greenhouse about January 1 and transplanted into the garden from February 15 to March 15. Both plants like full sun and average water.

Southeast/Gulf Coast: Common corn salad and Italian corn salad can be direct seeded from September 1 to October 1. Both plants like filtered or partial sun and average water, and overwinters in the garden with no special care. Common corns salad is a great green for winter here. Spring sowing is possible, but the plants bolt so quickly that it's hardly worth the trouble.

Upper Midwest: Common corn salad and Italian corn salad can be direct seeded in early April. Both plants like filtered or partial sun and average water.

Southwest: Not commonly grown in this region.

Southwest: Common corn salad and Italian corn salad are not commonly grown in this region.

Central West Coast: Common corn salad and Italian corn salad can be direct seeded about October 1-15. Both plants like full sun and average water, and overwinter in the garden with no special care. These are very easy crops that self-sow.

Maritime Northwest: Common corn salad and Italian corn salad can be direct seeded about April 1-15. Both plants like full sun and average water.

Valerianaceae

The entire process of gardening and seed saving is controlled to varying degrees by the vast array of regional climatic differences encountered throughout our country. For example, growing biennials to seed is a relatively easy process in mild winter areas, but the methods needed to overwinter those same biennials require monumental effort in regions where the ground freezes solid for months each winter. The addition of "Regional Growing Recommendations" to *Seed to Seed (Second Edition)* should help guide growers in developing and adapting seed saving techniques that are well suited to their own specific climatic situations.

Attempting to limit an area as vast as the United States to only seven climatic regions was not an easy task. In addition, our regional choices not only had to be geographic, but also depended on our ability to locate those rare and special growers who are experienced with saving seed from a vast range of different vegetables. Each of the following regional advisors has provided invaluable information based on their personal experience in growing and saving the seeds of vegetables profiled in this book. The scope of their horticultural knowledge and their commitment to developing methods for successful seed saving, in spite of climate limitations, is truly inspiring.

Will Bonsall (Northeast) and his family, who strive for a totally self-reliant, vegan lifestyle, live in a hand-built log home near Farmington in central Maine. Since about 1980, Will has operated Scatterseed Project, a genetic preservation project that distributes nearly 2,000 varieties annually through *Seed Savers Yearbook*. For more than two decades, Will has worked closely with the Seed Savers Exchange and is SSE's curator for potatoes (nearly 700 named va-

rieties field planted each year), peas, fava beans, runner beans, Jerusalem artichokes and biennials. He has developed about three acres of permanent gardens, mainly planted in wide rows, and conducts an extensive intern program each summer. Will's gardens and numerous isolation plots are surrounded by woods, resulting in ongoing problems with deer and drought. His ground is rocky, hilly land with terracing, and is routinely cover cropped for nutrients. The topsoil is thin, rocky and acid, but has good structure. Plants are started indoors during March and April, while work in the garden starts in late April and some years is not completely over until November 15. Will's favorite garden season is actually the dead of winter, when he is planning the new garden. His favorite vegetable is fava beans, because they are very beautiful and easy to grow, and so delicious to eat. Will is always drawn to crops that do especially well in his location and crops that no one else is maintaining.

As Director of Gardens and Grounds for the Thomas Jefferson Foundation, **Peter J. Hatch** (Mid-Atlantic) has been responsible for the maintenance, interpretation and restoration of the 2,000-acre landscape at Monticello since 1977. Peter has managed several important restoration projects, such as the eight-acre

Vegetable and Fruit Garden, The Grove (an ornamental forest of 18 acres), and establishment of the Thomas Jefferson Center for Historic Plants. His terraced gardens at Monticello are organized into 24 squares (30' x 40' growing plots) that border the back of the hill. That protected location allows for earlier planting and longer frost-free growing, which is ideal for varieties not normally grown to seed in the region. His garden soil is heavy red clay, nutrient rich but requiring lots of organic matter, so substantial time is spent making compost. He has ongoing problems with heat, drought and deer. Plants are started indoors from January 15 until March 15, and work in the garden runs from February 15 to November 1. Peter's favorite garden season is the fall, because the cool weather vegetables (brassicas and lettuce) do so well and the air is cool and clear. Crowder peas are his favorite vegetable and he especially enjoys growing plants that are historically significant to the region. Peter is the author of *The Gardens of Monticello* and *The Fruits and Fruit Trees of Monticello*, and the editor for *Thomas Jefferson's Flower Garden at Monticello*.

Barbara Pleasant (Southeast/Gulf Coast) lives in Huntsville, Alabama where her gardens cover 13 acres (acid clay soil), mostly in wide beds. Barbara can grow almost all garden crops, if planted at the right season, except for crops not hardy below 15° F. The

unique weather of her region results in ongoing problems with heat and high humidity, and subsequent fungal diseases. Up to 50" of rain are spread evenly year round. Her first frost is November 1-12 and last frost March 3-30. Plants are started indoors during February and March, and work in the garden usually starts with a break in the weather during February when salad greens are first planted, which are Barbara's favorite vegetables. Her favorite garden seasons are spring (for the salad greens) and fall (for *great* salad greens). Barbara is the Middle South Region columnist for nationalgardening.com, which also appears on Amazon.com and other web sites. She writes a weekly newspaper column ("Home Grown") for *The Huntsville Times*, a monthly column ("The Alabama Gardener") in *Neighbors* magazine, and is a contributing editor to *Organic Gardening* magazine. Barbara's books and articles appear regularly in Rodale, Storey, Meredith and National Home Gardening Club, and include: *Garden Stone, Care-Free Plants, Better Gardens – Less Work, Annual Flowers, Gardening Essentials, Beds and Borders, Container Gardens, Cutting Gardens, The Gardener's Weed Book, The Gardener's Guide to Plant Diseases, The Gardener's Bug Book*, and Rodale's *Complete Garden Problem Solver*.

Glenn Drowns (Upper Midwest) was born in Salmon, Idaho, when poultry and seed catalogs were filled with genetic diversity. Gardening in that harsh 90-day climate required hauling in 4" of soil. Moving to Iowa in 1984 and to his present farm in 1988 brought his gardening and poultry dreams into focus. Glenn is maintaining 2,000 vegetables, and 10 acres of his 40-

acre farm are in heirloom seed production using wide rows for Cucurbitaceae production. Glenn is also keeping 200 breeds of poultry and, with the help of his family, operates Sand Hill Preservation Center, a mail-order business specializing in heirloom seeds and rare poultry. He is a 7-12 Science Teacher at Calamus-Wheatland Schools, adjunct faculty member at Clinton Community College, and holds a M.S. in Biology from Western Illinois University. Glenn is SSE's longtime curator for cucurbits, corns and sweet potatoes. Garden problems include waves of summer insects, heavy rains in mid-summer, and high winds in spring and late summer. His soil is very sandy, sometimes causing seeds to dry out and seedlings to burn up, and requires lots of organic matter. Greenhouse planting is in late March, and garden season is from April 1 to October 31 with lots of variation every year. His garden interests include growing seed, seed saving techniques and plant breeding. His favorite garden season is summer when the melons (his favorite vegetable) are ready. Glenn is totally intrigued by the diversity in Cucurbitaceae.

Suzanne Nelson, Ph.D. (Southwest) is Conservation Director and Seed Bank Curator for Native Seeds/SEARCH, a Tucson-based non-profit that conserves

and promotes traditional crops and wild relatives in southwestern U.S. and northwestern Mexico. Suzanne's Ph.D. is in Agronomy and Plant Genetics from the University of Arizona in 1994, and her long-term focus is on the ecology, ethnobotany and conservation of native plants in the Sonoran Desert. She develops low-input cropping systems for semi-arid tropics, and directs projects that conserve crop genetic

Regional Advisors

resources and related traditional knowledge. Suzanne manages NS/S's Seed Bank (2,000 accessions of U.S. and Mexican crops and wild relatives) and oversees regeneration of the collection at NS/S's Conservation Farm near Patagonia, south of Tucson. The farm's 60 acres are great for growing, with wonderful loam soil and easy access to water. High temperatures and low rainfall during spring and early summer make it difficult or impossible to grow some crops. Monsoon rains usually begin in late June or early July, so May and June are poor planting months. At 4,000' elevation, first frost ranges from September 15 to November 15, and last frost from March 15 to May 15. Rainfall averages 7-14" from May 15 to September 15. Plants are started indoors February 15 to March 15, and in the garden May 15 to June 15. Suzanne's favorite vegetables are corn, beans and squash, because she enjoys growing and tasting varieties well adapted and culturally significant to the region.

Suzanne Ashworth (Central West Coast) and her husband live on her parents' family farm near Sacramento, California. She is an instructor at American River College, holds three Master degrees, is a consultant

for small farm crop development and an heirloom seed supplier. Suzanne's Mediterranean climate allows year round gardening, even most sub-tropicals with some protection (lows of 25-30° F.). Rainfall averages 18" from December-April. Her garden soil is loamy clay with good water retention. She has an acre of evaluation gardens in 5' x 100' beds, plus 10 acres of seed production in wide rows with drip irrigation. Suzanne is SSE's longtime curator for eggplants and ground cherries. She has grown, hand-pollinated and evaluated virtually all hard-shelled gourds that are available. During her initial research for *Seed to Seed*, she grew seed crops of 160 vegetables, and thoroughly researched and tested all seed saving and storage tech-

niques. Her continuing research involves medicinal herbs for small farm production, specialty crops for CSAs, and gourd use by indigenous peoples of Ecuador, Bali and Java. She starts plants indoors January 15 until March 15, and the only slow period during her gardening year is November 15 to January 15. Suzanne's favorite garden season is May-June when everything is finally planted, but not yet demanding more attention than there are hours in the day. Her favorite crops are eggplants and hard-shelled gourds. Suzanne enjoys growing crops that are a challenge, especially those others say are impossible.

John Navazio, Ph.D. (Maritime Northwest) started saving seed about 1980, while working as an organic farmer in Eugene, Oregon. In Bar Harbor, Maine he co-managed Beech Hill Farm and initiated classes in Sustainable Agriculture at College of the Atlantic. John's M.S. and Ph.D. are in Plant Breeding and Plant Genetics from University of Wisconsin at Madison. From there he became Research Director at Garden City Seeds in Montana, and then Senior Plant Breeder at Alf Christianson Seed Co. in Mt. Vernon, Washington, working with spinach, Swiss chard, beets and carrots. John's location in the maritimes allows year-round gardening, with major plantings from March 1 until October 1. His gardens cover 20 acres of raised wide beds, with irrigation from July 4 to September 4. About 45" of rain falls steadily from September 10 to July 4, causing problems with rot and slugs. His soil is silt/clay/loam with lots of compost incorporated. Western Washington is a major production area for cool season vegetable seed crops, including cabbage, table beets, Swiss chard, Chinese cabbage, arugula and rutabaga. These dry seeded crops must all be swathed, dried, threshed and out of the field by September 10, when the rains and possible winds start.

John's favorite season is fall, the easiest time for lush delicious greens. His favorites include all greens, especially spinach and kale. John is working with grassroots agricultural organizations, teaching organic seed farmers basic plant breeding and selection skills.

(Submitted Photos)

SEED SAVING ORGANIZATIONS

Seed Savers Exchange (SSE) - a non-profit, tax-exempt, publicly supported organization - is a network of 8,000 gardeners, orchardists and plant collectors who maintain and distribute endangered vegetables, fruits and grains. SSE's twin goals are to preserve "heirloom varieties" (passed down from generation to generation) that gardeners and farmers brought to North America when their families immigrated, and to greatly increase the genetic diversity available to gardeners and farmers growing healthy food for their families. Nearly three decades of unwavering and devoted effort by SSE is largely responsible for creating the heirloom seed movement, and the diligent efforts of our members are making rare heirloom varieties available to gardeners everywhere.

SSE's 8,000 members receive three publications each year: *Seed Savers Yearbook* (500 pages, mailed from February-June), *Summer Edition* (80-120 pages, mailed July-October) and *Harvest Edition* (80-120 pages, November-January). *Seed Savers Yearbook*, the greatest source of heirloom varieties in the world, contains the addresses of nearly 900 of SSE's members and listings for 12,000 rare varieties of vegetables and fruits they are making available to SSE's members. Since SSE was founded in 1975, its members have used Seed Savers' publications to distribute an estimated one million samples of rare seeds that were previously unavailable and often on the verge of extinction. SSE's publications have created a national awareness of heirloom varieties and the efforts to conserve them.

In 1986 SSE purchased its picturesque, 170-acre **Heritage Farm** - SSE's headquarters near Decorah, Iowa - where several collections of endangered food crops are on display to the public. Heritage Farm's genetic preservation projects include more than 20,000 varieties of rare vegetables, 700 19th century apples and 200 hardy grapes. Each summer 10% of each vegetable crop is grown (on a 10-year rotation) in order to produce fresh seeds. SSE's collections have provided the foundations for numerous alternative seed companies and are largely responsible for today's rapidly growing heirloom seed movement. SSE and Heritage Farm have provided the models for organizations and genetic preservation projects in more than 30 countries.

You don't have to already be keeping heirloom seeds to join SSE; your desire to try some of these beautiful, highly flavored varieties is enough. An annual membership in SSE, which includes the three issues described above, is $30 (with optional reduced rates of $25 for those on fixed incomes). Canadian and Mexican memberships are $35, and overseas $45.

SSE's three annual membership publications include about 700 pages of exciting horticultural information, and provide access to thousands of heirloom varieties not available elsewhere. Or, SSE's 80-page color seed catalog (including detailed membership information) is available free by sending your name and address to: Seed Savers Exchange, 3076 North Winn Road, Decorah, IA 52101 (phone: 563-382-5990; fax: 563-382-5872; web site: www.seedsavers.org).

The Flower and Herb Exchange (FHE), founded in 1989, was patterned after SSE but is a separate organization with its own yearbook. FHE's members are trying to locate, maintain and distribute flowers and herbs that are heirlooms or unusual, and are not commercially available. If you are keeping such plants and are willing to share their seeds with other gardeners (or if you are interested in growing rare flowers and herbs), FHE would be pleased to have you join our efforts.

Many seed savers are keeping heirloom flowers and herbs that hold special memories. FHE provides a system designed to help preserve this precious legacy and make it available to other gardeners who will treasure these plants and continue to exchange their seeds. Last year the 128-page yearbook of *The Flower and Herb Exchange* (mailed to about 2,000 members from March-May) contained the names and addresses of about 250 members and listings for more than 2,500 varieties of old-time flowers and herbs. The yearbook is filled with heirloom flowers whose simple beauty is seldom found in modern catalogs. FHE is very grateful to those families who had the respect and foresight to keep these living heirlooms from being lost. FHE is re-creating the garden landscapes of the past by reintroducing plants that once bloomed in our grandparents' gardens and yards.

FHE is a separate organization from SSE with its own yearbook and membership fee. To receive the annual yearbook of *The Flower and Herb Exchange*, send your name and address and $10 U.S. membership fee ($12 in Canada and Mexico, $15 overseas) to: The Flower and Herb Exchange, 3076 North Winn Road, Decorah, IA 52101. Detailed information about membership in FHE is also included in the center of SSE's seed catalog, described above, and on SSE's web site (www.seedsavers.org).

Native Seeds/SEARCH (NS/S) is a nonprofit seed conservation organization working to preserve traditional native crops of the U.S. Southwest and Northwest Mexico. For centuries Native American farmers have grown corn, squash, beans and other crops under a variety of growing conditions. NS/S encourages the continued use of these plants in their native habitats, and distributes them widely to home gardeners, researchers, and free of charge to Native American farmers. Wild relatives of crops - such as wild beans, chiles, gourds and cotton - are also included in NS/S's conservation efforts.

Annual membership in Native Seeds/SEARCH includes a subscription to their quarterly newsletter called *The Seedhead News*, the annual Seedlisting, and the holiday gift catalog. Members also receive a 10% discount on all purchases from the catalogs, web site and retail store in Tucson, Arizona. Membership starts at $25 per year. Profits from sales are used to support NS/S's conservation programs. Since 1983 - financed by member support, foundation grants and retail and catalog sales - NS/S has made nearly 2,000 desert-adapted southwestern crop collections. Membership helps make these seeds available, free of charge, to Native American gardeners.

The Seedhead News provides updates on NS/S's Conservation Farm and Seed Bank, in addition to tips from fellow gardeners, native food recipes, book reviews, features on Native American farmers, and previews of workshops and other special events. The Seedlisting offers for sale hundreds of crop varieties and many of their wild relatives, native food products and books, gardening tips, recipes and historical/cultural information about the plants. You can obtain NS/S's current seed catalog by sending $1.00 to: Native Seeds/SEARCH, 526 N. 4th Ave., Tucson, AZ 85705 (web site: www.nativeseeds.org).

Seeds of Diversity Canada (SoDC), formerly the Heritage Seed Program, is a registered Canadian charity organization whose mission is to promote the conservation and use of heritage and unique plant varieties. SoDC searches out, preserves, perpetuates, studies and encourages the cultivation of heirloom and endangered varieties of food crops, and also educates the public about the importance of heirloom and endangered crops and the need for their continued cultivation and preservation. SoDC's members are backyard gardeners, farmers, historical sites, museums, horticultural historians, botanical gardens, scientists and plant breeders.

The heart of SoDC is its network of growers who multiply endangered varieties in their gardens, practice proper seed saving techniques to keep the varieties pure, and save seeds that are made available to other members free of charge. In this way, someone somewhere is always growing these endangered varieties so they will not become extinct. Information is available through the organization on how to save your own seeds. SoDC is a living gene bank.

Three times each year (January, May and September), SoDC publishes periodicals containing articles about historic gardens, cooking with heritage varieties, cultural histories of fruits, vegetables, herbs and flowers, information about upcoming events, letters, photos and illustrations. Each January, SoDC publishes a *Seed Exchange Directory* of all varieties its members have to share. This listing is different from a seed catalog in that those requesting seeds from it are asked to grow the seeds, practice proper seed saving techniques and save seed to share with other members.

Anyone is welcome to join SoDC, even if they do not wish to become a grower, and your membership fee will help support SoDC's preservation projects. As a member you will receive three annual periodicals, including the yearly *Seed Exchange Directory* from which you can choose seeds you might wish to adopt. For membership information, write to: Seeds of Diversity Canada, PO Box 36, Station Q, Toronto, ON M4T 2L7, Canada (phone: 905-623-0353, e-mail: mail@seeds.ca, web site: www. seeds.ca)

——————— Foreign Seed Saving Groups ———————

Association Kokopelli, Quartier Saint Martin, 07200 Aubenas, France (phone: 33 4 75 93 53 34, fax: 33 4 75 93 37 75, e-mail: kokopelli.assoc@wanadoo).

Henry Doubleday Research Assn., Ryton Organic Gardens, Coventry CV8 3LG, Great Britain (phone: 024 7630 8210, e-mail: enquiry@hdra.org.uk).

Heritage Seed Curators Assn., P. O. Box 113, Lobethal, SA, 5241 Australia (phone: 08 8389 8649, e-mail: han.HSCA@b150.aone.net.au).

Irish Seed Saver Assn., Capparoe, Scariff, County Clare, Ireland (phone: 061 921866, e-mail: issa@esatclear.ie).

Koanga Gardens, R. D. 2, Maungaturoto, Northland Aotearoa, New Zealand (phone: 09 4312 145, fax: 09 4312 745).

Pro Specie Rara, Pfrundweg 14, CH-5000 Aarau, Switzerland (phone: 062 823 50 30, fax: 062 823 50 25, e-mail: obst@psrara.org).

Seed Savers' Network, P. O. Box 975, Byron Bay 2481, Australia (phone: 02 6685 6624, e-mail: info@seedsavers.net).

SELECTED REFERENCES

Allard, R. W. *Principles of Plant Breeding*. New York: John Wiley and Sons, 1960.

Andrews, J. Peppers: *The Domesticated Capsicums*. Austin: University of Texas Press, 1977.

Antunes, I. F., J. G. C. da Costa and E. H. Oliveira. *Natural Hybridization in Phaseolus vulgaris*. The 1973 Report of the Bean Improvement Cooperative, 1973.

Bailey, L. H. *Hortus Third, A Concise Dictionary of Plants Cultivated in the United States and Canada*. New York: Macmillan Publishing, 1976.

Bassett, Mark J. *Breeding Vegetable Crops*. Westport, Connecticut: AVI Publishing Company, 1986.

Bird, R. *Growing From Seed*. Jackson, New Jersey: Thompson & Morgan, 1988.

Bubel, Nancy. *The New Seed Starters Handbook*. Emmaus, Pennsylvania: Rodale Press, 1998.

Correll, D. S. *The Potato and Its Wild Relatives*. Renner, Texas: Texas Research Foundation, 1962.

Creech, J. L., and L. P. Reitz. "Plant Germplasm Now and for Tomorrow." *Advanced Agronomy* 23:1-43 (1971).

Culp, T. W., W. K. Bailey and R. O. Hammons. "Natural Hybridization of Peanuts, Arachis Hypogaea, in Virginia." *Crop Science* 8:108-111.

Dahlen, M., and K. Phillipps. *A Popular Guide to Chinese Vegetables*. New York: Crown Publishers, Inc., 1983.

Deppe, Carol. *Breed Your Own Vegetable Varieties*. Boston, Massachusetts: Libble, Brown and Company, 1993.

Doty, W. L. *All About Vegetables*. San Francisco: Chevron Chemical Company, 1973.

Dremann, C. C. *Ground Cherries, Husk Tomatoes, and Tomatillos*. Redwood City, California: The Redwood City Seed Company, 1985.

Elving, P. *Fresh Produce. A to Z, How to Select, Store & Prepare*. Menlo Park, California: Lane Publishing Company, 1987.

Erwin, A. T., and E. S. Haber. *Species and Varietal Crosses in Cucurbits*. Ames, Iowa: Agricultural Experiment Station, Iowa State College, 1929.

Fehr, W., and H. Hadley. *Hybridization of Crop Plants*. Madison, Wisconsin: American Society of Agronomy, 1980.

Fisher, H. *The Flower Family Album*. Minneapolis: The University of Minnesota Press, 1942.

Freeman, O. L. *Seeds: The Yearbook of Agriculture*. Washington, D.C.: The United States Government Printing Office, 1961.

George, R. A. T. *Vegetable Seed Production*. New York: Longman Inc., 1985.

Haplin, A. M. *Gourmet Gardening: 48 Special Vegetables You Can Grow for Deliciously Distinctive Meals*. Emmaus, Pennsylvania: Rodale Press, Inc., 1981.

Harrington, J. F. "Drying, Storing and Packaging Seed to Maintain Germination and Vigor." *Seedsmen's Digest* 11: 16-56 (1960).

Hedrick, U. P. *Sturtevant's Edible Plants of the World*. New York: Dover Publications, Inc., 1972.

Heiser, C. B. Jr. *The Fascinating World of the Nightshades: Tobacco, Mandrake, Potato, Tomato, Pepper, Eggplant, etc*. New York: Dover Publications, Inc., 1987.

Heiser, C. B. Jr. *The Gourd*. Norman: University of Oklahoma Press, 1985.

Heiser, C. B. Jr. *Of Plants and People*. Norman: University of Oklahoma Press, 1985.

Heiser, C. B. Jr. *The Sunflower*. Norman: University of Oklahoma Press, 1985.

Herklots, G. A. C. *Vegetables In South-East Asia*. London: George Allen & Unwin Ltd., 1972.

Hills, L. D. *Save Your Own Seed*. Essex, England: The Henry Doubleday Research Association, 1978.

Jabs, C. *The Heirloom Gardener*. San Francisco: Sierra Club Books, 1984.

Jardin, C. *Kulu, Kuru, Uru: Lexicon of names of food plants in the South Pacific*. Noumea, New Caledonia, 1974.

Johnson, C. *The Seed Grower*. Marietta, Pennsylvania- Redwood Seed Company, 1906.

Johnston, R. Jr. *Growing Garden Seeds*. Albion, Maine: Johnny's Selected Seeds, 1983.

Justice, O. L., and L. N. Bass. *Principles and Practices of Seed Storage*. Washington, D.C.: Agricultural Research Service, United States Department of Agriculture, 1978.

Knott, J. E. *Handbook for Vegetable Growers*. New York: Wiley and Sons, Inc., 1957.

Larkcom, J. *The Salad Garden*. New York: The Viking Press, 1984.

McGregor, S. E. *Insect Pollination of Cultivated Crop Plants*. Washington, D.C.: Agricultural Research Service, United States Department of Agriculture, 1976.

McLean, J. G., and F. J. Stevenson. "Methods of Obtaining Seed on Russet, Burbank and Similar Flowering Varieties of Potatoes." *American Potato Journal* 29:206-211 (1952).

Miller, D. C. *Vegetable and Herb Seed Growing for the Gardener and Small Farmer*. Boise, Idaho:

Seeds Blum, 1984.

Nieuwhof, M. *Cole Crops: Botany, Cultivation and Utilization.* London: Leonard Hill, 1969.

Owen, E. B. *The Storage of Seeds for Maintenance of Viability.* Bucks, England: Commonwealth Agriculture Bureau, 1956.

Proctor, M., and P. Yeo. *The Pollination of Flowers.* New York: Taplinger Publishing Company, 1972.

Pingry, P. A. *The Creative Gardener's Cookbook.* Kielefeld, West Germany: Ideals Publishing Company, 1985.

Proctor, M., and P. Yeo. *The Pollination of Flowers.* New York: Taplinger Publishing Company, 1972.

Rick, C. M. "The Role of Natural Hybridization in the Derivation of Cultivated Tomatoes of Western South America." *Economic Botany* 12:346-347 (1958).

Rick, C. M., M. Holle and R. W. Thorp. "Rates of Cross-Pollination in Lycopersicon pimpinellifolium." *Plant Evolution* 129:31-44 (1978).

Riley, J. M. "Solanaceae." *Solanaceae Quarterly.* Santa Clara, California, 1988.

Roberts, E. H. *Viability of Seeds.* London: Chapman and Hall Ltd., 1972.

Rogers, B., and B. Powers-Rogers. *Culinary Botany. The Essential Handbook.* Kent, Washington: Brant Rogers and Bev Powers-Rogers, 1988.

Rogers, M. *Growing and Saving Vegetable Seeds.* Pownal, Vermont: Garden Way Publishing (Storey Communications), 1978.

Ryder, E. J., Ph.D. *Leafy Salad Vegetables.* Westport, Connecticut: AV] Publishing Company, Inc., 1979.

Schneider, E. *Uncommon Fruits & Vegetables: A Commonsense Guide.* New York: Harper & Row, Publishers, Inc., 1986.

Shinohara, S. *Vegetable Seed Production Technology of Japan Elucidated with Respective Variety Development Histories, Particulars: Volume 1.* Tokyo, Japan: Authorized Agricultural Consulting Engineer Office, 1984.

Taylor, R. L. *Plants of Colonial Days.* Williamsburg, Virginia: Colonial Williamsburg, Inc., 1952.

Thompson, H. C., Ph.D., and W. C. Kelly, Ph.D. *Vegetable Crops.* New York: McGraw-Hill Company, Inc., 1957.

Vetmeyer, Noel, et al. *Lost Crops of the Incas.* Washington, D.C.: National Academy Press, 1989.

Vilmorin-Andrieux, MM. *The Vegetable Garden.* Berkeley: Ten Speed Press, 1885.

Whealy, K. *Fruit, Berry and Nut Inventory: Third Edition.* Decorah, Iowa: Seed Saver Publications, 2001.

Whealy, K. *Garden Seed Inventory: Fifth Edition.* Decorah, Iowa: Seed Saver Publications, 1999.

Whealy, K. *Seed Savers Yearbooks, Summer Editions,* and *Harvest Editions.* Decorah, Iowa: Seed Savers Exchange, 1975-2002.

Whitaker, T. W., and G. H. Davis. *Cucurbits.* New York: Interscience Publications, 1962.

Yamaguchi, M. *World Vegetables: Principles, Production, and Nutritive Values.* Westport, Connecticut: The AVI Publishing Company, Inc., 1983.

Yanovsky, E. *Food Plants of the North American Indians.* Misc. Publication 237. Washington, D.C.: U.S. Department of Agriculture.

GLOSSARY

Accession: A sample of seeds from a particular plant (or group of plants) entered into a collection or seed bank.

Aerial: Growing in the air instead of in soil or water.

Annual: Plants that are started from seed and produce seed themselves within one growing season.

Anther: Pollen-bearing structure supported by a filament, which together form the stamen of a flower.

Anthesis: The moment when a flower first opens, when the anthers and stigmas become functional.

Asexual Reproduction: Non-sexual reproduction, such as plants which are cloned from vegetative growth, cuttings, tubers, etc.

Biennial: Plants that require two growing seasons to complete a life cycle, usually exhibiting vegetative growth during the first year and producing seed during the second year.

Bolt: The development of a seed stalk, as in "hot weather caused the lettuce plants to bolt."

Bulbil: A small aerial bulb that forms on a flower stalk and is capable of forming a new plant, commonly seen in some types of onions.

Chaff: Pieces of stem, leaf and other debris that may be mixed with seed before the winnowing process.

Clone: A plant or group of plants produced from the same genetic parent using vegetative propagation (asexually) instead of from seed (sexually).

Cross-Pollination: Transfer of pollen from an anther on one plant to the stigma of a flower on another plant, and also often used to refer to situations that result in crossing between varieties.

Cultivar: An abbreviation for "cultivated variety," usually a named variety.

Day-Neutral: Plants which flower and produce fruit or seed regardless of the number of hours of sun.

Dioecious: A species that produces male flowers and female flowers on separate plants.

Dormancy: A state during which buds or seeds will not sprout even though conditions are favorable.

Edible: A portion of a plant that may be eaten, but is not necessarily palatable.

Family: A category of taxonomic classification ranking above a genus, forming a group of plants that includes one or more similar genera.

Fermentation: The natural microbial decomposition of fruit-bearing vegetables, sometimes induced deliberately to help clean the seeds and destroy seed-borne diseases.

Fertilization: The union of pollen with the ovule, which eventually produces seed.

Filament: The stalk of a stamen that bears the anther.

Genera: The plural of genus.

Genetic Diversity: The total range of genetic differences displayed by plants of the same species.

Genetic Erosion: The gradual, persistent loss of genetic resources.

Genetic Vulnerability: A condition which occurs when plants within a species become so genetically uniform that the continued evolution of the species is at risk.

Genus: A category of taxonomic classification ranking above a species, which forms a group of closely related species.

Germination: The sprouting of a seed, which marks the beginning of plant growth.

Germplasm: The total of the hereditary materials (inherited characteristics) within a species.

Heirloom Vegetable: A non-hybrid vegetable variety that has been passed down from generation to generation, usually a long-time family favorite.

Hilum: The scar on a seed, marking the spot where it was attached to the seed stalk or seedpod.

Hybrid: The offspring of a cross between parent varieties (usually of the same species) that are genetically different.

Imperfect Flower: A flower that has a stamen (stamens) or a pistil, but not both.

Inbreeding Depression: Loss of vigor and variation due to the crossing of two genetically similar plants.

Isolation: Separating one plant (or group of plants) from another to prevent any crossing.

Long-Day: Plants that flower or mature only when the length of daylight exceeds a certain minimum amount of time.

Monoecious: A species that forms male flowers and female flowers separately on the same plant.

Mutation: An unexpected inheritable genetic change.

Open-Pollinated: Non-hybrid plants produced by crossing two parents from the same variety, which in turn produce offspring just like the parent plants.

Ovary: The enlarged portion of the pistil, which contains the ovules (egg cells).

Ovule: A rudimentary seed that has not yet been fertilized.

Palatable: An edible portion of a plant that is pleasant or acceptable to the taste.

Peduncle: The stalk of a flower (or group of flowers) or, after fruit formation, the fruit-to-plant attachment as with squash.

Perennial: Any plant which lives more than two years, usually producing flowers and seeds from the same root year after year.

Perfect Flower: A flower that contains both a stamen (stamens) and a pistil.

Pistil: The female portion of a flower, which consists of an ovary, style and stigma.

Poison: A naturally occurring constituent in a plant or plant part that is capable of killing a human if eaten.

Pollen: The male spores or dust-like grains of reproductive material produced by the anthers.

Propagation: Increasing the number of plants by vegetative means or by planting seeds.

Raceme: An unbranched flower cluster consisting of a single central stem along which individual flowers grow on small stems at intervals.

Radicle: The embryonic portion of a seed which develops into the primary root.

Rogue: A non-typical, usually inferior plant within a varietal population.

Roguing: The removal of any plants that are not true-to-type in order to purify the variety.

Scape: A leafless flower stalk usually growing from the crown of the plant.

Scarify: To nick, cut into or abrade the hard coat of a seed, allowing water to enter in order to aid germination.

Seed: A fertilized and mature ovule capable of forming a new plant, typically consisting of an embryo with its protective coat and stored food.

Selection: The process, either natural or with human intervention, by which plants displaying desirable characteristics are retained within a population.

Self-Incompatibility: A trait associated with some perfect flowers whose pollen cannot grow in a flower on the same plant, but grows normally when transferred to a flower on another plant of the same variety.

Selfing: The transfer of pollen from one flower to another flower on the same plant.

Self-Pollination: The transfer of pollen from an anther to the stigma in the same flower, or to the stigma in another flower on the same plant.

Short-Day: Plants that flower or mature only when the length of daylight is shorter than a certain maximum amount of time.

Sibing: The transfer of pollen between flowers on different plants of the same variety.

Silque: A seedpod containing two segments or compartments on either side of a thin membrane bearing the seeds, especially characteristic of the Brassicaceae family.

Species: The units of taxonomic classification into which a genus is divided, each of which forms a maximum interbreeding group of plants that is reproductively incapable of crossing with other species.

Stamen: The male portion of a flower which produces the pollen grains, consisting of filaments and anthers.

Standard Variety: A non-hybrid variety, usually the end result of a breeding program cross, selected generation after generation until completely stabilized.

Stigma: The portion of the pistil that receives the pollen grains during fertilization.

Style: The elongated portion of the pistil that connects the stigma and the ovary.

Taxonomy: A system of arranging plants into related groups based on common characteristics, in descending order from most inclusive: kingdom, division, class, order, family, genus and species.

Threshing: Breaking the seeds free from the seedpods and other dry plant material.

Toxin: A natural constituent of a plant or part of a plant which, if eaten, will make humans sick, but not fatally.

True-to-Type: A plant (or group of plants) that conforms exactly to the known characteristics of that particular variety, the basis or standard for comparison.

Umbel: An umbrella-like cluster of flowers with stalks of nearly equal length radiating from the same point.

Variety: Closely related plants with nearly identical characteristics which form a subdivision of a species.

Vegetative Propagation: Reproduction by asexual methods, not from seed.

Vernalization: A period of cold temperatures that is necessary before some plants are able to form flowers for seed production.

COMMON NAME INDEX

Common Name Index

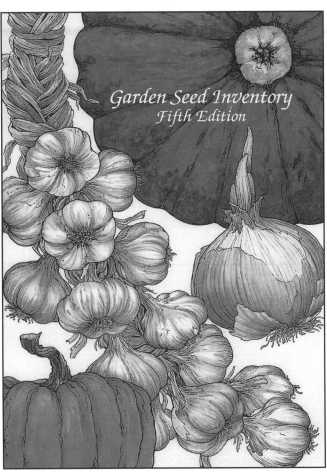

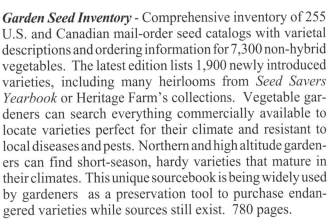

Garden Seed Inventory - Comprehensive inventory of 255 U.S. and Canadian mail-order seed catalogs with varietal descriptions and ordering information for 7,300 non-hybrid vegetables. The latest edition lists 1,900 newly introduced varieties, including many heirlooms from *Seed Savers Yearbook* or Heritage Farm's collections. Vegetable gardeners can search everything commercially available to locate varieties perfect for their climate and resistant to local diseases and pests. Northern and high altitude gardeners can find short-season, hardy varieties that mature in their climates. This unique sourcebook is being widely used by gardeners as a preservation tool to purchase endangered varieties while sources still exist. 780 pages.

Fruit, Berry and Nut Inventory - This newly revised "catalog of catalogs" is an essential reference for all backyard fruit growers and commercial orchardists who care about our rich heritage of fruits, berries and nuts. The sourcebook contains 75 sections divided by fruit type, source information for obtaining the catalogs of 280 mail-order nursery companies, and nearly 6,000 variety descriptions keyed to suppliers. This amazing cornucopia is the result of centuries of foreign collection and amateur development, further refined by the world's finest breeding programs. The apple section alone contains 1,500 varieties. 520 pages. **Available through Seed Savers' catalog and web site. Please see "Seed Saving Organizations" on page 221.**